Digital Activism in the Social Media Era

Bruce Mutsvairo
Editor

Digital Activism in the Social Media Era

Critical Reflections on Emerging Trends in Sub-Saharan Africa

Foreword by Herman Wasserman

palgrave
macmillan

Editor
Bruce Mutsvairo
Department of Social Sciences, Media Research Group
Northumbria University
Newcastle upon Tyne
United Kingdom

ISBN 978-3-319-40948-1 ISBN 978-3-319-40949-8 (eBook)
DOI 10.1007/978-3-319-40949-8

Library of Congress Control Number: 2016960574

Printed on acid-free paper

This Palgrave Macmillan imprint is published by Springer Nature
The registered company is Springer International Publishing AG
The registered company address is: Gewerbestrasse 11, 6330 Cham, Switzerland

Foreword

Digital technologies have disrupted the way media are practised and consumed globally—they have posed serious challenges to legacy media, increased the range of outlets for political discussion and debate, and brought the means of media production within the realm of the everyday.

Digital media have, on the other hand, also often served as channels for hate speech, intolerance, and increased the disempowerment of those citizens who lack access or the ability to use these platforms to full effect.

Both the positive and negative impact of digital media can be noted in the African context. But despite the often pessimistic accounts of connectivity levels in Africa, digital media have been appropriated and adapted to the African context with such speed and breadth that it is now clear that vibrant digital cultures and practices have developed in Africa despite infrastructural, political and economic obstacles (Mabewazara 2015, p. 1). While earlier approaches to digital media on the continent have often been biased towards a technologically deterministic focus on development impact, more recent studies of digital media on the continent have tended to shift the attention to the lived experience of African users of digital media and their appropriation, domestication and adaptation of these technologies to suit their economic, social and political circumstances. Simplistic assumptions about the direct democratizing effects that might result from the introduction of digital media have been thoroughly critiqued since the rise and wane of the 'Arab Spring', and have alerted us to the importance of studying digital activism within the specificities of context and the vagaries of history.

This book brings together examples of such assessments, spanning a range of countries, political environments and causes for activism, and rising to the challenge of exploring new theoretical frameworks and methodologies for analysis. These contributions are valuable illustrations of the broader theoretical argument that Africans engage with digital media in different ways, and in various dimensions of their lives, whether these are social, political, intellectual or personal.

Probably the most important platform for digital media in Africa today is the mobile phone. The penetration of mobile phones into the African continent remains one of the most astonishing examples of how media technologies are adopted and adapted to suit the specific contexts into which they are appropriated. It is now a well-established fact that mobile phones have enabled African societies to 'leapfrog' over the fixed line stage of telecommunication to become so pervasive in sub-Saharan Africa that mobile phone ownership is as common in South Africa and Nigeria as it is in the United States (Pew 2015). The uses of mobile phones in Africa extend beyond voice communication, to include text messaging, photo and video, banking, citizen journalism and, increasingly, accessing the internet. The latter, as this volume shows, is particularly important for engagement in political activities, democratic debate and social activism. Social networks like Twitter and Facebook, as well as messaging platforms such as Whatsapp, have become crucial spaces for the expression of dissent, the mobilization of activists and conduits to influence mainstream media agendas. This volume brings together a diversity of perspectives on such activism, and provides a range of examples from different African countries to illustrate how mobile phones have become vital tools for dissent, mobilization and activism. These avenues are especially important spaces in countries such as Zimbabwe, where the ability of formal media outlets to serve as platforms of critique are curtailed through political repression (see for instance Admire Mare's study of the Facebook phenomenon Baba Jukwa in that country), or where vast socio-economic inequalities have resulted in grassroots protests developing with such speed, and in locations out of earshot of elite sources, that the legacy media could not keep up (the student protests in South Africa discussed in Tanja Bosch's chapter is an example). Social media also have the potential of disrupting dominant hetero-normative narratives, which in many African societies are state-sponsored and culturally sanctioned. Several chapters in this volume illustrate how social media have managed to create spaces for African LGBTI communities to resist draconian legislation and counter oppressive mainstream discourses. Similar opportunities have arisen for feminist groups to puncture patriarchal narratives that dominate legacy media and formal political discussion.

In all these developments the youth are playing a central role. Whether using mobile phones to access reinvigorate political debate and discussion to counter widespread civil and political apathy (as Samuel Kamau argues in his chapter on youth, social media and civic engagement in Kenya) or where mobile phones are used to establish a hashtag politics in the South African #FeesMustFall movement, it is clear that African youth have appropriated mobile technologies in ways that are likely to shape the future of political engagement on the continent in future.

Although the majority of the chapters in this collection seem to take an optimistic view of the potential of digital media for activism and political engagement, there are also some that hint towards the flipside of these technologies. We should continue to remind ourselves that digital media can also reverse democratic gains through providing outlets for hate speech, amplify political repression through heightened surveillance strategies, or even just result in misguided involvement of extraneous actors that can undermine activists' intentions, as Currier and Moreau show in their discussion of African LGBTI organizing. We also know that the economic conditions on the continent continue to militate against premature celebrations of the potential of digital media to overcome centuries of economic oppression or to overturn authoritarian regimes overnight. The challenge for scholars of activism in Africa is to remain cognizant of both the potential and the pitfalls of digital media as they seek to better understand how these various forces interact in political practice, social activism and everyday life on this diverse continent.

University of Cape Town — Herman Wasserman

References

Mabweazara, H. (2015). Mainstreaming African digital cultures, practices and emerging forms of citizen engagement. *African Journalism Studies, 36*(4), 1–11.

Pew Research Center. (2015). Cell phones in Africa: Communication lifeline. Accessed 19 July 2016. http://www.pewglobal.org/2015/04/15/cell-phones-in-africa-communication-lifelne/

Contents

List of Figures

List of Tables

PART I

Political Engagements in Mediated Online Communities

CHAPTER 1

Dovetailing Desires for Democracy with New ICTs' Potentiality as Platform for Activism

Bruce Mutsvairo

INTRODUCTION

Mobile communication is increasingly playing a leading role in the mobilization of social and political protests around the world. There seem to be no known geographical boundaries for the digital revolution which the world is currently witnessing. From Chad to Chile, Mali to Myanmar, a new breed of digitally-based social initiatives have been gathering momentum for years, undoubtedly reinventing social activism as activists and ordinary people alike, eager to empower themselves politically and socially, embrace computers, mobile phones, and other web-based devices and technologies. With activists, mobile monitors, citizen journalists and digital story-tellers based in sub-Saharan Africa joining the fray, astutely bypassing hegemonic mass media gatekeepers by navigating through the online sphere to inspire collective political and social involvement across the continent, this highly

B. Mutsvairo (✉)
Department of Media & Communication Design, Northumbria University,
Newcastle upon Tyne, United Kingdom
e-mail: bruce.mutsvairo@northumbria.ac.uk

B. Mutsvairo (ed.), *Digital Activism in the Social Media Era*,
DOI 10.1007/978-3-319-40949-8_1

contested discipline of research has attracted more attention than ever before. In spite of this attention, regionally in sub-Saharan Africa, there has been a shocking lack of empirical accounts detailing who is doing what, why, where, when and with what impact. It is this gap that this book hopes to fill.

This book provides insights into the complexity of new media technologies and their relationship with aspirations for democratic and social changes in sub-Saharan Africa from the perspective of an activist. Thus, its main thrust is to examine what, with whose aid, how, with what impact and why a new breed of online-based activism is forcing political and social elites out of their comfort zones by seeking to facilitate social and political changes among different African groups such as gender-based and LGBT movements. If, indeed, digitally inspired forms of protests are manifesting into street demonstrations and internet campaigns, as witnessed in the Democratic Republic of Congo in 2015, the book critiques the real impact of online campaigning and civic engagements. Using a wide range of methodological perspectives, including surveys, social network analysis, online ethnography, interviews and participant observation, case studies in this volume assess trends and opportunities associated with the increasingly pervasive use of digital technologies. Henceforth, this book seeks to promote and advance our understanding of contemporary use of social media for the purposes of activism in present-day sub-Saharan Africa.

Conceptually, the book takes an inductive approach, seeking to interrogate new theoretical pathways representative of current trends in social media use and digital activism in sub-Saharan Africa. The reliance on inductive reasoning is preferred chiefly because this book, thanks to a series of case-by-case examinations of contemporary digital activism practices in a diverse range of countries including Nigeria, South Africa, Uganda, Kenya, Zimbabwe, Ethiopia, and Chad, is seeking a potentially universal theory that holistically determines current trends, challenges and opportunities for online activism across Africa. Presently, there is no such theory, with major studies favouring Western concepts when it comes to theoretical grounding (Mutsvairo 2015). The opportunities and challenges presented by social media to Africans should best be understood, the book argues, from an African perspective. That does not mean that there is something wrong with Western scholarship but l, as many who have been following debates in the discipline on how social media is changing societies would agree, context is key. Africa has its own history.

It arguably has its own political and social cultures. Differences in the way diverse groups on the continent are dealing with technological changes, particularly social media use in activism, is accordingly what this volume seeks to unpack.

Indeed some contributions in this book use Western theoretical underpinnings insofar as scrutinizing social media use and digital activism is concerned. However, such appraisals will seek to demonstrate experiences from an African viewpoint. For example, some cases analyse digital media-related concepts developed in the West, such as Fraser 's 'subaltern counterpublics' (1992), with a third eye, attempting to establish how relevant they are in the sub-Saharan African context and questioning whether new online-based activism tactics used by religious, political, gender-based and environmental groups are counter-hegemonic, as has been concluded in several Western studies (Ayres 1999; Castells 2001; Juris 2005; Van Laer and Van Aelst 2009).

With noticeable advancements in Information and Communication Technologies (ICTs), propose Surman and Reilly (2003), new opportunities for political activism have emerged. While we have seen few, or no, empirical studies investigating social media strategies used by advocacy groups for the purposes of activism in Africa, in other regions of the world researchers have been determinedly exploring this subject for a long time. Obar et al. (2012) and Obar (2014) have completed studies in both the US and Canada delving into the debate over new media technologies' ability to facilitate social and political activism, proving in both cases how profoundly and inherently extant the custom has become. Several other studies have also extensively examined the subject (examples include Polletta 2002; Tracy 2002; Reingold 2002; Sunstein 2003; Kampf 2010; Jansen 2010; McCafferty 2011; Castells 2012; Bertel and Stald 2013; Eltantawy 2013). In spite of this rich collection of studies, it's no straightforward task to conclude that new media platforms can potentially instigate political and social changes especially in sub Saharan Africa. Realizing its potential, Fuchs et al. (2011) argue that the internet has the ability to build communities. Even better, online platforms have become global nodes for collective action (Lievrouw 2011; Segerberg and Lance Bennett 2011). Yet as projected by Naughton (2011), three advantages for activists stand out when it comes to social media's increasingly enabling role: activists are empowered to easily connect; sympathizers can simply join in; citizens can watch and participate in real-life online activities. But social media can only facilitate protests, nothing more (Wolfsfeld et al. 2013). Further representing the sceptical school of thought, (Valenzuela 2013), based on his research in Chile, argues that social media does not craft new forms of protest but reinforces conventional techniques. Open internet access does not translate into political activism, as another sceptic (Morozov 2009) concludes. As scholars continue to debate the real essence of online activism, could such scepticism fit the cultural and geopolitical systems of sub-Saharan Africa?

By unveiling the network society, Castells (1997, 2009) and van Dijk (2005, 2006) provided an analysis of new information and communications technologies and their impact on different levels of interactions in society. Traditionally, activism has been reserved for 'activists', but in the information age dominated by the powerful presence of social media, ordinary citizens making use of mobile media and technological platforms consider themselves activists too (Hara 2008). To understand the power of social media, one has to look no further than representative digital uprisings that include the 2001 Manila protests in the Philippines, the 2004 demonstrations in Spain, the 2006 uprising in Belarus and the 2010 Red Shirt uprising in Thailand (Shirky 2011). However, there is no lack of scholarship suggesting the internet on a broader scale could *inhibit* democracy across the world (Gutstein 1999; Moore 1999; Wilhelm 1999; Graham 2000). The internet is a resource for activists, although reaching a broader audience is not always a guarantee of democratic success, which is why I argue that in some cases (mostly in Africa) the overarching belief that everyone with internet access is potentially an activist is fundamentally flawed.

Worse still, when it comes to activism, providing a platform for protests does not always mean everyone understands the content of a message or knows what action to take upon reading it. Yet social media and technological changes have made activism easier by providing (especially for those living under autocratic regimes) platforms for debate and knowledge-sharing while also enabling a message to reach its targeted audience in unprecedented fashion, within seconds. Globally, activists could practically be sharing the same methods, strategies and aims but the situation in sub-Saharan Africa does not always guarantee shared successes and experiences. In Africa and other regions of the world, traditionally demand-driven campaign methods, including protests, strikes and demonstrations, have customarily been successful in shaping and reshaping policy, practice or operations. How, then, are activists making use of the technological innovations to successfully push their agendas? It is against this background that this book attempts to clarify these differences in comparison to other regions of the world, endeavouring to show the extent to which (and why) activist experiences from other regions of the world may not always apply to the African case. More interestingly, within Africa itself, differences in experiences, norms, beliefs, circumstances (cultural and economic) are aplenty, hence the book's approach: detailing continent-wide, case-by-case analyses of digital activism, civil engagement and democratic discourses.

Activism in Africa: Towards an African Spring?

Conceptualizing activism in an African context requires a cross-disciplinary examination of factors facilitating and inhibiting its growth across the continent. While popular media, including comics and music, have traditionally been associated with the protest and resistance movement, media scholars including Willems (2010, p. 46) have boldly called such suggestions 'naive'. Similarly, Wasserman also warns of the 'naïve celebration of resistance' (2010, p. 10). Understanding digital activism in Africa requires a firm commitment to contextualizing the concept within a broad and diverse framework that underpins the continent's cultural, economic, geopolitical and historical backgrounds. African scholarship has sought to critique notions of using Western concepts in assessing the impact of new media technologies within their societies. For instance, dismissing Shirky (2010)'s cognitive surplus as 'clearly Western-centric' (Lewis et al. 2013, p. 46) have taken a stance against the scholar's 'effusive praise for the new connected age' arguing it 'ignores and fudges many complexities, contradictions and power relations' in an African state. While realizing its potential, they challenge commonly-held notions about the liberating capabilities of new media for women, concluding Fraser 's 'subaltern counterpublics' (1992) is a difficult concept when used in attempting to reconcile the difficulties faced by young South African women attempting to use new media technologies as an empowerment tool.

Furthermore, others such as Chuma (2006), Wasserman (2011) and Ndlela 2009) remain adamant that, in spite of the opportunities created by mobile media, judging the extent to which they can create an alternative politics and facilitate social change is very difficult, as the impact has not been predictable. A growing body of literature has examined the role of citizen journalism and mobile phones as key facilitators of activism in Africa (Moyo 2009; Banda 2010; Mano 2010; Moyo 2011; Wasserman 2011; Mutsvairo 2015). More and more in-depth studies looking into ICT's contributions towards the social and political state of affairs in African societies have also emerged in recent years (see Mudhai 2004, 2013; Paterson 2013). Some specifically deal with the influence and the changing dynamics of journalism in African online journalism (Mabweazara 2011, 2013; Skjerdal 2014) while others zoom in on the ethnographic impact of social media (Mare 2013). But again, while many in the West may rush to assume Africans are using the mobile phone for political and social emancipation, there is a need to understand that not everyone is privileged to own one and when they do, they may use it for purposes that have nothing to do with conventional politics. In the Western sense, mainstream media would generally been seen to be seeking to foster debate around social, economic, cultural and political issues. On the other hand, in Africa, media, including the so-called private media, does not always openly seek to foster debate among citizens. Fostering solidarity and unity in return for excellent perks and political favours is a key requirement of survival for some journalists. A window of opportunity may therefore be made available by social media even though a catalogue of factors, including power relations within the context of African society, could still hinder its ability to influence social and political changes. Besides, activism in Africa is hugely dependent on external donor funding, which provides another constraint as without foreign funds or links locally bred ideas may continue to be seen as lacking credibility and legitimacy.

To assume ICTs and the dynamics of digital mobilization have led to the 'normalization of protest' (see, Norris 2001; Walgrave and Van Aelst 2005) is somewhat problematic when you are living under the benevolence of an African dictatorship. There is always a price to pay for disobeying state-sponsored orders, and challenging the might of a despot remains tricky. This is why it is too soon to celebrate the 'opportunities' created by new media technologies especially when for some activists, participation in online activities has meant spending more time in a jail. When a culture is not ready to accept homosexuality as part of its societal norms, it remains difficult to measure the success of digital activism. Accepting is a light word for the current state of affairs—many societies in sub-Saharan Africa are fiercely opposed to the LGBT movement. The internet may thus provide an emancipatory route for individuals spotlighted for their sexuality but if they continue to live in fear or if they cannot come into the open to declare who they are, how democratic is this? How democratic and supposedly emancipatory is owning a mobile phone when you cannot afford to service it? Isn't it somewhat implausible to be expecting those finding it difficult to put food on the table to be active in online or offline activism? Under those circumstances, it is very clear their priorities will be somewhere else.

Again, the suggestion that social media platforms provide a potential to facilitate political and social changes is based on a misleading assumption that despotic regimes are not seeking to regulate and restrain these supposedly liberating spaces. African governments, especially those with a history of stifling freedom of association and assembly, will certainly be watching who is saying what on Facebook, which has been widely adopted as a mobile communicative tool across Africa. For example, President Yoweri Museveni's government forcefully reacted against social media-coordinated political protests in April and October 2011, banning protests and arresting organizers. In Zimbabwe, an activist was arrested in the second city of Bulawayo in March 2011 facing charges of using Facebook in his attempt to overthrow President Mugabe's government. The activist had written a message on what was believed to be ex-Prime Minister Morgan Tsvangirai's Facebook page making a reference to the Arab Spring protests in Egypt. As Zimbabwe's long-serving President Robert Mugabe endured non-stop antigovernment protests in 2016, he warned he would use Chinese technologies to cripple online dissent. The legitimacy of social media-led political activism has not just attracted debate in Africa. Indeed, the London riots in the UK in 2011 left many wondering whether they were indeed legitimate civic protests or criminal activities under the guise of activism.

Rethinking Activism

A global conceptualization of digital activism is necessary to understand opportunities and constraints for digital activism in Africa. Yang (2009) has defined activism simply as action for social, cultural, political, and nationalistic change. Digital activism, which has also been called 'online activism' (Alshehri 2016) and 'web activism' (Earl and Kimport 2011) has been defined by (Joyce 2010) as digital technologies used to expedite change in the political and social realms. Digital activism has benefited from its online discreetness which allows for political discussions to informally and escape elite controls and censorships (Dahlberg 2004). Mobilization forms a greater part of any course of activism as recognised by (Payne 1995). Driven by culturally shared beliefs and understandings (Zald 1996) and aided by economical forms of participation (Leizerov 2000), the mass mobilization of individuals to protest in the social media era has been called 'microactivism' by Marichal (2010). In some cases, the emergence of social media activism is in direct response to civil society deficiency and low levels of media development (Howard and Hussain 2013; Breuer et al. 2014). Research has shown an increasing participation of younger generations in Internet-based transnational advocacy (Nilan and Feixa 2006; Pleyers 2011). Activists are harnessing the power of alternative media because, as argued by McLeod and Hertog (1999), traditional media take a negative stance in their coverage of social movements, potentially hurting the activists' mobilization efforts. By ignoring ordinary citizen voices, especially those from counter-hegemonic movements, conventional media structures have unknowingly allowed digital activism to flourish (Cammaerts 2012) leading to what Yang (2016, p. 13) has called 'discursive protest on social media united through a hashtagged word, phrase or sentence'.

Still, it would be a misnomer to assume activism is a product of new media technologies; it's been there for as long as Africans have lived. We should not forget that not only has activism been central in defeating slavery within and outside the continent but it has also led to the inevitable confrontation and subduing of colonialism (at least on paper) as well as acting as the leading light to opposition to racism and other forms of gender or tribal discrimination. Western technology arrived in sub-Saharan Africa with Portuguese missionaries in the 15th century. By that time, activism had long existed among African groups, most of whom were engaged in fights over fertile land. Indeed, there have been many forms of activism across the continent, as depicted by different dimensions and analysis of the subject in various studies. Quansah and Fombad (2009), for example have analysed judicial activism in Botswana and South Africa in a comparative perspective, while Klopp and Orina (2002) have looked at student activism in Kenya. Mbali (2013) has provided an account of Aids activism in South Africa; Larmer (2015) has historicized colonial and post-colonial activism in sub-Saharan Africa and Van Der Vlies (2012) has assessed queer activism in South Africa. There is abundant library of literature dealing with activism-related developments in Africa (see Fine and Nicol 1995; Kennedy 2001; Nakaweesi-Kimbugwe and Mugisha 2009; Ekine 2010; Nakaweesi-Kimbugwe and Chigudu 2013).

But it is thanks to social networks that activism is rapidly experiencing a new transformation and direction. The availability of social media allows activists to post and share information anytime, anywhere (Hansen et al.

2011) with Facebook proving to be a very useful platform for the purposes of activism (Ellison et al. 2007; Neumayer and Raffl 2008). Not to be outdone, like-minded grassroots groups are also taking to YouTube, sharing common interests in a bid to advance political campaigning (Naim 2007). Castells (2003, p.139) paints a painstaking picture of digital optimism, 'in other instances, the technological vulnerability of the internet offers the opportunity for individual or collective expressions of protest to disrupt the websites of the electronic networks of government agencies or corporations targeted as representatives of oppression or exploitation'. A study by Ellison et al. (2007) shows a preference for online-based activism among the youths. Given all these promising accounts, it is possible to understand why there has been unimpeded belief that participatory tendencies in online activism provide a basis for a healthy democracy, even though such an assumption cannot go unchallenged. For example, it has been argued that participation tends to cripple democracy (see Vowles 1995). In the same vein, a study by Best and Wade (2009) found that the effects of the internet on democracy were limited in countries that were less developed and non-democratic. Yet in spite of the attention that social media has attracted as a decisive shining soul for modern activism, others have not just sponsored depressingly sceptical accounts on the internet's ability to encourage democracy but have also warned of (in the case of tyrannical regimes) state-sponsored will to chastise digital dissent (see Boas 2006; Zittrain 2008; Mozorov 2009a)

Digital Engagements: Lessons Learnt

While the availability of social media platforms has received plenty of attention worldwide, with frequent claims that this emergent form of communication is instigating social, environmental and political change, in sub-Saharan Africa, as proven by findings from various cases studies published in this volume, the success of online activism is reliant on several factors, chief among them, the effective coordination with offline activities. Even those who believe the internet was instrumental in determining the success of the Arab Spring would admit that had activists not taken to the streets, then perhaps, having typically overstayed his mandate, the ex-President of Egypt, Hosni Mubarak, would not have seen the need to give up. In line with this argument, Anduiza et al. (2009) have characterized activism in three different categories, drawing a distinction between activities that are only possible online, those only conceivable offline, and offline activities that can also be carried out online. While research from other regions of the world is concluding offline activism would be rendered impossible without the availability of online means (Juris 2005), in sub-Saharan Africa, where access to the internet is still very low in comparison to other regions of the world, the online–offline connection has yet to become universally plausible. Indeed there are pockets of evidence proving Gallagher (2009)'s claim that online mobilization is not only limited to raising awareness, but also provoking people to take action. In Malawi, for example, the government's decision to shut down pirate broadcasters and popular websites forced Malawians to turn to Twitter and Facebook for information during the 2012 protests (Mutsvairo and Harris 2016). Even though these platforms have been used to promote anti-government civic action across Africa, only a handful of countries across the continent openly tolerate dissent.

With several governments unwilling to tolerate political dissent, activists are taking the battle to social media networks. Unbelievable as it may sound, elites in Zimbabwe for example, consider street protests as something reserved for the less educated and less privileged. This is one reason among others why, apart from the successful labour-backed strikes of the 1990s, numerous calls for coordinated political or industrial action have continued to fail. But on the internet, people without previous knowledge of activism are joining in, openly saying what they want. Better still, for those living under repressive rule and fearing reprisals, social media platforms have made it possible for people to take part anonymously. It is therefore thanks to social networks, as (Shirky 2008, p. 181) pinpoints, that instead of telling people who care a little to do more, it is now possible to convince people who care a little to do a little. In other words, little is more. However, it is important to highlight that several governments in Africa will not be bothered by what people are saying online as long as they still control conventional media outlets such as radio, TV and newspapers because they know not everyone is able to understand social media especially for political purposes. Besides, they know they have the might of the police and military should activists attempt to take the government head-on, taking a cue from Van De Donk et al. (2004) who, despite seeing the benefits of the internet for activism, believe the element of being there is irreplaceable, declaring 'The Internet may facilitate the traditional forms of protest such as rallies, demonstrations, and collection of signatures, but it will hardly replace these forms' (p. 18).

In spite of a series of studies showing online activism is increasingly difficult to duck as it is fast becoming a reality globally, (see Myers 1994; McAdam 1996; McCarthy 1996;McPhail et al. 1998; Ribeiro 1998; Zunes et al. 1999; Leizerov 2000; Scott and Street 2000; Trigg 2000; Reilly 2003; Vegh 2003; Cardoso and Pereira Neto 2004; Kahn and Kellner 2004; Van De Donk et al. 2004; Rolfe 2005; Earl and Kimport 2011; Harlow 2011) perhaps the most formidable question to pose (especially in the case of Africa), is whether we are seeing the enhancement of political participation as a direct result of web-based activism. Ignoring the power of digital technologies is no longer an option for repressive regimes Obadare (2005) is keen to remind us, especially at a time when participation has been defined as any activity influencing society at large (Esaiasson and Westholm 2006).

Yet, as shown in some studies in this volume, it is so easy to underestimate the importance of internet literacy in the technology–democracy matrix, a point also supported by Sciadas (2003) and Beardon (2004). When it comes to Africa, not everyone who has access to social media is an activist, it must be noted. Moreover, as noted earlier on, not everyone with access to internet understands what it is and how to use it, a finding I consider to be a key takeaway from this book.

Nonetheless, McAdam et al. (1996) have argued that it is no longer possible to study democracy and democratization without paying specific attention to digital information technologies. Nothing new there—the tenacious relationship between technology and democracy has long been studied by various scholars (Lerner 1958). Habermas (1962)'s public sphere discourse has technological orientations to it. Some studies have even shown that the two work hand-in-hand. For example, Kedzie (1997) concluded, based on a 1993 study, that there was a strong correlation between democracy and the internet. Similarly, a 10-year study of 180 countries by Best and Wade (2009, p. 270) confirmed 'the existence of a positive relationship between democratic growth and Internet penetration'. Fuchs (2014) has taken things a step further by suggesting the availability of social media, specifically Twitter, has provided a new arena for the public sphere of political communication, which carries emancipatory connotations. It is still doubtful whether and how Habermas's suggestion that offline open talk and unhindered deliberations in a public sphere among citizens could lead to political solutions is applicable to Africa's online domains. Conclusions from studies in the West are significant, but several cases here make an attempt to deepen understanding of the African situation by questioning the applicability of these concepts in the technologically crippled continent.

Chapter Summaries

Key to understanding the impact of extemporaneous yet coordinated activist use of social media in sub-Saharan Africa is the ability to deal with a wide range of questions, which the 15 chapters seek to address. Divided in three thematic categories—Political Engagements in Mediated Online Communities; Digital Transformations: Civic Activism; and Gender and LGBT Movements Online: Emerging Debates, the volume investigates the potential to advance real-time activism in the digital age.

Chapters in Part I investigate the use and intersection of on- and offline techniques in advancing political changes among a new generation of networked political dissents. The introductory chapter deals largely with attempts both by state and non-state actors to comprehend the role that social media activism plays in advancing political change. This is followed by Iginio Gagliardone and Matti Pohjonen's attempt to probe the Ethiopian government's efforts to silence cyber-activists by appropriating online-based surveillance techniques under the guise of global anti-terrorism campaigns. They use a systematic analysis of 10,000 statements posted on Facebook between February 24 and June 24, 2015 to question the extent to which Ethiopians both online and offline are responding to these measures and with what impact. Seeking to outline the constraints of Facebook activism, Admire Mare follows up in Chap. 3 with a critical examination of the infamous Baba Jukwa Facebook page, which in its heyday made a name for releasing political secrets into the public social media domain, embarrassing officials ahead of the 2013 elections in Zimbabwe. In Chap. 4, Monica B Chibita profiles the dynamics of digital activism in Uganda, before Ibrahim Shaw and Di Luo give an account of cyber-activism in the Sierra Leonean blogosphere in Chap. 5, completing the first part of the book.

Part II looks not only at who is the leading force behind new online-based campaigns but also what strategies are being used and to what effect, thus measuring the potential as well as the problems that online activists face, zooming in on online-based civic campaigns. In Chap. 6, Sam Kamau provides an assessment of youth-inspired civic activism in Kenya. A collaboration between a musician and an anthropologist takes centre-stage in Chap. 7, where Mirjam de Bruijn and Didier Lalaye turn to ethnographical memoirs on the contemporary artist Layale's sometimes perilous confrontations with the political elite of Chad to show how Layale and other musicians' adaptation of new ICTs and other novel digital activities, is inadvertently spicing up the political battlefield in the former French colony. That is followed by Tanja Bosch's examination in Chap. 8 of the '#FeesMustFall' Twitter campaign in South Africa. Staying in South Africa and on Twitter, Glenda Daniels attempts to determine the social and political implications of the '#RhodesMustFall' campaign in Chap. 9, before Viola Milton endeavours to show how recent crises at the South African state broadcaster, SABC, are discursively constructed by civil society through its involvement in social media networks in Chap. 10.

Part III is made up of cohesive collection of chapters detailing and critiquing current trends and strategies used by the LGBT and gender-based movements across Africa. In Chapter 11 Ashley Currier and Julie Moreau explore digital methods and strategies associated with the LGBTI movement in sub-Saharan Africa. Chap. 12 delves into the intricacy of living in what Nhamo A. Mhiripiri and Bianca S. Moyo call 'homophobic Zimbabwean Society' as activists from The Gays and Lesbians of Zimbabwe (GALZ) use Facebook as an alternative Public Sphere to challenge prevailing political and social stigmas associated with their sexuality. Chap. 13 is based on Shepherd Mpofu's analysis of the online platform 'Her Zimbabwe' to demonstrate gender activism patterns Zimbabwe. In Chap. 14, Patience Mutopo takes a look at land reform in Zimbabwe from a media- and gender-based perspective. The final chapter is an examination by Dorothy Njoroge, dedicated to the '#BringBackOurGirls' Twitter campaign, which hogged the limelight early in 2014 as celebrities from across the globe sought to raise concern over the unknown fate of over 200 young girls abducted by Nigerian militant group Boko Haram. She uses the campaign to show complexities in the feminism discourses in Nigeria through a discourse analysis of over 500,000 tweets gathered between November 2014 and April 2015. The chapter questions the degree to which the #BringBackOurGirls social movement acts as a platform for producing alternative feminism discourse while assessing the state's response towards feminism discourse.

References

Alshehri, T. (2016). Challenges of digital activism in Saudi Arabia: The case of Raif Badawi. http://depts.washington.edu/tatlab/socialjustice/wp-content/uploads/2016/02/Alshehri-Challenges-of-Digital-Activism-in-Saudi-Arabia.pdf. Accessed 9 October 2016.

Anduiza, E., Cantijoch, M., & Gallego, A. (2009). Political participation and the Internet. *Information, Communication & Society, 12*(6), 860–878.

Ayres, J.M. (1999). From the streets to the Internet: The cyber-diffusion of contention. *Annals of the American Academy of Political and Social Science, 566*, 132–143.

Banda, F. (2010). *Citizen journalism and democracy in Africa: An exploratory study*. Grahamstown: Highway Africa.

Beardon, H. (2004). *ICT for development: Empowerment or exploitation?*. London: ActionAid.

Bertel, T.F., & Stald, G.B. (2013). From SMS to SNS: The use of the Internet on the mobile phone among young Danes. In K. M. Cumiskey, and L. Hjorth, (Eds.), *Mobile media practices, presence and politics: The challenge of being seamlessly mobile* (pp. 198–213). New York: Routledge

Best, M.L., & Wade, K.W. (2009). The Internet and democracy: Global catalyst or democratic dud?. *Bulletin of Science, Technology & Society, 9*, 255–271.

Boas, T.C., Zysman, J., & Newman, A. (2006). Weaving the authoritarian web: The control of Internet use in non-democratic regimes. In J. Zysman and A. Newman (Eds.), *How revolutionary was the revolution? National responses, market transitions, and global technology in the digital era*. Stanford, CA: Stanford Business Books.

Breuer, A., Landman, T., & Farquhar, D. (2014). Social media and protest mobilization: Evidence from the Tunisian revolution. *Democratization, 22* (4), 764–792.

Cammaerts, B. (2012). Protest logics and the mediation opportunity structure. *European Journal of Communication, 27*(2), 117–134.

Cardoso, G., & Pereira Neto, P. (2004). Mass media driven mobilization and online protest: ICTs and the pro-East Timor movement in Portugal. In W. Van De Donk, B. D. Loader, P. G. Nixon, and D. Rucht (Eds.), *Cyberprotest: New media, citizens and social movements* (pp. 147–163). London: Routledge.

Castells, M. (1997). *The rise of the network society. The information age: Economy, society and culture* (Vol. 1). Cambridge, MA: Blackwell.

Castells, M. (2001). *The Internet galaxy: Reflections on the Internet, business and society*. Oxford: Oxford University Press.

Castells, M. (2003). *The Internet galaxy: Reflections on the Internet*. Oxford: Business, and Society Oxford University Press.

Castells, M. (2009). *Communication power*. New York: Oxford University Press.

Castells, M. (2012). *Networks of outrage and hope: Social movements in the Internet age*. Cambridge, MA: Polity Press.

Chuma, W. (2006). The limits and possibilities of virtual political communication in transforming South Africa: A case study of *ANC Today* and *SA Today*. *Intercultural Communication Studies, XV*, 176–184.

Dahlberg, L. (2004). Net-Public sphere research: Beyond the "First Phase". *Javnost Ljubljana, 11*(1), 27–44.

Der Vlies, V. (2012). Van Der Vlies, Andrew, art as archive: Queer activism and contemporary South African visual cultures. *Kunapipi, 34*(1), 64–116.

Earl, J., & Kimport, K. (2011). *Digitally enabled social change. Activism in the Internet age*. Cambridge, MA: MIT Press.

Ekine, S. (2010). *SMS uprising: Mobile phone activism in Africa*. Cape Town: Pambazuka Press.

Ellison, N.B., Steinfield, C., & Lampe, C. (2007). The benefits of Facebook "friends:"Social Capital and college students' use of online social network sites. *Journal of Computer-Mediated Communication, 12*, 1143–1168.

Eltantawy, N. (2013). From veiling to blogging: Women and media in the Middle East. *Feminist Media Studies, 13*(5), 765–769.

Esaiasson, P., & Westholm, A. (2006). Deltagandets mekanismer. In P. Esaiasson, & A. Westholm (Eds.), *Deltagandets mekanismer: Det politiska engagemangets orsaker och konsekven- ser*. Malmo: Liber.

Fine, D., & Nicol, J. (1995). The lavender lobby: Working for lesbian and gay rights within the liberation movement. In E. Cameron and M. Gevisser (Eds.), *Defiant desire: Gay and lesbian lives in South Africa* (pp. 269–277). New York: Routledge.

Fraser, N. (1992). Rethinking the public sphere: A contribution to the critique of actually existing democracy. In C. Calhoun (Ed.), *Habermas and the public sphere*. Cambridge, MA: MIT Press.

Fuchs, C. (2014). *Social media: A critical introduction*. London: Sage.

Fuchs, C., Boersma, K., Albrechtslund, A., & Sandoval, M. (Eds.). (2011). *Internet and surveillance: The challenges of web 2.0 and social media*. New York: Routledge.

Gallagher, D.F. (2009, July 9). A blog's story gets a tweek in "Julie & Julia." *New York Times*.

Graham, S. (2000). Constructing premium network spaces: Reflections on infrastructure network and contemporary urban development. *International Journal of Urban and Regional Research, 24*(1), 183–200.

Gutstein, D. (1999). *E.con: How the Internet undermines democracy*. Toronto, ON: Stoddart.

Habermas, J. (1962). *The structural transformation of the public sphere: An inquiry into a category of bourgeois society*. Cambridge: MIT Press.

Hansen, D., Shneiderman, B., & Smith, M.A. (2011). *Analyzing social media networks with node XL: Insights from a connected world*. Burlington, MA: Morgan Kaufmann.

Hara, N. (2008). The Internet use for political mobilization: Voices of the participants. *First Monday*, 13(7). http://www.uic.edu/htbin/cgiwrap/bin/ojs/index.php/fm/article/view/2123/1976. Accessed 9 October 2016.

Harlow, S. (2011). Social media and social movements: Facebook and an online Guatemalan justice movement that moved offline. *New Media & Society, 14*(2), 225–243.

Howard, P. & Hussain, M. (2013). *Democracy's fourth wave?: Digital media and the Arab Spring*. Oxford: Oxford University Press.

Jansen, F. (2010). Digital activism in the Middle East: Mapping issue networks in Egypt, Iran, Syria and Tunisia. *Knowledge Management for Development Journal, 6*(1), 37–52.

Joyce, M.C. (Ed.). (2010). *Digital activism decoded: The new mechanics of change*. New York: International Debate Education Association.

Juris, J.S. (2005). The new digital media and activist networking within anti-corporate globalization movements. *Annals of the American Academy of Political and Social Science, 597*(1), 189–208.

Kahn, R., & Kellner, D. (2004). New media and Internet activism: From the "Battle of Seattle" to blogging. *New Media & Society, 6*(1), 87–95.

Kampf, C. E. (2010). Extending sociotechnical design to project conception: Knowledge communication processes for situating technology. In *Information Resources Management: Concepts, Methodologies, Tools and Applications* (pp. 868–882). IGI global: Hershey, PA.

Karpf, D. (2010). Online political mobilization from the advocacy group's perspective: Looking beyond clicktivism. *Policy and Internet, 2*(4), 7–41.

Kedzie, C. (1997). Communication and democracy: Coincident revolutions and the emergent dictator's dilemma. Unpublished Ph.D. diss., RAND Graduate School.

Kennedy, B. (2001). Homosexuals in the periphery: Gay and lesbian rights in developing Africa. *Nebraska Anthropologist*, Paper 21.

Klopp, J., & Orina, J. (2002). University crisis, student activism, and the contemporary struggle for democracy in Kenya. *African Studies Review, 45*(1), 43–76.

Larmer, M. (2015). Historicising activism in late colonial and post- colonial Sub-Saharan Africa. *Journal of Historical Sociology, 28*(1), 67–89.

Leizerov, S. (2000). Privacy advocacy groups versus Intel: A case study of how social movements are tactically using the Internet to fight corporations. *Social Science Computer Review, 18*(4), 461–483.

Lerner, D. (1958). *The passing of traditional society*. New York: The Free Press.

Lewis, D., Hussen, T.S., & Van Vuuren, M. (2013). Exploring new media technologies among young South African women. *African Femnist, 18*, 43–64.

Lievrouw, L. A. (2011). *Alternative and activist new media*. Malden, MA: Polity Press.

Mabweazara, H.M. (2011). Between the newsroom and the pub: The mobile phone in the dynamics of everyday mainstream journalism practice in Zimbabwe. *Journalism: Theory, Practice and Criticism, 12*(6), 692–707.

Mabweazara, H.M., Okoth, F.M., & Whittaker, J. (Eds.). (2013). *Online journalism in Africa: Trends, practices and emerging cultures.* London: Routledge.
Mano, W. (2010). Between vigilante and citizen journalism: ZimDaily's FairDeal campaing and the Zimbabwe crisis. Communicare. *Journal for the Communication Sciences in Southern Africa, 29*, 57–70.
Mare, A. (2013). A complicated but symbiotic affair: The relationship between mainstream media and social media in the coverage of social protests in southern Africa. *Ecquid Novi: African Journalism Studies, 34*(1), 83–98.
Marichal, J. (2010). Political facebook groups: Micro-activism and the digital front stage. https://thesocietypages.org/thickculture/2010/10/11/facebook-does-not-promote-activism-so-what/. Accessed 10 October 2016.
Mbali, M. (2013). *South African AIDS activism and global health politics.* Basingstoke: Palgrave.
McAdam, D. (1996). Conceptual origins, current problems, future directions. In D. McAdam, J. D. McCarthy and M. N. Zald (Eds.), *Comparative perspectives on social movements: political opportunities, mobilizing structures, and cultural framings* (pp. 23–40). New York: Cambridge University Press.
McAdam, D., McCarthy, J.D. & Zald, M.N. (1996). *Comparative perspectives on social movements: Political opportunities, mobilizing structures, and cultural framings.* New York: Cambridge University Press.
McCafferty, D. (2011). Activism vs. slacktivism. *Communications of the ACM, 54* (12), 17–19.
McCarthy, J.D. (1996). Constraints and opportunities in adopting, adapting, and inventing. In D. McAdam, J. D. McCarthy, and M. N. Zald (Eds.), *Comparative perspectives on social movements: Political opportunities, mobilizing structures, and cultural framings* (pp. 141–151). New York: Cambridge University Press.
McLeod, D.M., & Hertog, J.K. (1999). Social control, social change and the mass media"s role in the regulation of protest groups. In D. Demers & K. Viswanath (Eds.), *Mass media, social control and social change: A macrosocial perspective* (pp. 305–330). Ames, IA: Iowa State University Press.
McPhail, C., Schweingruber, D., & McCarthy, J. (1998). Policing protest in the United States: 1960–1995. In D. D. Porta and H. Reiter (Eds.), *Policing protest: The control of mass demonstrations in western democracies: Social movements, protest, and contention.* Minneapolis: University of Minnesota Press.
Moore R.K. (1999). Democracy and cyberspace. In B.N. Hague and B.D. Loader (Eds.), *Digital democracy: Discourse and decision making in the information age.* London: Routledge.
Morozov, E. (2009). Downside to the Twitter revolution. *Dissent, 56*(4), 10–14.
Moyo, D. (2009). Citizen journalism and the parallel market of information in Zimbabwe's 2008 election. *Journalism Studies, 10*(4), 551–567.

Moyo, L. (2011). Blogging down a dictatorship: Human rights, citizens journalists and the right to communicate in Zimbabwe. *Journalism: Theory, Practice and Criticism, 12*(6), 745–760.

Mudhai, O.F. (2004). Researching the impact of ICTs as change catalysts in Africa. *Ecquid Novi: African Journalism Studies, 25*(2), 313–335.

Mudhai, O.F. (2013). *Civic engagement, digital networks, and political reform in Africa*. New York: Palgrave Macmillan.

Mutsvairo, B. & Harris, S. (2016). Rethinking mobile media tactics in protests: A comparative case study of Hong Kong and Malawi. In R. Wei (Ed.), *Mobile media, civic engagement and civic activism in Asia: Private chat to public communication* (pp. 215–231). Springer: Dordrecht.

Mutsvairo, B. (2015). *Perspectives on participatory politics and citizen journalism in a networked Africa: A connected continent*. London: Palgrave Macmillan.

Myers, J.D. (1994). Communication technology and social movements: Contributions of computer networks to activism. *Social Science Computer Review, 12*, 251–260.

Naim, M. (2007). The YouTube effect. *Foreign Policy, 158*, 104.

Nakaweesi-Kimbugwe, S., & Chigudu, H. (2013). *The LGBTIQ and sex worker movements in East Africa*. Brighton: BRIDGE, IDS.

Nakaweesi-Kimbugwe, S., & Mugisha, F. (2009). 'Bahati's bill: A convenient distraction for Uganda's Government. *Pambazuka News,* p. 453.

Naughton, J. (2011, Sunday January 23) Yet another Facebook revolution: Why are we so surprised?, *The Guardian, The Observer*.

Ndlela, M.N. (2009). Alternative media and the political public sphere in Zimbabwe. In K. Howley (Ed.), *Understanding community media*. London: Sage Publications.

Neumayer, C., & Raffl, C. (2008). Facebook for global protest: The potential and limits of social software for grassroots activism. In *Proceedings of the 5th Prato community informatics & development informatics conference 2008: ICTs for social inclusion: What is the reality?*.

Nilan, P. & Feixa, C. (2006). *Global youth? Hybrid identities, plural worlds*. New York: Routledge.

Norris, P. (2001). *Digital divide: Civic Engagement, Information Poverty, and the Internet Worldwide*. New York: Cambridge University Press.

Obadare, E. (2005). The GSM boycott: Civil society, big business and the state in Nigeria. Civil Society Working Paper series, 23, Center for Civil Society, London School of Economics and Political Science.

Obar, J. A. (2014). Canadian advocacy 2.0: Social media adoption and perceived affordances by advocacy groups looking to advance activism in Canada. *Canadian Journal of Communication*, 39, 211–233. http://www.cjc-online.ca/index.php/journal/article/viewFile/2678/2447. Accessed 9 October 2016.

Obar, J.A., Zube, P., & Lampe, C. (2012). Advocacy 2.0: An analysis of how advocacy groups in the United States perceive and use social media as tools for facilitating civic engagement and collective action. *Journal of Information Policy*, *2*, 1–25.

Paterson, C. (2013). Editorial note: Journalism and social media in the African context. *Ecquid Novi: African Journalism Studies*, *34*(1), 1–16.

Payne, C. (1995). *I've got the light of freedom: The organizing tradition and the mississippi freedom struggle*. Los Angeles: University of California Press.

Pleyers, G. (2011). *Alter-globalization: Becoming actors in the global age*. Cambridge: Polity Press.

Polletta, F. (2002). *Freedom is an endless meeting*. Chicago: University of Chicago Press.

Quansah, E.K., & Fombad, C.M. (2009) 'Judicial activism in Africa: Possible defence against authoritarian resurgence?' http://ancl-radc.org.za/sites/default/files/Judicial%20Activism%20in%20Africa.pdf. Accessed 6 September 2015.

Reilly, P. (2003). Civil society, the Internet and terrorism: Two case studies from Northern Ireland. Paper prepared for the European Consortium for Political Research Joint Sessions of Workshops, Edinburgh.

Reingold, H. (2002). *Smart mobs: The next social revolution*. Cambridge, MA: Basic Books.

Ribeiro, G.L. (1998). Cybercultural politics: Political activism at a distance in a transnational world. In S. E. Alvarez, E. Dagnino, and A. Escobar (Eds.), *Cultures of politics, politics of cultures: Re-visioning Latin American social movements* (pp. 325–352). Boulder, CO: Westview Press.

Rolfe, B. (2005). Building an electronic repertoire of contention. *Social Movement Studies*, *4*(1), 65–74.

Sciadas, G. (2003). *Monitoring the digital divide... and beyond*. Montreal: Orbicom.

Sciadas, G. (Ed). (2005). *From the digital divide to digital opportunities: Measuring infostates for development*. Montreal: Orbicom.

Scott, A., & Street, J. (2000). From media politics to e-protest. *Information, Communication and Society*, *3*(2), 215–240.

Segerberg, A., & Lance Bennett, W. (2011). Social media and the organization of collective action: Using Twitter to explore the ecologies of two climate change protests. *The Communication Review*, 14, 197–215. http://research.fit.edu/sealevelriselibrary/documents/doc_mgr/921/Segerberg_&_Bennett_2011_Twitter_to_explore_ecologies_of_CC_protests.pdf. Accessed 9 October 2016.

Shirky, C. (2008). *Here comes everybody: The power of organizing without organizations*. New York City: Penguin Press.

Shirky, C. (2010). *Cognitive surplus: Creativity and generosity in a connected age*. London: Penguin.

Shirky, C. (2011). The political power of social media. *Foreign Affairs, 90*(1), 1–9.
Skjerdal, T. (2014). Online journalism under pressure: An Ethiopian account. In H. M. Mabweazara, O. F. Mudhai, and J. Whittaker (Eds.), *Online journalism in Africa: Trends, practices, and emerging cultures* (pp. 89–104). London: Routledge.
Sunstein, C. (2003). *Why societies need dissent.* Cambridge, MA: Harvard University Press.
Surman, M., & Reilly, K. (2003). Appropriating the internet for social change: Towards the strategic use of networked technologies by transnational civil society organizations. *Social Sciences Research Council.* http://marksurman.commons.ca/wpcontent/uploads/sites/2/Surman_2003_Appropriating_Internet_Social_Change.pdf. Accessed 10 October 2016.
Tracy, K. (2002). *Everyday talk.* New York: Guilford Press.
Trigg, R.H. (2000). *From sand box to "fund box": Weaving participatory design into the fabric of a busy non-profit.* Proc. of PDC, 174–183.
Valenzuela, S. (2013). Unpacking the use of social media for protest behavior: The roles of information. *Opinion Expression, and Activism. American Behavioral Scientist, 57*(7), 920–942.
Van De Donk, W., Loader, B.D., Nixon, P.G., & Rucht, D. (2004). Introduction: Social movements and ICTS. In W. Van De Donk, B. D. Loader, P. G. Nixon, and D. Rucht (Eds.), *Cyberprotest: New media, citizens and social movements* (pp. 1–25). London: Routledge.
Van Dijk, J. (2005). *The deepening divide: Inequality in the information society.* Thousand Oaks, CA: Sage Publications.
Van Dijk, J. (2006). *The network society* (2nd edn). London: Sage.
Van Laer, J., & Van Aelst, P. (2009). Cyber-protest and civil society: The Internet and action repertoires in social movements. http://uahost.uantwerpen.be/m2p/publications/1260489691.pdf. Accessed 10 September 2015.
Vegh, S. (2003). Classifying forms of online activism: The case of cyberprotests against the World Bank. In M. McCaughey and M. D. Ayers (Eds.), *Cyberactivism: Online activism in theory and practice* (pp. 71–95). New York: Routledge.
Vowles, J. (1995). Electoral participation. In J. Vowles, P. Aimer, H. Catt, J. Lamane, and R. Miller (Eds.), *Towards consensus.* Auckland: Auckland University Press.
Walgrave, N.S., & Van Aelst, P. (2005). Who demonstrates? Anti- state rebels, conventional participants, or everyone?. *Comparative Politics, 37*(2), 189–205.
Wasserman, H. (2011). Mobile phones, popular media and everyday African democracy: Transmissions and transgressions. *Popular Communication, 9*, 1–13.
Wasserman, H. (Ed). (2010). *Popular media, democracy and development in Africa.* Oxford and New York: Routledge.

Wilhelm, A.G. (1999). Virtual sounding boards: How deliberative is online political discussion? In Hague, B.N. and Loader B.D. (Eds.), *Digital democracy. Discourse and decision making in the information age* (pp. 154–179). London: Routledge.
Willems, W. (2010). At the crossroads of the formal and popular: Convergence culture and new publics in Zimbabwe. In H. Wasserman (Ed.), *Popular media, democracy and development in Africa* (pp. 46–62). London: Routledge.
Wolfsfeld, G., Segev, E., and Sheafer, T. (2013). Social media and the Arab spring: Politics comes first. *The International Journal of Press/Politics, 18*(2), 115–137.
Yang, G. (2009). *The power of the Internet in China: Citizen activism online.* New York: Columbia University Press.
Yang, G. (2016). Narrative Agency in Hashtag Activism: The Case of #BlackLivesMatter. *Media and Communication, 4*(4), 13–17.
Zald, M.N. (1996). Culture, ideology, and strategic framing. In D. McAdam, J.D. McCarthy & M.N. Zald (Eds.), *Comparative perspectives on social movements: Political opportunities, mobilizing structures.* Cambridge: Cambridge University Press.
Zittrain, J. (2008). *The future of the Internet—And how to stop it.* New Haven, CT: Yale University Press.
Zunes, S., Kurtz, L., & Asher, S. (Eds.). (1999). *Nonviolent social movements: A geographical perspective.* Oxford: Blackwell Publishing.

Bruce Mutsvairo is a Senior Lecturer in Journalism at Northumbria University Newcastle, UK. His research explores the role of digital media in advancing political participation in sub-Saharan Africa. His latest book *Perspectives on Participatory Politics and Citizen Journalism in a Networked Africa: A Connected Continent* (eds) was published at Palgrave in 2015.

CHAPTER 2

Engaging in Polarized Society: Social Media and Political Discourse in Ethiopia

Iginio Gagliardone and Matti Pohjonen

Ethiopia is a country of many paradoxes. It has some of the lowest levels of internet penetration in the world, yet it applies some of the most severe measures for surveilling and censoring online communication (Human Rights Watch 2014). It has charted new avenues of collaboration with emerging donors, especially with China, but also continues to be Africa's largest recipient of development aid from traditional, Western donors (Fourie 2015; Gagliardone 2014a). It has championed uses of Information and Communication Technologies (ICTs) that have later been adopted elsewhere in Africa, from videoconferencing for government communication to commodities exchanges, and yet it is considered backward when it comes to digital innovation (Rashid 2015).

In the case of digital activism, Ethiopia similarly displays many contradictions. During the events that followed the contested parliamentary

I. Gagliardone (✉)
University of the Witwatersrand, Johannesburg, South Africa
e-mail: iginio.gagliardone@wits.ac.za

M. Pohjonen
Africa's Voices Foundation, Cambridge, United Kingdom
e-mail: matti.pohjonen@gmail.com

B. Mutsvairo (ed.), *Digital Activism in the Social Media Era*,
DOI 10.1007/978-3-319-40949-8_2

elections of 2005, Ethiopian protesters combined new and traditional communication channels in ways that closely resemble the uses of the media that would characterize the 'Arab Spring' in 2011. Yet during these protests, Facebook was still in infancy, with no presence in Africa, and Twitter had yet to be launched. In 2005 it was bloggers who represented the critical node enabling innovative forms of communication to be experimented with. Already in the 1990s Ethiopians in the diaspora had created platforms allowing numerous bloggers to voice their opinions (i.e. 'nazret.com'), in ways that pre-dated the approach later adopted by online magazines such as *Slate* or *The Huffington Post*. While these early initiatives were dominated by individuals with a manifest adversarial agenda towards the Ethiopian government, by 2005 young journalists and activists (i.e. Enset, Ethio-Zagol) had begun to experiment with new ways of reporting that eschewed the most polarized tones (Skjerdal 2011), becoming representative of a new generation willing to embrace technology to promote political change. In a move that dramatically increased their reach, commentaries and political manifestoes published online began to be printed and were turned into leaflets for distribution on the ground in Ethiopia. Before and after the 2005 elections, mobile phones, and especially SMS, were also widely used to mobilize protest in real time and disseminate calls to action initially posted on web forums. As Eskinder Nega, editor and columnist of the popular newspapers *Menelik*, *Asqual*, and *Satenaw*, pointed out: 'We were publishing articles by prominent people in the diaspora. Fundamental debates were going on in websites such as 'Ethiomedia' and the 'Ethiopian Review' and we were translating them because we wanted to make sure they were known to the public in Ethiopia' (As quoted in Gagliardone 2014b).

This convergence of different media forms used in 2005 deeply resonates with the 'media relays' that characterized the protests in Tunisia and Egypt in 2010, when activists combined different media forms to reach those who had no access to the latest technologies (Wilson and Dunn 2011; Aouragh and Alexander 2011). Yet, in striking contrast to the media and scholarly attention given to the Arab Spring, similar use of new media in Ethiopia five years earlier received negligible international attention.[1] International news coverage mostly focused on the political violence around the elections and not on this revolutionary use of new media *avant la lettre*.

While international commentators did not understand or report on these early forms of digital activism in Ethiopia, the Ethiopian rulers took notice. So much so that, after the protests and the violence had subdued, the Ethiopian government started to progressively trim the complex communication network that had assembled different voices across a plurality of media forms. First, the SMS network was interrupted (June 2005); a few months later some of the most vocal Ethiopian journalists who challenged the results of the election and called for more democracy were arrested and their papers forced to close (November 2005); finally, a year after the contested election, the government started to block access to blogs and websites where dissenting opinions were found (May 2006).

This 'failed revolution' represented the beginning of a complex process of negotiation between the Ethiopian government and various generations of digital activists seeking to use new media to promote political change. This chapter traces the contours of this contested relationship through the analysis of one of the most critical events in the recent history of digital activism in Ethiopia—the arrest of six members of the Zone9 blogging collective and the global campaign launched for their release. The case of the Zone9 bloggers does not only offer insights on the opportunities and risks of digital activism in Ethiopia, but also highlights some of the contradictions that characterize digital activism in closed regimes and its international ramifications.

Zone 9 Bloggers—Seeking a Shrinking Middle Ground

Kality, south of the Ethiopian capital Addis Ababa, is one the country's most notorious prisons, where many prominent political prisoners have been held. It is divided into eight zones. The name Zone9 was chosen in 2012 by a group of bloggers to refer to an imaginary 9th detention area existing beyond Kality's walls—Ethiopia itself.[2] Despite their name, the criticism moved by the Zone9ers—Abel Wabella, Atnaf Berhane, Mahlet Fantahun, Natnail Feleke, Zelalem Kibret, Befekadu Hailu, Soleyana S. Gebremichael, Endalk Chala, and Jomanex Kasaye—towards the Ethiopian government sought to distance itself from older grievances and accusations. The bloggers tried new avenues instead, advocating reform from within, rather than beyond, the political framework created by Ethiopia's ruling party, the Ethiopian People Revolutionary Democratic Front (EPRDF). Unlike bloggers posting on diaspora-led platforms such as 'nazret' or 'ethiomedia', they decided not to attack core elements of the EPRDF's ideology—e.g. ethnic federalism and revolutionary democracy. The Zone9ers, on the contrary, asked Ethiopian rulers to #RespectTheConstitution, the hashtag used for one of their campaigns pressuring the government to live up to the principles it had established to rebuild the nation after the civil war, including the right to freedom of expression. Following the motto 'We blog because we care', the Zone9ers produced stories that aimed to progressively build an 'alternative independent narration of socio-political conditions in Ethiopia'.[3] In contrast to many bloggers in the Ethiopian diaspora who tended to write in English, most Zone9ers privileged Amharic in their posts, signalling a willingness to contribute to national debates and reach a broader audience within Ethiopia. Rather than considering Ethiopian rulers as enemies to confront and attack, they exploited the power of social networking platforms such as Twitter to initiate conversations with those in power, for example, engaging in unprecedented debates with Foreign Minister Tedros Adhanom, the government's most active presence on social media.

Despite the efforts to build a middle ground from which to engage with the Ethiopian government, and calling for reform from within rather than an overthrow of the regime, on the 25th of April, 2014, six of the bloggers were arrested—Abel Wabella, Atnaf Berhane, Mahlet Fantahun, Natnail Feleke, Zelalem Kibret, Befekadu Hailu—along with three other journalists—Asmamaw Hailegeorgis, Tesfalem Waldyes and Edom Kassaye.[4] The initial charges included working with international human rights organizations and taking part in digital security training. The group was subsequently also charged with terrorism. The accusations included collaborating with outlawed opposition groups such as Ginbot 7 and conspiring with foreign organizations to use social media to destabilize Ethiopia. Some of the evidence given in support of the terrorist activity during the court cases included the use of Tactical Technology Collective's 'Security in a Box: Tools and Tactics in Digital Security' and blog commentary on Wael Ghonim's book 'Revolution 2.0' about the use of social media during the Arab Spring and its potential relevance for Ethiopia.[5]

The arrests stirred a high-profile international social media campaign to free the arrested bloggers, which spread online behind the #FreeZone9Bloggers hashtag. The popularity of the campaign was unprecedented in Ethiopia.[6] After its launch, the campaign gained visibility internationally, including the first African-wide 'tweetathon' organized in solidarity by Nigerian and Tanzanian bloggers, and legal petitions addressed to the African Union and the United Nations' Human Rights Council. The campaign was especially active during the initial months of the imprisonment and was promoted by international human rights and freedom of speech organizations such as the Committee to Protect Journalists (CPJ), Human Rights Watch, Global Voices, the Media Defense Legal Initiative, the Electronic Frontier Foundation, and Reporters Without Borders. After tens of delayed court hearings and over 500 days in prison without charge, the Zone9 bloggers were finally acquitted of terrorism charges in October 2015, even if a few charges remain.

Methodology

In order to explore these contradictions underpinning digital activism in Ethiopia, and especially the shifting boundaries between national and global forms of digital activism, we compared data collected from two distinct and high-profile campaigns linked to the Zone9 bloggers in Ethiopia. The first dataset includes the first 30 days of tweets posted using the hashtag #RespectTheConstitution, consisting of a total of 1625 tweets published between 4 December 2012 and 3 January 2013. The second dataset comprises the first 30 days of tweets published using hashtag #FreeZone9Bloggers, consisting of a total of 38,487 tweets produced between 25 April 2014 and 25 May 2014.

Our research methodology was developed in three phases, combining quantitative and qualitative methods. During a first phase, we imported all tweets using the hashtags #RespectTheConstitution and #FreeZone9Bloggers through the Twitter data reseller GNIP. We then employed the open-source data-analysis tool Elasticsearch, and its visual interface Kibana, to provide a background analysis of both datasets to gain a comparative understanding of the overall communicative dynamics of both campaigns. In this process we sought to identify some of the 'communicative metrics' developed by Bruns and Stieglitz (2012) to systematically analyse Twitter hashtag conversations:

- The number of tweets in the hashtag dataset;
- The number of unique users contributing to the hashtag dataset;
- The percentage of original tweets in the hashtag data set (i.e., tweets that are neither @replies nor retweets);
- The percentage of genuine @replies in the hashtag data set (i.e., @replies that are not retweets);

- The percentage of retweets in the hashtag data set;
- The percentage of tweets in the hashtag data set that contain URLs.

In addition to these metrics, we identified additional variables that would help better understand the communicative dimensions characterizing the campaigns.

- We focused on the time–frequency distribution of the tweets to help identify events during which there was a significant increase or decreased in the number of tweets produced.
- We also identified the most active users in both of the campaigns in terms of the tweets produced.
- We also identified users who were the most retweeted by others in both of the campaigns.
- Wherever possible, we also tracked the geolocations of the tweets provided in the author profile of the users involved in both Twitter campaigns. As Twitter does not often provide reliable geographical data, this also required cross-verifying the location with the stated location found in the user's Twitter profiles where necessary.
- Finally, we defined the most influential actors for further analysis by employing a combination of three different criteria: (a) most tweets produced; (b) most retweeted; and (e) most followed users.

During the second part of the research, we combined this background research and carried out a social network analysis of both datasets. In particular, we exported the data to Gephi, the open-source social network analysis/visualization tool, and employed social network analysis algorithms to better understand the local, regional and global dimensions of both campaigns. Based on these, we then mapped out visually some of the key relationships and actors in both campaigns. We especially focused on the following relationships found in the Twitter data:

- *RT-relationships*: We looked at the relationships in all the retweets.
- *'@'-mention relationships*: We looked at all the instances of @mentions and relationships behind these.
- *Follower relationships*: Finally, we also extracted follower-relationships for the five most influential participants in the #FreeZone9Bloggers campaign and analysed the connections between more than 30,000 followers and relationships amongst them.

In addition to this, we also did basic text mining to understand the word frequency of different terms used in them and the hashtags associated with them.

Finally, we complemented the quantitative part with more qualitative discourse analysis and interviews. This consisted of semi-structured interviews with the key stakeholders involved in the #FreeZone9Bloggers campaign as well as with media professionals and journalists familiar with the media environment in Ethiopia. Eleven interviewees were selected through snowball sampling based on existing research engagement in Ethiopia as well as identifying the most influential Twitter users found in the social network analysis. From both the discourse analysis and interview questions, we were especially interested in identifying the relationship between the global and local dimensions implicated in these two digital activist campaigns, and especially how the government had responded to the #FreeZone9Bloggers campaign as well as whether there has been any convergent spill-over effects of the global campaign to other local media forms in Ethiopia.

Campaigning Locally and Globally

The #FreeZone9Bloggers campaign was an unprecedented event in the history of digital activism in Ethiopia, especially because of its volume, persistence and international visibility. Fig. 2.1 visualizes the results of the social network analysis performed on the collected tweets, based on node centrality[7] and community detection[8] algorithms. It indicates how the campaign was animated by a number of loose twitter 'communities'. In the bottom left corner, the global free speech activist community can be identified, formed around the influential Twitter accounts of freedom of speech organisations such as @africamedia_CPJ, @globalvoices, @advox and @feathersproject. In the centre, are some of the diasporic Twitter users involved in the campaign, revolving around the prolific @_emi_m, who has a central role in the network cluster. Next, are some of the people closely involved with the Zone9 collective such as @jomanex and @zone9ers, and writers and researchers based in Ethiopia such as @halelule and @debirhaner. Finally, on the right side, are various Twitter users sharing a base both in Ethiopia and its diaspora, and who tend to usually cover issues related to popular culture.

Even though the boundaries cutting across different groups are porous, the analysis reveals how the #FreeZone9Bloggers campaign brought

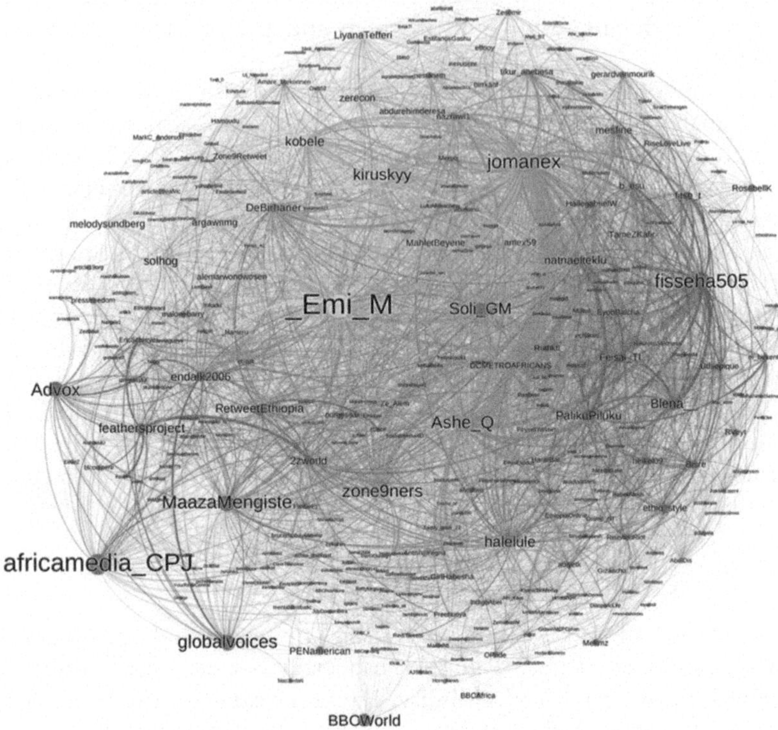

Fig. 2.1 Retweets behind the #FreeZone9bloggers campaign

together fragmented and separate communities, with a significant presence of actors with a global reach.

This pattern stands in stark contrast with the second campaign we analysed, #RespectTheConstitution, which represented the most ambitious initiative launched by the Zone9 bloggers on Twitter. Tweets using this hashtag criticized the government's record especially on issues related to freedom of expression (Fig. 2.2):

As illustrated in Fig. 2.3, this campaign produced fewer retweets and tended to be dominated by the Zone9 bloggers themselves (at the centre of the graph) and their immediate social networks. Around them, divergent and smaller sub-communities were also involved, composed of some diasporic bloggers, such as @semhar and @palikupiluku, as well as

Fig. 2.2 Tweets addressing the Ethiopian government to #RespectTheConstitution

small sub-communities in Ethiopia such as the nexus of Oromo online news sites such as @gadaa and @opride.

Even if the campaign succeeded in attracting the attention of programmes such as Aljazeera Stream, produced by Aljazeera English to

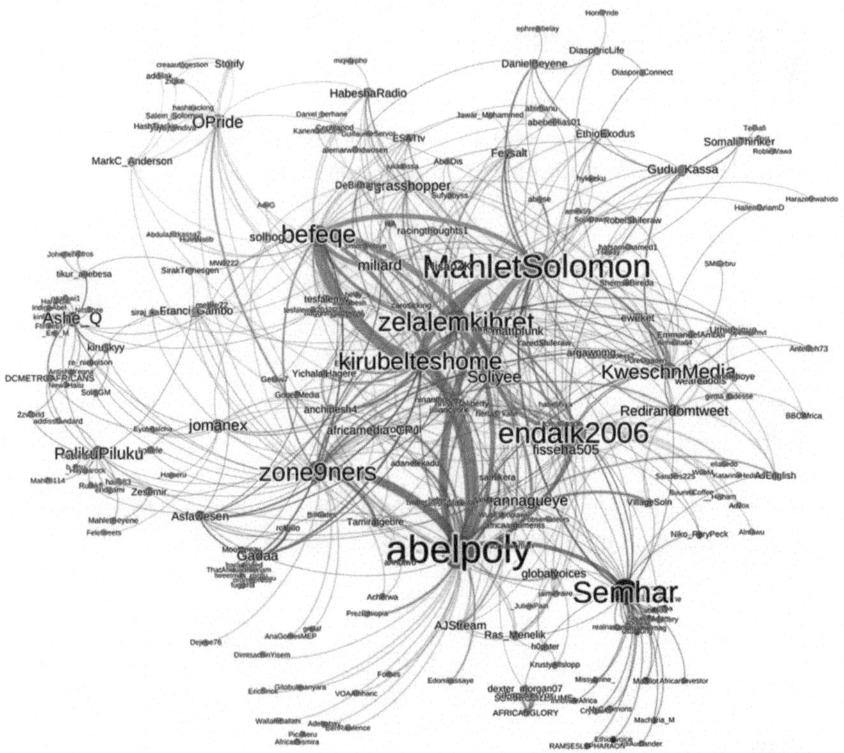

Fig. 2.3 Retweets in the #RespectTheConstitution campaign

follow digital tendencies in different parts of the world, the campaign nonetheless reached only a few actors with global influence. In general, few nodes were involved beyond the Zone9 bloggers themselves and their immediate network.

An even clearer picture of the localized and relatively limited nature of the #RespectTheConstitution campaign emerges from our analysis of @-mentions (Fig. 2.4). Most of the mentions occur within the Ethiopian community associated with the Zone9 bloggers and its diasporic supporters. The central role played by Zone9 bloggers in these networks is also visible, surrounded by small pockets of other users involved in the Ethiopian media scene.

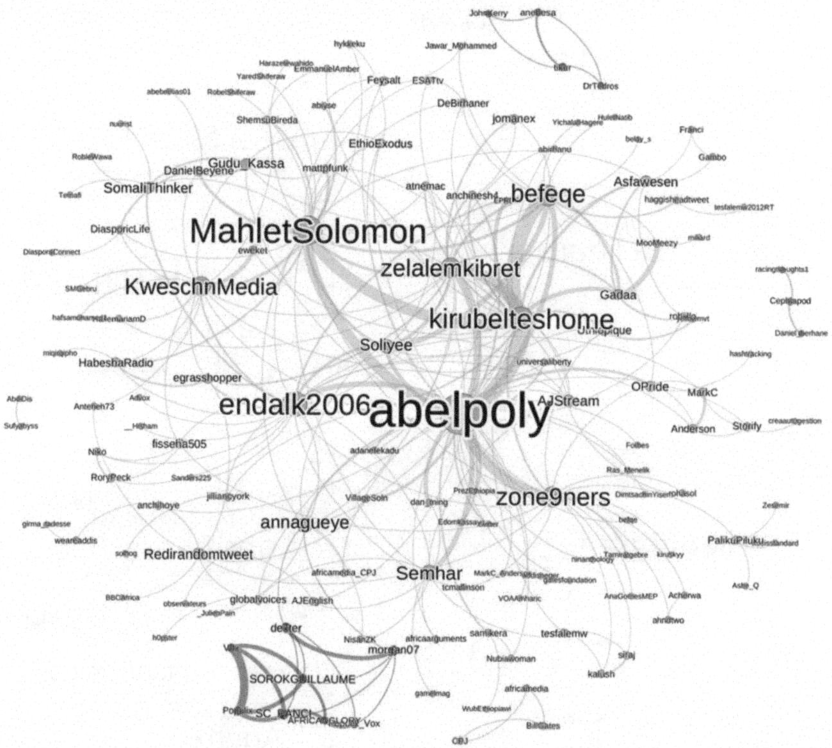

Fig. 2.4 @-Mentions in the #RespectTheConstitution campaign

It is also worth noting that in the top-right corner is a small cluster which includes institutional figures who were called upon by the campaigners, such as @DrTedros, Ethiopia's Minister of Foreign Affairs, and @JohnKerry, the USA Secretary of State who had planned a visit to Ethiopia later in 2014.

If we shift attention back to the #FreeZone9Bloggers campaign and comparatively analyse the @-mentions that characterized it, it becomes evident how greater much efforts were made in this case to call upon or get the attention of the same figures (Fig. 2.5).

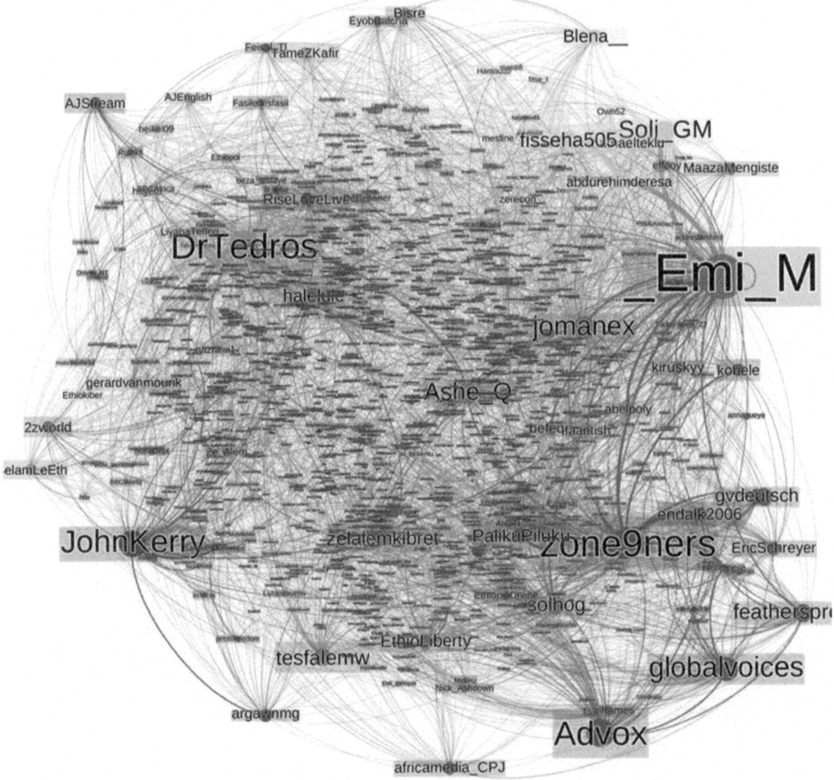

Fig. 2.5 @-Mentions in the #FreeZone9Bloggers campaign

The reason behind the shift in the relevance for the @JohnKerry twitter handle can be explained the fact that, in a move that surprised most national and international observers, the Zone9Bloggers were arrested just days before the planned state visit by the US Secretary of State to Ethiopia. Despite concerted efforts to call upon Kerry to put pressure on the Ethiopian government, he only briefly mentioned the arrest in his official speech and the incident had no detrimental consequences on the relationship between the USA and Ethiopia.[9] This illustrated the complexities and difficulties of those forms of digital activism that seek to appeal to national and international players who present themselves as bulwarks of digital rights, but which are also interested in maintaining good relationships with countries like Ethiopia that are considered partners in the war against terrorism in the region and efficient in making use of development aid. Tedros Adhanom, on his part, was called upon because of the engaging conversations he had earlier had with some of the bloggers, via Twitter, as well as personally. Most users asked him to come forward in support of the bloggers, given the favourable words he had of them in the past. He never responded to such requests and continued to be silent on the bloggers' arrest.[10]

A final element that offers a revealing comparison of the differences in the communicative dynamics of the two campaigns, is the analysis of the share of tweets posted respectively by lead users (top 1 % most active users), highly active users (next 9 % of active users), and least active users (the remaining 90 % of users: the 'long tail' of the user base), and the relationship between original tweets and retweets implicated in both datasets. As Bruns and Stieglitz (2012) explain, these metrics help understanding the nature and significance of different types of campaigns carried out on Twitter. As the previous graphs indicate, while the #RespectTheConstitution campaign was dominated by lead users (see the thickness of the links connecting only a few users when compared to the thin links outside of the centre of the network cluster), in the case of #FreeZone9Bloggers there was a greater balance among tweets posted by different types of users. If we further analyse the ratio between original tweets and retweets, most tweets produced by the #RespectTheConstitution campaign consist of original commentary, whereas the majority of tweets using the #FreeZone9Bloggers are retweets (Figs. 2.3, 2.4, 2.6 and 2.7).

Taken together, then, these metrics point towards two distinctly different types of campaigns. The #RespectTheConstitution campaign displays characteristics of those types of conversations occurring around events that are well known to participants, such as popular TV programmes or elections. According to Bruns and Stieglitz (2012), these conversations aim not as much to disseminate urgent information, but rather to address a topic or an event within a community of like-minded users. The #FreeZone9Bloggers campaign, instead shows communicative characteristics that are closer to campaigns such as #Kony2012, for example, where a broader number of users around the world supported a cause and contributed to its visibility, without knowing one another or being knowledgeable enough about the issue at stake to offer original commentaries.

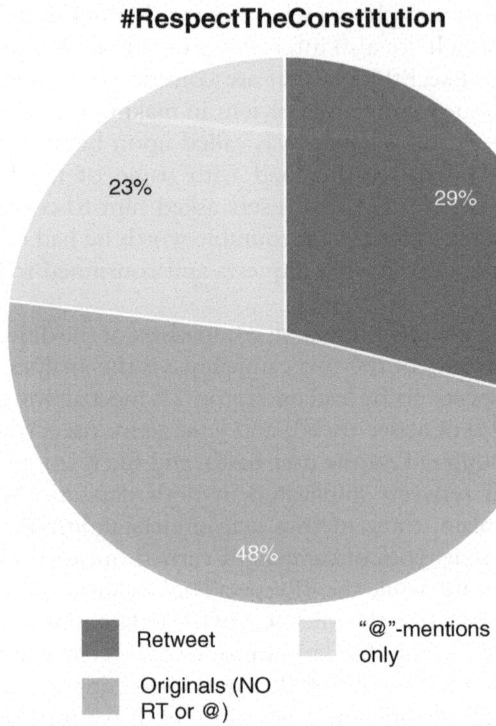

Fig. 2.6 Proportion of original tweets and retweets #RespectTheConstitution

Discussion

The comparative analysis of the two campaigns highlights some the tensions and paradoxes that have characterized the relationship between the Zone9bloggers, the Ethiopian government, and a multiplicity of international actors (from NGOs such as CPJ to the US government) that became involved with the campaign after the bloggers' arrests. It also indicates some broader contradictions underpinning digital activism in Africa, especially in closed regimes. We focus on two in particular, connecting national and international forms of activism.

One of the core accusations filed against the Zone9 bloggers was that they had collaborated with 'external agents' to promote political change in Ethiopia. Yet as the analysis of the #RespectTheConstitution campaign

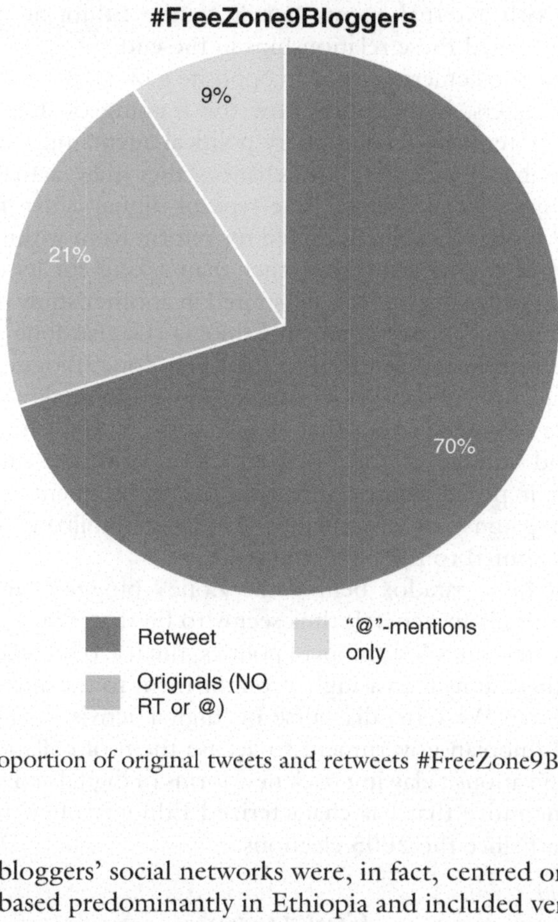

Fig. 2.7 Proportion of original tweets and retweets #FreeZone9Bloggers

reveals, the bloggers' social networks were, in fact, centred on individuals and groups based predominantly in Ethiopia and included very few actors with a global reach. The distinctly local flavour of the kind of digital activism carried out by the Zone9 bloggers is further substantiated by the style and content of their writings as a whole.[11] As the analysis of the actors involved in #FreeZone9Bloggers campaign suggests, it seems the arrest itself produced the result of projecting the bloggers closer to the sphere of action of human rights organizations with whom the Ethiopian government had historically entertained hostile relationships. This phenomenon highlights a first paradox, connected to the ability of the actions pursued by the Ethiopian government against its opponents to act as a 'self-fulfilling prophecy'. The accusations that the bloggers entertained relationships with external agents hostile to the Ethiopian government actually strengthened these relationships in the end.[12]

A second paradox emerges from an opposite gaze at events surrounding the Zone9 bloggers, highlighting how the framing of digital media as powerful and potentially revolutionary political agents may act as a 'self-impairing prophecy', reducing the chances they may actually serve to produce lasting political change. The type of digital activism promoted by the Zone9 bloggers explicitly aimed for reform from within the framework established by the EPRDF, rather than asking for its replacement with a different order. As we have illustrated in another study detailing the tone of social media conversations in Ethiopia (Gagliardone et al 2016), almost all the conversations linked to the #FreeZone9Bloggers campaign were engaging, rather than polarizing, stressing the quality and innovativeness of the bloggers, rather that attacking the Ethiopian government. The reach and volume of the #RespectTheConstitution campaign also indicates that it posed limited threat to the government—yet the fear that such campaigns could somehow have a destabilizing potential in Ethiopia contributed to the bloggers' arrest.

The overarching paradox behind the Zone9 bloggers, and of digital activism in Ethiopia in general, thus seems to be that, while the aims are rooted deeply in domestic Ethiopian politics, the use of new media as way to carry out these aims increasingly brought them to the ambit of a more global (and often Western) discourse of 'digital activism'. This in, turn, allowed the Ethiopian government to accuse them of collaborating with 'foreign organizations', clawing back new forms of digital activism into the pre-existing narrative that has characterized Ethiopia's new media environment at least since the 2005 elections.

Conclusion

Closed regimes seem to have progressively learned how to exploit the contradictions of an international agenda seeking, but often failing, to balance between development effectiveness, respect of human rights, and fight against terrorism. The case of the Zone9 bloggers represents a dramatic, but not uncommon, example of how forms of digital activism seeking to promote change from within these types of regimes are being severely affected by these contradictory strategies.

In accordance to what Jean Francois Bayart (2000) argued in the case of many African countries interacting with the international system, the

Ethiopian government has relied on extraversion to achieve its goals, manipulating its unequal relationship with the external environment in its own favour. The accusations of terrorism moved towards the government's opponents under the Anti-Terrorism law are one of the clearest example of this course of action. Numerous international organizations, including the Committee to Protect Journalists, Reporters without Borders, Amnesty International and Human Rights Watch have accused the Ethiopian government of taking advantage of a law they label as 'deeply flawed' (Human Rights Watch 2013) in order to silence critical voices. The government has responded to this criticism by re-asserting the legitimacy of its acts and how the law has been passed in compliance with UN Security Council Resolution 1373, which requires states to ensure 'terrorist acts are established as serious criminal offences in domestic laws' (UN Security Council 2001, p. 2). As Ethiopia's Prime Minister Hailemariam Desalegn remarked answering a question on the arrest of the Zone9 bloggers 'I don't think becoming a blogger makes somebody immune, if someone involves into this terrorist network that destabilizes my country'.[13]

Analysis of the kind we offered in this chapter aims at using evidence to offer empirically grounded counter-arguments to these types of assertions and, by highlighting some of the contradictions between international and national forms of activisms, assert the need for new paths that can support, rather than put at risk, the work of local agents of change.

Notes

1. It must be noted that in 2005 Internet penetration in Ethiopia was just 0.22 %, and mobile penetration was just 0.55 %, but as Wilson and Dunn pointed out (2011), at the time of the protest in Egypt the twitter population was 0.001 %, and this did not prevent some international media talking about a social media revolution.
2. An account of the origins of the name Zone9 can be found in the Zone9's acceptance speech for the 2015 International Press Freedom Award (https://cpj.org/awards/2015/zone-9-bloggers-ethiopia.php)
3. http://www.zoneniners.com/. Accessed on 14 May, 2016
4. Two members of the collective, Endalkachew Chala and Soliana Shimeles, were charged *in absentia*.
5. https://trialtrackerblog.org/2014/08/12/full-translation-of-zone9ers-charge-sheet/. Accessed on 14 May 2016.

6. See http://www.bbc.com/news/blogs-trending-272124728. Accessed on 14 May 2016.
7. We used Eigenvector centrality algorithms to measure the influence of a node in a network, indicated by their size in the social network.
8. Modularity algorithms measures the strength of division of a network into groups, clusters or communities. We coloured different communities based on this to illustrate the complex relationships behind the #FreeZone9Bloggers campaign.
9. When we interviewed the organizers behind #FreeZone9Bloggers, lobbying John Kerry was the key strategic aim in the first few days of the campaign when it exploded in popularity
10. There was also anecdotal evidence that the arrests themselves reflected a lack of consensus within the Ethiopian government about how to control social media in preparation for the 2015 elections. It is still unclear who authorized the arrests even if there are unverified accounts that this was carried out by the National Intelligence and Security Services (NISS) without the explicit knowledge of the Office of Government and Communication Affairs (OFGCA) who is usually in charge of media policy.
11. A translation of some of the most important writings of Zone9ers before the arrest can be accessed at http://trialtrackerblog.org. A counterargument could be that while acting locally, the bloggers could have been funded or directed by external actors. Given the transparency that has always characterized the work of the Zone9 bloggers, and the information we collected through interviews with a number of individuals that who close to, but also wrote in opposition to the Zone9bloggers, we feel confident to rule out these types of hypotheses. An additional indication of the absence of external influencers is the fact that the prosecutor himself has consistently failed to provide evidence of such links during the trials.
12. Once released, many of the bloggers sought to fend off the power of this strategy, and, while they accepted some of the awards offered to them by influential international NGOs, they also decided to keep a low profile, rather than posing as darlings of Western-based organizations.
13. Hailemariam Desalegn, quoted in Fortin (2014)

References

Aouragh, M., & Alexander, A. (2011). The Arab spring|the Egyptian experience: Sense and nonsense of the internet revolution. *International Journal of Communication*, *5*, 15.

Bayart, J.-F. (2000). Africa in the world: A history of extraversion. *African Affairs*, *99*(395), 217–267.

Bruns, A., & Stieglitz, S. (2012). Quantitative approaches to comparing communication patterns on twitter. *Journal of Technology in Human Services, 30*(3–4), 160–185.

Fortin, J. (2014) Ethiopia: Bloggers and journalists are charged as terrorists. *The New York Times*, July 18. http://www.nytimes.com/2014/07/19/world/africa/ethiopia-bloggers-and-journalists-are-charged-as-terrorists.html. Accessed 28 Aug 2014.

Fourie, E. (2015). China's example for Meles' Ethiopia: When development "models" land. *The Journal of Modern African Studies, 53* (03), 289–316.

Gagliardone, I. (2014a). Media development with Chinese characteristics. *Global Media Journal, 4*(2), 1–16.

Gagliardone, I. (2014b). New media and the developmental state in Ethiopia. *African Affairs, 113*(451), 279–299.

Gagliardone, I., Pohjonen, M., Beyene, Z., Zerai, A., Aynekulu, G., Bekalu, M., Bright, J., Moges, M.A., Seifu, M., Stremlau, N., & Taflan, P. (2016). Mechachal-online debates and elections in Ethiopia. Working paper three: From hate speech to engagement in social media.

Human Rights Watch. (2013). Ethiopia: Terrorism Law Decimates Media. http://www.hrw.org/news/2013/05/03/ethiopia-terrorism-law-decimates-media.

Human Rights Watch. (2014). *"They Know Everything We Do". Telecom and internet surveillance in Ethiopia*. New York: Human Rights Watch.

Rashid, S. (2015) Commodity exchanges and market development: What have we learned? https://www.researchgate.net/profile/Shahidur_Rashid/publication/283018014_Agricultural_Commodity_Exchange_and_Market_Development_What_Have_we_Learned/links/5626ae7908aeabddac935e82.pdf. Accessed 9 May 2016.

Skjerdal, T. S. (2011). Journalists or activists? Self-identity in the thiopian diaspora online community. *Journalism, 12*(6), 727–744.

UN Security Council 2001 Resolution 1373.

Wilson, C., & Dunn, A. (2011). Digital media in the Egyptian revolution: Descriptive analysis from the Tahrir data sets. *International Journal of Communication, 5*, 1248–1272.

Iginio Gagliardone is Lecturer in Media Studies at the University of Witwatersrand and Associate Research Fellow in New Media and Human Rights at the University of Oxford. His research and publications focus on media and political change, particularly in Sub-Saharan Africa, and on the emergence of distinctive models of the information society worldwide. He has led numerous research projects, from examining the role of Information and Communication

Technologies in peace-building and state-building in Eastern Africa, to understanding the increasing role of emerging powers such as China in the media and telecommunication sectors in Africa, to analyzing the nature and significance of hate speech online ahead of elections. He completed his PhD at the London School of Economics and Political Science, investigating the relationship between development and destabilization in Ethiopia.

Matti Pohjonen is Research Fellow for the VOX-Pol Network of Excellence, a European academic research network focused on researching the prevalence, contours, functions, and impacts of violent online political extremism and responses to it. He is a digital media anthropologist whose work focuses on developing new research methods and theoretical approaches to understand emerging digital cultures in the developing world. He worked previously for the Programme for Comparative Media Law and Policy (PCLMP), at the University of Oxford, for a project mapping online debates in Ethiopia. He finished his PhD from the School of Oriental and African Studies (SOAS), where he was also an AHRC-funded Post-Doctorate Research Fellow (2013), Teaching Fellow (2007–2010) and Research Fellow in Digital Culture (2003–2006).

CHAPTER 3

Baba Jukwa and the Digital Repertoires of Connective Action in a 'Competitive Authoritarian Regime': The Case of Zimbabwe

Admire Mare

Introduction and Background of the Study

Most of the studies (Gerbaudo 2012; Lim 2014; Švelch and Štětka 2016; González-Bailón et al. 2011) conducted the during and after the Arab Spring, the Occupy Wall Street movement in America, Occupy Nigeria and Spanish *indignados* suggest that activists and social movements (henceforth, SMs) are increasingly making use of Facebook pages and WhatsApp groups as well as Twitter hashtags to mobilize support,

---

It refers to a hybrid regime type in which formal democratic institutions are widely viewed as the primary means of gaining power, but in which fraud, civil liberties violations and abuse of state and media resources so skew the playing field in favour of the incumbent (Levitsky and Way 2010, p. 5).

A. Mare (✉)
Department of Film, Television and Journalism, Faculty of Humanities, University of Johannesburg, Johannesburg, South Africa
e-mail: admiremare@gmail.com

B. Mutsvairo (ed.), *Digital Activism in the Social Media Era*,
DOI 10.1007/978-3-319-40949-8_3

coordinate demonstrations and circulate protest action frames. Research (see Neumayer and Raffl 2008; Harlow 2012; Valenzuela 2013; Švelch and Štětka 2016) has been carried out on the creative use of Facebook pages in several North and South American, European and Australasian countries. In the case of the Spanish *indignados*, the movement's online diffusion was accompanied by the offline diffusion of behaviour (González-Bailón et al. 2011). Similarly in Colombia, the 'One Million March against FARC' Facebook page was used to mobilize a lot of people against FARC (Neumayer and Raffl 2008). Using the *Justicia Rodrigo Rosenberg* and *Movimiento Cívico Nacional* Facebook pages in Guatemala, Harlow (2012) argues that the SM transitioned from operating online towards offline spaces thereby helping to catalyse political change.

In Chile, the Student Federation of the University of Chile (FECH), utilized Facebook mainly to call for protest actions, to highlight the achievements of the movement, and to indicate their opponents (Valenzuela 2013). Facebook pages like the Spanish Real Democracy Now (DRY) and We Are All Khaled Said (WAAKS) have also received widespread scholarly attention for their roles in the *indignados* movement and Arab Spring (Gerbaudo 2012, 2016; Lim 2014). In authoritarian regimes, Facebook pages and groups have been found to allow activists and SMs to bypass offline public spaces which are generally repressed and fear-infested (Gerbaudo 2012; Lim 2014). These social media platforms have also been seen to expand the discursive and public spheres in liberal democracies. For Švelch and Štětka (2016), Facebook pages have become a primary conduit for emotional protest, which can be subsequently taken to the streets. Collectively, these studies show that SM actors are appropriating new media to recruit, engage, organize and communicate with its various constituencies.

Cognisant of the blurring nature of the relationship between physical and online public spaces, Lim argues that modern SMs oscillate from 'real to the virtual (and back again)'. The point is that digital media and physical public spaces have become interdependent dimensions of SMs (Lim 2014). Ayres (1999) has focused on what he terms 'from the streets to the internet' which is suggestive of the transformation of SMs from being offline consummated towards an online presence. In the same vein, Gerbaudo (2012) observes that SMs in 'liquid modernity' (Bauman 2004) start online before building and recruiting offline volunteers. It is arguable that the process is cyclical: SMs can start online before moving offline or vice versa depending on the political opportunity structures. These foregoing arguments further corroborate the idea that contemporary activism has shifted from generally being street-orientated to encapsulate online spaces as venues and tools for instigating political change.

As in other parts of the globe, studies (Mare 2014; Mutsvairo and Sirks 2015; Bosch 2016; Gerbaudo 2016) focusing on the deployment of social media platforms by activists and SMs have also sprouted in Africa. Bosch (2016) discusses about the South African student-led campaign known as Rhodes Must Fall (#RMF) to explore youth activism and counter-memory via Twitter. In Egypt, research (Herrera 2012; Gerbaudo 2012; Honwana 2013) has demonstrated that the 'We are all Khaled Said' Facebook page which was created in June 2010 to protest against the police-inflected death of Said, played an instrumental role in the instigation of the Egyptian uprising. In Tunisia, a Facebook page 'Mr President, Tunisians are setting themselves on fire' was established which also played an invaluable role in organizing and galvanizing country-wide protests (Honwana 2013). Most of the research in Africa suggests that Facebook pages provide the means to bypass traditional news gatekeepers, thereby enabling movement participants to publish their own information and publicize activities which are often overlooked by the mainstream media.

In Zimbabwe, very few studies (Mare 2014; Mujere and Mwatwara 2015; Mutsvairo and Sirks 2015) have discussed the impact of Baba Jukwa (henceforth, BJ) Facebook page on offline political processes. For instance, Mutsvairo and Sirks (2015) looked at the contribution of the BJ Facebook page in reinforcing political participation in Zimbabwe. They found that that in spite of the page's ability to encourage Zimbabweans to openly discuss and share thoughts, there simply is no evidence that BJ has helped facilitate increased democratic participation (Mutsvairo and Sirks 2015). Although Mutsvairo and Sirks (2015) described BJ's Facebook page as an epitome of online political activism, they did not address the issue from the perspective of SM theory. This chapter seeks to fill this gap. As Agarwal et al. (2012) note, there is a fundamental lack of fundamental research on the formation and transformation of cyber-collective SMs. In this context, the critical examination of the BJ Facebook page may also help to show how some internet-enhanced SMs fail to make it to the streets.

SMs and the Internet

SMs refer 'to informal networks, based on shared beliefs and solidarity, which mobilize about conflictual issues, through the frequent use of various forms of protest' (Della Porta and Diani 1999, p. 16). Scholars

(Melucci 1996; Della Porta and Diani 1999) also observe that SMs constitute an organized set of constituents pushing for the implementation of certain policies or specific changes in society's structure or values in order to achieve a specific social goal. They tend to emerge in response to situations of inequality, oppression and/or unmet social, political, economic or cultural demands. Besides mobilizing resources, framing their grievances and proposing new models and visions for economic and political power relations (Della Porta and Diani 1999), SMs also deploy 'repertoires of collective action' (Tilly 1978). These are the set of means that are effectively available to a given set of people and which they use to act collectively in order to make claims on individuals and groups (Tilly 1978).

In recent years, the proliferation of new media technologies has transformed the way in which political action is imagined, experienced and organized by SMs (Diani 2000; Van Laer and Van Aelst 2010; McCaughey and Ayers 2003). Scholars (van de Donk et al. 2004) have theorized about the way the internet and other new media technologies are actually changing the internal and external organization of SMs. 'Physical' organizations within the movement are appropriating the internet while new 'virtual' social movements are entering the field (Edwards 2004). SMs which are 'internet-supported and enhanced' (Van Laer and Van Aelst 2010) have been characterized as 'cyber-movements' (Palczewski 2001), 'cyber-enabled' social movement organizations (Mao and Wang 2012), 'networked movements' (Castells 2012) and cyber-collective social movements (Agarwal et al. 2012). It is important to underscore that although the availability of new communication technologies makes traditional SMs somewhat dispensable for mobilization purposes, a certain institutionalization remains necessary in order to exert a more lasting political influence (Van Laer and Van Aelst 2010).

Cyber-enabled social movement organizations (CeSMOs) have been defined as a group of people, facilitated by the internet or mobile technologies, that assembles to lead, participate in, discuss and implement social behaviour centred on a defined topic/interest or concerning a particular event/grievance/ issue (Mao and Wang 2012). These SMs are characterized by their volunteerism and activism roots, perplexing self-organizing patterns, sudden and unpredictable onsets, rapid dynamic growth, complex interactivity between online and offline activities and the potential reach to a large number of users. As Edwards (2004, p. 164) notes, the internet makes new, virtual organization patterns possible that are characterized by place-independent cooperation between persons or organizations. These movements tend to have a relatively heterogeneous constituency, fluid character, 'leaderless' networks and horizontal and symmetrical participation structures (Castells 2012).

A never-ending debate has ensued within academic literature pitting cyber-optimists and cyber-pessimists focusing on the potential for new media to deliver political change. Cyber-optimists (Shirky 2011; Diamond 2010; Papacharissi 2010) celebrate social media's revolutionary and democratizing potential in ways that resonate with technological deterministic discourses. New media technologies are viewed as enabling social movement actors to report news, expose wrongdoing, express opinions, mobilize protest and monitor elections. Social media are also touted as spawning new repertoires of collective action (Castells 2012) like 'connective action' (Bennett and Segerberg 2012) at the local, national and transnational level.

Cyber-pessimists (Gladwell 2010; Morozov 2011) question the revolutionary potential of the social media in bringing about social change. They show that new media platforms are being used by authoritarian regimes to track, suppress, and silence dissidents. They also highlight that online activism instead of helping activists actually distract them from engaging in real physical protests and allows authoritarian regimes to conduct create Orwellian modes of state surveillance over individual and group behaviour (Lim 2012). Morozov (2011, 2014) criticizes cyber-optimism for promoting the gospel of 'technological solutionism'[1] where technical fixes are seen as an answer to democratic challenges (Morozov 2014). According to him, technological solutionism 'impoverish[es] and infantilize our public debate' (Morozov 2014, p. 43). As Morozov (2011) observes, this type of activism gives those who participate in 'slacktivist'[2] campaigns an illusion of having a meaningful impact on the world without demanding anything more than joining a Facebook group.

An Overview of Social Movements in Zimbabwe

In Zimbabwe, SMs have been active since the days of the colonial struggle through the post-colonial era (Moyo 1993; McCandless 2009; Muzondidya 2014;). SMs were instrumental in mobilizing people for struggles against racial inequality, discrimination, oppression and land expropriations (Win 2004; Zeilig 2008; Muzondidya 2014). However the dawn of independence led to a situation where SMs went to bed with the ruling elite, thereby abdicating on their role as the 'voice of the voiceless.' As cheerleaders, SMs adopted positions, which can be characterized as: 'complementing government efforts; working only on development; working hand in hand; and not against the government' (Win 2004, p. 20). The new government also sought to contain the mobilization agency of labour by subordinating it to the state. In rural areas, the government organized public action through government-controlled Village and Ward Development Committees in order to contain the growth of SMs (Zeilig 2010). This situation, however, changed in the late 1980s when militant student and trade unionism cut its umbilical cord from the political society paving way for radical activism. Given the weak political opposition at that particular juncture, SMs metamorphosed from being 'praise singers' of the ruling oligarchy to become the 'surrogate opposition'. Trade unions protested against the imposition of the World Bank-sponsored Structural Adjustment Programmes (SAPs) and the authoritarian tendencies associated with the ruling elite. Student unions, on their part, focused on the deleterious effects of SAPs especially with regards to the privatization of catering and housing services at tertiary institutions (Bratton and Masunungure 2011). The government reacted by passing draconian legislation aimed at restricting dissent to tolerable levels.

In the mid-1990s, consumer associations also joined the protest spectacle, raising grievances related to the worsening food inflation, devaluation of the local currency and introduction of cost recovery measures. The thousands of war veterans who had been demobilized at independence in 1980 also regrouped and mobilized their members under the weight of the economic and social burdens of the 1990s (Kriger 2003). The second decade after political independence was characterized by the institutionalization of the protest culture. The social activism of the 1990s culminated in the formation of the National Constitutional Assembly (NCA) (a civic grouping of labour, women, youth, students, intellectuals and the unemployed). The NCA turned into one of the most powerful SMs in the late 1990s, which forced the government to embark on a constitution-making process in 1999. Frustrated with the government's slow pace of land reform and confronted by diminishing access to land, demographic pressures, deteriorating productivity of available land and generalized decline in sources of income (Zeilig 2010), the rural SMs applied underground social pressure, including land occupation, to force land redistribution onto the policy agenda.

Despite huge strides made in the late 1990s, since the early 2000s there has not been any significant growth in SMs. SMs have actually become 'socially thin' and disengaged in community mobilization (Muzondidya 2014). There are multiple reasons for this decline in social mobilization and activism. These include: donor fatigue, repression, loss of organic linkages to the grassroots, co-option of vocal social movement actors, diasporization of activists, political disengagement, risk aversiveness amongst the people, polarization of society and the rise of youth vigilante groups. As Muzondidya (2014) aptly avers, political co-option of SMs delivered a mortal blow to their capacity to mobilize society across political party loyalties. The co-option of both the Zimbabwe Congress of Trade Unions (ZCTU) and NCA into the Movement for Democratic Change (MDC) after the formation of the party in 1999 as well as the Zimbabwe African National Union-Patriotic Front's (ZANU-PF) systematic control and co-option of war veterans and the rural land movements, for instance, not only resulted in a huge loss in critical leadership but also deflated SMs' capacity to mobilize and organize autonomously.

The signing of the global political agreement (GPA) in 2008 also sounded a death knell to most SMs that were in bed with the powerful political parties in the country (Muzondidya 2014). The blurring between the incumbency and opposition created a serious crisis of legitimacy for most SMs, which were used to the discourse of polarized politics. They found themselves sandwiched between a hard place and a rock. SM actors in alliance with the ZANU-PF found it difficult to criticize the inclusive government without also attacking their own party. Similarly, those who backed the MDC-T and MDC-N also experienced a similar quandary. This phase between February 2009 and August 2013 can be best described as an era of civic vacuum where SMs went underground, others muted into political parties (for instance, the NCA) while some lost steam of the struggle. This hollowing out of SMs resulted in a huge civic vacuum which BJ attempted to fill.

Civic Vacuum and the Emergence of Baba Jukwa

Baba Jukwa as a Facebook phenomenon gripped Zimbabwe ahead of the 2013 elections. The page was created on March 22, 2013—almost two years after the start of the uprisings which gripped Tunisia and Egypt, generally believed to have been fuelled by social media, although more sober accounts point to a combination of political, economic and technological factors (see Aouragh 2012; Gerbaudo 2012). Upon its creation, it evoked euphoric expectations about the possibility of the 'Zimbabwean

Winter'. The international media described BJ as Zimbabwe's Julian Assange and Andrew Snowden, reminiscent of the two advocates of free speech and transparency's disclosure of official secrets. On his Facebook page, BJ presented himself as a 'Concerned father, fighting nepotism and directly linking community with their Leaders, Government, MPs and Ministers'. The page metamorphosed from a muckraking and whistle-blowing space to a SM counter-framing outlet. The mysterious Facebook character exposed a number of public officials like Dumiso Dabengwa, Constantine Chiwenga, Obert Mpofu, Saviour Kasukuwere, Fidelis Fengu and Ignatius Chombo. BJ's posts focused on a looting spree of state resources, electoral fraud, personal problems of ZANU-PF politicians and classified information about politburo meetings.

There are unverified claims that the ZANU-PF government had offered USD300,000 as a reward for the unmasking of BJ. Although Phillip and Edmund Kudzayi were arrested on suspicion that they were the creators and administrators of the BJ Facebook page, they were acquitted in 2015 after the state failed to prove its case beyond reasonable doubt. By the time of its first closure in 2013, the page garnered had over 470,000 followers. Notably, its audience was more than the aforementioned figure because some followers chose to access the page anonymously (Mutsvairo and Sirks 2015). In spite of government claims that they had unmasked and apprehended BJ, the Facebook mole continued to update the page until mid-August 2014, when the page abruptly disappeared from the web. The page resurfaced in 2015 before disappearing again. The popularity of the page was aided by the massive uptake of mobile internet and ADSL services in Zimbabwe (ZAMPS 2013). The fact that a Facebook page created 3 months before a penultimate election became so prominent and generated digital enthusiasm 'provides evidence of the extent to which online networks can help challenge the competitive advantage of traditional players' (González-Bailón et al. 2011, p. 961). The page also managed to plug the gap left by the waning investigative journalism and the retreat of the SMs from contentious politics.

Conceptual Framework

The analysis of this study is guided by the social movement framing theory (Benford and Snow 2000). This theory is concerned with the strategic aspects of symbolic meaning work which constitutes a central part of communicative strategies used by SM actors to construct collective and individualized self-representation. As Williams (2004, p. 93) adds, framing theory focuses on the 'symbolic' dimensions in the action of social movements, as frames 'articulate grievances, generate consensus on the importance and forms of collective action to be pursued, and present rationales for their actions and proposed solutions to adherents, bystanders, and antagonists'. It puts emphasis on the intentional ways in which movement activists (administrator(s) of the BJ Facebook page) seek to construct their self-presentations so as to draw support from others points to critical processes in SMs. As such, the administrator[s] of the BJ Facebook page can be viewed as signifying agents actively engaged in the production and maintenance of meaning for constituents, antagonists, and bystanders or observers (Benford and Snow 2000).

By acknowledging the link between SMs' frames and mobilization, framing analysis provides a basis for bridging the gap between the ideational and symbolic dimensions of collective action and direct forms of mobilization (Benford and Snow 2000). Framing theory also provides a suitable framework with which to link online communication with offline action. It allowed me to better analyse how Facebook's potential and specific technological characteristics contributed to BJ's mobilization efforts.

Framing theory provides a way to link ideas and social construction of ideas with organizational and political process factors. Like a picture frame, SM actors (administrator(s) of the BJ Facebook page) exclude some things while focusing attention on others. As Benford and Snow (2000) posit, SM framing theory attempts to understand the way in which SMs and SM actors create and use meaning, or how events and ideas are framed. For Benford and Snow (2000, p. 614), 'collective action frames are action-oriented sets of beliefs and meanings that inspire and legitimate the activities and campaigns of a social movement organization (SMO)'. Therefore, SM actors (administrator(s) of the BJ Facebook page) deploy collective action frames in order to create a set of meanings which would inspire people to act collectively toward some goal.

SM framing theory foregrounds four broad areas: the creation and use of collective action frames, framing processes, opportunities and constraints, and the effect of framing on movement outcomes and other processes (Benford and Snow 2000, pp. 612–613). With regards to collective action frames, Benford and Snow (2000) argue that they have three main framing tasks: 'diagnostic framing', 'prognostic framing', and 'motivational framing'. Diagnostic framing deals primarily with 'problem identification and attributions,' wherein 'injustice frames' (i.e., identifying victims and amplifying victimhood) constitute the main part of the framing process (Benford and Snow 2000, p. 615). It also pinpoints the 'sources of causality, blame and culpable agents'. Prognostic framing involves the 'articulation of a proposed solution to the problem or at least a plan of attack and the strategies for carrying out the plan' (Benford and Snow 2000, p. 617). Motivational framing provides a 'call to arms' or 'rationale for engaging in ameliorative collective action, including the construction of appropriate vocabularies of motive' (Benford and Snow 2000, p. 617). By pursuing these core framing tasks, movement actors attend to the interrelated problems of 'consensus mobilization' and 'action mobilization' (Klandermans 1984). This study sought to find out if the administrator(s) of the BJ used the Facebook page for motivational, diagnostic and prognostic framing.

Methodology

This study deployed a combination of social media ethnography and qualitative content analysis to answer the three research questions. Social media ethnography as a variant of online participant observation was used to obtain first-hand experience of how BJ deployed his Facebook page for digital activism in a country where offline street protests have become rather muted due to repression. As Postill and Pink (2012) observe, social media ethnography encapsulates observing the activities and interactions of administrator[s], fans and followers on a Facebook page. Although I did not actively participate on Baba Jukwa Facebook page through commenting, liking, sharing and replying posts, I was a habitual 'listener' and 'lurker' on the page throughout its life-cycle. My ethnographic fieldwork revolved around three overlapping routines: observing, exploring and archiving. Using both electronic and manual archiving systems, I collated status messages, comments, and various metrics for the periods between March 22, 2013 and August 31, 2013. This time-frame was chosen because the page was created in March and ran up to the end of August 2013 uninterrupted. Most of the status updates and comments were written in English and Shona which I am proficient in. In total, I collected over 3,200 status updates posted by the page administrator(s) during the data-collection phase.

To analyse the BJ Facebook page, qualitative content analysis was conducted on a selection of the posts made by the administrator on Facebook. As part of the qualitative content analysis, I established categories of status updates posted by the BJ Facebook page administrator(s) based on the three framing tasks identified by Benford and Snow (2000):

motivational, diagnostic and prognostic framing. In line with Facebook's fair use policy, the posts and comments are presented with the following identifiers: name, date and timestamp. The research questions were as follows:

1. How was the Facebook page deployed by Baba Jukwa to advocate for political change in Zimbabwe?
2. What kinds of collective action frames did the BJ Facebook page use to mobilize people to engage in political action in Zimbabwe?
3. Which digital repertoires of contention were foregrounded by the administrator(s) of the BJ Facebook page?

The results are discussed below.

Discussion and Analysis of Findings

How was the Facebook Page Deployed by Baba Jukwa to Advocate for Political Change in Zimbabwe?

This study found that BJ utilized his Facebook page for different purposes in his fight for democratization, freedom of expression and a corruption-free society. Social media ethnography revealed that BJ used his Facebook page for virtual recruitment, soliciting financial donations, mobilization, information dissemination, choreographing of emotional assembly and as a venue for activism. Mobilization refers 'to the process by which a passive collection of individuals in a society is transformed into an active group in the pursuit of political, social and ideological change' (Nedelman 1987, p. 181). In this regard, the Facebook page was instrumental in urging people to go out and register to vote. For instance, in one of his numerous posts, BJ wrote the following:

> Please go out in numbers and register to vote. We are still welcoming plenty of Vapanduki (rebels from ZANU-PF) and we expect more by the end of the day [Baba Jukwa, 22 April 2013 at 8:23 a.m.].

In the above post, BJ urged his fans and followers to go out and inspect their names on the voters roll as well as to go and cast their votes during the 2013 harmonized elections. This was despite the long queues and chaos that characterized the mobile voter registration exercise. The page also mobilized people to take action against corruption, electoral fraud and political killings.

Online observations suggest that BJ also appropriated Facebook for virtual recruitment of volunteer and donors. Virtual recruitment entails the act of signing up to a campaign through liking or joining a Facebook group or fan page. The purpose of virtual recruitment is to stay in touch with people that supports the campaign and start them on the path to becoming donors and volunteers. In one of his daily blizzard of posts, BJ claimed that he was the head of a grouping of persons from the revolutionary party totalling 30,000 called Vapanduki (rebels) who were working hard to ensure ZANU-PF lose the 2013 elections. Below is another post which indicates the recruitment and group formation potential of the Facebook page:

> Baba Jukwa
>
> June 7, 2013 at 13:41 p.m.
>
> Zimbabwe we are shooting from all angles. I am happy to confirm that the Jukwa family in the administration has grown beyond 500 people and I am happy with your support; and your constant following and encouraging fighting for change. What makes our struggle succeed is that we have people in all sectors/parastatals across the country. I am happy to tell you that we have managed to bring in 50 people working from the foreign desk of my party is all sectors as well. These evil people have no chance at all. The more they search for one Baba Jukwa, the more Baba Jukwa recruits administrators. Bravo to those people in the police, prisons, army and intelligence who are now our administrators. Together we deliver the country
>
> Asijiki
Ndatenda
Baba Jukwa

Online observations indicated that BJ also used Facebook to solicit financial donations and crowd-funding. Crowd-funding denotes the practice of funding a project or campaign by raising monetary contributions from a large number of people via the internet and other digital technologies (Prive 2012). Online fundraising is also viewed as enabling for the mobilization and recruitment of donors, who may be unreachable through offline methods. In the case of BJ, the Facebook page was used to mobilize financial resources. PayPal details were placed on the Facebook page for fans and followers to donate money to the cause. For instance, the two posts below are insightful:

Baba Jukwa
July 12, 2013 at 10:53 a.m.
Please let's not forget to donate to strengthen the cause of exposing and removing evil from our beautiful soil on our way to a New Zimbabwe.
I will give you more details in the next hour
Ndapanduka Zvamuchose (I have rebelled for good)

Asijiki
Ndatenda (Thank You)
Yimi (Yours) Baba Jukwa

Both posts suggest that Facebook was also utilized for fundraising purposes in order to 'push my struggle forward'. Posts on the page suggested that the money was going to be used to grow teams on the ground so that every region would be covered for daily information.

The administrators of the page also utilized it to aggregate content from various sources including professionally and user-generated content. The BJ Facebook page provided space for fans and followers to comment and contribute content, as well as access comments made by other fans or followers. Like 'Letters to the editor', BJ invited his fans and followers to email and inbox their own leaks and disclosures. He also urged people to expose corrupt people from their own areas. One of the posts read as follows:

Baba Jukwa
June 21, 2013 at 20:12 p.m.
Don't forget to inbox us names of those victimizing you countrywide so we setup a good example to the evil people and its security henchmen. Our account is babajukwaaa2013@gmail.com. Together we will reform the party and achieve a new Zimbabwe. Ndapanduka Zvamuchose, Asijiki, Ndatenda (Thank You).

In response to the above, some of the fans and followers sent their own testimonials and user-generated content which were in turn published on the BJ Facebook page. An example is below:

Baba Jukwa
July 15, 2013 at 13:56 p.m.
Here is an unedited letter from Mberengwa
Hesi BJ Pano parikuRiggiwa paChingechuru Pry School,vanhu varikuVoter through writing names pazvipepa saka vanhu vagara vari pazvigaro sana

> Jorum Gumbo naZimuto Naison ndivo varikungozoWinner coz ndivo vane mazita anozivikanwa nemaVoters chete,vana Major Shava havasikanwi maNames avo,apa hapana paakanyorwa maNames fo as to choose. Publicise this baba Jukwa pliz we r tired of Jorum and people are disappointed but vamwe vedu havazive zita remukwikwidzi wake.
>
> Asijiki

In the letter addressed to the administrator above, the author from Mberengwa indicated that there was rigging going on at ZANU-PF primary elections where people were being asked to write names of their preferred candidates on a piece of paper as opposed to secret ballot. The process was therefore rigged in favour of well-known politicians like Jorum Gumbo and Naison Zimuto. The author urged BJ to publicize the rigging process because people in Mberengwa are sick and tired of non-performing candidates like Jorum Gumbo.

In terms of frame articulation, the administrators of the BJ Facebook page deployed non-textual tools like hyperlinks and allowed fans and followers to email testimonials and letters to the editor. The problem of publishing unedited letters in the context of citizen journalism and user-generated content is that it simultaneously makes it more difficult to differentiate accurate information from fabrication: conspiracy theories may be as prominent as well-substantiated claims (Garret 2006).

The BJ Facebook page was also important in terms of ensuring access to information. Like Wikileaks (a 'whistleblower' website), BJ solicited information, including classified information, and published that information in its primary form. At first the information was primarily leaked through the Facebook page but later newspaper columns (on *The Zimbabwean*) and websites (babajukwanews.com). Like Assange and Snowden who used the legacy media and internet websites, BJ also deployed social media platforms and newspaper columns to expose politicians for their alleged covert operations and gave out internal communication memos, public officials' emails and contact numbers, so that fans and followers could contact them. In short, BJ replicated the Wikileaks model in a context where media repression is endemic thereby rendering communication sovereignty obsolete. Facebook allowed BJ to have his 'own' means of communication and self-representation. As intimated above, he also utilized the mainstream diasporic print media (*The Zimbabwean*) in order to communicate beyond the cosy circle of like-minded sympathizers.

> Baba Jukwa
>
> June 7, 2013 at 12:38 p.m.
>
> Good day my fellow countrymen, as I said yesterday go out in numbers and buy The Zimbabwean newspaper ($1 and R6) here at home also in South Africa, Botswana, Swaziland, Zambia, UK among other countries to have an update on my column where I exposed everything.
>
> Asijiki

In the post above, BJ urged his fans and followers to buy *The Zimbabwean* (a UK-published newspaper which was sold in Zimbabwe and neighbouring countries) in order to read about more disclosures on his column. As Mujere and Mwatwara (2015) observes, the case of BJ is very interesting as far as it exposes how citizen journalism can cause despondency within the camp of those considered powerful.

The page also proved to be an invaluable space for everyday political talk. Everyday political talk as 'non-purposive, informal, casual, and spontaneous political conversation voluntarily carried out by free citizens, without being constrained by formal procedural rules and pre-determined agenda' (Kim and Kim 2008, p. 53). As such, it was a space in which citizens deliberated about their common affairs, hence, an institutionalized arena of discursive interaction. The BJ Facebook page constituted a 'venue of magnetic gathering or a trending place' (Gerbaudo 2012). In the build-up to 31 July 2013, the BJ Facebook page managed to generate what Gerbaudo (2016, p. 255) calls 'moments of digital enthusiasm'. This refers to necessarily transient phases of intense, positive emotional mood emerging in political online conversations in proximity to major event (Gerbaudo 2016). It also engendered an 'imagined community' (Anderson 1991) where people were able to freely express themselves without fear of reprisal, although media reports suggests that a number of his fans and followers were picked up for questioning by the police. In imagined communities 'the members of even the smallest nation will never know most of their fellow-members, meet them, or even hear of them, yet in the minds of each lives the image of their communion' (Anderson 1991, p. 6).

The BJ Facebook page was not only an arena for the formation of discursive opinion but also a platform for the formation and enactment of collective identities. Melucci (1989, p. 34) defines collective identity as a 'shared definition produced by several interacting individuals who are concerned with the orientations of their actions as well as the field of opportunities and constraints in which their actions take place'. Baba Jukwa used a number of floating signifiers to construct collective identity on his Facebook page. For instance, statements like 'We know who they are it's the devil', 'Our Facebook Page', 'our Gmail account', 'We need our country back', 'No one can stop our revolution' and 'vapanduki zvamuchose (Rebels Forever) orchestra band', 'My children we are being threatened', and 'Pasi navanhu vakaita sana (Down with people like)' evoked perceptions of 'We-ness' and a common people united by their oppression. Most of his posts addressed fans and followers first as 'Great Zimbabweans' and famously ended with 'Asijiki' (an isiNdebele word which means 'No Retreat' in English). The use of 'Asijiki' by BJ can be conceptualized as an attempt to construct collective identity in the online space. As Melucci (1989) observes, the use of slogans and militant language is necessary for identity formation.

BJ Facebook Page and Collective Action Frames in Zimbabwe

New technologies have helped to create new networks over which collective action frames can be propagated (Garret 2006). These 'invented spaces of participation' (Cornwall 2002) allowed social movement actors like Baba Jukwa to avoid distortion and bypass filters associated with 'invited spaces of participation' (Cornwall 2002). Mass media outlets tend to exhibit a bias favouring established institutions and figures of authority. These entities are more likely than activists to have their positions accurately and completely represented in the news (Gitlin 1980). Qualitative content analysis established that BJ used Facebook to advance diagnostic (how did the post define the problem?), prognostic (what solutions were suggested?) and motivational (was the post a call to arms or motivating?) framing.

As discussed earlier, diagnostic framing deals primarily with 'problem identification and attributions,' wherein 'injustice frames' (i.e., identifying victims and amplifying victimhood) constitute the main part of the framing process (Benford and Snow 2000, p. 615). A number of posts made by BJ identified several problems bedevilling Zimbabwe. These include: the breakdown of rule of law, electoral manipulation, corruption, lack of internal democracy and muzzling of the public media. For instance, Baba Jukwa wrote the following with regards to the shenanigans from ZANU-PF to rig elections:

> All opposition parties must know that my evil party is registering every Zimbabwean with an ID especially those in the Diaspora, they went through the immigration office and took names of those outside the country and registered them countrywide and their so-called cell chairpersons will vote on behalf of everyone to give my evil party more numbers [Baba Jukwa, May 12, 2013 at 15:27 p.m.).

The aforementioned post catapulted the MDC-T into action calling for transparency in voter registration process. BJ claimed that ZANU-PF through Registrar-General, Tobaiwa Mudede, was in the process of deleting suspected MDC members from the voter's roll as well as adding ghost names who would be fraudulently made to 'vote' for ZANU-PF. Through this, diagnostic framing served to identify not only the roots of the disputed elections in Zimbabwe, but also what could be done to address it, particularly by ensuring transparency in the voter registration process.

Motivational framing provides a 'call to arms' or 'rationale for engaging in ameliorative collective action, including the construction of appropriate vocabularies of motive' (Benford and Snow 2000, p. 617). The bulk of motivational framing on the BJ Facebook page focused on urging Zimbabweans to take action. For instance, some of the posts urged people to call named and shamed politicians and public officials, to join the 'Vapunduki' and the Brigadier Nhlela groups as well as donating to the cause. Although media reports suggest that people heeded the call and phoned some politicians, fear militated against sustained street protests against ZANU-PF. As Gamson (1992, p. 60) argues, mobilizing people to take direct action is a daunting task because of a 'structural impediment to collective action' that can be reinforced by 'a political culture that operates to produce quiescence and passivity'.

Qualitative content analysis established that BJ exhorted his fans and followers not to be engrossed in 'slacktivist' campaigns but to take action in their locations. Besides encouraging people to go out and vote, the administrator(s) of BJ Facebook implored people to demand justice from the named and shamed politicians and public officials. The posts below are instructive:

> Zimbabwe don't just be happy here, we need action. Help us in building a better country (Baba Jukwa, August 5, 2013 at 21:34 p.m.).
>
> Baba Jukwa
>
> July 27, 2013 at 22:13 p.m.
>
> I urge you to call the Paymaster General on 04-708 281 and ask him why he has cancelled the deduction facility and prevent us from buying goods on credit, whilst allowing one company to milk us.
>
> Asijiki
> Ndatenda

Prognostic framing involves the 'articulation of a proposed solution to the problem or at least a plan of attack and the strategies for carrying out the plan' (Benford and Snow 2000, p. 617). In this regard, BJ saw his mission as to 'to reform my party and bring democracy to my country'. The solution to the diagnostic frame according to BJ was to ensure media, security, governance, constitutional and electoral reforms. Without these raft of measures, BJ indicated that a 'new Zimbabwe' would not born. Below is a post which is illustrative:

> Baba Jukwa
>
> June 25, 2013 at 16:17 p.m.
>
> I want to reveal to you today that Herald lies too much, take your seats and see how I tell the truth unfolding and how they try to lie to the country. We have to reform Zimpapers soon as well.

In the case of *The Herald* (a government owned daily newspaper) doggedly known for publishing propaganda, BJ suggested that Zimpapers should be reformed. This ties in neatly with his call for widespread media reforms of all government owned print and broadcasting entities.

Baba Jukwa and Digital Repertoires of Connective Action

Tilly defines repertoire of contention as 'the range of strategies, methods, tools, and tactics that group members use to make claims on other individuals or groups'. Because street demonstrations in Zimbabwe are regulated by the Public Order and Security Act[3] (POSA), which makes it extremely difficult for protesters to be granted the right to protest, administrator(s) of the BJ page popularized digital repertoires of connective action. Garret (2006) define digitally based acts of civil disobedience as tactics aimed at upsetting the status quo by disrupting the normal flow of information, thereby attracting attention to their cause and message. Online observations established that the administrator(s) of the BJ Facebook page encouraged his fans and followers to deploy a variety of digital repertoires of connective action. Some of the digital repertoires of connective action include: defacement of Facebook pages, email bombing, calling and SMSing exposed politicians and public officials, boycotting certain political parties and unliking or unfriending certain Facebook pages. In the context of BJ, Facebook and mobile phones were used as platforms for civil disobedience. Administrators of BJ Facebook page did not, however, encourage their fans and followers to engage in distributed denial of service (DDOS) actions, hackvitism, virtual sit-ins in which government and corporate web sites are blocked, preventing legitimate usage. BJ also urged his fans and followers to use their mobile phone as a tool of protest in its own right. BJ had the habit of brandishing telephone numbers of the person or persons involved in criminal and corrupt practices, encouraging web users to call them up, and demand an explanation. As such, new media technologies (Facebook and mobile phone) were used in particular to amplify and extend conventional modes of social action.

BJ also incited his fans to engage in email bombing and defacement of the Facebook page belonging to the then Malawian President Joyce Banda. Thousands of BJ followers heeded his call by posting expletives and insulting messages on her official Facebook page titled Her Excellency Dr Joyce Banda. This followed a post by Baba Jukwa directed at Banda alleging that Zimbabweans were aware that she had signed an agreement with ZANU-PF to rig elections. Dr Joyce Banda was forced to issue a press statement where she said: 'These are malicious allegations only meant to destroy someone's reputation. We will never meddle with the affairs of another country.' In this case, Facebook allowed Zimbabweans to advance political causes that are difficult to undertake in physical space.

Conclusion

This chapter has argued that besides acting as a channel of citizen journalism, Baba Jukwa symbolized a cyber-movement with no physical meetings but which made use of a whole gamut of technologies within the wider communicative ecology. These include mobile phones, emails, Facebook, newspapers and websites. Facebook afforded the administrator(s) of the BJ page the means to shape repertoires of contention, frame the issues, propagate unifying symbols, and transform individualized activism into connective action. It has also highlighted the problems associated with most of the digital repertoires of contention utilized especially as it pertains to exposing fans and followers to communication surveillance, leaving off digital data traces and use of real names as well as pseudonyms. It has argued that online activism backed by limited offline activism feeds into the cult of armchair activism, free-rider problem and neglects the importance of face-to-face mobilization and strategic planning.

Notes

1. Technological solutionism refers to the treatment of 'all complex social situations either as neatly defined problems with definite, computable solutions or as transparent and self-evident processes that can be easily optimized—if only the right algorithms are in place' (Morozov 2014; xiii).
2. Slacktivism has come to represent a pejorative term that refers to supposedly inauthentic, low-threshold forms of political engagement online, such as signing an e-petition or 'liking' a Facebook page.
3. The Act criminalizes the distribution of political posters, pamphlets or other such material in public places and private homes without the permission from the police. Noteworthy to highlight that contravention of POSA attracts a jail sentence of up to five years. POSA also requires people to notify the police 14 days before holding a public event, thereby giving the police excessive powers in terms of determining 'legitimate' and 'illegitimate' gatherings. The irony about POSA is that it makes people's right to protest subject to the approval of their adversaries (the police, who are subservient to the current government).

References

Agarwal, N., Lim, M., & Wigand, R.T. (2012). Raising and rising voices in social media: A novel methodological approach in studying Cyber-collective movements. *Business and Information systems Engineering*, *4*(3), 113–126.

Anderson, B. (1991). *Imagined communities: Reflections on the origin and spread of nationalism* (Rev. edn.). London and New York: Verso.

Aouragh, M. (2012). Social media, mediation and the Arab revolutions. *TripleC, 10*(2), 518–536.

Ayres, J.M. (1999). From the streets to the Internet: The cyber-diffusion of contention. *Annals of the American Academy of Political and Social Science, 566*, 132–143.

Bauman, Z. (2004). *Wasted lives*. London: Polity Press.

Benford, R.D., & Snow, D.A. (2000). Framing processes and social movements: An overview and assessment. *Annual Review of Sociology, 26*, 611–639.

Bennett, W.L., & Segerberg, A. (2012). The logic of connective action. *Information, Communication & Society, 15*(5), 739–768.

Bosch, T. (2016). Twitter activism and youth in South Africa: The case of #RhodesMustFall. *Information, Communication & Society*, 1–12.

Bratton, M., & Masunungure, E. (2011, January). *The anatomy of political predation: Leaders, elites and coalitions in Zimbabwe*, 1980–2010. The Developmental Leadership Program (DLP).

Castells, M. (2012). *Networks of outrage and hope. Social movements in the Internet age* (p. 786). Cambridge: Polity Press.

Cornwall, A. (2002). Making spaces, changing spaces: Situating participation. Development. IDS Working Paper. Brighton: Institutive of Development Studies.

Della Porta, D., & Diani, M. (1999). *Social movements: An introduction*. Oxford: Basil Blackwell.

Diamond, L. (2010). Liberation technologies. *Journal of Democracy, 21*(3), 69–83.

Diani, M. (2000). Social movement networks virtual and real. *Information, Communication and Society, 3*(3), 386–401.

Edwards, A. (2004). The Dutch women's movement online: Internet and the organizational infrastructure of a social movement. In W. van de Donk, B. D. Loader, P. G. Nixon, and D. Rucht (Eds.), *Cyberprotest: New media, citizens, and social movements*. New York: Routledge.

Gamson, W.A. (1992). The social psychology of collective action. In A.D. Morris, & C.M. Mueller (Eds.), *Frontiers in social movement theory*. New Haven, CT: Yale University Press.

Gamson, W.A., & Meyer, D. (1996). Framing political opportunity. In D. McAdam, J.M. McCarthy, & M. Zald (Eds.), *Comparative perspectives on social movements*. Cambridge, UK: Cambridge University Press.

Garrett, R.K. (2006). Protest in an information society. *Information, Communication and Society, 9*(2), 202–224.

Gerbaudo, P. (2012). *Tweets and the streets: Social media and contemporary activism*. London: Pluto Press.

Gerbaudo, P. (2016). Rousing the Facebook crowd: Digital enthusiasm and emotional contagion in the 2011 protests in Egypt and Spain. *International Journal of Communication, 10*, 254–273.

Gitlin, T. (1980). *The whole world is watching*. Berkeley, CA: University of California Press.

Gladwell, M. (2010, October 4). Small change. Why the revolution will not be tweeted. *The New Yorker*. Retrieved from http://www.newyorker.com/reporting/2010/10/04/101004fa_fact_gladwell. Accessed 18 November 2011.

González-Bailón, S. et al. (2011, December 15). The Dynamics of protest recruitment through an online network. *Scientific Reports*, *1*(197). doi: 10.1038/srep00197.

Harlow, S.D. (2012). Social media and social movements: Facebook and an online Guatemalan justice movement that moved offline. *New Media & Society*, *14*(2), 225–243.

Herrera, L. (2012). Youth and citizenship in the digital age: A view from Egypt. *Harvard Educational Review*, *82*(3), 333–352.

Honwana, A. M. (2013). *Youth and revolution in Tunisia*. London: Zed Books.

Kim, J., & Kim, E.J. (2008). Theorizing dialogic deliberation: Everyday political talk as communicative action and dialogue. *Communication Theory*, *18*(1), 51–70.

Klandermans, B. (1984). Mobilization and participation: Social-psychological expansions of resource mobilization theory. *American Sociological Review*, *49*, 583–600.

Kriger, N. J. (2003). *Guerrilla veterans in post-war Zimbabwe: Symbolic and violent politics*, 1980–1987. Cambridge: Cambridge University Press.

Levitsky, S., & Way, L.A. (2010). *Competitive authoritarianism: Hybrid regimes after the cold war*. Cambridge: Cambridge University Press.

Lim, M. (2012). Clicks, cabs, and coffee houses: Social media and oppositional movements in Egypt, 2004–2011. *Journal of Communication*, *62*, 231–248.

Lim, M. (2014). Seeing spatially: People, networks and movements in digital and urban spaces, *International Development and Planning Review*, *36*(1), 51–72.

Mao, W., & Wang, F. (2012). *New advances in intelligence and security informatics*. Oxford: Zhejiang University Press.

Mare, A. (2014). Social media: The new protest drums in Southern Africa? In B. Pătruţ and M. Pătruţ (Eds.), *Social media in politics: Case studies on the political power of social media. Public administration and information technology*. Canton of Bern: Springer.

McCandless, E. (2009). *Polarization and transformation in Zimbabwe: Social movements, strategy dilemmas and change*. Durban, University of KwaZulu-Natal Press.

McCaughey, M., & Ayers, M.D. (Eds.). 2003. *Cyber activism: Online Activism in theory and practice*. New York: Routledge.

Melucci, A. (1989). *Nomads of the present: Social movements and individual needs in contemporary society*. London, UK: Hutchinson.

Melucci, A. (1996). *Challenging codes: Collective action in the information age*. Cambridge: CambridgeUniversity Press.

Morozov, E. (2011). *The net delusion: The dark side of internet freedom*. New York: Public Affairs.

Morozov, E. (2014). *To save everything, click here: The folly of technological solutionism*. New York: Public Affairs.

Moyo, J.N. (1993). Civil society in Zimbabwe. *Zambezia*, *20*(1), 1–13.

Mujere, J., & Mwatwara, W. (2015). Citizen journalism and national politics in Zimbabwe: The case of the 2008 and 2013 elections. In B Mutsvairo (Ed.),. 2015. *Perspectives on participatory politics and citizen journalism in a Networked Africa:* A *connected continent*. London: Palgrave Macmillan.

Mutsvairo, B., & Sirks, L. (2015). Examining the contribution of social media in reinforcing political participation in Zimbabwe. *Journal of African Media Studies*, *7*(3), 329–344.

Muzondidya, J. (2014). *Zimbabwe beyond July 2013: Prospects for rebuilding vibrant social movements*. Durban: HSRC.

Nedelman, B. (1987). Individuals and parties–changes in processes of political mobilization. *European Sociological Review*, *3*(3), 181–202.

Neumayer, C., & Raffl, C. (2008). Facebook for protest? The value of social software for political activism in the anti-FARC rallies. DigiActive Research Series, December 2008. Retrieved from http://www.digiactive.org/wpcontent/%20uploads/research1_neumayerraffl.pdf. Accessed 13 April 2011.

Palczewski, C.H. (2001). Cyber-movements, new social movements, and counterpublics. In R. Asen and D. C. Brouwer (Eds.), *Counterpublics and the state*. Albany: State University of New York Press.

Papacharissi, Z. (2010). *A private sphere: Democracy in a digital age*. Cambridge: Polity Press.

Postill, J., & Pink, S. (2012). Social media ethnography: The digital researcher in a messy web. *Media International Australia*, *145*, 123–134.

Prive, T. (2012). What is crowd-funding and How does it benefit the economy. http://www.forbes.com/sites/tanyaprive/2012/11/27/what-is-crowdfunding-and-how-does-it-benefit-the-economy/. Accessed 23 March 2015.

Shirky, C. (2011). The political power of social media. *Foreign Affairs*, *90*(1), 28–41.

Švelch, J. & Štětka, V. (2016, January). The coup that flopped: Facebook as a platform for emotional protest. *First Monday*, *21*, (1–4).

Tilly, C. (1978). *From mobilization to revolution*. London: Longman.

Tarrow, S. (1998). *Power in movement: social movements, collective action and politics* (2nd edn.). Cambridge: Cambridge University Press.

Valenzuela, S. (2013). Unpacking the use of social media for protest behavior: The roles of information, opinion expression, and activism. *American Behavioural Scientist*, *57*(7), 920–942.

van de Donk, W., Loader, B.D., Nixon, P.G., & Rucht, D. (Eds.). (2004). *Cyberprotest: New media, citizens and social movements*. London, UK: Routledge.

Van Laer, J., & Van Aelst, P. (2010). Internet and social movement action repertoires: Opportunities and limitations. *Information, Communication and Society, 13*(8), 1146–1174.

Williams, R.H. (2004). The cultural contexts of collective action: Constraints, opportunities, and the symbolic life of social movements. In D.A. Snow, S.A. Soule, & H. Kriesi (Eds.), *The Blackwell companion to social movements.* Malden, MA: Blackwell Publishing.

Win, E. (2004). When sharing female identity is not enough: Coalition building in the midst of political polarisation in Zimbabwe. *Gender and Development, 12*, 1.

Zeilig, L. (2008). Student politics and activism in Zimbabwe: The frustrated transition. *Journal of Asian and African Studies, 43*(2), 215–237.

Zeilig, L. (2010). Zimbabwe: Struggle, dictatorship and the response of the social movements. Links, 28 June. http://links.org.au/node/1768. Accessed 30 November 2016.

Zimbabwe All Media Products Survey (ZAMPS). (2013). Harare: Zimbabwe advertising research foundation.

Admire Mare is a Research Associate at the Faculty of Humanities, University of Johannesburg, South Africa. He holds a PhD in Journalism and Media Studies from Rhodes University. Mare has published articles on business journalism ethics in Africa, the creative appropriation of ICTs by pirate radio stations in Zimbabwe, and the intersection of social and mainstream media in the coverage of social protests in Southern Africa. His research interests include the intersection of journalism and social media, social media and youth activism, social movements and new media technologies.

CHAPTER 4

Digital Activism in Uganda

Monica B. Chibita

Introduction

Since the current NRM government came into power in 1986, there has been significant growth in the availability of public channels of communication, and in legislation to guarantee freedom of expression and access to information. The country has also opened up to multi-party democracy after nearly four decades of military rule or a one-party state. Both mobile phone and internet use have grown and citizens have used these avenues to network, to express themselves, to mobilize and to advocate for causes. Over the years, there has been growing opposition to the manner in which the country is governed in particular aspects such as the conduct of elections, poor management of natural resources, lack of fiscal discipline and poor service delivery which has been expressed through the media, and most recently the new media. There is also growing evidence of government discomfort with citizens' use of the new media platforms to express discontent.

This chapter discusses the growing tension between the Ugandan government and its citizens as the latter's activism migrates from the mainstream to the new media platforms to advance various causes in the face of shrinking space for self-expression in the mainstream media. The

M.B. Chibita (✉)
Uganda Christian University, Mukono, Uganda
e-mail: mbchibita@gmail.com

B. Mutsvairo (ed.), *Digital Activism in the Social Media Era*,
DOI 10.1007/978-3-319-40949-8_4

methodology of the chapter includes document analysis, in-depth interviews with key activists, and qualitative analysis of online content. The goal of the chapter is to document and tease out patterns that throw light on the trajectory of digital activism in Uganda.

Activism and Digital Activism

According to Permanent Culture Now, activism refers to 'taking action to effect social change'. Such change may be in the social, political, economic or environmental domain. Activism is normally associated with social movements. The most common types of activism include grassroots activism, letter writing and petitions, direct lobbying, litigation, demonstrations, civil disobedience, digital activism and others. Often activism progresses along a continuum with letters and petitions being on one side and aggressive activities like protests, disobedience and 'hacktivism' being on the other (see Watson 2005). Hacktivism refers to the subversive use of computers or computer networks to achieve the goals of activism and is often linked to cyber-terrorism. Any or a combination of these tactics may be used to demand a solution to a problem by taking an oppositional stance; creating alternatives to the dominant system through effecting some form of behaviour change (e.g. walking to work to protest pollution) or taking revolutionary action aimed at 'toppling' major institutions of society. For purposes of this discussion, activism may be categorized as online, or offline.

Vegh (2003) defines online activism (also known as or related to digital activism, cyber-activism or e-activism) as 'a politically motivated movement relying on the internet'. Online activism, according to Vegh, is proactive, aims at achieving certain goals, and is usually targeted at 'the controls and authorities imposing them' (2003, p. 72).

Joyce (2010, p. viii) defines online or digital activism as 'the use of digital technologies: mobile phones and internet-enabled devices, for example-in campaigns for social and political change' Digital activism strategies may either be internet-based, or simply internet-enhanced. Vegh says in internet-based strategies the internet is used for activities that are only possible online, like virtual sit-ins, or hacking. Internet-assisted strategies, on the other hand, only use the internet to enhance the traditional media's role in the campaign. This may include extending the boundaries of awareness, or increasing efficiency (Vegh 2003, p. 71).

Vegh further categorizes online activism into three. The first type, awareness/advocacy activism is where individuals or independent organizations seek to highlight information or news that the mainstream media, either by commission or omission have misreported, under-reported or ignored. The second type, organization/mobilization refers to activism which uses the internet to call for offline action such as a march, call for transfer of a typically offline action online (for instance sending your local Member of Parliament an email instead of a letter by post or instead of meeting him/her in person). This category of activism can also call for an action that is only possible online such as 'spamming' a targeted person or organization's website. The third category which Vegh calls action/reaction mostly relates to deliberate destructive online action such as hacking to draw attention to a cause or to cripple the targeted person or organization (2003, pp. 73–75).

Digital activism as we know it has been largely enabled by the new media, and more specifically the phenomenon of social media. The new media in question here are the internet, and mobile telephone technology that makes the internet accessible on the move. Kaplan and Haenlein (2010, p. 61) define social media as 'a group of internet-based applications that build on the ideological and technological foundations of Web 2.0 and that allow the creation and exchange of user-generated content'. Examples of the most popular social media sites include Facebook, Twitter, LinkedIn, Pinterest, Google Plus+, YouTube, Tumblr, Instagram, Flickr and WhatsApp.

For a long time, the research focus in Africa was on the traditional media (particularly radio and TV) and their democratic and developmental potential. However, what we refer to today as the social media experience is made possible by new means of communication, particularly the internet and mobile phones. In the last two decades, the research emphasis has shifted towards the various new media because of their immense popularity, particularly among the 'millennials'. The potential of new media technologies in Africa has been hailed by many scholars and development partners. Socha and Eber-Schmid (2012), for instance, argue that new media 'holds out a possibility of on-demand access to content anytime, anywhere, on any digital device, as well as interactive user feedback, creative participation and community formation around the media content'. They talk about the new media's 'democratization' of the creation, publishing, distribution and consumption of media content' and the death of the gate-keeper. Scholars such as Diamond (2010) have, as a result, named these media 'liberation' media. The internet falls under this category, as do certain types of mobile phones that meet the above criteria.

In Africa, the new media have been credited for the improvement of information gathering, processing, distribution, storage, and engagement between political leaders and their populations. They have been praised for empowering ordinary people and enabling them to mobilize and to participate in public discourse on subjects pertaining to 'democracy' and 'development' (see, for instance, Underwood 2005; Banda et al. 2009; Diamond 2010). The most basic forms of new media uses have given ordinary people access to power-centres that that they had never had before, and expanded the parameters for ordinary people to participate in important discourses. Hadji (2016, p. 74) contends that through the use of social media policy analysis, evaluation, and monitoring can be promoted and political no-go areas can be penetrated. He says,

> the use of social media provides for better and faster means to, firstly, get help and support through publicity of events, to, secondly access related help from various sources including networks, and, finally to frame issues in a fluid manner that allows for focus and shifting of concerns with the reality on the ground without having to wait for the 24-hour news-cycle.... They provide an alternative space for reviving a dormant public consciousness into sentient, dynamic, social discourse (Hadji 2016, p. 75, 77).

CIMA (2008, p. 10) puts the possible import of these technological developments for democracy this way: 'The overarching theme ... is the rise of a pluralized, diverse and multi-mediated public sphere, with individuals, groups, corporations, governments, and other entities freely co-mingling to influence public opinion.'

However, other scholars have questioned the magic that these technologies are able to work in African contexts. Castells and Ince (2003), for instance, caution against excessive enthusiasm. Other scholars including Alzouma (2005), Tumusiime (2007) and Duncan (2013) all caution against getting carried away with the 'magic' of the new technologies without due consideration of the social, economic and political contexts within which these technologies are appropriated.

A significant proportion of findings from empirical studies of the use of the new media technologies in African contexts cite challenges related to lack of access, costs of connectivity, availability of network coverage and lack of skills to optimize the use of the new media technologies. While economies of scale have brought down internet prices in many developed countries, purchasing power, illiteracy and language barriers in African countries keep the numbers low and the prices high. Furthermore, while the number of users on the continent among a certain social class is rising steadily (Global Internet Report 2015), the sheer price of a mobile phone, or a computer, or the cost of connectivity, put these devices beyond the reach of the majority of citizens. Thus Brodock (2010, p. 21) argues, 'while digital activism promises to increase the effectiveness of grassroots efforts around the world, the digital divide hinders this process by limiting participation'. Other obstacles include illiteracy and language. Government surveillance is also cited as a major obstacle. There is reason to suspect that as governments have sought to engage people through the social media, they have used this as an excuse for monitoring social media activity with the ultimate aim of censorship.

The Pew Internet and American Life Project (2009) puts it even more appropriately, even if the report refers to an American context:

> whether they take place on the Internet or off, traditional political activities remain the domain of those with high levels of income and education.... Contrary to the hopes of some advocates, the Internet is not changing the socio-economic character of civic engagement in the United States. Just as in offline civic life, the well-to-do and well-educated are more likely than those less well off to participate in online political activities.

In situations where there is intolerance to diverse political views, there is evidence to indicate that restrictive media policies also constitute a major obstacle to digital activism. Ironically though, the same polices play a part in driving activism to the internet and mobile phones where individuals and organizations with various causes perceive more opportunities for free expression. Ushahidi, a Kenyan civil society initiative that pioneered the adoption and use of Google Maps to map out violence 'hotspots' during the period following the contentious Kenyan 2007 elections provides a fresh example of this (see Goldstein and Rotich 2008; Cullum 2010, p. 57). Khamis et al. (2012) document the digital strategies used in the Egyptian and Syrian political uprisings of 2011. Baguma and Eilu (2015) list ways in which the mobile phone can be combined with social media to accomplish things which may not otherwise be possible in less than free political environments such as typify many African countries.

Given that the political space in African contexts tends to be more highly contested than other spaces, Baguma and Eilu (2015, p. 15) indicate that a combination of mobile telephones and social media have demonstrated the potential to accomplish the following during elections:

send politically themed ringtones for callers to hear or download onto their phones; recruit supporters for rallies and other campaign events using short code; raise money from supporters by charging instant donations to their phone bill or mobile money for countries where it exists and encourage supporters to forward text messages, ring tones, links and short codes to friends and family. According to Cullum (2010, pp. 50–52), mobile phones have also been used to facilitate movement before and during rallies, encourage people to take action, sign petitions, or simply demonstrate support. Cullum highlights the element of speed that gives an edge to mobile phone communication in digital activism:

> Using mobile technology, a joke, rumour, political message or link can spread contagiously like an epidemic. When a person forwards a text message with the instructions or information to those in his phone's address book, it is received by individuals who personally know and trust the sender. If the receiver believes the message to be true and important, he or she will then likely forward the message to others. As such messages go viral and it becomes harder for authorities to stop them.

Thus the literature reveals that the new media have tremendous potential for digital activism but the obstacles relating to the infrastructure, access, skills and security are real and may impinge on the optimization of these technologies for activism.

Prospects for Digital Activism in Uganda

According to World Internet Statistics, by 30 November 2015, 1.8 million of 34.8 million Ugandans had access to the internet. According to the State of Internet Freedom in Uganda: Survey on access, privacy and security online (CIPESA 2015), most Ugandans used email, WhatsApp, Mobile SMS, Facebook and Mobile Chats. In an attempt to make the internet more accessible to rural Ugandans, the government put in place the Uganda Rural Development Fund. This has enabled the establishment of hundreds of internet points of presence (POPs), equipping of rural school laboratories and training in ICT skills. Such efforts notwithstanding, the high cost of access and infrastructural bottlenecks still lock out many Ugandans, especially in the rural areas. There are also challenges of basic literacy as well as technological literacy (Baguma and Eilu 2015, p. 9). The above notwithstanding, statistics from World Internet Statistics (2015) indicate that in the last decade, mobile-phone usage in Uganda has expanded rapidly, and with it the use of social media, especially among people below 35.

However, perhaps the most salient challenge to the freedoms associated with the advent of the new media is government intervention to curtail freedom of expression offline and online. Although the social media are gaining popularity as a means of disseminating news and information, in Uganda, therefore, CIPESA (2015) reports that there have been many attempts by the Ugandan government to curtail its citizens' ability to optimize the social media for mobilization and social action. This has been particularly pronounced around election periods but has also featured whenever government has suspected that either civil society or sections of the public are getting too critical of the actions of government using the available media platforms. There have, therefore, been attempts by government to curtail freedom of expression online in other instances as well, such as in the case of the Save Mabira environmental protest of 2007/2011, the walk-to-work protest of 2011 or the 2016 elections. It is worth noting that in curtailing online activity, the Ugandan government has largely invoked existing laws. The next section provides an overview of some of these laws.

Mixed Messages on Freedom of Expression, Access to Information and the Right to Privacy

The current National Resistance Movement (NRM) government took over power from the previous government by force of arms in 1986. In 1995, a progressive constitution (Uganda 1995) came into force. Article 29 (a) of that constitution states:

Every person shall have the right to:

(a) Freedom of speech and expression, which shall include freedom of the press and other media;
(b) Freedom of thought, conscience and belief which shall include academic freedom in institutions of learning.

Article 41 of the Constitution of the Republic of Uganda guarantees the right of access to information, even though it places the emphasis on access to information in the possession of the state.

The laws of Uganda provide for privacy in article 27 which states in part that 'No person shall be subjected to interference with the privacy of his home, correspondence, communications or other property.'

The above three provisions are related to the extent that the right to privacy helps guarantee the enjoyment of freedom of expression, and access to information makes freedom of expression in the broadest sense of the term, a reality.

The freedoms promised by Article 27, 29 (a) and 41 of Uganda's constitution must, however, be read in the context of Article 43 which sets the boundaries within which media freedom and the right to access to information should be enjoyed. Article 43 states: 'In the enjoyment of the rights and freedoms enshrined in the constitution, no person shall prejudice the fundamental or other human right and freedoms of others or the public interest'. While the media, civil society and the public tend to cite Article 29 and 41 often when they perceive a threat to their rights and freedoms, the state has tended to lean towards article 43 and invoked the 'public interest' in curtailing people's freedom to access information and express themselves in 'other media'. This in spite of the caution embedded in section c of Article 43 (c) which states 'Any limitation of the enjoyment of the rights and freedoms (prescribed by this Chapter) must not be beyond what is acceptable and demonstrably justifiable in a free and democratic society, or what is provided for in the Constitution.

As Joyce observes,

> ... repressive and authoritarian governments do not limit themselves to legal channels when shaping the digital activism environment. In these countries, even activists who have access to digital technologies have difficulties using them because of government-imposed limitations. These governments track online political speech and block applications used by digital activists. Often such online obstruction leads to offline persecution and even imprisonment (Joyce 2010, p. 6).

Circumscribing Activism

Uganda held its first local government elections under the new government in 2011. However, these were held under the 'umbrella' of the ruling NRM, as political parties at the time were banned. The ban was lifted in 2005 and the country held its first multi-party elections in 2006.

In the lead-up to the 2006 elections, the Uganda Communications Commission (UCC), the converged regulator for the broadcast and telecommunications industry, ordered the shut-down of www.radiokatwe.com, a site which had waged a campaign against the incumbent President Museveni, the first family and some government officials who they variously accused of corruption, nepotism and inefficiency. The UCC's defence was that Ugandan law 'empowers the commission to direct any telecoms operator to operate networks in such a manner that is appropriate to national and public interest' (Committee to Protect Journalists 2006). A spokesman for the ruling NRM told the *New Vision* newspaper that the site was publishing 'malicious and false information against the party and its presidential candidate'. The site, according to Open Net Africa, had received 71,000 hits in one day. Although Ugandans managed to by-pass the ban using proxy servers, the shut-down sent a message that no platform was beyond surveillance or regulation.

On 30 May 2015, the president of Uganda threatened with immediate arrest people who were circulating video-recordings on social media pitting two ethnic groups (the Bahima and the Bakiga) against one another. Section 41 of Uganda's Penal Code Act defines promoting sectarianism as the act of printing, publishing, making or uttering any statement likely to '(a) degrade, revile or expose to hatred or contempt; (b) create alienation or despondency of; (c) raise discontent or disaffection among; or (d) promote, in any other way, feelings of ill-will or hostility among or against, any group or body of persons' on the grounds of religion, tribe, ethnic or regional origin. It is important to note that the president belongs to the Bahima ethnic group and his ex-prime minister who was also running for president the same year comes from the Bakiga ethnic group.

Section 25 of the Computer Misuse Act (Uganda 2011) states, 'Any person who willfully and repeatedly uses electronic communication to disturb or attempt to disturb the peace, quiet or right of privacy of any person with no purpose of legitimate communication whether or not a conversation ensues commits a misdemeanour.' In 2015, in the lead up to the 2016 elections, Police ransacked the home of Robert Shaka. They confiscated electronic equipment and then arrested and charged him with intruding on the privacy of the president. Shaka, a media critic, had been mistaken for a notorious social media activist known as TVO (for Tom Voltaire Okwalinga) who had repeatedly posted negative messages about, among other things, the health status of President Museveni. Shaka was released on bail a week after his arrest. This was a signal to people who use the internet to be careful what they post because the 'long arm of the law' would occasionally catch up with them.

It is worth noting that recently, when the government of Uganda has shut down mainstream media houses, it has also shut down or disrupted their websites. For instance, in 2006, the government blocked access to 93.3 KFM, a privately-owned radio station, and the website of its sister newspaper the *Daily Monitor* for publishing election results without the authority of the Electoral Commission. The blockage was only removed after the official results from the Electoral Commission had been declared. Subsequently, the FDC, the leading opposition party, complained that the blockage had stopped their agents from transmitting results and cast doubts on the authenticity of the results declared by the electoral commission.

The Ugandan government has also sought to maintain a degree of surveillance over the social media by setting up monitoring bodies. In 2013, a national Computer Emergency Response Team (Ug-CERT) was set up to 'provide[s] information and assistance to its constituents in implementing pro-active measures to reduce the risks of computer security incidents as well as responding to such incidents when they occur [sic]'. (Uganda Computer Emergency Response Team-UG-Cert) The team is housed under the National Information Technology Authority (NITA-U), one of several regulators for the Information Technology sector.

Doing Digital Activism in Uganda

This section takes a close look at three campaigns: the 'Save Mabira' protest aimed at preventing government from de-gazetting one third of the county's largest natural forest in 2007 and then in 2011; the opposition Forum for Democratic Change (FDC)'s protest aimed at forcing a change in the country's leadership and epitomized by the 'walk-to-work' protests of 2011 and the FDC's campaign to remove Museveni from the presidency in 2016.

The Save Mabira Campaign 2007/2011

On 8 August 2006, *The Monitor* newspaper published a story stating that President Museveni had instructed the minister in charge of the environment to give away 7,100 Hectares of land to Mahendra Mehta, a Ugandan investor of Indian extraction, to enable him to plant more sugar-cane.

It emerged in this and other reports that followed, that the deal involving approximately one-third of Uganda's largest tropical rain forest had been cut in secret between Museveni and Mehta in the period leading up to the February 2006 elections. The Mehta group which Mahendar Mehta heads owns several companies in Uganda including the Sugar Corporation of Uganda (SCOUL). Because the Ugandan government had de-gazetted other forest land including a section of Bugala forest to make way for another foreign investor to plant oil palm despite widespread protests, civil society reacted immediately. Under the leadership of the National Association for Professional Environmentalists (NAPE) and with the support of international NGOS, they formed a coalition and mobilized thousands of Ugandans to protest against the proposed give-away. The protest was originally led by Non-Governmental Organizations (NGOS) including National Association of Professional Environmentalists, Advocates Coalition for Development and Environment (ACODE), Greenwatch, Environmental Action Network, Environmental Alert, Anti-Corruption Coalition of Uganda, Nature Uganda and National Association of Professional Environmentalists (NAPE) which played the coordinating role. Other participants included international environmental NGOs, politicians from government and the opposition, religious institutions including a range of churches under the Uganda Joint Christian Council (UJCC), the Muslim community, and cultural institutions including Buganda and Busoga where the forest was located, affected communities, Traders led by the Kampala City Traders Association (KACITA), the Media and the International Community. This according to many accounts, was the broadest coalition in Uganda ever formed to deal with a single environmental issue.

At the local level, NAPE and ACODE were the lead agencies with regards to strategy and responding to government litigation as well as initiating strategic litigation. According to the former Executive Director of one of the leading NGOS in the coalition, the goal of the coalition was to Save Mabira Forest, but more importantly, to stop the de-gazetting of natural forests. At a deeper level, Mabira was a political issue like any other. Thus as one network system specialist and civil society activist who played a key role in the coordination of the online campaign observed, 'the politics around Mabira was centred around sugar, but it was actually about land – the irregular give-away of land' (S. Mubiru, Personal Communication, 11 May 11 2016). Mabira thus became a 'symbol' or an issue around which activists could mobilize. Unlike previous similar moves by government to de-gazette forests, Mabira was large, and centrally located, so it was easier to mobilize the whole country around it. The organizing committee claims to have mobilized up to two million Ugandans using both traditional and new media.

The Campaign in the Media

The coalition sought to raise awareness about the importance of Mabira forest and highlighted the fact that given its proximity to Lake Victoria and River Nile the forest is a major catchment area. They also argued that it is a source of livelihood for many people. Furthermore, they emphasized the fact that it is a source of important medicinal plants, firewood and construction material for the local communities. They pointed out that it is a source of important and unique information for researchers, as well as a popular eco-tourism site. The forest's destruction, therefore, they argued, would contribute greatly to climate change, affect many livelihoods and species and have an adverse effect on the economy. Above all, they argued that the de-gazetting would set a precedent for government impunity (Child 2009, pp. 248–251).

Two of the coalition leaders interviewed admitted there was no planned or agreed overall communication strategy. However, another key informant who was more new-media-savvy said there was a strategy, although the members from civil society were not that involved in its formulation. The coalition, nevertheless ran an effective campaign that optimized both the traditional and the new media. As one of them said, they 'simply took advantage of every opportunity that presented itself on radio, television, the print media, the internet and mobile telephones' (G. Tumushabe, Personal Communication, 4 May 2016). Interviews with the former executive director of an environmental NGO, a leading environmental activist who played a central role in the Save Mabira campaign and a female communication strategist for the campaign all confirm that the print media played a key role, with both the major national papers (*The New Vision* and the *Daily Monitor*) publishing several news stories, editorials and analytical pieces on the protest as it gained ground. *The Independent* magazine played a particularly pro-active role, strategically publishing key stories highlighting the gravity of the problem or analysing the implications of the give-away. The protestors identified several friendly journalists whom they embedded with major media organizations to ensure the Mabira story stayed on the agenda, since the majority of Ugandans accessed the mainstream media, and particularly radio, and policy-makers were key targets of the newspapers and television. A leading local environmentalist puts it this way: 'The rest of the print media regularly reported on the issue, keeping the need to stop the give-way on the public's minds. What we appreciated the most is that unlike other stories, the media stayed with this story for a long time, making it possible to influence public opinion' (F. Muramuzi, Personal communication 5 May 2016).

The coalition's engagement strategy was two-pronged: while they were in constant dialogue with government agencies like the National Environmental Authority (NEMA) and the National Forestry Authority (NFA), they at the same time liaised with sympathizers living abroad to raise the issue of the Mabira Forest give-away at key international fora whenever the opportunity arose. Besides the print media, the activists also took every opportunity to appear on interactive radio and talk shows, and to leverage on the mainstream media's online presence hence expanding their reach.

New Media

All activists interviewed pointed out that in 2007, the use of Facebook, Twitter and other social media platforms was only beginning to take root in Uganda so the leaders of the campaign (mostly local NGOS) did not utilize them much. Young people mostly used Facebook to discuss lifestyle not issues 'pertinent to the development of this country', according to Shawn Mubiru (Personal Communication, 11 May 2016). The focus was more on lifestyle. This notwithstanding, some individuals maintained active blogs and debated the Mabira give-away. Some academics were also active on Facebook. A search on Wordpress alone yielded 168,000 blogs that mentioned or discussed the Mabira give-away. Several Facebook groups were formed around the issue. One such group was 'Save Mabira Now.' Several young people came on board. This page attracted civil society to Facebook which hitherto they had not used much. Another page created by one David Onen on 23 August 2011 'Save Mabira: Boycott Lugazi Sugar.' To date, this group boasts of 441 members. Some of the members include prominent media personalities Ronnie Mich Egwang, a renowned television host, Harry Sagara, a famous satirical writer and James Onen (alias Fatboy), a seasoned morning show radio presenter with one of Uganda's leading English radio stations; Sanyu FM.

The key messages in the conversations pertaining to the Save Mabira protest included calls for the boycott of Lugazi Sugar, as well as of the ruling NRM government. Other members of the group reduced the issue to race. Some members of the group used this opportunities to vent their anger against Asians in general, accusing them of stealing Ugandans' land. The Facebook conversations betrayed deep-seated emotions of anger and frustration with President Museveni, the government and foreign investors, and in particular Asians. Some group members expressed a sense of betrayal by their government which had been entrusted with an important natural resource.

A few members expressed their support of the forest giveaway. These, however, were outnumbered and drew the wrath of other Ugandans who labelled them 'traitors' and 'unpatriotic'. The momentum was in the opposite direction and such pro-give-away posts which also came from government operatives drew insults from the supporters of the Save Mabira Campaign.

The use of micro-blogs like Twitter was more limited and confined to the more highly educated elite. Using hashtags like #Mabira and #Save Mabira, discussions on Twitter attempted to link the give-away to a range of concerns that included race and labour relations, environmental degradation, possible tax-evasion, lack of transparency in share-holding in the sugar industry, and campaign financing.

Websites were used to raise awareness, call for action (both from government, for instance to find alternative sources of land for SCOUL) and from activists (for instance to join the protest march that took place in April 2007). According to the leader of one local environmental NGO who became the face of the campaign, websites helped bring the Mabira issue to the outside world. In October 2006, the Coalition launched a petition on *petitiontime.com*. According to Child (2009, p. 247), the petition was immensely successful, registering on average 2,000 signatures a day within a month of its launch. At the peak of the campaign in April 2007, the signatures per day had more than doubled. The NGO's created links to as many partner local and international organizations' website as possible and called on all partners to do the same.

> Many of the coalition partners had websites. We were able to post the objectives of the campaign and the campaign strategy. We also used the website to post updates. This created a worldwide distribution of the message – what we would call a multiplier effect (F. Muramuzi, Personal conversation, 5 May 2016).

The coalition built up large and international mailing lists which they used to post updates, and to call for action including asking people to pass the message on, and to contact the 'enemies' of Mabira and stop the give-away. According to one of the coalition's communication strategist, the activists also used email to mobilize. Email was, in addition, also used to encourage people to engage their members of parliament, and to share agreed actions. This was supplemented with thousands of letters written to various members of parliament and other key politicians and other 'power centres'. Their method, according to the former executive director of an environmental NGO interviewed, was 'Donald Rumsfeld, former American Secretary of Defense's, "shock and awe."'

The key local strategists in the Save Mabira Campaign focused their new media campaign on SMS. Mobile phones were just gaining currency and the majority of Ugandans did not own smart phones. However, SMS was well known and used across the different socio-economic classes. 'We knew that very many Ugandans were hooked to their phones', said one communication strategist interviewed. At the same time, the activists knew that there would be serious consequences from government if any of them was identified as the source of the messages. The coalition therefore colluded with one of the large telecommunications companies to obtain a dedicated line that would guarantee them anonymity. The coalition designed a short message that read: 'Save Mabira Forest. Do not buy Lugazi sugar.' The message also urged people to pass it on to several others. The SMS message according to activists quickly went viral. This helped the coalition by-pass the challenges of internet connectivity and helped build momentum. It also ensured anonymity. Police started off by trying to trace the source/sources of the SMS. Eventually, according to several activists interviewed, they abandoned this and started forwarding the boycott message themselves.

Apart from websites, Facebook, Twitter, email and SMS, activists also utilized YouTube to post audio-visual information and persuasive material. In this the locally based activists were assisted by partners abroad who had better capacity to research, update and upload timely and accurate data.

The March

The Save Mabira campaign came to a climax in a march on 27 April 2007 which paralysed business in parts of the capital city, Kampala. The march set out to cover over the 83 km from Kampala to Mabira Forest and attracted over 1,000 people according to the Global Non-Violent Action

Database (2007). However, after a few kilometres, the march turned rowdy, with some protestors shouting racial slurs and shoving the police. Police shot in the air, causing a stampede. In the chaos that ensued, three lives were lost and several people injured. Over 20 activists, including the leaders, were arrested.

The Save Mabira campaign utilized the new media platforms, and in particular mobile phones, to great effect as a way of bypassing limitations on expression in the mainstream media. In the end government reversed its decision to give away the section of the protected forest (GlobalVoices 2011).

The victory of the activists, was, however, short-lived. On August 13 2011, while addressing district leaders and agriculturalists, President Museveni resurrected the debate on Mabira when he announced once again that government would give away a section of Mabira Forest in the interest of development. He blamed the shortage of sugar in the country on the fact that environmental activists had blocked his plan to give away part of Mabira forest to facilitate growth of more sugar-cane in 2007. He referred to the activists as 'anti-development', 'economic saboteurs'.

This time, however, the activists were better prepared. The networks and mailing lists from 2007 were still in place. Several new Facebook groups came up and the discussion was more diffuse. Because many more people had acquired the means and skills to be active on the digital platforms, the coordination of the conversation was less centralized. Offline activities such as T-shirts, poster, bumper stickers, talk-shows, editorials etc. augmented the online campaign. With the help of their partners, the Coalition released a study explaining the economic cost of the proposed forest land give-away (NatureUganda 2011) and drafted a fresh petition. However, government withdrew its decision to give away the land before the petition was signed. For the second time, the give-away of part of Mabira forest was averted.

Achievement of the Save Mabira Campaign

Taking the Mabira campaign online, according to Mubiru, managed to interest young people online in 'politics'. This carried on offline. 'The people who were not online received the message more than the people online [sic]. There were many people who, online, promised to join offline activities, but out of fear, just did not show up.' It took some persuasion. As Mubiru puts it, 'We explained to them that "without politics, you cannot have your lifestyle".' Eventually, there were many people saying the same thing. The diaspora became even more active on the social media, so the activists reached out to them. They developed a long 'befriend' list and started sending out email messages about meetings and strategy. Each time they sent out a message, they asked the people to reach out to their friends in the diaspora. This way, they built a large community. They also invited people to sign the petition and many did. They invited people to plant trees, and the NFA picked it up and started offering tree seedlings free of charge. The King of Buganda offered free land to SCOUL to save Mabira Forest.

It is important to note the synergies. Civil society had the message and the resources. The job of the online activists was to 'pick up civil society's message and disseminate it.' (S. Mubiru, Personal Communication, 11 May 2016.)

Challenges of the Mabira Campaign

Digital activism in Uganda, as in many other developing nations, takes place among real challenges online and offline. In 2011, government operatives joined the conversation online, mainly to ridicule and insult the activists into silence. Some messages contained threats like: 'Do you know who you are trying to challenge?' (referring to the president) and activists were threatened with 'disappearance'. Three of the key informants and several other people were arrested and questioned by the Criminal Investigation Department and the Inspector General of Police several times. They were accused of crimes ranging from inciting violence, inciting the public to loot, intent to overthrow the government of Uganda and treason. Many journalists were threatened, often with anonymous calls. As a result of this, one key informant said, 'There was a high attrition rate.'

The Walk-To-Work Protests of 2011 and the 2016 Elections

The 'walk-to-work protests' followed the 2011 presidential elections in Uganda where Kizza Besigye's FDC lost for the third time in a row to the incumbent, President Museveni. This loss, and rising public anger against rising food prices, fiscal indiscipline and deteriorating service-delivery provided fertile ground for protest. The anger among the opposition was exacerbated by President Museveni's responding to complaints about rising fuel prices by advising people to be economical with fuel and not 'drive to bars'. In the words of Shawn Mubiru, . . . , 'Everyone was bruised.' The resultant unrest, and the opposition's repeated call to citizens to stand up for change in their leadership culminated in the 'walk-to-work' protests of 2011 (News 2011).

The protests started with a meeting in Bunga, a suburb of Kampala which was attended by a small number of people. 'We wanted to engage government and make them respond to the concerns of the people', said one young activist interviewed. The group agreed to ride on the symbolism of Museveni's 'advice' and mobilise people to walk to work.

The easiest group to reach were politically like-minded people so one of the female activists called upon the FDC to mobilise to walk to work. Because she was heading the communications of the FDC, it was difficult for her to coordinate this effort as well, so another member of parliament came in. The group initially brought on board several other key FDC and Democratic Party (DP) members. Finally, FDC publically came out and owned the campaign. The campaign then started shifting into the hands of politicians.

The 'walk-to-work' protests drew in Members of Parliament, religious leaders, civil society and people from all walks of life. Led by a coalition of opposition members named Action for Change (A4C), the protest walks started on 11 April. Besigye, Norbert Mao, the Head of the DP and several other protestors were arrested on the first day as police sought to stop the protests. The protests quickly turned violent as police faced off with civilians. Protestors were harassed and arrested several more times before the protests died down. According to various reports, 5–9 people died including a two-year-old girl who was shot in the head and chest by police. Because government was intent on stopping the 'walk-to-work' protests after the Mabira experience, many young activists who were not necessarily active politicians retreated to the online platforms to vent their disgruntlement with their country's governance and call for change.

The Campaign in the Media (2016)

The 'walk-to-work' protests, coming four years after the Save Mabira protest, utilized all the digital media platforms used in the Save Mabira campaign and more extensively, attracting intervention by the statutory Communications Regulator, UCC. By this time many more Ugandans were connected to the internet and a large number owned mobile phones. At the height of the 'walk-to-work' protests, UCC instructed Internet Service Providers (ISPs) to block access to Facebook and Twitter for

24 hours. This followed an earlier order where UCC had instructed telecom companies to block and regulate SMS (short message service) that could 'instigate hatred, violence and unrest' during the presidential election period. The regulator had flagged 18 words that constituted 'red flags' and were likely to invite surveillance or blockage. The words included 'Egypt', 'bullet', 'people-power', 'Tunisia', 'Mubarak', 'dictator', 'teargas', 'army', 'police', 'gun', 'Ben-Ali', 'UPDF' (which stands for the national army, the Uganda People's Defence Force) and some words in the local languages (Biryabarema 2011). Although there is no sufficient documentation to show that any media organization complied with these directives, they sent a message to would-be digital activists that government was watching.

The 2016 Elections

The build up to the 2016 elections was particularly tense because President Museveni, who had been power for three decades, was standing against his long-time rival Kizza Besigye but also his former Prime Minister, Amama Mbabazi. The population was polarized. The issues raised by the FDC in 2011 were on the agenda again and were vigorously discussed on the social media. On 17 February, on the eve of Uganda's February 2016 polls, the Communications regulator once again instructed ISPs to switch off Facebook, Twitter and WhatsApp, as well as mobile money transfer services, again in the interests of 'public order'. President Museveni said the shutdown was intended as 'a security measure to avert lies . . . intended to incite violence and illegal declaration of election results'.

The ban was condemned by many as plain censorship. This time, though, Ugandans were able to get around the ban by using encrypted Virtual Private Networks (VPNs).

The Campaign in the Media (2016)

The online campaign drew attention to the same issues as the 'walk-to-work' campaign had done, only this time amplified. Using their newly created Facebook page, My FDC, to launch their policy agenda the FDC articulated their commitment to democracy. They quoted president Museveni on key pronouncements and unfulfilled promises. They concentrated on ensuring that as they approached the 2016 election it was 'cool' to be associated with the FDC. They engaged a team of young people and trained them about keeping the message simple, clear and focused. 'We let them know that this was about the message, not just posting', said one communications strategist interviewed.

Because they were largely dealing with a young demographic—Uganda's population is the youngest in the world with 77 % aged below 30, the activists emphasized formatting, creativity and visuals. They used a multi-media approach, posting audio, photos, video clips etc. from the campaign trail. Using mobile phones, supporters posted many photographs and videos via WhatsApp with commentary, drawing attention to the issues of the campaign. They had people hold up posters of Kizza Besigye and take photographs with them which were then posted on Facebook. The party also posted their campaign programme online which raised curiosity and interest. There were daily updates and news flashes. All messages had a call to action. The most basic message was 'If you agree with this message, pass it on' and this, according to activists interviewed, did a lot to drive traffic to the FDC pages.

The campaign concentrated on the rural areas, with Besigye doing up to ten rallies a day, many of which were recorded and transmitted on multiple digital platforms. They made it a habit of posting 'thank you' notes for supporters in their own languages after each rally, which was significant in Uganda where there are different languages or dialects spoken in every region, many of which do not get space in the mainstream media.

The FDC online team also set up Twitter handles including #WesigeBesigye (Trust Besigye) and #Freemyvote. #WesigeBesigye in particular enabled aggregating of opinion and sharing. However, these were not as popular as the Facebook pages.

Challenges

President Museveni won the 2016 election. Kizza Besigye, who came second, was placed under house arrest for over a month. During that time, he was unable to put together an election petition. The candidate that came third, former Prime Minister Amama Mbabazi petitioned the High Court and lost for lack of evidence. Since the conclusion of the 2016 elections, the social media have been switched on and off several times. There have been many arrests, and many opposition politicians are under surveillance. The memory of the social media shut-down is still fresh on peoples' memory and Ugandans are more aware of government surveillance in a previously relatively surveillance-free space. Activists interviewed think the shut-down had a significant impact on the elections. In the words of one of them, 'The shut-down really, really, really impacted on the outcome of the election . . . There was no money to buy internet bundles even if people had VPN. Teams were disconnected. Telephone services were jammed and there were many dropped calls. The shut-down created voter apathy. The opposition was discouraged. . . . If the blockage had not happened, Museveni would have had to declare himself president by force'.(S. Mubiru, Personal conversation, 11 May 2016).

Conclusion

The Save Mabira campaign in Uganda may be seen as a watershed. Coming in 2007, right after an election, and just as the most popular social media platforms took root in Uganda, the campaign opened up a new area for activism that drew in the hitherto younger and less vocal demographic of the country. For the most part, digital activism in Uganda since 2007 has been 'internet-enhanced rather internet-based' (Vegh 2003, p. 72), largely due to the fact that although there is a growing portion of the population able to access the internet, these are by no means the majority. Thus, for the foreseeable future, both from the sender and the receiver side, internet-based activism is only likely to involve a small portion of stakeholders. However, although one may not be able to say that the digital media are *the* new watchdog, at least one may refer to them as *a* new watchdog.

The findings of this chapter suggest that the most common type of activism in Uganda since 2007 has been Vegh's first type: awareness/advocacy. This is the simplest type as it mostly involves making information available and ensuring it is widely disseminated. Hence the SMS message in the Save Mabira Campaign, and the change message followed by 'If you believe this, pass it on' in the 2016 elections. In the initial stages, awareness raising and advocacy was most commonly done using websites and Facebook because (1) It was easy for the lead organisations like NAPE and ACODE to set up websites and link them with their wide NGO network and (2) Facebook was available to people on a range of devices, including relatively simple mobile phones. As digital activism in Uganda has evolved, activists have embraced WhatsApp, which considered 'dark' and is immensely popular with younger people, and YouTube which enables activists to by-pass obstacles to broadcasting erected by government against the mainstream media, reaching many more people than they would have otherwise reached. A combination of YouTube and mobile phone technology also allows activists to receive footage from all their constituencies and make it available across geographical borders in a relatively short time.

Clearly, digital technology has had a liberating effect on a certain category of Ugandan society (mostly the young and educated). However, Ugandan digital activism is still plagued by the perennial logistical and structural barriers that Brodock (2010) and Hadji (2016) highlight. Most prominent among these obstacles has been government's increasingly direct intervention to block access to and use of the social media at peak political moments. Activists have mitigated some of the logistical obstacles by using VPNS. They have used the most accessible technologies to convey the basic message about the cause at hand (as in the case of the Mabira campaign) and left the more sophisticated discourse for Facebook, for instance. They have simplified and translated messages to make them accessible to more people; they have 'befriended' journalists to ensure constant (and favourable) coverage and they have utilized multimedia strategies to ensure the message gets to as many Ugandans as possible (as in the case of the 2016 campaigns). However, for as long as certain structures remain in place, subversion can only go so far, and using existing laws and extra-judicial means, government still has the potential to hold activism in check. While there may be what Hadji (2016, pp. 75–77) calls the revival of 'a dormant public consciousness into sentient, dynamic social discourse', therefore, the might of government has been demonstrated in the most unequivocal ways and is likely to have an impact on what risks the average Ugandan is willing to take in the name of digital activism.

References

Alzouma, G. (2005). Myths of digital technology in Africa: Leapfrogging development?. *Global Media and Communication*, 339–356.

Baguma, R., & Eilu, E. (2015). Using mobile phones in elections in developing countries: Opportunities and challenges. In G. Abdoulaye (Ed.), *Computing in research and development in Africa* (pp. 251–265). New York, NY: Springer doi:10.10071978-3-319-08239-4_12.

Banda, F., Mudhai, O. F., & Tettey, W. J. (2009). New media and democracy in Africa – A critical interjection. In O. Mudhai, W. Tettey, and F. Banda (Eds.), *African media and the digital public sphere* (pp. 1–20). New York: Palgrave Macmillan.

Brodock, K. (2010). Economic and social factors: Digital activism in closed and open societies. In M. Joyce, (Ed.). *Digital activism decoded: The new mechanics of change* (pp. 71–84). New York, NY and Amsterdam: Internaltional Debate Education Association.

Castells, M., & Ince, M. (2003). *Conversations with Manuel Castells.* London: Polity.

Centre for International Media Assistance. (2008). Scaling a changing curve: Traditional media development and the new media. A Report to the Center for International Media Assistance.

Child, K. (2009). Civil society in Uganda. The struggle to save the Mabira Forest Reserve. *Journal of Eastern Africa Studies, 3*(2), 240–258. doi:10.1080/17531050902972659.

CIPESA. (2015). State of internet freedom in Uganda: Survey on access, privacy and security online. In *CIPESA ICT Policy Research series 08/15.* http://www.cipesa.org/?wpfb_dl=209. Accessed 12 October 2016.

Committee to Protect Journalists (CPJ). (2006). https://cpj.org/2006/02/critical-site-still-blocked-on-eve-of-president.php. Accessed 12 October 2016.

Cullum, B. (2010). Devices: The power of mobile phones. In J. Mary (Ed), *Digital activism decoded. The new mechanics of change* (pp. 47–70). New York: International Debate Education Association.

Diamond, L. (2010). Liberation technology. *Journal of Democracy, 21*(3), 69–83. doi:10.1353/jod.0.0190.

Duncan, J. (2013). Mobile network society? Affordability and mobile phone usage in Grahamstown East. *Communication: South African Journal for Communication Theory and Research, 39*(1), 35–52.

Elias, B. (2011). Uganda bans SMS texting of key words during poll. Kampala. Reuters. Thurs Feb.17, 2011. 1.08.

Global Internet Report. (2015). www.internetworldstats.com/stats.htm. Accessed 8 October 2016.

Global Non-Violent Action Database (2007). http://nvdatabase.swarthmore.edu/content/ugandans-save-mabira-forest-sugarcane-plantation-2007. Acessed 8 October 2016.

GlobalVoices. (2011). https://globalvoices.org/2011/08/19/uganda-ugandans-take-fight-to-save-a-rainforest-to-internet/. Accessed 12 October 2016.

Goldstein, J., & Rotich, J. (2008). *Digitally networked technology in Kenya's 207-2008 post- election crisis.* Cambridge, MA: The Berkman Centre for Internet and Society.

Hadji, A. (2016). Breaking boundaries. The opportunities for using social media in civil society networking, activism and civic engagement. In M. Kamp (Ed.),

Reality check: Assessing the impact of social media on political communication and civic engagement in Uganda (pp. 72–88). Kampala: Konrad Adenauer Stiftung.
IRIN News. (2011, April). Uganda's chaotic walk-to-work protests put Uganda in the spotlight. http://www.irinnews.org/report/92615/uganda-chaotic-walk-work-protests-put-kampala-spotlight. Accessed 12 October 2016.
Joyce, M. (Ed.). (2010). *Digital activism decoded: The new mechanics of change* (pp. 71–84). New York, NY and Amsterdam: IDEA.
Kaplan, A. M., & Haenlein, M. (2010). Users of the world unite: The challenges and opportunities of social media. *Business Horizons, 53*, 59–68.
Khamis, S., Gold, P. B., & Vaugh, K. (2012). Beyond Egypt's "Facebook Revolution" and Syria's "YouTube" uprising: Campaign political contexts, actors and communication strategies. Arab media and society. http://www.arabmediasociety.com/?article=791.
NatureUganda. (2011). The economic valuation of the proposed de-gazettement of Mabira Central Forest Reserve. www.natureuganda.org/downloads/Mabira/mabiradegazettementrepport.pdf. Accessed 8 October 2016.
Permanent Culture Now. www.permanent-culture-now/what is activism. Accessed 8 October 2016.
Socha, B., & Eber-Schmid. (2012). What is new media? Defining new media isn't easy. http://www.newmedia.org/what-is-new-media.html.
Tumusiime, J. (2007). Investigating a rural community's use of communication technology: A study of Nakaseke Community Multi-media Centre in Uganda J. MA thesis, Rhodes University.
Uganda. (1995). The Constitution of the Republic of Uganda. www.ulii.org/node/23824. Accessed 22 February 2016.
Uganda. (2011). The Computer Misuse Act. www.ulii.org/ug/legislation/act/2015/2-6.
Uganda Computer Emergency Response Team-UG-Cert. http://www.ug-cert.ug/data/smenu/14/UgCERT.html. Accessed 11 October 2016.
Underwood, M. (2005). The internet as public sphere. http://www.zip.com.au/~athornto//links.htm
Vegh, S. (2003). Classifying forms of online activism: The case of cyber-protests against the World Bank. In M. McCaughey and A. Michael (Eds.), *Cyberactivism: Online activism in theory and practice*. New York: Routledge.
Watson, O. R. (2005). You decide: The dictator watch guide to social and environmental activism. http://www.activism101.org/dwguide/guidetofc.html
World Internet Statistics. (2015). www.worldinterentstats.com/htmeferences

Monica B. Chibita is an Associate Professor and Head of Department at the Mass Communication Department, Uganda Christian University (UCU). She holds a D. Litt. et Phil. (Communication) (University of South Africa), an M.A. in

Journalism (University of Iowa), and B.A/Education (Makerere University). She served in various capacities (Lecturer, Senior Lecturer, Associate Professor and Acting Head of Department) at Makerere University between 1994 and 2011, and has served on several boards including Uganda's Broadcasting Council, the New Vision Printing and Publishing Corporation, the East African Communication Association (EACA) and the African Centre for Media Excellence. Her research interests are in the broad area of media and democracy with specific interest in regulation and participation. She is Associate Editor of the Journal of African Media Studies (JAMS) and serves on the editorial boards of several other journals in the field.

CHAPTER 5

Citizen Journalism, Cyber-Activism, and 'Crowdsourcing': Discussing the Sacking of Sierra Leone's Vice President Sam Sumana on Facebook and Twitter

Ibrahim Seaga Shaw and Di Luo

This chapter critically explores the role of citizen journalism in the context of social media or social networking sites (SNS) in the 'democratic empowerment' of ordinary citizens within the framework of 'participatory politics'. It builds on recent work by Shaw (2016) which offered a human rights journalism (here after HRJ) critic of the 'democratic deficit' of citizen journalism (here after CJ) in the social media framing of the Ebola epidemic in Sierra Leone. However, while that work focused on the deficits of CJ in the promotion of human rights and development, this chapter focuses on its deficits as an alternative journalism paradigm to radical democratic empowerment and participatory politics within a human rights framework.

I.S. Shaw (✉) · D. Luo
Newcastle, United Kingdom
e-mail: ibrahim.shaw@northumbria.ac.uk; di.luo@northumbria.ac.uk

B. Mutsvairo (ed.), *Digital Activism in the Social Media Era*,
DOI 10.1007/978-3-319-40949-8_5

Yet ever since the emergence of the digital revolution, many scholars, not least Bird (2009), Held (2004, 2006), Frazer (2007) and Castells (2006) have remained upbeat about the power of the internet in ushering in much more democratically empowered public spheres in both national and global contexts. Mark Poster (2001, p. 175) sees the internet as empowering 'previously excluded' communities', while Agre (1994) sees it as ushering in a renaissance of democracy. Stuart Allan praises it for ensuring 'bottom up coverage' as citizen journalists offering their first hand reports about what is going on around them (Allan 2006, p. 7). In short, most scholars have celebrated how CJ has narrowed down, or addressed, what Hackett (2005) has called the 'democratic deficit' of traditional journalism. Moreover the internet has led to the increasing blurring of the lines between the production and consumption of news (Rosen cited in Bird 2009, Geniets 2013). This new process therefore changes the role of the audiences from passive consumers of news to active producers and consumers while enjoying their democratic freedom of expression and participation. These dramatic changes have made some media scholars to call for a rethink of media and journalism studies in the twenty-first century, while others such as Chaffee and Metzger went the extra mile and published their controversial article in 2001 — 'The End of Mass Communication?'. In the article, they argued that with the new media landscape it is no longer business as usual with traditional media theories, such as agenda-setting, media effects on audiences, and the information divide. However, as this chapter seeks to demonstrate using quantitative content analysis of the coverage of the controversial sacking of Sierra Leone's Vice President Sam Sumana in March 2015, which provoked demonstrations in Freetown, London and Washington, the news agenda of cyber-activists on social media is still largely set by mainstream journalists. This raises the question of the potential of citizen journalism to address the democratic deficit of mainstream journalism. Of course, there are few recent studies by Goode (2009), Curran et al. (2013), Shaw (2016) etc. that have asked questions about the democratic potential of CJ. However, what makes this chapter unique is that it is the first to offer a human rights journalism critique of the potential or deficiency of CJ to provide democratically empowered public spheres that draws on social media framing of a controversial political event—in this case, the sacking of a VP in one of West Africa's fledging post-conflict democracies.

This chapter has three main sections: Citizen Journalism and radical democratic empowerment—change or continuity in media audience and agenda-setting; the internet, social media and democracy in Sierra Leone; and Facebook and Twitter discussions of the sacking of VP Sam Sumana in Sierra Leone.

Citizen Journalism and Radical Democratic Empowerment: Change or Continuity in Media Effects and Agenda-Setting

This section explores whether or not we have experienced any fundamental change in traditional media theories such as media audience effects and agenda-setting in our new media environment. Shaw (2016) offers a critique, through a human-rights journalism lens, of the shortcomings of CJ in serving as counterhegemonic journalism to mainstream journalism in the reporting of human rights and development, using a Sierra Leone anti-Ebola Facebook discussion forum as a case study. In this chapter we go further. Not only do we use a human rights journalism lens to interrogate the democratic deficits of CJ in democratic empowerment and participation involving a constitutional and political crisis provoked by the sacking of a seating VP but also we use human rights-based principles of human rights standards, participation, empowerment, accountability, and non-discrimination (Shaw 2012; see also Beman and Calderbank 2008) as effective alternatives to addressing these deficits.

First we want to engage briefly with the debates regarding the conceptualization of CJ. The concept has recently expanded beyond the scope of the process of creating content for formal online news outlets such as blogs or independent news websites, including those for traditional media outlets, to include citizens' follow-up participation in the news production process, such as social media posting, reposting, linking, tagging, commenting and rating (Goode 2009; Kim and Lowery 2015). Thus, while news websites and blogs run by citizen journalists attracted much earlier scholarly attention, cyber-activism or citizen journalism activities randomly carried out on social media platforms such as Facebook and Twitter are becoming 'increasingly relevant and important'. However, from the foregoing conceptualization of CJ there appears to be some ambiguity in the scholarly understanding of what CJ is, or who is a citizen journalist. It seems as if online journalism, that is a type of journalism practiced by mainstream professional journalists using multi-media technologies, is simply, but problematically, being conflated with citizen journalism, which Kolodzy (2012) described as a 'random act of journalism' based on the creation of content by users in response to their consumption of content generated either by mainstream journalists on their traditional news media platforms or content generated by fellow users in the blogosphere or on social media platforms.

Part of the aim of this chapter is to address this conceptual ambiguity of CJ and restore its true meaning as an alternative public-driven, public-owned and public-interest news platform. It makes sense to see CJ as purely journalism by, for, and of the people, that is the traditional news consumers, now turned prosumers in the new media environment, and for those members of the public whose interests mainstream journalists or politicians claim to represent. This conceptual clarity of CJ as opposed to online journalism becomes even more relevant when contrasted with mainstream professional journalism. In traditional news production, professional gatekeeping routines such as 'selecting, writing, editing, positioning, scheduling, repeating and otherwise massaging of information' (Shoemaker and Vos 2009, p. 73) are followed, whereas, in new media news production such traditional boundaries are blurred, which means anyone with access to the internet can participate (Shaw 2016, see also Benkler 2006; Bruns 2008; Jenkins 2006).

The blurring of the lines between production and consumption has forced most journalists to provide more participatory and audience-centric news to keep the news production process rolling. This means that journalists are increasingly seeing themselves as convergent journalists involved in both 'pushing' the story out to the audiences in whatever form they want it, and in the 'pulling in' of information 'from members of the public who want to share their situation with others to add to the collective knowledge'(Shaw 2016). This has changed the whole relationship between the producers (journalists) and consumers(readers or audiences) from what Rosen called vertical (top-down—one to many), to horizontal (bottom-up—citizen to citizen), with the journalist more or less playing the role of the facilitator of the conversation of the networked community. This new process changes the role of the audiences from passive consumers of news to active producers and consumers while enjoying their democratic freedom of expression and participation. The user-generated content (UGC) created in the conversation between citizens (horizontal) on one hand, and between citizens and mainstream journalists (reverse vertical) in a bottom-up way is fed back to the collective pool of knowledge available to the citizen journalist or mainstream journalist for onward dissemination to the public. Meanwhile, the new process changes the role of the audience from passive recipients of information to active partners in its production and consumption. The citizens pulled into participate in the news production process are now increasingly constituting what has come to be called 'crowdsourcing' (Shaw 2016). This blurring of the lines between production, distribution, and consumption of news content, be it on news web sites of legacy or new media, or on SNS, may be partly responsible for the ambiguity over the conceptualization of CJ. This could also have provoked the controversial article by Chaffee and Metzger in 2001 titled: 'The End of Mass Communication?' in which they argued that media theories such as agenda-setting, media effects, and information or digital divide associated with legacy media no longer apply in the new media environment, because, according to them, the power of the internet has made the legacy media less important. Chaffee and Metzger (2001) no doubt belong to school of media scholars cited in the introduction who are over the moon with the power of the internet to provide democratically empowered public spheres needed to address the democratic deficits of mainstream journalism which is more or less modelled on the classical western liberal democracy paradigm.

On the contrary, this chapter, largely following the 'political economy of the media' tradition, takes a more pessimistic position on the power of the internet, and by extension CJ, to address the democratic deficits of mainstream journalism. A study by Curran et al. (2013) dismisses as a myth the widely held claim of the internet as an 'empowering tool' for otherwise marginalised publics. The Curran et al. (2013) research, which studied news websites, TV and the press from nine different countries, found online news as 'being very similar to the news of other media in being heavily reliant on state representatives (such as government ministers and public officials) and on experts'(886) as sources of information. The research, albeit based on the study of hard news, found these dominant sources representing '70 percent of the sources of online news compared with 64 percent of press sources and 60 percent of television news sources (886)'. The research also found that the websites studied reflected the voices of opposition politicians and civil society less than those in traditional media (Curran et al. 2013). Business and expert sources were rated a bit more at 10.98 % and 25.87 %, respectively, which suggests that business and expert voices were better articulated than civil society ones. These findings are interesting in that they challenge the myth of the internet serving as an alternative to traditional media, which, according to a maze of research (Hall et al. 1978; Bennett 1990;

Mermin 1999; Manning 2001; Davis 2009; Curran 2011), has been acknowledged as relying too much on elite political and business sources in setting the news agenda in the US and the UK (Shaw 2016). The Curran et al. (2013) research suggests that not much has actually changed in journalism as a result of the recent media technological changes. It resonates with Curran's remark 'All media were once new media' which suggests more continuity than change in journalism in the digital age. However, no African country is included among the nine countries studied in the Curran et al. (2013) research, a gap which this chapter also aims to address. We argue that CJ as it stands is not enough to perform this role of addressing these gaps and that it needs to be complemented by human rights journalism to do this well. Thus, we go along with the critical re-evaluation of Chaffee and Metzger's controversial article in 2001: 'The End of Mass Communication?' little over a decade later by Weimann et al. (2014) where they concluded that although media theories may change to accommodate the changes of the new media environment, it does not mean the 'old' issues of power, resistance, structure, and ownership have disappeared overnight.

The rest of this section will briefly explore the claims and counterclaims of change and continuity in agenda-setting and media audience effects in the new media environment. Normatively speaking, CJ is different from mainstream journalism in that it is among other things centred around people more than around elites; democratic more than profit-centred; more partisan and empathic; and more participatory, engaging and empowering (Shaw 2012, 2016). At least this is the view of the internet optimists such as Chaffee and Metzger (2001) who believe that the internet has fundamentally altered the existing media theories and the power relations between the producer and consumer of news in terms of who is really calling the shots. However, at the other end of the spectrum—the pessimists—such as the authors of this chapter, Weinmann et al. (2014) and others earlier cited believe that although minor changes have occurred in the media theories these do not reflect any fundamentally changes in the power relations in the production and consumption of news.

Let us first look at the Media Audience theory to see how new media has changed it to the extent of altering the power relations between the producers and consumers of news. Chaffee and Metzger (2001) claim that, contrary to the idea of legacy media audience as unified and mainly passive mass, the audience in new media is seen as a diffuse group encompassing those who consume and produce news at the same time. This new audience is now called 'users' because it is made up of people who actively use and produce content rather than just passively consuming it. This change means that the direct effect of news content on users is replaced by conditional effect since the users now have agency to reject this in real time and provide an alternative they deem represents the reality better in their estimation. For example, uses and gratification research shows an expansion of the glorifications supplied by the media due to the unique facets of internet use (LaRose and Eastin 2004). Moreover, the interpretive activities of users have made them to be more media-literate and therefore more empowered to make informed judgement on what news they consume and how and why they consume it (Jenkins et al. 2009). However, Weinmann et al. (2014) argue that, although users now have more agency in the new media environment this does not necessarily translate into their democratic empowerment beyond the community of users they are participating in. 'Audiences are still susceptible to the impact of the media on their attitudes and behaviours; restricted as content creators by established media institutions, and prefer to be engaged, media wise, within their own social, communal, and political perimeters' (Weinmann et al. 2014, p. 807).

In the case of the agenda-setting theory, Chaffee and Metzger (2001) asserted that new media may give more power to users whose voices are normally excluded in legacy media. They argued that the agenda-setting theory will change from 'what issues the media tell people to think about' to 'what issues the people tell the media they want to think about'. Users can now form their own agendas and then find others who share their agendas. As Tomaszeski (2006) suggested, such users can be bloggers who are being sourced by the traditional media, who are taking original content from them and incorporating it into their own messages to the public. However, according to Weinmann et al. (2014), there is scholarly evidence to suggest that new media has weakened and at the same time strengthened traditional media-agenda setting process. An extensive study of agenda-setting between 1956 and 2004 by Tan and Weaver (2013) found no evidence to support the view that the agenda-setting effect between the *New York Times* and the public has become weaker over time. Moreover, a study by Coleman and McCombs (2007, p. 503) looking at the effects of agenda-setting on various groups of individuals concluded that 'different media use among the young did not seem to influence the agenda-setting effect much at all'.

The Internet, Social Media and Democracy in Sierra Leone

Sierra Leone is a small West African country with a population of about six million. Sierra Leone gained its independence from Britain on April 27 1961. The country became a multi-party democracy in 1996 following the election of Ahmed Tejan Kabbah of the SLPP as president. The first major test of this fledgling democracy came in 2007 when for the first time in the country's history a ruling party (the SLPP) was defeated in an election which brought the current president, Ernest Bai Koroma of the APC party, to power. President Koroma went to win his second and final term in 2012. His running mate in both terms was VP Sam Sumana, a businessman previously based in the US, whom he controversially sacked on 17 March 2015. The country went through an 11 year civil war which officially ended in January 2002. There are about 40 newspapers, including 15 dailies. The majority of newspapers are privately operated and are often critical of the government. There is relative press freedom, although there are some taboo subjects and journalists generally observe self-censorship for fear of going against the 1965 Criminal and Seditious Libel Act. Radio is by far the most popular and trusted medium in the country with 85% of people having access to radio and 72 % of people in the country listening to radio daily.

Internet access has been very low in the country but this situation dramatically changed from 2008 following the introduction of Wi-Fi and 3G mobile phones. The capital, Freetown, has a city-wide internet connection and internet access is also available for a small fee in cafeterias, hairdressers, as well as in dedicated internet cafes. However, Sierra Leone still has one of the lowest internet penetrations in Africa, standing at 4.4 %, according to World Internet Statistics research in November 2015.

Sierra Leoneans, especially the young, are very active on social media, especially on Facebook, which is the SNS with most users (94.96 %) with 260,000 active users in the country in November 2015 (World Internet Stats). Twitter is not as popular as Facebook in Sierra Leone although it is the second most used SNS in the country with 3.56 %. But the statistics would be far different if Sierra Leonean users based overseas were to be factored in. Few of the leading newspapers are present on Facebook, with *Awoko* leading the number of Facebook likes (6,158) as of 12 May 2016, followed by *Global Times* (3,915) and *Awareness Times* (2,843). Some

Sierra Leone news websites are also present on Facebook, with *Sierra Loaded* having the most likes (6,375) followed by *MySierraLeone online.com* (4,266), *Peep* (1,702), and *Sierra Leone Breaking News* (930). The news website with the most Twitter followers is *Sierra Leone Times* (2,243) followed by *Sierra Loaded* (600).

Discussing the Sacking of Sierra Leone's Vice President on Facebook and Twitter

Having explored the changes and continuities of media audience and agenda-setting theories in the context of citizen journalism and cyber-activism, and briefly discussed the internet, social media and democracy in Sierra, we will now focus on analysing the discussion of the controversial sacking of Sierra Leone's VP Sam Sumana on Facebook and Twitter to determine the extent to which these changes and/or continuities of these media theories play out. We draw on quantitative content analysis focusing on the manifest texts in the posts on Facebook and Twitter discussing the sacking on 17 March 2015. The aim is to investigate the democratic empowering potential of the posts to determine whether anything has fundamentally changed in the power relations, agency and agenda-setting in favour of grass roots citizens, or whether it is business as usual. As we noted in the first section of this chapter, the study by Curran et al. (2013) disagrees with the widely held claim that the internet has empowered the otherwise voiceless members of the public as it found the news websites studied from nine countries used more elite (state, business, and expert) sources than grassroot sources, even more than the mainstream presses in those countries. This chapter, therefore, aims to contribute to this research and others such as Shaw (2016) to test the validity of the empowering role of the internet and CJ and at the same time test the validity of the claim made by Chaffee and Metzger that traditional media theories of audience and agenda-setting are becoming irrelevant in the new media environment.

We draw on De Bonville's model of quantitative content analysis (2000) on the basis of quantitative measurement of the aggregate data of posts on Facebook and Twitter collected using the search phrase 'sacking of Sam Sumana' covering the period from the date of the sacking, 17 March 2015, to 8 May 2016. In all, 24 Facebook posts and 24 Twitter posts were retrieved and coded. Facebook and Twitter were selected for this study because they are the two most popular SNSs used in Sierra

Leone. We decided to look at posts spanning a little over one year in order to capture everything about the sacking of the VP from when it happened to the recent Supreme Court ruling which confirmed the constitutionality of the sacking.

For research design, similar but slightly different ways are used to organise the posts gathered from Facebook and Twitter. For Facebook, data collected include user/poster's name, date of the post; type of the post; description of the post, how many people comment, how many people share, and how many views. For Twitter, data include: user/poster's name date of the tweet; content of the tweet; where the tweet linked to if there is a linked followed at the end of the tweet; how many people reply; how many retweets; and how many tweet 'likes'.

We will explore the following research questions:

RQ1: Were posts by grassroot sources more than those by elite sources?
RQ2: Were User-Generated Content (UGC) posts more than posts from mainstream media?

RQ1 will investigate the claim about who actually sets the agenda between the elites, including journalists, and audiences or users of content on social media to determine whether traditional agenda-setting theory is still relevant. RQ2 will investigate who, between the mainstream journalist and the audience/user, has got more power, agency and influence over the other in the production of news content to determine whether traditional media audience theory is still relevant.

Grassroot Versus Elite Posts

We start by answering RQ1: Were posts by grassroot sources more than those by elite sources? Elite sources include mainstream media, state/ruling party, opposition party(ies), NGOs, and development/relief agencies while grass-root sources include ordinary citizens, communities, and civil society groups or activists. For this study the sources of the posts are quantified into the following categories: users/posters include news/media publishing/organization (including websites and other media organizations in community format) and the public; sources of the posts include grassroots sources from the general public and elite sources from the news/media organizations or state agencies.

Discussion of Results: Facebook and Twitter

Facebook: Of 24 posts on Facebook, 16 are from elite sources, and only eight are from grassroot sources. And, in fact, of the eight posts from grassroot sources, six are based on information originally generated by elite sources who are either from news organizations or state agencies. Only two are posts from users on the Facebook forum called 'Sam Sumana for President 2017' (see Fig. 5.1).

As we can see in Fig. 5.1, a very large majority of posts are actually from elite sources (67 % compared with 33 % grassroot). This clearly shows elite sources continue to set the agenda of news and views posted on social media almost the same way they do in mainstream media. This contrasts very sharply with the optimistic views of Held, Frazer, Castells, Chaffee and Metzger (2001) etc. who have been celebrating the potential of the internet to empower and engage excluded voices. Moreover, contrary to the claim by Chaffee and Metzger (2001) of the 'reverse agenda-setting' coming to

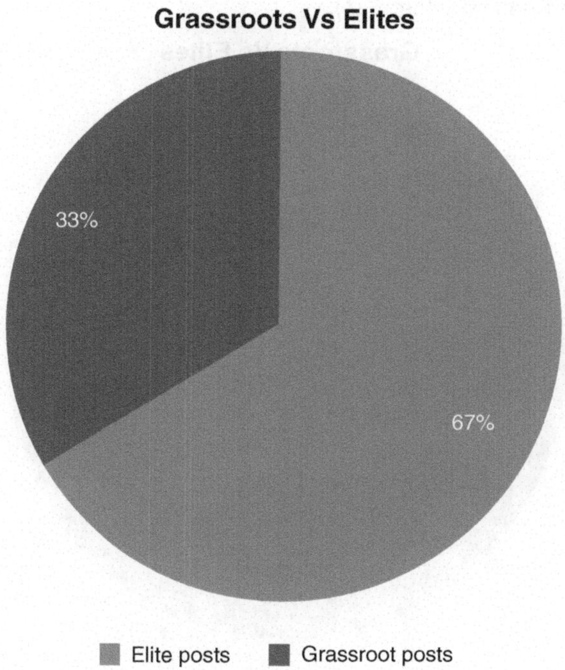

Fig. 5.1 Grassroots and elites on Facebook

pass with the public instead of the media calling the shots, the above results show that it is in fact business as usual in terms of the media setting the agenda for the public discussions on social media. Another even more interested finding is the fact that only two out of the total of eight posts identified as grass-root posts are actually directly contributed by users while the other six come from users but based on information indirectly contributed by elite sources, including mainstream media. This shows that some cyber-activists who participate in crowdsourcing pools may not after all be citizen journalists in the strict sense of the word of users generating their own content but rather online journalists who may just be helping to share content that is often generated by people affiliated to elite establishments (Shaw 2016; Platon and Deuze 2003).

Twitter: Out of 24 posts analysed, 15 are from elite sources, and only nine are from grassroot sources. And in fact out of nine individual grassroot users, three posted information from elite sources, either from news media or state agency. Six of them are independent posts generated directly from users (see Fig. 5.2).

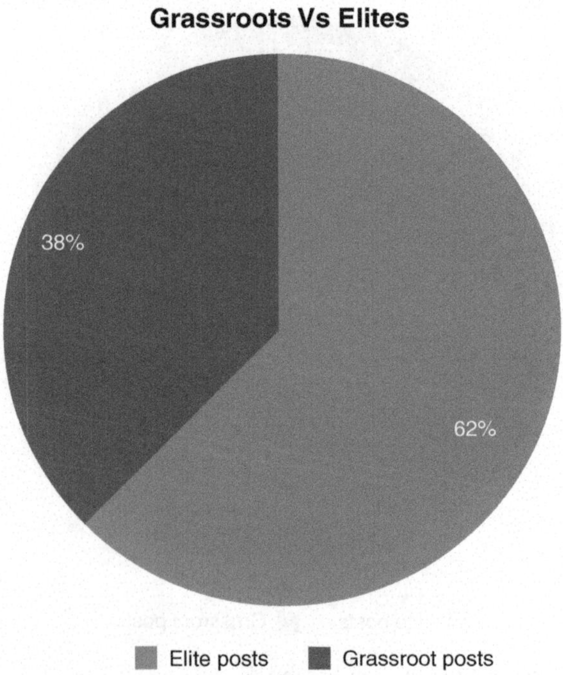

Fig. 5.2 Grassroots and elites on Twitter

As we can see in Fig. 5.2, the pattern is very similar Fig. 5.1 on Facebook in that the majority of posts come from elite sources (62 % compared to 38 % grassroot). This shows that powerful elites still enjoy the lion's share of power relations between them and the rest of the public on Twitter almost the same way as on Facebook. However, the results show that Twitter (38 %) did slightly better than Facebook (33 %) in the percentage of grassroot posts. Moreover, Twitter did far better in terms of having more posts (six) directly posted by grassroot users than Facebook (2). These results show that Twitter has slight advantage over Facebook in terms of narrowing the agenda-setting gap between powerful elites and grassroots.

User-Generated Content Vs Mainstream Media Content

We now examine RQ2: Were User-Generated Content (UGC) posts more than posts from mainstream media? This question will find out whether drawing on the analysis of posts from users and mainstream media, the media audience theory, which gives the edge to news producers over news consumers in the power relations, is still relevant in the new media environment.

Discussion of Results: Facebook and Twitter

Facebook: Posts from mainstream media often attract the most comments, shares and views, for example, the video posted by the 'Sierra Network Salone' generated nine comments, 104 shares and 4,300 view clicks (updated to 8 May 2016). However, at the other end of the spectrum, UGC posts seldom attract comments, shares, or views. For example further results show mainstream media posts (16) on Facebook on the sacking are far more numerous than those generated by users (8). Hence, even though Facebook is commonly thought to be a social media that is popular among citizen journalists on discussing 'the sacking of Sam Sumana' it is actually dominated by the traditional mainstream media.

As we can see in Fig. 5.3, there are far more MMC posts than UGC posts (67 % : 33 %), which shows the very wide disparity in terms of power relations, agency, and influence between ordinary users of Facebook and mainstream journalism users. It shows that it is business as usual in terms of media audience and direct effect they experience from the use

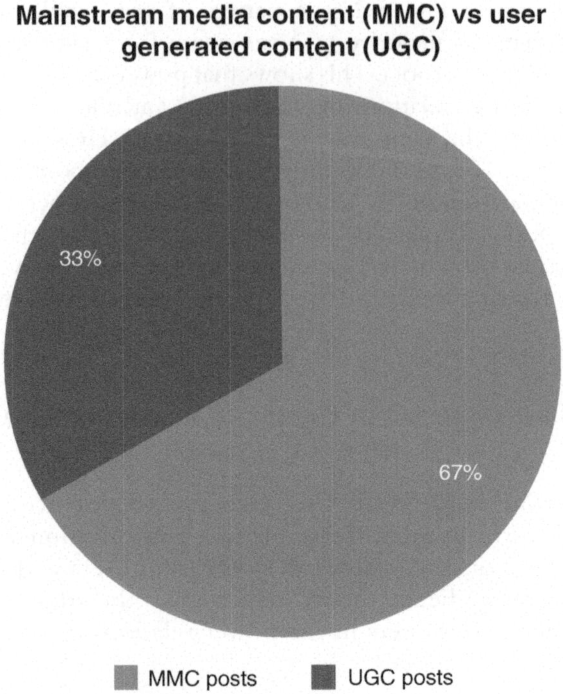

Fig. 5.3 MMC vs UGC on Facebook

of media content they access on SNS platforms such as Facebook, which sharply contrasts with the claim by Chaffee and Metzger (2001) that new media will tip the balance in favour of users of content produced by mainstream media.

Twitter: Of a total of 24 posts, MMC contributed slightly more than UGC (13 : 11). Some of the MMC posts were contributed by news websites operating only in the diaspora, such as *Sierra Loaded* while others were contributed by journalists and bloggers attached to mainstream media (print and broadcast) operating online and locally for example *Politico* and *Standard Times.*

As we can see in Fig. 5.4, the margin between MMC posts and UGC posts on the twitter discussion is very small compared to that between MMC posts and UGC posts on the Facebook discussion. These results

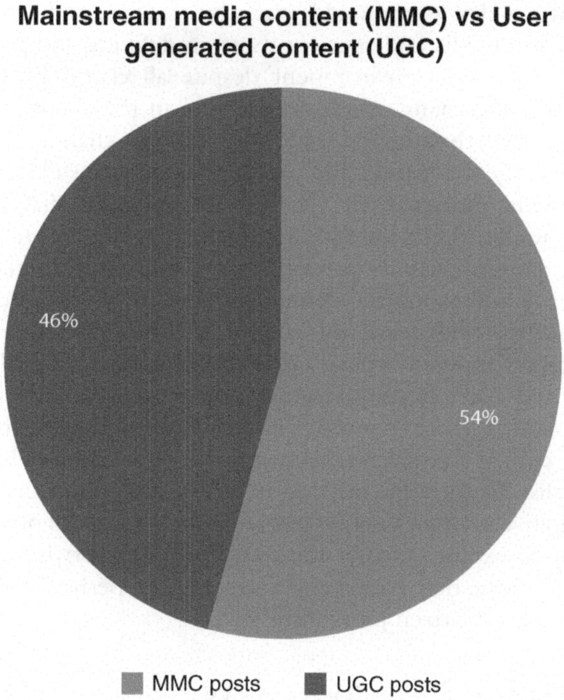

Fig. 5.4 MMC vs UGC on Twitter

show that, although it is business as usual in terms of the mainstream media enjoying the lion's share in terms of power relations and influence over the media audiences on both Facebook and Twitter, we see that, at least on Twitter, there is evidence of a significant shift of power from mainstream media to citizen journalism. This is important because it means that the change in media audience theory predicted by Chaffee and Metzger (2001) could hold sway at least when it comes to some SNSs such as Twitter.

Conclusion

To conclude, our quantitative content analysis of the Facebook and Twitter discussions or posts on the sacking of Sierra Leone's vice president Sam Sumana shows that very little, if anything, has changed in the power relations between elite sources and grassroot sources, and between mainstream media and media audiences or users, in defining and producing the news in the new media environment despite all claims by Chaffee and Metzger (2001) and many others cited earlier in the chapter. The results of our analysis show that despite some very minimal changes, legacy media theories such as agenda-setting and media audience are still highly relevant in the new media environment. These results suggest that CJ needs to inculcate the human-rights journalism principles of human rights standard, participation, empowerment, accountability, and non-discrimination to make it better in addressing the democratic deficits of mainstream journalism. Moreover, the evidence in this chapter that it is sometimes difficult to tell the difference between ordinary users posting their original content on social media and users posting content originating from established elite sources shows that there is need for more research to clarify the true definition of citizen journalism, or perhaps to determine who is really a citizen journalist. Despite the methodological limitation of this study using only a quantitative content-analysis research method, it will provide a useful starting point to explore further the relevance or otherwise of traditional media theories in the new media environment, and perhaps a much clearer conceptualization of citizen journalism.

References

Agre, P. (1994). Networking and democracy. *The Network Observer*, *1*(4). Online. Available at www.polaris.gseis.ucla.edu/pagre/tno/april-1994.html.

Allan, S. (2006). *Online news*. Maidenhead: Open University Press.

Beman, G., & Calderbank, D. (eds.). (2008). *The human rights-based approach to journalism: Training manuel Vietnam*. Bangkok: UNESCO.

Benkler, Y. (2006). *The wealth of networks: How social production transforms markets and freedom*. New Haven: Yale University Press.

Bennett, W. L. (1990). Toward a theory of press-state relations in the United States. *Journal of Communication*, *40*(2), 103–125.

Bird, E. S. (2009). The future of journalism in the digital environment. *Journalism*, *10*(3), 293–295.

Bruns, A. (2008). *Blogs, wikipedia, second life, and beyond: From production to produsage*. New York: Peter Lang Pub.

Castells, M. (2006). *The power of identity: The information age: Economy, society and culture*. Oxford: Blackwell Publishing.

Chaffee, S. H., & Metzger, M. J. (2001). The end of mass communication?. *Mass Communication and Society*, *4*(4), 365–379.

Coleman, R., & McCombs, M. (2007). The young and agenda-less? Exploring agerelated differences in agenda setting on the youngest generation, baby boomers and the civic generation. *Journalism & Mass Communication Quarterly, 84*(3), 495–508.

Curran, J. (2011). *Media and democracy*. London: Routledge.

Curran, J., Coen, S., Aalberg, T., Hayashi, K., Jones, P. K., Splendore, S. et al. (2013). Internet revolution revisited: A comparative study of online news. *Media, Culture and Society, 35*(7), 880–897.

Davis, A. (2009). Journalist-source relations, mediated reflexivity and the politics of politics. *Journalism Studies, 10*(2), 204–219.

De Bonville, J. (2000). *L'analyse de contenu des médias*. Paris: De Boeck & Larcier.

Fraser, J. (2007) Open Complimenting Closed? [Online] Available at: http://eduspaces.net/josiefraser/weblog/169960.html.

Geniets, A. (2013). The global news challenge: Market strategies of International Broadcasting Organizations in developing countries. London: Routledge.

Goode, L. (2009). Social news, citizen journalism and democracy. *New Media and Society, 11*(8), 1287–1305.

Hackett, R. (2005). Is there a democratic deficit in US and UK journalism. In S. Allan (Ed.), *Journalism: Critical issues* (pp. 85–97). New York: Open Society Press.

Hall, S., Critcher, C., Jefferson, T., Clarker, J., & Roberts, B. (1978). *Policing the crisis. Mugging, the state and law and order*. London: Macmillan.

Held, D. (2004). *Global covenant*. Cambridge: Polity.

Held, D. (2006). *Models of Democracy* (3rd edn.). Cambridge: Polity.

Jenkins, H. (2006). *Convergence culture: Where old and new media collide*. New York: New York University Press.

Jenkins, H., Purushotma, R., Clinton, K., Wiegel, M., & Robison, A. J. (2009). *Confronting the challenges of participatory culture: Media education for the 21st century*. Cambridge: MIT Press.

Kim, Y., & Lowery, W. (2015). Social media environment? Personal and social determinants of citizen journalism activities. *Digital Journalism, 3*(2), 298–314.

Kolodzy, J. (2012). *Practicing convergence journalism: An introduction to cross-media storytelling*. London: Routledge.

LaRose, R., & Eastin, M.S. (2004). A social cognitive theory of Internet uses and gratifications: Toward a new model of media attendance. *Journal of Broadcasting & Electronic Media, 48*(3), 358–377.

Manning, P. (2001). *News and news source*. London: Sage.

Mermin, J. (1999). *Debating war and peace*. Princeton: Princeton University Press.

Platon, S., & Deuze, M. (2003). Indymedia journalism: A radical way of making, selecting and sharing news?. *Journalism, 4*(3), 336–355.

Poster, M. (2001). *What's the matter with the internet?*. Minneapolis: University of Minnesota Press.

Shaw, I. S. (2012). *Human Rights Journalism. Advances in Reporting Humanitarian Interventions.* Basingstoke: Palgrave.
Shaw, I. S. (2016). *Business journalism: a critical political economy approach.* London: Routledge.
Shoemaker, P. J., & Vos, T. P. (2009). *Gatekeeping theory.* New York: Routledge
Tan, Y., & Weaver, D. H. (2013). Agenda diversity and agenda setting from 1956 to 2004: What are the trends over time? *Journalism Studies, 14*(6), 773–789.
Tomaszeski, M. S. (2006). A baseline examination of political bloggers: Who they are, their views on the blogosphere and their influence in agenda-setting via the two-step flow hypothesis. http://195.130.87.21:8080/dspace/bitstream/123456789/402/1/examinationofpoliticalbloggers.pdf.
Weimann, G., Weiss-Blatt, N., Mengistu, G., Tregerman, M. M., & Oren, D. (2014). Reevaluating the end of mass communication? *Journal of Mass Communication and Soceity, 17*(6), 803–829.

Dr Ibrahim Seaga Shaw is a senior lecturer in Media and Politics at Northumbria University. He holds a PhD from the Sorbonne and is Secretary General of the International Peace Research Association (IPRA). He is author of four books, including two monographs: *Human Rights Journalism* (Palgrave Macmillan, 2012) and *Business Journalism: A Critical Political Economy Approach* (Routledge, 2016). He is also author of many book chapters and journal articles with leading publishers such as SAGE, Palgrave and Routledge. He has a background in journalism spanning 20 years, having worked in Sierra Leone, Britain and France.

Di Luo is an international PhD student from China currently studying at Northumbria University. Her research interest focuses on the news reporting and human rights reporting in China. She is currently in her third year of the PhD programme, and looking forward to finishing up by the end of 2016. She holds a Master degree from Northumbria University, UK and an undergraduate degree from South Australia University, Australia. In her three years' PhD studying time, she had submitted and presented papers to a couple of conferences, including the ones hosed by the International Association for Media and Communication Research. She is also working on two more journal articles to be published in the next year time. Apart from her academic work, she is also the administrative assistance for the 2016 International Peace Research Association Conference, the president for the Chinese Students and Scholars Association (CSSA) at Northumbria University, and member of the Northern Britain Chinese Entrepreneurs Association.

PART II

Digital Transformations: Civic Activism in the Africa Blogsphere

CHAPTER 6

Engaged Online: Social Media and Youth Civic Engagement in Kenya

Samuel C. Kamau

Introduction

The internet's potential for increasing civic and political participation has been met with both expectation and explicit scepticism Tedesco (2004).

'Techno-optimists', (Woody and Weare 2004), believe that the internet will stimulate and increase participation by creating new opportunities for involvement. Coleman (2001) argues that the internet is having a transformative effect on participation by giving access to previously inaccessible information, developing spaces for unmediated public deliberation and changing the way representatives perform (Coleman 2001, p. 118). The internet's capacity to bypass the grip of traditional mainstream media facilitates a horizontal flow of information, which enhances citizens' ability to directly engage with each other and with their leaders (Barber et al. 1997). The boundless nature of the internet empowers the ordinary citizen through unlimited access to information and the space to voice opinions, positions to a wider audience (Tedesco et al. 1999).

On the other hand the sceptics or 'techno-pessimists' believe the internet offers no real chance of altering traditional politics, arguing that it will only

S.C. Kamau (✉)
Aga Khan University, Nairobi, Kenya
e-mail: kamau.samuel@aku.edu

B. Mutsvairo (ed.), *Digital Activism in the Social Media Era*,
DOI 10.1007/978-3-319-40949-8_6

serve to reinforce the established political communication patterns, transferring the traditional offline communication habits to the online platform (Bucy and Gregson 2001, p. 357).

The internet has become so central to young people's interactions that is now impossible to conceptualize their life without taking account of the internet (Zhao 2006). It has become a major source of news and information, which has seen increased presence of youth online (Madden 2006).

Currently, 3.3 billon people have access to the internet across the world, and Africa has 331 million internet users, representing 26 % of the population.[1] Internet access has also grown steadily in Kenya, with the latest data by the Communication Authority of Kenya (CAK) indicating that internet penetration stands at 31.9 million or 69.9 % of the Kenyan population (CAK 2016)

Social Media

Social Networking Sites (SNS), the love-children of the internet, have experienced explosive growth in the couple of years and have been widely adopted across the globe, especially among youth (Boyd and Ellison 2007). Steinfield et al. (2012) define SNS as 'web sites that enable users to articulate a network of connections of people with whom they wish to share access to profile information, news, status updates, comments or other forms of content' (p. 2). Currently, SNS have 2.22 billion users, up from 1.22 billion users in 2011, with Facebook alone having over 1.5 billion users and Whatsapp 900 million.[2] Social media use is growing rapidly in Africa with about 124 million Facebook users (ITU, 2015, ICT facts and Figures) and Kenya about 5 million active Facebook users and 700,000 twitter users. SNS have become important tools for managing relationships among large and diverse groups of people and help in sharing information and other resources (Boyd and Ellison 2007; Ellison 2007).

Boyd and Ellison (2007) summarised the use of SNS in four broad areas: impression management and friendship performance; networks and network structures; bridging online and offline networks; and the management of privacy. They allow their users to connect with 'friends' with whom they can communicate, share content and view each other's profile. Members can also join virtual groups based on common interests (Ellison 2007).

Beyond social connections, SNS are now being seen as powerful tools for social change as people and organizations use them to raise awareness and mobilize around social issues. In Kenya SNS have been used to coordinate industrial action (the #Peremende movement), raise funds for building a spinal injury hospital (#BringZackHome), fight against corruption (#KickCorruptionOutKenya), raise funds for cancer patients (#MilliForJadudi), raise awareness on miscarriages and infant death (#StillAMum) demand for the release of arrested journalists (#FreeNgirachu and #FreeMutai), raise money for humanitarian interventions (#WeAreOne and #KenyansForKenya) demand for political and social accountability (#ArrestWaiguru) among others.

Problem

Declining enthusiasm and growing apathy among the young in political participation has been a concern among scholars who have noted the high levels of cynicism in the youth (Bennet 1997). The last 30 years have witnessed significant decline in civic engagement among young people (Capella and Jamieson 1997; Carpini 2000; Flanagan and Levine 2010; Syvertsen 2011).

Traditionally, young people have been considered as disengaged from politics and less likely to participate in political activities (Wattenberg 2008; Bauerlein 2008). Carpini (2000) found that youth are significantly less likely to participate in community organizations designed to address public problems through collective action, which points to a decline in the 'civic infrastructure' during formative years of political socialization when these young people are developing 'civic habits'.

With the emergence of SNS, there is renewed hope and expectation that they will increase participation and enhance democracy. It is argued that SNS remove the barriers that hinder collective action and empower citizens to influence and monitor policy makers by offering a low-cost forum to participate (Outlook 2006).

Social media have been praised for their ability to reach many people. SNS facilitate the sharing of personalized content in public spaces which helps to connect people. However, real doubts abound whether SNS actually bring new people into the realm of civic and political participation. The debate focuses on the transition from online reach to offline action (Sheedy 2011). Learning of something online does not necessarily lead to action because uncommitted people can join SNS and follow an event from home without being motivated to go out and join the action (Papic and Noonan 2011).

Additionally, it has been noted that the imbalances experienced in traditional communication channels are also replicated online due to unequal access. Social media platforms can exacerbate the existing differences in participation (Prior 2005). Citizens who are politically active in the traditional sense are also the same who are likely to use the internet for political participation.

In most cases, SNS users do not go online to look for political information, rather, the information finds them online (Kohut 2008).

Objectives

The study sought to explore the relationship between reliance on Social Networking Sites and civic engagement:

1. To establish the nature of offline and online civic engagement among youth.
2. To investigate the relationship between reliance on social media and civic engagement.
3. To examine ways in which SNS support campaigns for social change.

LITERATURE

Kenyan Political Culture, Systems and Youth Participation

Kenyan youth have faced numerous challenges which has seen them remain on the periphery of social and political life of society (Wanjala 2002; Kagwanja 2005). The Kenyan environment often precludes youth from participating in policy discussions (Youth Agenda 2008). The political system has throughout history conspired to limit youth participation in politics (KEDOF 2008): young people tend to be frequently excluded from the national public debates on account of inexperience (UNDP Kenya Report 2009), and youth participation for a long time was limited to executing political violence in rallies, with no meaningful roles (KNHCR 2008; KEDOF 2008). Limited youth participation is a threat to democracy and leads to the under-representation of young people in the socially and politically active structures of society (Oriare 2009). Technological advances have created new opportunities and spaces for political mobilization especially among the young (Zhang et al. 2010). Against this backdrop, this study explored ways in which political mobilization of youth can be enhanced, specifically focusing on the role of social media.

The Internet in Political Communication

Communication online is very different from the one-way communication of traditional media (Sheedy 2011). The internet has been labelled a 'master medium' because of the ability to create a hybrid of the traditional vertical one-way medium and a two-way communication horizontal feedback (Selnow 1998). Similarly, the internet is free from the stringent controls and gatekeeping aspects that define traditional print and broadcast media (Margolis et al. 1997).

As the internet continues to grow and dominate communication about politics (Selnow 1998), its value and potential in the political process is being more widely recognized. Barber et al. (1997) identifies several possibilities for online and electronically enhanced democracy. These include: (1) inherent interactivity; (2) potential for lateral and horizontal communication; (3) point-to-point and non-hierarchical modes of communication; (4) low cost to users; (5) rapidity as a communication medium; (6) lack of national or other boundaries; and (7) freedom from the intrusion and monitoring of government.

Social Networks, Social Capital and Engagement

Networks are regarded as effective mechanisms for creating feelings of solidarity (Granovetter 1982) among people. Putnam (1995) argues that social connections generate the social trust which in turn strengthens community relations and enables local participation. Through these connections, people are drawn around common interests which stirs public engagement (Jones 2006). These networks drive discussions among people especially those with shared interests (McLeod et al. 1999, in Halpern 2013). Conversely, the absence of ties and social networks serves to discourage civic participation (Huckfeldt and Sprague 1995).

Bourdieu and Wacquant (1992) define social capital as 'the sum of the resources, actual or virtual, that accrue to an individual or group by virtue of possessing a durable network of more or less institutionalized relationships of mutual acquaintance and recognition' (p. 14). The social relations in a community generate the necessary energy for social action within that community. Growth in social capital enhances commitment to a community and improves the ability of that community to mobilize collective actions (Ellison et al. 2009), which results in positive social outcomes (Adler and Kwon 2002). Access to useful information, personal relationships and the capacity to organize groups are some of the benefits an individual can draw in a community (Paxton 1999; Helliwell and Putnam 2004). Lin (2001) believes that individuals engage and interactions strategically with a focus on desired outcomes.

Civic and political participation are related in many ways and hard to unlink. Zhang et al. (2010) look at civic and political participation as consequences of social capital. Wilkins (2000) found that 'civic participation is a positive predictor of political participation'. Putnam (1995) argues that people are more likely to participate in civic and political activities when social capital is high and this happens when people are tightly bound in an association and their level of trust is high among each other (Brehm and Rahn 1997).

Social Networking Sites and Social Capital

Social media have transformed the way relationships are formed and maintained (Rosenfeld and Thomas 2012). They are associated with opportunities for information flow, social influence and democratic revolution (Lewis et al. 2014). The internet has been associated with both the growth and the decline of social capital (Ellison et al. 2007). Some argue that the internet use replaces face-to-face contact between people, especially the heavy users (Nie 2001), while others claim that online interactions eventually lead to face-to-face contact between the people (Parks and Floyd 1996). Still others argue that the internet in combination with other communications methods supports offline interactions and social capital development (Quan et al. 2004).

Questions abound on whether SNS enhance a sense of community among the users. Trends indicate that people mostly use SNS sites to maintain contact and interaction with friends and acquaintances and also gather information about friends and people they meet in real life (Boyd and Ellison 2007). SNS users mostly attempt to communicate with people with whom they have an online communication more than complete strangers (Lampe et al. 2006; Lenhart and Madden 2007). However, beyond supporting the maintenance of existing social ties they also aid in the formation of new connections (Ellison et al. 2009). In some instances, online and offline social networks overlap like when online connections result in face-to-face meetings (Parks and Floyd 1996).

Both online and offline interactions are part of an integrated communication activities among people. SNS sites do not necessarily remove people from their offline world but they can be used to support relationships and keep people in contact, even when physically removed from each other. Different groupings like neighbourhood communities, extended families, organization employees and classmates, among others, use SNS to maintain relationships (Ellison et al. 2009). In a more recent study, Ellison et al. (2012) reviewed previous research and concluded that:

> SNS can contribute to the formation and maintenance of both forms (bridging and bonding) of social capital: Those involving connections to a larger heterogeneous network of weak ties can be conduits for information diffusion, and those involving connections to stronger ties that can provide emotional, and important material support. (p. 8)

SNS Connections, Discussions and Engagement

Much of what happens on SNS sites is interpersonal communication as friends continue with their interactions online (Boyd 2006; Ellison 2007; Lampe et al. 2007). Communication plays a central in driving engagement (McLeod et al. 1999) and maintaining an active citizenry. Through communication, citizens learn about issues and ways to participate (McLeod et al. 1999; Eveland et al. 2005). Interpersonal communication about politics increases political knowledge, helps in crystallizing political opinion and spurs the desire to participate (Huckfeldt and Sprague 1995; Scheufele et al. 2004; Kwak et al. 2005).

Social media conversations are mostly informal exchanges of short messages among friends (Boyd 2006; Thelwall 2009). People use these sites to manage a relatively loose network of friends (Steinfield et al. 2008), they are able to communicate with each other in a variety of ways and the messages can be private or public (Palen & Liu 2007). On social media platforms, 'friend' could actually mean close friend, more distant friend, acquaintance or nothing (Boyd 2006; Thelwall 2009).

SNS have been credited with accelerating political discussions (Warner et al. 2012). They have created a platform for engagement especially for the younger citizens, who are not known to follow political talk on other media (Albarran et al. 2007). Daniel Halpern (2013) notes that social media triggers civic engagement through news consumption and political discussions. MacLeod et al. (1999) in their study found that when people engage in frequent issue-specific political discussions they are likely to have a better understanding of politics and they are also likely to be more politically sophisticated.

While social media create an ideal platform for political discourse and sometimes encourages the expression of diverse views (Williams & Gulati 2008; Clarke 2010; Zhang et al. 2010), these discussions on SNS have been undermined by a variety of factors. Uncivil behaviour, characterized by 'vigorous attack and humiliation' has been observed in some online forums (Davis 1999; Kushin 2009). This can discourage polite and respectful people from participating in the discussion, leaving it to the abrasive and belligerent. Davis (1999) used the term 'flaming' to describe posts made in online discussions that personally attack a participant or his ideas. Online political discussion has been criticized for discouraging disagreeing persons from engaging in discussions (Kushin & Kitchener, 2009). Additionally, online conversations on SNS are mostly male-dominated and at times discourage women from actively participating. Susan Herring in her research found that 'online communication remains gendered and dominated by the aggressive and adversarial nature of the male style' (Herring 1999).

The structure of the internet has also been found to create conditions conducive to selective exposure to media content (Bimber and Davis 2003). People tend to expose themselves to information that aligns with their pre-existing views. Scholars have noted that virtual communities are fairly homogeneous in terms of values and viewpoints (Dahlberg 2001), and that the participants in online discussions often hold comparable political perspectives (Wilhelm 1998). On the flip-side, other studies have recognized the internet's ability to expose people to diverse viewpoints compared with face-to-face connections like family, friends and co-workers (Horrigan et al. 2004). Exposure to conflicting views is essential for democracy (Mutz 2002), heterogeneous networks increase the chances of such exposure. The internet broadens 'exposure to diverse views, especially for individuals who do not have partisan leanings' (Kahne et al. 2011, p. 496).

Social Media and Online Participation

Youth have manifested lower levels of civic engagement compared to adults (Bennett et al. 2009), however, they tend to manifest a higher level of engagement in online spaces (Thakery and Hunter 2010). SNS have often been used to mobilize people during crisis and disasters (Palen and Liu 2007). Due to the emotional connection, Social media can be used to easily rally people around a cause. Additionally, people online tend to form groups around shared causes and interests (Mainwaring 2011). Active online users tend to participate in group activities, which makes it easier to target them.

From Disengaged Citizens to Effective Political Actors: Online Vs Offline Participation

The disruption caused by social media has significantly altered traditional patterns and practices of civic participation (Brandtzaeg et al. 2015). Traditional patterns of civic engagement are hierarchical and too formal, limiting the effectiveness of efforts to reach young people (Montgomery 2008); they are attracted to informal, spontaneous and non-institutional forms of expression.

Research has shown a positive relationship between offline and online civic engagement (Smith et al. 2009). Ordinary citizens and civil society organizations have used social media to raise awareness and generate support for particular causes, engage decision-makers and hold governments to account (Clarke 2010). Some studies have established that SNS played a key role in mobilizing and encouraging to participate in the Arab Spring (Storck 2011; Tufekci & Wilson 2012). Governments have also embraced social media as a public engagement tool to solicit citizen's input in policy making and encourage public debate (Norton and Citron 2010).

Brandtzaeg et al. (2012) however, argue that though SNS engage people in sporadic episodes of civic participation, they are not specifically designed for that. Debatin et al. (2009) capture it more vividly 'the critical design choices underlying those sites do not communicate clear conceptions of citizenship, nor are they concerned with developing the civic skills of users' (p. 408). In general however, young people have been found to be more active in taking up social media for political and civic activities (Warren et al. 2014). This implies that the potential to engage youth using these new channels remains, but may not have been fully exploited.

Internet Access and the Digital Divide

Central to the debate on the potential and role of the internet in stimulating political participation is the question of access and the digital divide. There is an obvious disproportionate representation of those with greater access or technical ability, especially in the developing world. Only about 9.8 % of the 940 million people living in the Least Developed Countries (LDC) have access to the internet, and 4 billion people from the developing world remain offline

Generally, the internet population is never representative of the national population. Pew internet research revealed that the US internet population is younger, more educated and wealthier and more male than female than the general population (Pew Research 2008, 2010). Sparks (2001) observes that level of education, age, gender and income levels are important indicators of the divide between the information 'haves' and the information 'have nots'. Differences in infrastructural development have ensured gaps remain between the politically active and politically inactive, between the economically privileged and underprivileged and between Urban populations rural populations (Garramone et al. 1986; Hacker 1996). However with increased internet access, government support and lowering of costs, this gap is narrowing across the world (Hindman 2000).

Summary

From the review of the relevant literature, a combination of certain conditions and features are necessary to facilitate youth engagement.

- Equal access to the internet and the online forums and spaces is key to effective participation. Some people are at a disadvantage based on certain factors like socio-economic status or gender.
- The necessary resources and skills to facilitate access and participation—economic, connectivity to the internet, time to participate and the technical skills to access and operate the in the online social media forums.
- Openness of communication and discussions, healthy debates even where there are contrasting views—this includes choices between different options.
- Informed and intellectually competent citizenry. This includes access to relevant information and is made possible through education and the media.
- Focus on relevant issues—discussions are centred on issues relevant to the political process and civic life.
- Functional horizontal connections between the participants. This facilitates the creation of social capital.

- Vibrant civil society that constantly engages the people and the government on civic issues and at the same time provides a platform for discussions.
- Open government that is open to receive and release information—access to those in power and a channel of complaints or opinions.

The Study

To respond to the research question, a survey of 600 university students was conducted. The study used self-reported questionnaires to test the relationship between reliance on social networking sites and civic engagement.

The sample yielded 512 responses, which represents an 85.3 % response rate, with 53 % female respondents and 47 % male respondents.

The researcher also conducted in-depth interviews with key informants and held focus group discussions.

The Questionnaire

The questionnaire first asked demographic questions, then questions about internet and social media use and access, and finally, about online and offline civic engagement activities.

Internet and social media usage: This sought to establish the extent of social media usage and the scope of young people's activities online.

Reliance on social networking sites: the extent of individual users' attachment and dependence on SNS. This was measured by several items within the questionnaire (Cronbach's alpha = 0.85).

Civic Participation: The nature and frequency of involvement in civic activities was measured using an index of seven items on a six-point scale (Cronbach's alpha = 0.90.)

Data Analysis Procedures

Data analysis was conducted at several levels. The first level was a basic descriptive analysis. Next, the frequencies were run on the political variables and reliance on social networking sites. A hierarchical regression analysis in which measurement was done at different levels of aggregation.

Results

Social Media Usage and Reliance

The results provide an overview of the respondents' patterns of social media usage, forms and levels of civic participation and then examine the relationship between reliance on social media and civic engagement. The study established a high usage and reliance on SNS. Almost everyone surveyed (98 %) indicated they use social media. Facebook was by far the most popular social media platform with 82 % of the participants indicated they visit the site several times a day. Fifty three per cent of the respondents consider themselves highly reliant on SNS with only 8 % reporting they were not reliant at all.

Civic Participation among Kenyan Urban Youth

Civic participation was defined as activities that address community concerns through non-governmental or non-electoral means. In general, the study found limited or low participation in civic activities among the surveyed young people, pointing to a level of disconnect or apathy towards what is happening in society.

Male respondents were more active than their female counterparts in all the civic activities measured in this study. This can be partly explained by historical and cultural factors that hinder active participation by women in civic affairs (Kariuki 2010). In general, women are less active in political spaces as the patriarchal nature of the African society places leadership and problem solving largely in men's hands with women are mere spectators (Kasomo 2012).

Table 6.1 summarizes the scope of civic participation among youth. The majority of young people do not volunteer in organizations that seek to address community concerns. Only one-third of the sampled male youth and one-fifth of the female youth indicated they had volunteered in organizations dealing with community problems. More than half registered either zero or low participation in volunteering.

Lobbying local and national government leaders is not common among urban youth. Only about 19 % of males and 6 % of females reported ever having spoken or written to local leaders on local problems and needs. There was limited collective action to address local problems or needs. Demonstrations and organized protests to address local or national concerns are not very popular among urban youth. The

Table 6.1 Scope of civic participation among youth

Civic activity	*Male (%)*	*Female (%)*
Volunteering in organizations that deal with local needs and problems	34	21
Lobbying government leaders and workers about local needs	19	6
Working with others to solve community problems	34	17
Engaging in protests and demonstrations on local issues	16	5
Taking part in forming an action group	37	19
Mobilizing others for a cause	40	27

Source: Self

majority of the respondents (63 %) have never participated in such demonstrations. Table 6.2 summarizes the scope of young people's online civic activities. The most common participatory activities include: fundraising, building community or solidarity movements, advocacy, sharing information, mobilizing or calling for action, lobbying and online petitions.

The results indicate varying levels of online participatory activities among youth on social media. Social media is very effective in raising awareness and exposing people to information about social causes. Eighty-two per cent of the respondents indicated they had come across campaigns or information supporting social change on SNS. About half (49 %) reported having posted information in support of a social cause while 40 % had joined a group online supporting a social cause. Lobbying local and national leaders (7 %), signing online petitions (9 %), donating money (14 %) were far less common. Curiously, only 6 % of the respondents indicated they had actually responded with actual offline activity to an online call for action.

Hierarchical regression model for civic participation

Hierarchical regression analysis was performed to test the relationship between the dependent variable 'civic participation' and the predictor variable 'reliance on SNS sites' after controlling for the effect of the demographic variables 'age' and 'gender' and the political variables ' political interest' and 'political knowledge' (Table 6.3).

The analysis could not establish a significant relationship between 'reliance on SNS sites' and civic participation ($\beta = -0.42$, $P \geq 0.05$). This implies reliance on SNSs does not have any significant impact on offline

Table 6.2 Online civic participation

In the last three months, have you……..	*YES %*	*NO %*	*NOT SURE/no response (%)*
Given money in support of a cause shared online	14	84	2
Tweeted/retweeted/favourite a post with a hashtag calling for action	41	57	2
Posted information (status update/video/meme/ photo to support a cause	49	48	3
Joined a group on Facebook around a cause	40	57	3
Created a group around a social cause	2	98	0
Engaged in discussions about a social concern on Social Media?	36	61	3
Invited/added a friend to join an online group supporting a social cause on Social Media?	26	72	2
Discovered/came across a social good campaign on Social media?	82	14	4
Signed(clicked) and online petition calling for action or social change	9	86	5
Mobilized other people to action using social media	8	89	3
Shared/commented another person's post supporting a cause or calling for action	41	54	5
Contacted/Engaged/Lobbied a local or national leaders about an issue on social media	7	91	2
Shared a blog/link to a story calling for action or raising awareness	36	61	3
Responded to an call for action by attending a meeting/joining a protest	6	93	1

Source: Self

civic participation. However, the more people discuss politics with others, the more they are likely to participate in civic activities ($\beta = 0.24$, $P < 0.001$). This implies interpersonal discussion of politics and social issues has a positive impact on civic participation. Correlation analysis also reveals that reliance on SNSs is not significantly related to civic participation as defined in this study. The analysis reveals a very weak positive correlation between reliance on SNS and civic participation (0.074) which is not statistically significant ($P \geq 0.01$) (Table 6.4).

Reliance on SNS and Civic Participation

This finding contradicts some previous studies that found reliance on SNSs has a significant influence on civic participation (Zhang et al. 2010).

Table 6.3 Table of regression coefficients (Civic participation)

Coefficients[a]						
Model		*Unstandardized coefficients*		*Standardized coefficients*	*T*	*Sig.*
		B	*Std. Error*	*Beta*		
4	(Constant)	3.740	0.549		6.813	0.000
	Gender	0.717	0.132	0.251	5.428	0.000
	Age	0.001	0.115	0.000	0.005	0.996
	Political efficacy	-0.117	0.062	-0.088	-1.896	0.059
	Political knowledge	-0.310	0.202	-0.073	-1.534	0.126
	Interest in politics	0.001	0.055	0.001	0.026	0.979
	Interpersonal discussion	0.259	0.057	0.236	4.546	0.000
	SNS Reliance	-0.042	0.026	-0.074	-1.629	0.104

[a]Dependent variable: Civic participation
Source: Self

Table 6.4 Correlation between reliance on SNS and Civic participation

		SNS Reliance	*Civic participation*
SNS reliance	Pearson correlation	1	0.074
	Sig. (2-tailed)		0.116
	N	457	448
Civic participation	Pearson correlation	0.074	1
	Sig. (2-tailed)	0.116	
	N	448	456

Source: Self

Discussion

Civic Participation

The alarmingly low level of civic participation among the surveyed youth, with the majority appearing uninterested when it comes to collective action to address local problems or needs can be explained by several factors. First, the absence of structured forums for engagement in Kenya. Many young people do not have avenues to express their views and grievances to the government. Secondly, citizens generally expect the government to do everything and solve all community problems, they do not see a role for themselves. This thinking is underscored by a common Kenyan phrase '*tunaomba serikali*' (We are asking the government) whenever confronted with challenges and problems, even those that people can adequately handle on their own. Third, the tendency to leave all civic action to political, religious and civil society leaders. In Kenya, most citizens leave demonstrations and protest activities to civil society activists, preferring to watch from afar. Protest activities tend to occur when people want policy-makers to address pressing social, economic or political concerns in a more timely fashion than other modes of participation might allow (Resnick and Casale 2014). A recent demonstration, the '*Unga Revolution*', demanding lower prices for essential commodities, left the majority of citizens uninterested despite the fact that the protests had a direct bearing on their living standards. Fourth, most educated youth are disconnected from the general societal concerns as long as those issues do not directly affect them. Some studies have found a higher likelihood of participation among more educated people (Pettersen and Rose 1996) but this is not replicated in this study. Lastly, the culture of tokenism and hand-outs is well entrenched in Kenyan society. Kenyan youth generally expect some of monetary reward for any service rendered in the society (Kagwanja 2006). The culture of volunteering or working for the common good is not common. Additionally, the findings show low participation among female students compared to males in all civic activities. This is explained by historical and cultural factors that hinder active participation by women in civic affairs (Chesoni, Muigai & Kanyinga 2006; Kariuki 2010; Kasomo 2012).

Social Networking Sites and Civic Participation—Offline vs Online Engagement

Kenyans on social media, especially Twitter, are very active in using social media to mobilize for action on a variety of issues. The disconnect between online activities and offline action is puzzling—it contradicts previous studies that have associated reliance on SNSs with civic engagement (Baumgartner and Morris 2010; Zhang et al. 2009; Smith 2013).

While SNS provide opportunities for youth to be involved in civic activities online, this is not replicated offline. Hashtags are popularly used to: create awareness around issues, to mobilize for funds, pressure government, expose or fight corruption, coordinate protests among others. But despite being fairly active in online spaces, the same youth are inactive offline. The transition from online reach to offline action remains elusive.

Lenhart et al. (2010) argued that it is best to reach youth using SNS, where they spend most of their time online. Kim et al. (2007) found young people to be relatively active in online spaces as opposed to offline. This is partly because traditional patterns of civic engagement are hierarchical and formal, limiting the effectiveness of efforts to engage youth (Montgomery 2008). Online participation appeals to youth because it is spontaneous, informal and less structured. Low participation levels are not a reflection of social media but rather of a general unwillingness to participate in social causes.

SNS can also be associated with a false sense of involvement, equating tweeting, posting or sharing with engagement. The abundance of information flowing on SNS could lead to over-stimulation and knowledge without any action. Learning of something online does not necessarily lead to action because uncommitted people can join SNS and follow an event from home without being motivated to go out and join the action (Papic and Noonan 2011).This explains why in the study very few people had actually donated money (14 %) or responded offline to an online call for action (6 %) despite being exposed online to information about social campaigns.

Conclusion

At the core of the whole debate surrounding the political uses of SNS is the question of what effect, if any, these new technologies have on civic and political participation. The evidence in this regard is mixed. Optimistic supporters argue that social media technologies 'promote accountability, transparency and public engagement with political institutions and figures' (Clarke 2010). Sceptics on the other hand argue that social media only reinforces established patterns of engagement.

Social media came with a promise to reinvigorate democracy and citizen participation in politics especially among young people. While this promise and potential is yet to be fully realized, there is growing evidence, as seen from this study that indeed SNSs are engaging young people in civic and political activities, and their role and influence will continue to increase as more people join social media with increased access to the internet.

Even though this study found the level of influence and impact on civic and political participation is limited, there is compelling evidence from other studies that and social media are increasingly playing a prominent part in engaging youth (Smith 2013), raising hopes that online spaces can be used to mobilize them in the future. The process of social transformation involves information acquisition, knowledge development, transfer and sharing, ideation and thought leadership, empathy and emotional connection and the spread of credible ideas that inspire cognitive dissonance which in turn spurs action (Leggio 2008), and social media appears equipped to drive this process (Boyd 2010)

The hope of youth participation must be tempered by the fact that virtual space is not actual space and online engagement amounts to nothing if not supported by offline activities (Kann et al. 2007). The most effective movements use online platforms to support offline efforts. As internet access and penetration levels grow and more people join SNS, their potential to engage youth will grow, and the full benefits may progressively become manifest in the civic and political sphere.

Limitations and Suggestions for Further Studies

1. The sample for this study involved undergraduate students from two universities in Nairobi. This is a unique population and the participation habits of students are definitely not generalizable to the broader Kenyan population, even the youthful population. Students were sampled because of their high use of social media and ease of accessing the sample. Future studies should consider non-student populations that also use social media.
2. The data in this study is cross-sectional. As such, it is hard to prove causality or establish the direction of causality. Better strategies to establish causality and direction will prove useful in future studies.
3. This study looked at SNS collectively and may have ignored recent social media platforms like Whatsapp, Telegram, Snapchat among others that are gaining popularity. Future studies can isolate the role each of these platforms plays in engagement.
4. Future studies can seek better measures of civic engagement that are more relevant to the Kenyan and African context. The popular measures used in most studies are more Western and may not be relevant to the African context.

Notes

1. www.internetlivestats.com
2. www.statista.com.

References

Adler, P. S., & Kwon, S.-W. (2002). Social capital: Prospects for a new concept. *Academy of management review, 27*(1), 17–40.

Albarran, A.B., Anderson, T., Bejar, L.G., Bussart, A.L., Daggett, E., Gibson, S., ... Horst, J.L. (2007). "What happened to our audience?" Radio and new technology uses and gratifications among young adult users. *Journal of Radio Studies, 14*(2), 92–101.

Barber, B.R., Mattson, K., & Peterson, J. (1997). *The state of "electronically enhanced democracy": A survey of the internet*. New Brunswick, NJ: Wath Whitman center for the culture and politics of democracy, Department of Politics Science, Rutgers University.

Bauerlein, M. (2008). *The dumbest generation: How the digital age stupefies young Americans and jeopardizes our future (or, don't trust anyone under 30)*. New York: Penguin.

Baumgartner, J. C., & Morris, J. S. (2010). MyFaceTube politics: Social networking web sites and political engagement of young adults. *Social Science Computer Review, 28*(1), 24–44.

Behnke, P. (2010). *Social media and politics: Online social networking and political communication in Asia*. Singapore: Konrad-Adenauer-Stiftung.

Bennett, S.E. (1997). Why young Americans hate politics, and what we should do about it. *PS: Political Science & Politics, 30*(01), 47–53.

Bennett, W.L., Wells, C., & Rank, A. (2009). Young citizens and civic learning: Two paradigms of citizenship in the digital age. *Citizenship Studies, 13*(2), 105–120.

Bimber, B., & Davis, R. (2003). *Campaigning online: The Internet in US elections*. New York: Oxford University Press.

Boyd, D. (2006). Friends, friendsters, and myspace top 8: Writing community into being on social network sites. *First Monday, 11*, 12.

Boyd, D. (2010). Streams of content, limited attention: The flow of information through social media. *EDUCAUSE Review, 45*(5), 26–36.

Boyd, D., & Ellison, N. (2007). Social network sites: Definition, history, and scholarship. *Journal of Computer Mediated Communication, 13*, 210–230.

Bourdieu, P., & Wacquant, L. J. (1992). An invitation to reflexive sociology: University of Chicago press.

Brandtzæg, P.B., Følstad, A., & Mainsah, H. (2012). Designing for youth civic engagement in social media. Paper presented at the Proceedings of the IADIS International Conference of Web Based Communities and Social Media, Lisbon.

Brandtzæg, P.B., Haugstveit, I.M., Lüders, M., & Følstad, A. (2015, April). Participation Barriers to Youth Civic Engagement in Social Media. In *Ninth International AAAI Conference on Web and Social Media*, Oxford, UK.

Brehm, J., & Rahn, W. (1997). Individual-level evidence for the causes and consequences of social capital. *American Journal of Political Science*, *41*(3), 999–1023.

Bucy, E.P., & Gregson, K.S. (2001). Media participation a legitimizing mechanism of mass democracy. *New Media & Society*, *3*(3), 357–380.

Capella, J.N., & Jamieson, K.H. (1997). Spiral of Cynicism: The Press and the Public Good. Oxford: Oxford University Press.

Chesoni, A., Muigai, S., & Kanyinga, K. (2006). *Promoting Women's Human Rights and Enhancing Gender Equality in Kenya*: Sida

Clarke, A. (2010). *Social media: Political uses and implications for representative democracy*. Ottawa: Library of Parliament.

Cohen, C. J., & Kahne, J. (2011). *Participatory politics. New media and youth political action*. Chicago, IL: MacArthur Foundation.

Coleman, S. (2001). Online campaigning. *Parliamentary Affairs*, *54*(4), 679–688.

Communications Authority of Kenya (CAK). (2016). Quarterly statistics report, first quarter sector statistics. Report for the Financial year 2015–2016, Nairobi.

Dahlberg, L. (2001). Extending the public sphere through cyberspace: The case of Minnesota E-Democracy. *First Monday*, *6*(3). doi:10.5210/fm.v6i3.838.

Davis, R. (1999). *The web of politics: The Internet's impact on the American political system*. New York: Oxford University Press.

Debatin, B., Lovejoy, J.P., Horn, A.K., & Hughes, B.N. (2009). Facebook and online privacy: Attitudes, behaviors, and unintended consequences. *Journal of Computer-Mediated Communication*, *15*(1), 83–108.

Delli Carpini, M. X. (2000). Gen. com: Youth, civic engagement, and the new information environment. *Political Communication*, *17*(4), 341–349.

Ellison, N. B. (2007). Social network sites: Definition, history, and scholarship. *Journal of Computer-Mediated Communication*, *13*(1), 210–230.

Ellison, N., Steinfield, C., & Lampe, C. (2007). The benefits of Facebook "friends": exploring the relationship between college students' use of online social networks and social capital. *Journal of Computer-Mediated Communication*, *12*, 1143–1168.

Ellison, N. B., Lampe, C., & Steinfield, C. (2009). Feature social network sites and society: Current trends and future possibilities. *Interactions*, *16* (1), 6–9.

Ellison, N., Steinfield, C., Lampe, C., & Vitak, J. (2012). Online social network sites and the concept of social capital. *Frontiers in New Media Research, 15*, 115.

Eveland, W.P., Kwak, N., Shah, D.V., & Cho, J., (2005). Information and expression in a digital age modeling internet effects on civic participation. *Communication Research, 32*(5), 531–565.

Feldman, O., & Kawakami, K. (1991). Media use as predictors of political behavior: The case of Japan. *Political Psychology, 12*, 65–80.

Flanagan, C., & Levine, P. (2010). Civic engagement and the transition to adulthood. *The future of children, 20*(1), 159–179.

Garramone, G.M., Harris, A.C., & Pizante, G. (1986). Predictors of motivation to use computer-mediated political communication systems. *Journal of Broadcasting & Electronic Media, 30*(4), 445–457.

Granovetter, M., Marsden, P., & Lin, N. (1982). *Social structure and network analysis. Social structures and network analysis* (pp. 105–130). Beverly Hills, CA: Sage.

Gueorguieva, V. (2008). Voters, Myspace, and Youtube the impact of alternative communication channels, *26*(3), 288–300.

Hacker, K.L. (1996). Missing links in the evolution of electronic democratization. *Media, Culture & Society, 18*(2), 213–232.

Halpern, D., & Gibbs, J. (2013). Social media as a catalyst for online deliberation? Exploring the affordances of Facebook and YouTube for political expression. *Computers in Human Behavior, 29*(3),1159–1168.

Helliwell, J.F., & Putnam, R.D. (2004). The social context of well-being. *Philosophical Transactions-Royal Society of London Series B Biological Sciences, 359*, 1435–1446.

Herring, S.C. (1999). The rhetorical dynamics of gender harassment on-line. *The Information Society, 15*(3), 151–167.

Hindman, D.B. (2000). The rural-urban digital divide. *Journalism & Mass Communication Quarterly, 77*(3), 549–560.

Horrigan, J., Garrett, K., & Resnick, P. (2004). The Internet and Democratic Debate. Pew Internet and American Life Project. http://www.pewInternet.org/pdfs/PIP_Political_Info_Report.pdf.

Huckfeldt, R.R., & Sprague, J. (1995). *Citizens, politics and social communication: Information and influence in an election campaign*. Cambridge: Cambridge University Press.

Jones, K.S. (2006). Giving and volunteering as distinct forms of civic engagement: The role of community integration and personal resources in formal helping. *Nonprofit and Voluntary Sector Quarterly, 35*(2), 249–266.

Kagwanja, P.M. (2005). Clash of generations? Youth identity, violence and the politics of transition in Kenya, 1997–2002. Vanguards or vandals: Youth, politics and conflict in Africa, 83–108.

Kagwanja, P.M. (2006). 'Power to Uhuru': Youth identity and generational politics in Kenya's 2002 Elections. *African Affairs, 105*(418), 51–75.

Kahne, J., Middaugh, E., Lee, N.-J., & Feezell, J.T. (2011). Youth online activity and exposure to diverse perspectives. *New Media & Society, 14*(3), 492–512.

Kann, M.E., Berry, J., Grant, C., & Zager, P. (2007). The internet and youth political participation. *First Monday, 12*(8).

Kariuki, C.G. (2010). Women participation in the Kenyan society. *The African Executive, 296*(3), 17–30.

Kasomo, D. (2012). Factors affecting women participation in electoral politics in Africa. *International Journal of Psychology and Behavioral Sciences, 2*(3), 57–63.

Kenya Elections Domestic Observation Forum [KEDOF]. (2008). Preliminary press statement and verdict of 2007 Kenya's general elections. http://www.iedafrica.org/documents/KEDOF-statement-31-12-07.pdf. Accessed 31 December 2008.

Kenya National Commission on Human Rights [KNHCR]. (2008). *On the brink of the precipice: A human rights account of Kenya's post-2007 election violence.* Nairobi: KNCHR.

Kim, B.J., Kavanaugh, A.L., Zin, T.T., Rosson, M.B., Carroll, J.M., & Schmitz, J. (2007). Local groups online: Political learning and participation. *Computer Supported Cooperative Work* (CSCW), *16*(4–5), 375–395.

Kohut, A., Keeter, S., Doherty, C., & Dimock, M. (2008). *Social networking and online videos take off: Internet's broader role in campaign 2008.* TPR Center, The PEW research center.

Kushin, M.J., & Kitchener, K. (2009). Getting political on social network sites: Exploring online political discourse on Facebook. *First Monday, 14*(11).

Kwak, N., Shah, D.V., Cho, J., & Eveland, W.P. (2005). Information and expression in a digital age modeling Internet effects on civic participation. *Communication Research, 32*(5), 531–565.

Lampe, C., Ellison, N., & Steinfield, C. (2006). *A Face (book) in the crowd: Social searching vs. social browsing.* Paper presented at the Proceedings of the 2006 20th anniversary conference on Computer supported cooperative work.

Lampe, C., Ellison, N.B., & Steinfield, C. (2007). The benefits of Facebook "friends:" Social capital and college students' use of online social network sites. *Journal of Computer-Mediated Communication, 12*(4), 1143–1168.

Leggio, J. (2008). Mumbai attack coverage demonstrates (good and bad) maturation point of social media. CBS Interactive, 28.

Lenhart, A., Madden, M., Macgill, A. R., & Smith, A. (2007). Teens and social media. http://www.pewinternet.org/pdfs/PIP_Teens_Social_Media_Final.pdtime. Accessed 30 November 2016.

Lenhart, A., Purcell, K., Smith, A., & Zickuhr, K. (2010). *Social media & mobile internet use among teens and young adults.* Washington, DC: Millennials, Pew Internet & American Life Project.

Lewis, K., Gray, K., & Meierhenrich, J. (2014). The structure of online activism. *Sociological Science, 1*, 1–9.

Lin, N., Cook, K.S., & Burt, R.S. (Eds.). (2001). *Social capital.* Chicago, IL: Aldine de Gruyter.

Madden, M., Lenhart, A., & Hitlin, P. (2006). *Teens and technology: Youth are leading the transition to a fully wired and mobile nation.* Washington, DC: Pew Internet and American Life.

Mainwaring, S. (2011). Exactly what role did social media play in the Egyptian revolution? *Fast Company*, 14.

Margolis, M., Resnick, D., & Tu, C.-c. (1997). Campaigning on the internet parties and candidates on the World Wide Web in the 1996 primary season. *The Harvard International Journal of Press/Politics, 2*(1), 59–78.

McLeod, J.M., Scheufele, D.A., & Moy, P. (1999). Community, communication, and participation: The role of mass media and interpersonal discussion in local political participation. *Political Communication, 16*(3), 315–336.

Montgomery, K.C. (2008). Youth and digital democracy: Intersections of practice, policy, and the marketplace. In W.L. Bennett (Ed.), *Civic life online: Learning how digital media can engage youth* (pp. 25–49). Cambridge, MA: The MIT Press.

Mutz, D.C. (2002). The consequences of cross-cutting networks for political participation. *American Journal of Political Science, 46*(4), 838–855.

Nie, N.H. (2001). Sociability, interpersonal relations, and the internet reconciling conflicting findings. *American Behavioral Scientist, 45*(3), 420–435.

Norton, H.L., & Citron, D.K. (2010). Government speech 2.0. *Denver University Law Review, 87*, 899.

Oriare, P. (2009). *The impact of mass media on youth political participation in the 2007 Kenya general elections in Nakuru district* (Unpublished Doctoral Thesis). University of Nairobi.

Outlook, A. E. (2006). OECD Publication. *Paris: African Development Bank.*

Palen, L., & Liu, S.B. (2007). *Citizen communications in crisis: anticipating a future of ICT-supported public participation.* Paper presented at the CHI '07: Proceedings of the SIGCHI conference on Human factors in computing systems. San Jose, CA, ACM, pp. 727–736.

Papic, M., & Noonan, S. (2011). Social media as a tool for protest. *Stratfor Global Intelligence*, 3.

Parks, M.R., & Floyd, K. (1996). Making friends in cyberspace. *Journal of Computer-Mediated Communication, 1*(4). http://onlinelibrary.wiley.com/doi/10.1111/j.1083-6101.1996.tb00176.x/full. Accessed 30 November 2016.

Paxton, P. (1999). Is social capital declining in the United States? A multiple indicator assessment 1. *American Journal of Sociology, 105*(1), 88–127.

Pettersen, P.A., & Rose, L.E. (1996). Participation in local politics in Norway: Some do, some don't; some will, some won't. *Political Behavior, 18*(1), 51–97.

Prior, M. (2005). News vs. entertainment: How increasing media choice widens gaps in political knowledge and turnout. *American Journal of Political Science, 49*(3), 577–592.
Putnam, R.D. (1995). Bowling alone: America's declining social capital. *Journal of Democracy, 6*(1), 65–78.
Quan-Haase, A., & Wellman, B. (2004). How does the internet affect social capital. *Social Capital and Information Technology, 113*, 135–113.
Resnick, D., & Casale, D. (2014). Young populations in young democracies: Generational voting behaviour in sub-Saharan Africa. *Democratization, 21*(6), 1172–1194.
Rosenfeld, M.J., & Thomas, R.J. (2012). Searching for a mate the rise of the internet as a social intermediary. *American Sociological Review, 77*(4), 523–547.
Scheufele, D.A., Nisbet, M.C., Brossard, D., & Nisbet, E.C. (2004). Social structure and citizenship: Examining the impacts of social setting, network heterogeneity, and informational variables on political participation. *Political Communication, 21*(3), 315–338.
Selnow, Gary W. (1998). *Electronic whistle-stops: The impact of the Internet on American politics.* Westport, CT: Praeger.
Sheedy, C.S. (2011). Social media for social change: A case study of social media use in the 2011 Egyptian revolution. A Capstone Project Presented to the Faculty of the School of Communication, American University.
Smith, A. (2013). Civic engagement in the digital age. *Pew Internet & American Life Project.*
Smith, A.W., Schlozman, K.L., Verba, S., & Brady, H. (2009). *The Internet and civic engagement.* Washington, DC: Pew Internet & American Life Project.
Sparks, C. (2001). The Internet and the global public sphere. In L.W. Bennett and R.M. Entman (eds) *Mediated Politics: Communication in the Future of Democracy* (pp. 75–95). Cambridge: Cambridge University Press.
Stanley, J.W., & Weare, C. (2004). The effects of internet use on political participation. *Administration & Society, 36*(5), 503–527.
Steinfield, C., Ellison, N. B., & Lampe, C. (2008). Social capital, self-esteem, and use of online social network sites: A longitudinal analysis. *Journal of Applied Developmental Psychology, 29*(6), 434–445.
Storck, M. (2011). The role of social media in political mobilisation: A case study of the January 2011 Egyptian uprising. *University of St Andrews, Scotland, 20.*
Syvertsen, A.K., Wray-Lake, L., Flanagan, C.A., Wayne Osgood, D. & Briddell, L. (2011). Thirty-year trends in U.S. adolescents' civic engagement: A story of changing participation and educational differences. *Journal of Research on Adolescence, 21*, 586–594.
Tedesco, J.C. (2004). Changing the channel: Use of the Internet for communicating about Politics. In L.L. Kaid (Ed.), *Handbook of Political*

Communication Research (pp. 507–532). Mahwah, NJ: Lawrence Erlbaum Associates.

Tedesco, J.C., Kaid, L.L., McKinney, M.S., & Gaddie, K. (1999). Journalistic responsibility and political advertising: A content analysis of coverage by state and local media. *Communication Studies*, *50*(4), 279–293.

Thackeray, R., & Hunter, M. (2010). Empowering youth: Use of technology in advocacy to affect social change. *Journal of Computer-Mediated Communication*, *15*(4), 575–591.

Thelwall, M. (2009). Social network sites: Users and uses. *Advances in Computers*, *76*, 19–73.

Tufekci, Z., & Wilson, C. (2012). Social media and the decision to participate in political protest: Observations from Tahrir Square. *Journal of Communication*, *62*(2), 363–379.

UNDP. (2009). *Road to 2015: Driving the MDGs*. UNDP Kenya Annual Report. Nairobi.

Wanjala, S. (2002). Elections and the political transition in Kenya. In Mute, et al., (Eds.), *Building an open society – The politics: A developmental approach*. Boston and Toronto: Little Brown and Company.

Warner, B.R., McGowen, S.T., & Hawthorne, J. (2012). Limbaugh's social media nightmare: Facebook and Twitter as spaces for political action. *Journal of Radio & Audio Media*, *19*(2), 257–275.

Warren, A.M., Sulaiman, A., & Jaafar, N.I. (2014). Social media effects on fostering online civic engagement and building citizen trust and trust in institutions. *Government Information Quarterly*, *31*(2), 291–301.

Wattenberg, M.P. (2008). *Is voting for young people?: With a postscript on citizen engagement*. New York: Pearson PTR.

Wilhelm, A.G. (1998). Virtual sounding boards: How deliberative is on-line political discussion? *Information Communication & Society*, *1*(3), 313–338.

Wilkins, K.G. (2000). The role of media in public disengagement from political life. *Journal of Broadcasting and Electronic Media*, *44*, 569.

Williams, C., & Gulati, G. (2008). What is a social network worth? Facebook and vote share in the 2008 presidential primaries. In *Annual meeting of the American Political Science Association* (pp. 1–17). Boston, MA: APSA.

Yamamoto, M., Kushin, M. J., & Dalisay, F. (2013). Social media and mobiles as political mobilization forces for young adults: Examining the moderating role of online political expression in political participation. *New Media & Society*, *17*(6), 880–898. 1461444813518390.

Young, I. M. (2000). *Democracy and inclusion*. New York: Oxford University Press.

Youth Agenda. (2008). *Who's guilty? Youth perspective on the 2007 pre-polls electoral violence in Kenya*. Nairobi: The Youth Agenda.

Zhang, W., Johnson, T. J., Seltzer, T., & Bichard, S. L. (2009). The revolution will be networked: The influence of social networking sites on political attitudes and behavior. *Social Science Computer Review, 28*(1), 75–92.

Zhang, W., Johnson, T. J., Seltzer, T., & Bichard, S. L. (2010). The revolution will be networked: The influence of social networking sites on political attitudes and behavior. *Social Science Computer Review*. 28:75–92

Zhao, S. (2006). Do internet users have more social ties? A call for differentiated analyses of Internet use. *Journal of Computer-Mediated Communication, 11*(3), 844–862.

Samuel C. Kamau is a faculty member at the Graduate School of Media and Communication, Aga Khan University, Nairobi. Previously, Samuel taught at the University of Nairobi, School of Journalism and Mass Communication. He is also a research consultant, media critic, communication trainer, and an avid blogger. His teaching and research interests include; New Media technologies, political communication, digital journalism, and development communication.

CHAPTER 7

An Engaged Chadian Artist's Digital Itinerary Towards Political and Civic Success: Pitfalls of Oppression

Mirjam de Bruijn and Didier Lalaye

The Chadians who make some furore in the outside world, outside Chad, are maybe not more than two: Croquemort and Beral; Beral and Croquemort

(Patrick Giraudo, IFT, 1 June 2015, Ndjaména)

Introduction

In this paper we will present a biography in context, to understand the itinerary and career of Didier Lalaye, alias Croquemort, who is an engaged slam artist from Chad. Didier is co-author of this paper. It is an itinerary in which choices are related to various vital conjunctions, an itinerary that does not always follow a common pattern (Johnson-Hanks 2002). Didier

M. de Bruijn (✉)
Leiden University, Leiden, Netherlands
e-mail: m.e.de.bruijn@hum.leidenuniv.nl

D. Lalaye
Utrecht Medical Centre, Utreucht University, Utrecht, Netherlands
e-mail: lalaye84@gmail.com

B. Mutsvairo (ed.), *Digital Activism in the Social Media Era*,
DOI 10.1007/978-3-319-40949-8_7

participates in many different 'social fields' (see Sally Falk Moore 1973), which are woven together in his person and his networks. These fields are his artistic world, the world of medicine—he is a doctor—his family and friends, and the international relations in which he participates representing Chadian youth. Behind and hidden in these fields and decisions is the person and his/her psychology, but always in context; a specific context of Chad, of Central Africa and of Africa in the world. Didier's career should be situated in a Chadian context—both its historical context and the present day artistic scene. This is an 'engaged' itinerary in which reflections on society go hand in hand with the production of 'parole', or 'political engagement' in the public sphere of Chad and Africa, and gradually also in Europe. A political imagination, as a reflection on society and a possible political and social future, emerges from his creations, which are based on experiences in his various social fields, facilitated by the use of new Information and Communication Technologies (ICTs).

Using the biographical method (life history in context), we try to elicit what have been crucial moments in defining the course of the itinerary and the choices of creation. From the story of the person to the context of oppression and upcoming ICTs, we sketch changes in the decision-making and imaginations of the person and how these are related to (an interpretation of) the socio-political environment. One of the characteristics of so-called change-makers or entrepreneurs is their ability to connect and access information. As Castells stated (2009), connectivity and communication are power. In this paper, we demonstrate the importance of connectivity and communication, new ICTs, in giving people the power to change their life itinerary by creating opportunities and appropriating new information and ideas. Art is an expression of the power of communication and artists are often change-makers.

Context

Presidential elections were held in Chad on 10 April 2016. There was no outright majority for the outgoing president, Idris Déby, who has been in power since 1990. Instead, other candidates were positioned and a second round of elections is being prepared. The result shows that the logic of dictatorship, that is, automatic triumph of the president, has been countervailed in Chad. Civil society organizations reached a turning point in March 2015, when protests against the obligatory wearing of a helmet by motorcyclists (which in itself is a good measure but here became a cause of the levying of high fines on the motocyclists) revealed a long-hidden but clear disapproval of the dictatorial regime and its politics of impoverishment. Civil society showed its decisiveness during the elections of 10 April when one-third voted against President Déby. At time of writing, we are still waiting for the definitive outcome of the process. Finally, it seems, the Chadian people are trying to take their destiny into their own hands. The emergence of civil society is tentative given long-standing oppression and many civil wars that have coloured post-colonial Chad, but it is clear that the tide has turned.

Since 2000, mobile telephony and the internet have been increasingly available in Chad. Although the government has a policy of discouragement, by keeping prices up and only allowing two ICT (Information and Communication Technology) companies into the country, they have not been able to stop people accessing the internet and using telephones to access information, news, and to relate to others, organize movements, etc. This has certainly played a role in the recent developments in Chad. It is no coincidence that the government closed down the internet during the elections, a tactic used on previous occasions during periods of unrest. As several online publications inform us, the government has established a very oppressive regime (see for instance the blog of an expelled Chadian blogger www.makaila.fr). Although access to social media is still very low (see Akinyoade et al., forthcoming 2017), it is on the rise and increasingly (young) people are accessing Facebook. Indeed, the influence of Facebook 'activism' by the diaspora on discussions can no longer be neglected. In addition, artists and engaged others are active on Facebook and portray themselves with their identity of choice. In this paper, we will see how this is also the case for the itinerary of the engaged artists.

Less often mentioned in discussions on new ICTs and socio-political change are the effects this has had on other domains in society, like the production of music. It cannot be denied that the digitalization of cameras, of music, etc. has facilitated the tasks of music producers. Studio equipment has become cheaper and easier to access, but also the skills and capacity to handle the technology are now accessible for a larger group of people. In short, the digitalization of the music industry has been an important factor in the promotion of popular music and urban cultural expression. This digitalization can be viewed as one of those crucial moments in history when the lives of artists change and they are given the space and room to voice their ideas and to make their imaginations of the world heard by others.

Interpreting and Meeting

Mirjam has been working on several research projects in Chad since 2001. These projects have brought her to the terrains of, among other things, conflict research and poverty analysis. Chad is not the most peaceful country in the world, with civil wars since 1965, a policy of non-development, and, since becoming an oil-producing country in 2005, increasing inequalities between various population groups. Despite its new-found oil income, the country is still listed at the bottom of most good governance (development, etc.) indexes. The country's logic is inspired by imminent violence and the impossibility of escaping it (Debos 2012). Understanding how and why people developed the lives they lead in such a country has been Mirjam's quest. From 2008, her project has added new ICTs to the mix. The perspective of technology and society opened a new direction in her research, shifting her focus to possibilities for change, and voice. One of the leading questions became: How do change-makers living in oppressive environments build their careers and take the chance to develop a future? How do they shape their (political) imagination of past and future?

To discover this social process of decision-making, we follow here a biographical method. Despite criticism of this method that it is too specific to develop historical insights (Banner 2009) we adopt the approach of Apitzsch and Siouti (2007, p. 3) who maintain that biographies have 'proven to be an excellent way of making theoretical sense of social phenomena', and that this method 'is particularly suited to the analysis of social phenomena as identifiable processes [. . .]' and therefore it is very much a tool for understanding how identity changes in relation to contextual changes. And they continue: 'The focus of biographical analysis is not only the reconstruction of intentionality, which is represented as an individual's life course, but the embeddedness of the biographical account in social macro structures' (idem, 7), that is, in our examples, information technologies over time. Hence, the biography of one person in context will give us insight into the deeper social and historical processes at play.

It is impossible to present a biography in one chapter. Therefore, here we search for moments of success and decisions that build a future under an oppressive regime. We will examine specific biographical moments in the life of one person that are crucial for the itinerary's shape. Johnson-Hanks (2002) describes these moments as vital conjunctures: 'moments when seemingly established futures are called into question and when actors are called on to manage durations of radical uncertainty [...] navigated in reference to their horizons—the imaginable futures that are hoped for or feared' (Johnson-Hanks 2002, p. 878). A vital conjuncture implies a (temporal) space of uncertainty in which choices need to be made for the course of the (near) future, whether this is always consciously done so or not. And although these choices are personal, the imagined futures are socially constructed, depending on social, cultural, political and economic opportunities or 'horizons'.

Constructing the Biography

Didier, alias Croquemort, and Mirjam met for the first time in May 2013. A colleague, Remadji Hotondji, facilitated contact between Mirjam and a group of engaged musicians, including Beral and Croquemort. We discussed their drive to be musicians and their ways of expressing themselves. Out of this meeting grew the idea for a project to give a voice to engaged people in countries where this is not easy. In March 2014, Mirjam contacted the group again. At that time, Croquemort was in Ndjaména and so they met in a bar on the Boulevard de Sao, where they deliberated possibilities of embarking on a trajectory of mutual understanding and research into the music scene. They engaged in this itinerary, recognizing a shared enthusiasm and activism. Mirjam's subsequent visits to Chad, then, were to follow the music scene and to discuss the many different aspects of Didier's life, gradually getting to know his family. This personal and emotional encounter blurs methodology with friendship and deep knowledge of a person that becomes problematic in terms of 'research' and 'data'. Framing the collaboration as one between the musician and the 'researcher' is one of the ways to avoid this ethical question, as the two authors decide on the publication.

Croquemort's life is not only about music and text, he is a doctor, political activist, youth leader, social entrepreneur, father, friend and so on. He allowed Mirjam to share these fields of his life. Gradually, by becoming involved in some of Mirjam's projects, and vice versa, he also became involved in Mirjam's life. A mutual understanding developed in which the *tour d'horizon* for the construction of the biography was being made. Mirjam was in Chad in September and December 2014, January, February, May and October 2015 and in March 2016. In November 2014, Didier visited Sweden for one of his projects and he combined this with a visit to Leiden University. Didier visited the Netherlands again in June 2015 for a writing residence of 3 months. The co-production of Didier's (auto)biography has become one of the main kernels of this research project.

A Biographical Note on the Artist: Croquemort—A Character that Makes It Go

Berceau

Didier Lalaye, alias Croquemort is a writer and a medical doctor. His writing is the basis of the songs and music he makes. Writing and language is his *devoir*. As a young boy he was constantly reading. He was brought up in a family that valued study and language highly. His father, an education inspector, stimulated his children to study and to be attentive. Didier's youth was divided between Pala, the family's '*berceau*' and the Chagoua neighbourhood of Ndjamena. Although he does not like divisions and oppositions, it is clear that he has been born and raised in a country where oppositions and inequality are inherent to the everyday and the organization of society. Being from Pala makes one a southerner, Chagoua is a quarter of *sudistes*. The North–South opposition has played an important role in Chadian history and has been mentioned as one of the main reasons for the country's cleavages, etc. Being born under the Habré regime—the former dictator, Hissène Habré, who was trialed in Senegal, May 2016—raised under the arbitrary regime of Déby and frequently confronted with injustice certainly shaped the character of the intelligent, well-informed and intrinsically justice-seeking person, that is Didier.

Betrayal

One word pops up regularly in our discussions: *trahison*—that is, betrayal. Basic trust relations are difficult to develop in a worn and torn, oppressed society, where the secret service is well organized and daily survival is a struggle (see Debos 2012; Heitz Tokpa, 2014). As a small boy, Didier was already confronted with this deeply rooted character of Chadian society. Betrayal was the reason that he was expelled from university for two years, from 2010 to 2012. It is beyond the scope of this paper to explain the exact reasons for this incident, but what is important is that Didier protested in defence of his co-students. While others retreated and went back to class, Didier, along with 30 others, was accused of conspiring against university leaders and he was expelled. Despite the fact that they won the case against the university, there was no justice. Didier/Croquemort experiences this betrayal of his fellow students as a deep scar.

These experiences, and many others, make him reflect and say that this regime has killed the youth and their possibilities of developing a good future. An untroubled youth was not possible for Didier. His opportunities were limited, he learned too soon that life was hard and people are difficult to trust.

Texts

The writer/musician Croquemort wants to awaken society and make people reflect on who they are and how their society is a clear example of inequality and neglect. His creations have developed from the hip-hop music of his youth to the genre of slam poetry. Slam is urban engaged poetry originating from Chicago in the 1990s. In Africa, the genre is still new but steadily growing. His newest album, *Apprenons à les comprendre*, contains philosophical texts; like *Prisonier*: we are all imprisoned, which refers to real prison, but asks whether we make the prison ourselves? The song text of *Apprenons à les comprendre* raises the idea of human beings, and all their strange characteristics, being impossible to comprehend. These texts go together with his poems that refer to the daily life of Chadians, a quotidian that is recognizable in other African countries and, of course, elsewhere in the world. The core of Croquemort's texts criticize inequality and demand rights, but employ an analytical prose/poetry that questions and mirrors. Are we not all entitled to a nice life, with at least a provision of basic needs? Often Chadian families are deprived of such fundamentals. These songs appeal to the Chadian public. Croquemort's concerts are sold out, and his CDs are popular. His musical and text qualities are highly esteemed by international observers of Chad as well.[1]

During his last concert, March 18, 2016, he introduced four new songs that were a clear commentary on present-day Chad, in which civil society is increasingly protesting against President Déby, who has been in power for 26 years, and where drinking water and good roads are still a dream. In the run up to the elections of 10 April, the concert on 18 March was a moment of reflection for society, but especially for Croquemort.

Prizes and Invitations

A coincidence on the terrace of a small bar in Ndjamena on 31 March 2016 provides an insight into the start of Croquemort's international career. The person in question overheard our conversation, in which we discussed the making of a documentary (I was with a Chadian photographer and film maker) and he asked to be interviewed. He shared his first encounter with Croquemort in 2011, when Croquemort was part of the Radio France Internationale (RFI) programme *Couleurs Tropicales*, where Croquemort's song *Cousin de l'U(nion)E(uropéenne)* was nominated for a prize. This song criticizes the way Europeans view Africa. Even now, this is one of Croquemort's most famous songs. Before 2011, Didier had won several prizes in writer's competitions, but after 2011 an international scene started to open up for him. He went to different summer schools, was invited to the Forum de la Francophonie, and participated in several slam festivals in West and Central Africa. It brought him to Canada, France, the Netherlands, Sweden, Mali, Burkina Faso, Tunisia, Dakar and Ivory Coast.[2] His first album was created in that year, and his second album was produced in 2015.

His prizes and invitations allowed him to get foot on the ground on the international Slam scene. It is interesting to note that he invested a lot in this career during the period he was expelled from university. His position as an engaged singer in Chad does not make it easy to pursue this path, as became fully clear in 2016, when, for reasons of neutrality, around election time he was not allowed to receive the promised financial contribution to his national Chadian tour by the French Embassy, nor to sing the songs he wanted to sing during a concert in Canada for which he was invited, but for which the Chadian government would have paid.

Constraints and Possibilities

Inspiration

'The world is there to be analysed! It is analysing that I do.'

Growing up in Chad either makes one very critical and angry, or the opposite: lethargic. Croquemort is certainly on the observation side of the scale, criticizing and analysing his society and trying to extend his analysis to the world beyond Chad. Croquemort's song texts reflect his Chadian environment, an environment coloured by censorship, violence, mistrust, and lack of a cultural policy. But talented young people like Croquemort fight hard to overcome these barriers, which ironically, become a source of inspiration.

Media and Culture Policy: Censorship and 'Fear'

Didier/Croquemort is one of the few engaged artists from Chad able to reach international circles. He is part of and creator of the up-and-coming music scene in Chad, which, due to war, political choices, censorship, but especially a non-musical environment, was semi-absent until a decade ago (see Alhassim 2016). Chadian music and artists were hardly known in the international world, in contrast to other African countries like Cameroon, Mali and Senegal. Some rare artists like El Hadj Ahmat Pecos did sing protest songs, but had no international exposure. It is likely that this is related to the Chadian regime, which does not allow protest music to be played on national radio or TV channels. It has been, and still is, one of the most oppressive regimes in Central Africa, despite the promise of democracy and openness that came with the coup d'etat in 1990, instigated by Idris Déby who has held power ever since. Freedom of speech is certainly not the rule in Chad. Since 2009, there have been claims of a gradual liberation of speech (Seli 2014), but recent developments around the appearance of jihadist movements and more open protest have given the Chadian regime another incentive to control the population. We could relate this to ICT politics, which deny access to high-speed internet. The broadband cable (*cable haute debit*) was stopped at Chad's borders. Until now, internet connectivity in the country has been poor, but compared to a decade ago it has improved. Compared to the period before 2008, the role of internet access and social media has increased tremendously in shaping life, especially of young Chadians.

This is clearly related to the poor development of media in Chad. Other than national TV and radio, which are highly censored, until recently there have been few alternatives, with the exception of Radio Liberté, which plays alternative music and on which some discussion is allowed. In rural areas, there are some very local (often set up by catholic missions) radio stations, but there is clearly no venue for alternative music. The arrival of mobile telephony and media technology has improved the situation slightly. Bluetooth and other technology allow for the diffusion of music. Internet channels such as YouTube, Facebook, etc. are increasingly integrated into artists' strategies for dissemination, but these channels have a limited public. Access to YouTube requires good internet. Hence, these venues are mostly for urbanites and for the diaspora. In the urban media scene things are changing as private channels are opening due to easy-access technology. It is now much easier to make TV programmes. However, so far these are rather neutral enterprises, and there is hardly room for protesting voices. Independent channels such as Electron TV and Vox Africa do broadcast work of Croquemort, and they have broadcast several interviews with him and some of his concerts.

Censorship seems to be limited, but as Croquemort stated himself: 'we are free to say what we want but not on "their radio"'. After his concerts, Croquemort almost goes into hiding, adopting a low profile, but this is probably less for fear of reprisals from the government but rather to escape public attention.

(No) Presence of International NGOs in Chad

The activity of international players in the 'development' field of Chad is relatively low and since 2003 has concentrated on the oil production and its consequences (see De Bruijn 2008). The development of culture is not very high on the agenda. Its presence is mainly in the major cities like N'djaména, Moundou and Abéché. Most artistic funds are released by the IFT, Institut Francaise Tchadien. Another player is Radio France International (RFI) whose internationally recognized competitions push some artists into the international world. The BBC has also developed a number of activities. Recently, telephone companies have become involved in music competitions, but they all adopt a neutral role as they depend on government relations for their business. Nevertheless, their competitions do influence the artists and their exposure to the outside world. One can only conclude that an important part of the protest music scene auto-develops in relation to the wishes and ideologies of some entrepreneurial and convinced young people.

Culture Infrastructure

As a consequence of the absence of a clear cultural policy and the absence of international players in the field, a cultural infrastructure is lacking: concerts in Ndjamena are held at the Institut Francaise du Tchad (IFT), Centre Baba Moustapha or in bars; government buildings like la Normandie (a cinema) are not allowed to host concerts by engaged artists. There is no real concert hall, or even a small concert room. IFT and Baba Moustapha organize these concerts and other artistic manifestations, also international exchanges, mainly for those artists that have already made a name for themselves on a national, and often international level. But they are not creating a 'breeding ground'. There is no space for the youth to develop, although the Maison du Quartier (a youth house in Chagoua, funded by the IFT and French Embassy) is a beginning in this sense (cf. Alhassim 2016). For the past few years the organisation of festivals may be listed under culture infrastructure. But as the organization of Croquemort's festivals 'Ndjam s'enflamme en Slam' have shown, it is really a struggle to receive enough funding for such events. These festivals are also a statement of young people who want to develop culture in their country.

Possibilities and Opportunities: Auto-Development

Facebook and Other Social Media

> 'Je suis collé à mon ordinateur; je fouille tous qui est possible: c'est ça qui a commencé de me faire sortir du Tchad.'

Croquemort takes his connectivity seriously. As a young boy, at a time when, for the majority of people in Chad, the internet was simply not known, he was already eager to get access to games, etc. Computers hold few secrets for him, and his use of phone and smartphone is daily and constant. Croquemort has his own Facebook pages and he is online on a daily basis. His posts react to recent developments in his country, like the protest march in March 2015, the attacks in Ndjaména in the summer of 2015 and the aforementioned elections (10 April 2016). He does not shy away from criticizing the government or the acts of bureaucrats/ministers, etc. He has a lot of followers. 'It is very important to be strict when it comes to Facebook and followers; they should be taken seriously as they are my public.' Hence, following up on internet activity is almost a full-time occupation for Croquemort. It is important to know, however, that this form of communication is difficult to control, although technologies for controlling it are gradually improving in Chad.

But the internet is not only a platform for the public, it is, in particular, an information source. Indeed, Croquemort spends at least an hour a day searching the internet for opportunities to engage in competitions, etc.

The Appearance of Studios

> 'C'est bien aussi grâce à Preston; qui l'a poussé qui l'a fait écouter les titres slam; studio d'une radio ou il travaillait, A qui je dois tout.
> Il y a eu Makris, côté technique
> Anderson; première album'

In addition to an absence of music venues, there is also an absence of music production infrastructure. The producers of official TV and radio are not open to assisting the protest scene (for obvious reasons). Other structures are emerging, but only very recently. The scene of our in-depth research is the neighbourhood of Chagoua, the breeding ground of Mali's hip-hop scene. Studios have been set up and have started producing urban music, and creating radio and, more recently, TV programmes. A year ago, IFT funded a '*maison de quartier*' where the young of the neighbourhood meet, shop and receive training. Photography exhibitions and presentations of music and art are part of the organization of the *maison de quartier*. One of the better-equipped studios is Preston Concept. The owner of this studio, Paulin Preston, has a business-like attitude. He self-financed the studio and developed his own festival. Whereas originally he was clearly involved with protest music, in recent months we have seen him moving to a lighter music style, that is not per se political or protest, as he says it gives more chances to the youth. He has experienced the hardships of the politically engaged and the difficulties faced by such artists seeking to make it in the public domain in Chad's oppressive regime (Alhassim 2016). These studios developed in the rhythm of the development of ICTs and digital technology for the production of music (cameras, audio), etc. They collaborate a lot with Cameroon, where the production of CDs is far more developed than in Chad.

Interestingly, people like Preston can earn enough nowadays to buy the digital equipment needed. This is also an effect of the reduction of prices of this material and, of course, also his drive to develop the music scene as an almost political and social act. He is an engaged person who feels that the development of the music scene may help Chadian youth. But he is also a realist and his latest move to produce more commercially oriented music might have to do with his assessment of the situation in Chad and the possibilities for earning money.

Didier/Croquemort's first single: *Je voudrais devenir un star* was produced by Black Label, Anderson, in 2010. His last album was produced by Preston. The CD was launched with a big concert, held at IFT, at the end of January 2015. Croquemort is now at a possible turning point in his career. His new CD has given him new impetus. Invitations for concerts and participation in music-related events and projects keep coming. How will this develop? And what are the most important steering factors? Are these factors the same ones that have pushed him so far, or will there be new or different ones?

Conclusion: Moments of Decision M/Taking

We opened the paper with the idea of the biography in context. What have been moments of choice, and moments of change? How has Didier sculpted his future in the context of oppression and difficulties encountered in the production of culture? Crucial moments have included his expulsion from school, the arrival of better internet and social media, the creation of studios in Ndjamena. This is the context in which the production of music and text was possible, but the creation of artistic production also needs an environment and, in the case of Didier/Croquemort, it seems that the environment of poverty and oppression, which he experiences on a daily basis, is one of these sources. It is the confrontation with this environment that makes him imagine a future, through his texts. These texts, his words, now reach beyond Chad and, thus, will become a Voice for Chad and possibly an important platform for his career. Indeed, his itinerary has been developed on the crossroads between new ICT development, the context of oppression and poverty, and personal capacities and opportunities.

Croquemort has created his own international scene through the prizes he has won and the invitations he receives. He is always eager to participate in competitions. What has certainly helped here is the circle of family and friends in France, and the attitude of his father, who studied in the UK, speaks English and taught his children that the world is bigger than Chad. The context of Chad, the difficult living conditions, its ranking on the lowest end of poverty indexes, is also part of this itinerary. This may sound cynical, but it has certainly inspired the song texts and the deep emotions that one feels while listening to these texts, hence it is an important input for his success.

Returning to the idea of biography as method: in this chapter we have tried to show how the biography of a person gives insight into itineraries of success. It is clear that much depends on personal initiatives and not, per se, on a common development path. For Didier, there is an argument to be made that change follows vital conjunctures that are perceived and interpreted by the individual. For him, these were his expulsion from the university, of living in a family of learning, of being aware of the appearance of internet and, indeed, being able to appropriate this technology and use it to its fullest, and, finally, to be able to relate to the right persons who can assist in the development of his itinerary. The internationalization of Didier has been crucial to this itinerary. The prizes won, and his subsequent links to the Netherlands, are not simply coincidences, but well-taken decisions at a moment when opportunities arose. A vital conjunction is not always perceived as such by everyone. Those who are bold enough to recognize them and take the opportunity will be rewarded!

To conclude this paper, I cite part of an interview that I held with Croquemort in November 2014:

Mirjam: So, it is through IFT that you have been able to make a career?

Croquemort: No, what do you think, they 'discovered' me when I was already on the scene?

Mirjam: So what did push you after all to become the artist you are, entering gradually into the international scene?

Croquemort: I am 'glued' to my computer; I search for all that is possible; that is what makes me leave Chad. But it is certainly also thanks to Preston, who has pushed me to enter into Slam, he made me listen to Slam. He also developed that studio that allows us to produce. And he used the radio where he works to disseminate my music. *C'est Preston à qui je dois tout.* And of course there are other people, like Makris, who is a good technician. And my friend Z. helped me to find opportunities on the internet and proposed my first song to RFI. Of course, structures like IFT have been very helpful, and then there is now the project Voice4Thought: I was able to have a concert in Amsterdam, and this summer to work in a professional studio, etc. This is a very interesting frame for my work.[3]

But art is above all content! And that is what I find now here during my stay in the Netherlands; I have found my calm, my space for reflection!

'Je voudrais devenir star!'

Mirjam: And a last question; what about your experience at the University? Your removal/expulsion for 2 years?
Croquemort: Yes, ironically that has given me time to develop an international career.[4]

The context of Chad is a source of inspiration, but that same space for inspiration is difficult to find in Chad, simply because of the circumstances: these are the pitfalls of oppression.

Notes

1. See also www.croquemort.biz
2. Invitation to events in the Francophone context:

    - Media jeunesse et francophonie, Yaoundé Cameroun (2009)
    - À l'école d'été de la Tunisie (2010, première scène de Slam)
    - Forum mondial des emplois verts, Niamey (2012)
    - Forum mondiale de la langue française Québec, Canada (2012)
    - Mali, Festival de slam et humour (2015)
    - In 2014, 2015 and 2016: Invitation to the Netherlands and France (concerts, participation in debates, residence)

    Prizes:

    - Couleurs talent (RFI) 2011
    - Ndjam Vie (2011)
    - Forum mondial de la langue française (juillet 2012)
    - Forum des emplois verts (janvier 2012)
    - Cote d'Ivoire Dakar festas HH 2013)
    - Canada (2014)
    - Prix de novelles/littéraire. Lille (twice); Lyon, Toulouse

3. See.voice4thought.org
4. Omitted from our discussion:

    (Je suis collé à mon ordinateur; je fouille tous qui est possible: c'est ça qui a commencé de me faire sortir du Tchad; C'est bien aussi grâce a Preston; qui l'a poussé qui l'a fait écouter les titres slam; studio d'une radio ou il travaillait, A qui je dois tout.)

    Il y a eu Makris, cote technique Anderson; première album;

    Amis: Zyzou qui s'est occupé à suivre RFI, c'est lui qui a mis RFI au courant de la musique de croquemort.

CCF, qui a donné beaucoup de pousse (Patrick)

Voice 4 thought...j'arrive à avoir concert à Amsterdam, studio professionnelle; cela donne un cadre quand même; l'art c'est d'abord la matière; ma réflexion a changé, calme etc...ce qui manque au Tchad.

References

Akinyoade, A, De Bruijn, M., et al. (forthcoming 2017). Social media and political agency in Chad, outcome of a survey.

Alhassim, B. (2016). Pratique et perception du hip-hop dans le quartier du Chagoua, Chad, MA thesis en Antropologie.

Apitzsch, U., & Siouti, I. (2007). *Biographical analysis as an interdisciplinary research perspective in the field of migration studies.* Frankfurt am Main: Johann Wolfgang Goethe Universitat.

Banner, L.W. (2009). Biography as history. *The American Historical Review, 114* (3), 579–586.

Castells, M. (2009). *Communication power.* Oxford: Oxford University Press.

De Bruijn, M.E. (2008). The impossibility of civil organizations in post-war chad. In A. Bellagamba and G. Klute (Eds.), *Beside the state: Emergent powers in contemporary Africa* (pp. 89–105). Cologne: Rüdiger Köppe Publishers.

Debos, M. (2012). *Le métier des armes.* Paris: Karthala.

Heitz Tokpa, K.E. (2014). Trust and distrust in Rebel-Held Cote d'Ivoire, social life during violent conflict in the region of Man, Western Côte d'Ivoire (2002–2010). PhD dissertation, University of Basel.

Johnson-Hanks, J. (2002). On the limits of life stages in ethnography: Toward a theory of vital conjunctures. *American Anthropologist, 104*(3): 865–880.

Moore, S.F. (1973). Law and social change: The semi-autonomous social field as an appropriate subject of study. *Law & Society Review, 7*(4), 719–746.

Seli, D. (2014). *(Dé)connexions identitaires hadjeray: Les enjeux des technologies de la communication au tchad.* Leiden and Bamenda: ASC/Langaa.

Mirjam de Bruijn was appointed Professor of Contemporary History and Anthropology of Africa at Leiden University's Faculty of Arts as of June 15, 2007. She also works as a senior researcher at the African Studies Centre Leiden. Mirjam de Bruijn is an anthropologist whose work has a clearly interdisciplinary character. She has done fieldwork in Cameroon, Chad and Mali and an important theme throughout is how people manage risk (drought, war, etc.) in both rural and urban areas. Her programme 'Mobile Africa Revisited', which started in 2008, is a comparative study of the role of Information and Communication Technologies (ICT) and ICT's interrelationship with agency, marginality and mobility patterns in Central and West Africa. In 2012 she was awarded a research grant for four years for the project www.Connectin-in-times-of-duress.nl, in which she researchers the realstionship between conflict, connectivity and society. She developed a valorazation project www.voice4thought.org in which she develops alternative forms of publication and disemmination, combining artisticand academic work.

Didier Lalaye is a PhD student at Utrecht University. He is a medical doctor (graduated 2015) and artist (writer and musician). The Chadian-born artist goes by the name, Croquemort. Didier won several prizes, both for his essays and for his music/slam (urban poetry). He is director and coordinator of an e-medicine programme in southern Chad. He developed a method by using mobile telephony to reach out to villages where health provision is still very poor.

CHAPTER 8

Twitter and Participatory Citizenship: #FeesMustFall in South Africa

Tanja Bosch

Introduction

The Fees Must Fall (#FMF) movement was a national, student-led protest which began in South Africa during mid-October 2015, in a response to fee increases at South African universities. The protests began at the University of the Witwatersrand (Wits) and rapidly spread to other tertiary institutions around the country, including technical colleges. The protests should be considered against a broader background of declining government funding for higher education, together with widespread socio-economic inequalities and racial conflicts. Since the end of apartheid, community protests in South Africa have increased sharply. The country has experienced a range of protests, sometimes violent, related to the inadequate provision of services, most often water, housing and sanitation. Over the last decade community protests have increased in frequency, largely due to tensions resulting from high levels of economic inequality. High levels of unemployment,[1] limited access to housing, water and sanitation, electricity, and healthcare, together with corruption within municipal administrations, and growing crime, have

T. Bosch (✉)
Centre for Film and Media Studies, University of Cape Town, Cape Town, South Africa
e-mail: tanja.bosch@uct.ac.za

B. Mutsvairo (ed.), *Digital Activism in the Social Media Era*,
DOI 10.1007/978-3-319-40949-8_8

all been listed as reasons for the protests, often described a bottom-up 'rebellion of the poor' (Alexander 2010). Moreover, specific groups e.g. women, have remained disempowered, and excluded from formal participation mechanisms. South Africa lacks strong civil society structures that can represent the interests of the majority; thus civil society cannot be 'radical' because it is 'a terrain seen to include social movements, political parties and capital' (McEwan 2005, p. 975).

In an analysis of online coverage of the #FMF protests, research and monitoring organization Media Tenor found that the #FMF hashtag generated nearly 1.3 million tweets during the last two weeks of October; and that Twitter was the most used social media platform for the campaign.[2] By comparison, Facebook only generated 6,000 posts on the topic over the same time period.[3] The #FMF campaign took place several months after the Rhodes Must Fall (#RMF) campaign, which started at the University of Cape Town, and developed into a national and collective project of resistance to normative memory production (Bosch 2016). Also student-led, the #RMF campaign similarly used Twitter as a vehicle of communication, demonstrating how social media often affords youth an opportunity to participate in political discussions, as well as discussions of broader socio-political issues of relevance in contemporary South African society, reflecting a form of sub-activism (Bakardjieva 2010) and participatory citizenship. This chapter extends the research on #RMF and youth activism to explore how the #FMF protests played out on social networking site Twitter, in the context of protest in South Africa, as well as the global growth of so-called 'Twitter activism' and wide-scale online political participation.

This chapter recognizes the widespread scholarly critiques of techno-optimistic narratives, which hail the internet as the key to social protest, coining terms such as 'Twitter revolutions'. More sceptical approaches take into account deeply sedimented histories and politics of place in order to understand the dynamics of protest in concrete locales or the tendency for social movements to organize through decentralized, diffuse, and leaderless networks since at least the 1960s, if not long before (Juris 2012). We are also reminded that many protesters at the centre of so-called Twitter revolutions such as Tahrir Square in Egypt did not have internet access and were equally mobilized through face-to-face networks. Morozov (2011) has denounced what he refers to as 'slacktivism', which allows individuals to 'participate' in social activism at the click of a button; arguing that social networking sites like Twitter are more suited to entertainment than political organizing. Similarly, journalist and author

Malcolm Gladwell has argued that social media provide weak ties and are therefore unsuitable for revolutionary action.[4]

Despite these critiques, it remains that digital tools and platforms are being widely used in political campaigns and have become influential channels through which politics and political debate is mediated (Jungherr 2015). Moreover, as Gerbaudo (2012) has argued, 'the process of mobilization cannot be reduced to the material affordances of the technologies it adopts but also involves the construction of shared meanings, identities and narratives' (p. 9). Acknowledging potential limitations in drawing conclusions from digital trace data, Jungherr (2015) points out that access to this new data does not always mean that researchers know how to meaningfully interpret patterns. However, Jungherr (2015) presents a framework, drawn on in the present chapter, which interprets data traces collected on Twitter as a mediated reflection of political reality, albeit one 'skewed by the attention, interests, and intentions of politically vocal Twitter users' (p. viii). This chapter thus argues that despite the limitations of social media research and the fact that Twitter is not widely used by all citizens in South Africa (even though usage is growing); studying Twitter in the context of #FMF can shed light on youth protest politics.

Of a total population of 54.73 million, there are 26.84 million active internet users in South Africa, with a 20 % growth of social media usage between 2015 and 2016, and most accounts accessed via mobile.[5] Twitter has 7.4 million users.[6] Given that most Twitter (and social media) users tend to belong to the young adult demographic,[7] together with the fact that #FMF generated such a large number of tweets, studying this phenomenon reveals something about the online discourse around and online component of the protests, even if online discussions are dominated by the most vocal users.

Methodology

The methodology for this study comprised a content analysis of a dataset comprising over a million tweets collected at the height of the protests, in order to identify key actors and conversations. Tweets were collected using NodeXL. NodeXL is a free, open-source network analysis and visualization software package for Microsoft Excel 2007/2010/2013, intended for users with little or no programming experience to allow them to collect, analyse, and visualize a variety of networks. NodeXL can help researchers to visualize the structure of conversations about various topics.

Tweets were also collected via a software package created as part of the Media, Conflict and Democratisation project (MeCoDeM)).[8] Both sources of data allowed the researcher to retrieve a stream of all tweets matching the Fees Must Fall hashtag searchers through the Twitter API. As Bruns and Stieglitz (2013) argue, such datasets 'can be analysed subsequent to the event, issue, or topic they discuss, or even while it continues, to extract information about the shape of the conversation, identify the main participating users, examine major themes, highlight key links to external resources, and establish other, more context-specific facts about the exchange'. In addition to looking at broad patterns in terms of the tweets and the tweeters, an exploratory qualitative content analysis of selected tweets explored the purpose and nature of the online conversations via the hashtag #FeesMustFall.

> The dynamic nature of conversations within hashtag communities provides fascinating insights into the inner workings of such ad hoc issue publics: it enables researchers to trace the various roles played by individual participants (for example, as information sources, community leaders, commenters, conversationalists, or lurkers), and to study how the community reacts to new stimuli (such as breaking news and new contributors). Such observations also offer perspectives on the interconnection of the community with other communicative spaces beyond Twitter itself and on the relative importance of such spaces; in all, they point to the overall shape of the event. (Bruns and Burgess 2015, p. 23).

This is initial preliminary research, which is primarily descriptive, and which will be later complemented with a more expansive social network analysis to further explore connections and relationships. Further research might also triangulate the social media data with qualitative interviews with student protesters.

The campaign gained momentum rapidly and reached a peak on 23 October 2015 when protestors marched to the Union Buildings. The qualitative analysis focuses only on tweets from this day. The top 1,000 tweets of 23 October were exported to an excel spreadsheet and coded. Much scholarly work on Twitter uses hashtags to identify tweets, to highlight particular conversations and communicative exchanges. This study also explored the frequency of retweets in order to analyse extended conversations. The practice of retweeting means messages spread virally through networks of followers within minutes of the original tweet (Jeffares 2014).

This chapter thus attempts to map the nature of the Twitter discourse around the hashtag #FMF, providing a descriptive account of what was happening on Twitter at the height of the protests. The central question framing the study was: to what extent virals such as #FeesMustFall strengthen or undermine public discourse, and whether political reality is framed by such virally shared digital content. In this instance, the chapter argues that Twitter afforded students an opportunity to participate in politics and set mainstream news agendas. Youth are increasingly using social networking sites like Twitter to develop a new biography of citizenship which is characterized by more individualized forms of activism, deliberately setting their struggles outside the party political realm. While South African youth may not be participating in mainstream party politics, as evidenced by the decline in voting numbers in national elections, youth political participation on Twitter, an already familiar space, shows that they are politically active in different ways (Bosch 2016).

While South Africa's transition to democracy in the 1990s was not marked by violent revolution, rising social inequality has resulted in ongoing community protests, and the student protests can be seen within this context. Revolutionary student movements have always been a feature of transitional societies, and are appearing with increasing frequency in Western societies. This chapter attempts to contribute to an increased understanding of the role of the internet in fostering political participation and activism. Taking into account critiques of the internet by scholars such as Morozov (2009, 2011) and Dean (2005), Gladwell and others, the proposed chapter explores the collective experiences of social media within the context of #FeesMustFall. An examination of this specific localized protest could help researchers shed light on an important political moment in post-apartheid South Africa; and also helps researchers develop an understanding of (student) protest in an African context, particular with reference to the increased role played by new technologies, social media in particular, as tools for political mobilization. As Isin and Ruppert (2015) argue, the internet can bring citizen subjects into being through online performance and speech acts.

Findings and Discussion

Hashtag Politics

The complete dataset studied contains 123,497 tweets posted between 15 October 2015, when the protests began, until 29 November 2015. During this period a range of hashtags were widely used, with #FMF at the centre, allowing users to contribute to a national conversation around the topic, and contributing to the 'symbolic construction of a sense of togetherness' (Gerbaudo 2012, p. 9). While a number of additional hashtags emerged and were used simultaneously, most tweets contained the #FMF hashtag, demonstrating the power of the hashtag in constituting and linking a particular public, 'where publics are understood as being formed, re-formed and coordinated via dynamic networks of communication and social connectivity organized primarily around issues or events rather than pre-existing social groups' (Bruns and Burgess 2015). The term hashtag politics (see Davis 2013; Jeffares 2014) has been used to describe the increased role of Twitter as a political source, particularly its influence in placing issues on the agenda for national debate and deliberation. Using the hashtags meant that users could address a specific imagined community of users who were following the topic.

When Twitter users follow or post tweets using hashtags it makes it possible for them to communicate with a broader community of interest around the hashtag topic without needing to establish a mutual follower/followed relationship with any of the other participants (Bruns and Burgess 2015). During the height of the protests, the most frequently used hashtag was #feesmustfall, followed by #nationalshutdown. Twitter users often used multiple hashtags in order to reach various overlapping constituencies (Bruns and Burgess 2015). Other related hashtags were used to indicate the localized nature of the protests as they spread to various tertiary campuses. These included #uctfeesmustfall (University of Cape Town), #stelliesfeesmustfall (Stellenbosch University), #uwcshutdown (University of the Western Cape); as well as some variants such as #witsfeesmustfall (University of the Witwatersrand), #ujshutdown (University of Johannesburg), and the more straightforward #freeeducationforall and #freeeducation.

The total number of tweets tagged with the hashtag #feesmustfall was 123,497. Following only the #feesmustfall hashtag, 52,024 original tweets were posted at the height of the protests, on 23 October 2015. However, counting retweets in addition to original tweets, 199,953 tweets were posted on 23 October 2015. The large number of tweets on this particular day can probably be attributed to the fact that on 23 October thousands of students marched to the Union Buildings in Pretoria where student leaders met with President Zuma. Following the meeting, the President announced that there would be a 0 % fee increase for 2016.

In this particular case study, the hashtag played a central role in the national political discussion. 'Fees Must Fall' was a phrase widely referred to by the general public, and also widely used by the mainstream print and television news in their coverage of the protests. Later the 'must fall' component of the hashtag was carried over to other slogans, including #BladeMustFall (reference to Blade Nzimande the Minister of Higher Education) and later, #ZumaMustFall, the public citizen driven campaign calling for the resignation of President Jacob Zuma. The hashtag thus clearly both organizes but also amplifies attention from both citizens and the media. Small (2011) has argued that the primary function of political hashtags is usually simply informing versus political dialogue and reporting.

Davis (2013) has argued that Twitter's intertexuality contains the potential for igniting widespread political activism by encouraging voices from all sectors of society to be heard. Intertexuality refers to the notion that all utterances are dialogic and exist within a complex web of interconnected meanings and messages, whilst acknowledging the polyphony of discursive voices in which no single voice can be objectively distinguished from others (Davis 2013). As such, 'Twitter embodies an intertextual exchange of messages and opinions by which each tweet is connected with another, whether written in response to an event or another's post. None exists in isolation, unlike Facebook status updates, because each can be categorized and aggregated through its evaluative and ideational language' (Davis 2013, p. 18). The #FMF Twitter activity must thus be viewed as part of a larger social media ecosystem which includes mainstream news coverage, posts on personal communication and private WhatsApp groups, face-to-face meetings, discussions and so on. Twitter can be viewed as a complementary tool, one of many, in the orchestration of the protests, as discussed further below. Most tweets were posted from mobile platforms, demonstrating the importance of mobile telephony and the mobile internet in fostering online political participation. It should also be noted that the large majority of tweets posted, and the ensuing discussions, were in English. This excludes non-English speakers in a country where there are 11 official languages, and first-language English speakers only number 4.9 million (out of 50.9 million) (Census 2011). However, it should also be noted that the mainstream media is also predominantly in English, with few vernacular language mainstream newspapers; thus one might argue that studying Twitter as a site of political discussion is no different to studying mainstream mass media, and that in fact it might be even more inclusive, given youth participation in social media.

Twitter as a 'Choreography of Assembly' for #FMF

During the height of the #FMF campaign, Twitter was used both as an organizing tool by students, and also as a space for national debate around related issues. On the one hand, students used it to mobilize others and to coordinate meetings, marches, sit-ins and other face-to-face meetings and gatherings. On the other hand, it was used to disseminate information, share stories about students who had been financially excluded from tertiary studies, and raise awareness about the issue in order to frame the protests in a positive light by providing personal narratives to justify the political activity. The new social media tools such as Twitter thus enable new forms of group formation, which result in rapid communication together with an increased speed in group actions (Shirky 2008). Students could use Twitter to quickly mobilize large groups of supporters for mass meetings and marches, as well as to gain media coverage, and raise public awareness.

At the University of Cape Town for example, Twitter was used to mobilize students to occupy Bremner Building, the administrative block of the university. Similarly, Wits University students occupied Senate House and the fees office in January 2016, to protest registration fees. Gerbaudo (2012) has argued that contemporary popular movements are focused on the idea of unity and the adoption of practices of 'centring', with the most common manifestation being 'the tactic of the mass sit-in, the physical occupation of public space which often evolves into a semi-permanent protest camp' (p. 11). In this instance, Twitter played a central role in mobilizing protesters to 'occupy' university spaces and in broadcasting information about the occupation. One of the main purposes of tweets thus appeared to be coordinating face-to-face meetings, protests, sit-ins and other gatherings. Gerbaudo (2012) argues that 'the crucial element in understanding the role of social media in contemporary social movements is their interaction with and mediation of emerging forms of public gatherings and in particular the mass sit-ins which have become the hallmark of contemporary popular movements' (p. 5). This 'choreography of assembly' was largely coordinated via a series of hashtags, with #FMF often at the centre. Moreover, during the height of the campaign, during the student leader meetings with government officials, information was spread via Twitter. Similarly, student protesters used Twitter to inform other users about incidences of police brutality; while other student users posted information about locations of barricades and whether or not campuses were accessible or whether they were being closed off by protesters.

During the Fees Must Fall protests, Twitter also played a key role in conveying information to dispersed groups and individuals. Students and other individuals would often send out tweets asking others to provide information about activities taking place on specific days, and others would respond with specific information about meeting times and venues. This reflects the role of Twitter, in this instance, as a 'choreography of assembly', 'directing people towards specific protest events, in providing participants with suggestions and instructions about how to act, and in the construction of an emotional narration to sustain their coming together in a public space' (Gerbaudo 2012, p. 12). The overwhelming narrative was one of support for the protests and the actions of protestors, with those individuals tweeting complaints about the disruptive or violent nature of the activities quickly shut down by others. Twitter was also often used by individuals simply to express solidarity with the protests, sometimes by individual posts, and other times simply by re-tweeting existing posts.

Turner's (1978) notion of social drama is also useful here, with the term referring to a political process (in this case #FMF) that originates within a social group but can spread across a wider intergroup field unless appropriate 'redressive action' is taken. In this instance, the campaign had begun to garner support from academics, who also spoke up and marched in support of students across various campuses; as well as parents—with some social commentators speculating that the #FMF protests could result in more widespread national political activism against government policies beyond tertiary fees. Social dramas undergo four stages: (1). Breach, (2). Crisis, (3). Redressive action and (4). Either reintegration or schism. To some extent the redressive action comprised the implementation of a zero percent fee increase; but the social drama is ongoing as student protests flared up again in early 2016. Twitter might thus be considered a liminal space (drawing on Turner 1978), as an unstructured, temporary state, which allows people from different sectors of society to come together and participate in temporary relationships, where traditional social hierarchies can be temporarily dismantled.

#FMF as a Viral Campaign

Moreover, the growth of and widespread use of the hashtag #FMF can be described as a viral campaign, as the term is used by Postill (2012, 2013), to describe the rise of a viral culture marked by the acceleration of news cycles. The main features of a viral campaign include tweets with catchy slogans, together with 'explosive growth, social drama liminality, real-time participation, multiple online and face-to-face arenas and intense but ephemeral news media coverage' (179). This is one theoretical frame through which the Twitter engagements might be analysed. Another useful frame comes from Victor Turner (1978) who coined the term social drama to refer to 'a political process that originates within a social group but can spread across a wider intergroup field unless appropriate 'redressive action' is taken'. Social dramas undergo four stages: (1) breach; (2) crisis; (3) redressive action; and (4) either reintegration or schism. At its height, the #FMF campaign could be considered an example of ongoing social drama, much of it taking place online via social media. Each day, students and citizens would establish via Twitter what activities were planned for that particular day; and whether university campuses could be accessed or whether they were closed due to protest action. The discussion around examinations at the University of Cape Town for example, and whether or not they would be postponed (they eventually were postponed) was another aspect of the drama that played out on Twitter; with individuals discussing and weighing the options and then sharing the final news. Postill (2013) suggests that 'social media are viral media. That is, they are designed and actively used to spread digital contents epidemically, from peer to peer, through routinized activities such as 'liking' a Facebook photograph, retweeting a political slogan, or emailing a YouTube hyperlink to friends' (p. 6). This chapter considers the #FMF campaign as a viral campaign, defined by Postill as one which 'achieves popularity by spreading from person to person, especially by digital means' (p. 7).

The use of the hashtag by mainstream news media is discussed further below. The protests were covered by intense but ephemeral news media coverage, which died down soon after the announcement of a 0 % fee increase; despite the fact that protests continued on many tertiary campuses for other aspects of the campaign e.g. the call to end outsourcing of workers. However, it should also be noted that according to the Media Tenor research report, more than half of the mainstream media coverage was negative.

The top three most tweeted posts during the 15–29 October time range, incorporating all related hashtags were as follows, with the top tweet retweeted over 26,000 times:

1. White students knew police wouldn't hurt them so they made a human shield for black protesters. #uctshutdown (posted by @douniatee, 23 October 2015, 10.42am). 26, 843 tweets, 27, 319 likes.

This tweet was accompanied by a photograph showing white students forming a human shield, to 'protect' fellow black student protests https://twitter.com/douniatee/status/657613021049696256

2. 'Education is the most powerful weapon we can use to change the world.' #FeesMustFall (posted by @Caspar_Lee, 19 October 2015, 5.46am), 4299 retweets, 9, 391 likes. https://twitter.com/Caspar_Lee/status/656089044372365312
3. It's so hard for some to understand #FeesMustFall but this article from @khayadlanga is really powerful (posted by @Trevornoah, 22 October 2015, 9.16 am), 3,926 retweets, 2455 likes. This tweet was accompanied by a link to an opinion piece by columnist Khaya Dlanga, which ends with 'Because blacks do not have these privileges, expensive university fees shut blacks out—the end result, no transformation in the workplace—no economic freedom. We end up being second-class citizens in our own country. Let the kids liberate us from our own blindness, Viva youth of 2015 viva!'.[9]https://twitter.com/Trevornoah/status/657229097551175682

It is interesting to note that the top tweets are by users who are popular celebrities and not political figures, political commentators, or journalists. Dounia is a musician, Caspar Lee is a comedian and YouTube vlogger, and Trevor Noah is a comedian. Interestingly, a popular poll recently showed Trevor Noah to be the 'most admired' South African personality. This may be indicative of a trend for South Africans to have less faith in mainstream party politicians (or even mainstream media organizations), and instead embracing popular culture and the 'cult of celebrity'.

However, if we look at the top retweeted tweeters, these individuals still feature, but mainstream news media are also prevalent here, raising questions about the role of media in the Twitter debates on #FMF. The most retweeted user was Eye Witness News, with the E-News channel falling in 6th position, and the Daily Vox and News24 at 9th and 10th. The tweets posted by news media were 'on the ground' tweets posted by journalists covering and live-tweeting the events. If we look at the users who received the most replies, then E-News channel still features as number 1, though this is followed by the official ANC Twitter account. News media again feature widely here with radio journalist Redi Thlabi at number 3, followed by Eye Witness News at number 4, News24, PowerFM, PowerFM news, and ANN news channel at numbers 7–10 respectively. The responses to MyANC were all hostile, with users responding critically to ANC tweets purporting to support the student protests as a manifestation of freedom within a democracy. Conversely, the user responses to news organizations were usually complimentary, with users expressing enthusiasm at protest developments, or support for the protest activities being reported.

FMF, Twitter and Citizenship

The emergence of #FMF as a viral campaign on Twitter raises its potential as an emergent space of radical citizenship in response to citizen (youth) exclusion from formal spaces of political participation. The emergence of social media platforms and related practices challenges traditional understandings of citizenship. As McEwan (2005) has argued, radical spaces emerge organically out of common interests and concerns as a result of popular mobilization or individuals joining together in common aims. The #FMF engagements on Twitter reveals that social media can thus emerge as one such site of radical possibility as it was constituted by individuals themselves, and is also transient, meaning 'durability is dependent on people wanting to participate in them' (McEwan 2005, p. 980).

Considering #FMF within a broader South African context, it is one of many struggles which is

> becoming progressively more organized, with strong local, national, and international networks forming between communities, labour, women's, youth, environmentalist, and other social movements. These are potentially radical and enabling spaces because the people themselves have chosen to be part of them and are responsible for their existence. Transient and organic citizenship spaces might also be spaces of resistance, bringing together diverse groups of people around particular issues and facilitating more radical kinds of participation (McEwan 2005, p. 980).

In the case of #FMF, this chapter argues for Twitter as a vehicle which creates a space for people to argue different positions, 'thus generating political freedom and meaningful realisation of citizenship' (McEwan 2005, p. 980). Despite concerns around the digital divide, Twitter is beginning to emerge in Africa as a virtual space for people to resist, challenge existing conditions, and propose alternatives.

Conclusion

Discourses of citizenship in South Africa have focused on deepening the democratic debate through empowerment, which involves 'moving out of constrained places and isolated spaces, widening the scope for action and multiplying potential sites for engagement' (Cornwall 2002, p 2). While participation in mainstream spaces can be limited due to differing social and economic contexts, this chapter has attempted to show that the Twitter interaction around the #FMF student protests reveal social media as a new site for engagement. At the same time the 'issue public' (Bruns and Burgess 2015, p. 22) which formed on Twitter in the case of #FMF, existed in parallel to related issue publics existing in other public spheres such as Facebook, or mainstream news media. For youth who are traditionally disengaged from traditional party politics, social networking sites, Twitter in the case of #FMF, offers a vehicle for the participation in digital activism. This case study raises the possibility for Twitter to result in the formation of a 'digital citizen' (Isin and Ruppert, 2015). The preliminary trace data found on Twitter reflects a mediated notion of South African political reality, even if it only reflects the voices of the most vocal. As McEwan (2005) has argued, 'Paradoxically, alternative citizenship spaces are rarely inclusive and often rely on oppositional processes of identity formation for the creation of a common purpose' (p. 980).

Notes

1. http://businesstech.co.za/news/finance/122985/massive-jump-in-south-african-unemployment-rate/
2. https://www.scribd.com/doc/287690577/Media-Tenor-Feesmustfall-Analysis
3. http://www.financialmail.co.za/mediaadvertising/2015/11/05/social-media-feesmustfall-tweets-rule
4. http://www.newyorker.com/magazine/2010/10/04/small-change-malcolm-gladwell
5. http://www.htxt.co.za/2016/04/29/the-stuff-south-africa-26-8-mil-internet-users-spend-most-their-time-doing-online/
6. http://www.worldwideworx.com/socialsa2016/
7. http://www.pewinternet.org/2015/08/19/the-demographics-of-social-media-users/
8. http://www.mecodem.eu/
9. http://www.news24.com/Columnists/Khaya-Dlanga/Why-I-too-am-angry-along-with-the-young-ones-20151021

References

Alexander, P. (2010). Rebellion of the poor: South Africa's service delivery protests–a preliminary analysis. *Review of African Political Economy*, *37*(123), 25–40.

Bakardjieva, M. (2010). The internet and subactivism: Cultivating young citizenship in everyday life. In T. Olsson and P. Dahlgrem Ed., *Young people, ICTs and democracy*. Sweden: Nordicom.

Bosch, T. (2016). Twitter activism and youth in South Africa: The case of #RhodesMustFall. *Information, Communication and Society*, *14*(6), 757–769.

Bruns, A., & Burgess, J. (2015). Hashtags from ad hoc to calculated publics. In N. Rambukkana (Ed.), *Hashtag publics: The power and politics of discursive networks*. New York: Peter Lang. 13–28.

Bruns, A., & Stieglitz, S. (2013). Towards more systematic *Twitter* analysis: Metrics for tweeting activities. *International Journal of Social Research Methodology*, *16*(2), 91–108.

Census (2011). Available at http://www.statssa.gov.za/census/census_2011/census_products/Census_2011_Census_in_brief.pdf. Retrieved 12 May 2016.

Cornwall, A. (2002). Making spaces, changing places: Situating participation in development. ISD Working Paper 170, IDS: University of Sussex.

Davis, B. (2013). Hashtag politics: The polyphonic revolution of# Twitter. *Pepperdine Journal of Communication Research*, *1*(1), 4.

Dean, J. (2005). Communicative capitalism: Circulation and the foreclosure of politics. *Cultural Politics*, *1*(1), 51–74.

Gerbaudo, P. (2012). *Tweets and the streets: Social media and contemporary activism*. New York: Pluto Press.

Isin, E., & Ruppert, E. (2015). *Being digital citizens*. London: Rowman & Littlefield International.

Jeffares, S. (2014). *Interpreting Hashtag politics: Policy ideas in an era of social media*. Hampshire, UK: Palgrave Macmillan.

Jungherr, A. (2015). *Analysing political communication with digital trace data: The role of Twitter messages in Social Science Research*. Switzerland: Springer International Publishing.

Juris J. (2012). Reflections on #Occupy everywhere: Social media, public space, and emerging logics of aggregation. *American Ethnologist*, *39*(2), 259–279.

McEwan, C. (2005). New Spaces of Citizenship? Rethinking gendered participation and empowerment in South Africa. *Political Geography*, *24*, 969–991.

Morozov, E. (2009). The Brave New World of Slacktivism. *Foreign Policy* (blog), 19 May http://neteffect.foreignpolicy.com/posts/2009/05/19/the_brave_new_world_of_slacktivism

Morozov, E. (2011). *The net delusion: The dark side of internet freedom*. New York: Public Affairs.

Postill, J. (2012). Digital politics and political engagement. In H. A. Horst and D. Miller (Ed.), *Digital anthropology*. London/New York: Berg.

Postill, J. (2013). Democracy in an age of viral reality: A media epidemiography of Spain's indignados movement. *Ethnography*, 1–9. http://eth.sagepub.com/content/early/2013/10/08/1466138113502513.abstract.

Shirky, C. (2008). *Here comes everybody: The power of organizing without organizations*. New York: Penguin Press.

Small, T. A. (2011). What the hashtag? A content analysis of Canadian politics on Twitter. *Information, Communication & Society*, *14*(6), 872–895.

Turner, V. (1978). *The ritual process: Structure and anti-structure*. Chicago, IL: Aldine Publishing

Tanja Bosch is a senior lecturer and researcher in the Centre for Film and Media Studies at the University of Cape Town, South Africa. She completed her MA in International Affairs while a Fulbright Scholar at Ohio University, where she also graduated with a PhD in Mass Communication. Tanja teaches broadcast journalism, media theory and qualitative research methods. Her areas of research and publication include talk radio, community media, and youth use of mobile media and online social networks.

CHAPTER 9

Scrutinizing Hashtag Activism in the #MustFall Protests in South Africa in 2015

What role did media play in hashtag activism during the #RhodesMustFall and #FeesMustFall protests in South Africa in 2015?

Glenda Daniels

Introduction

The hashtag, signified with the symbol #, is used on the social media platform Twitter[1] for publics to engage on a particular topic, spread news or opinion, stir critical debates which have sometimes led to protests and radical activism—and in some cases the overthrow of governments. This article examines the use of the hashtag during two of the biggest protests in post-apartheid South Africa: #RhodesMustFall and #FeesMustFall. It further interrogates to what extent journalists from traditional media were engaged in this activism in the protests at South African universities in 2015.

G. Daniels (✉)
University of the Witwatersrand, Johannesburg, South Africa
e-mail: Glenda.Daniels@wits.ac.za

B. Mutsvairo (ed.), *Digital Activism in the Social Media Era*,
DOI 10.1007/978-3-319-40949-8_9

Twenty-one years after democracy, two major campaigns—or mini-revolutions—shook the complacent but dissatisfied political landscape in South Africa. The first was the #RhodesMustFall campaign at the beginning of 2015 at the University of Cape Town (UCT), which brought down the statue of Cecil John Rhodes, a major and larger-than-life symbol of colonialism and racism in South Africa; the second was the #FeesMustFall protest at the end of 2015 which achieved the reduction of fee increases at South African universities from 10 % to 0 %.

The first protest, which began at UCT in Cape Town in February 2015, organically led to the creation of the hashtag #RhodesMustFall which in turn fuelled a mini-revolution, forcing the hand of the university administration to action: to raise the statue from its plinth, let it teeter dramatically in mid-air, before lowering it on to a truck to be escorted to a place of safety. The action was symbolic and was not just about the statue: the statue was a symbol of a lack of transformation, white superiority (Ngcaweni 2015) and colonial thinking, patriarchy, sexism and racism.[2] Social media, particularly Twitter, assisted the call to action through the hashtag. The questions of how, to what extent, and what role traditional media played, will be the focus of this research and analysis.

On 9 March 2015, a student activist, Chumani Maxwele staged a political protest against the lack of racial transformation at UCT, using human excrement. It was meant to attract attention, cause offence and show the humiliation and degradation of the apartheid past, but also the continued hurts of racism, a lack of transformation, and new hashtag #Whiteprivilege, 21 years after the fall of the apartheid regime.

Thousands of students joined the #RhodesMustFall protest which spread nationwide, so that every university was out on boycott of classes, coining another hashtag, #Nationalshutdown, leading to the complete shutdown of universities, in October 2015.

In tandem, activism at the University of Stellenbosch in the Cape, where black students protested against racism and being taught in Afrikaans, led to the hashtag #OpenStellenbosch where a video titled 'Luister' (Afrikaans for Listen) about black students' experiences went viral nationally and spread around the world.

The next major protest, also assisted by the hashtag in social media, began at the University of the Witwatersrand in Johannesburg in September 2015. This was ignited when the university announced a 10 % increase in fees for the year 2016, and the hashtag #FeesMustFall was organically formed. The wave of protests beyond the immediate issue of fees linked this economic struggle of the 10 % fee increase to other simmering issues such as #Whiteprivilege, calls for the decolonization of the curriculum, transformation of the university's race and gender composition and rage against the devaluing and exclusion of black voice and culture. The protests which deployed the hashtag #FeesMustFall culminated in the storming of both Parliament in Cape Town and the Union buildings (the seat of government) in Pretoria, and police and student violence. And, like the success of the statue of Rhodes falling, fees fell from their own plinth too, to a 0 % increase.

This article examines how students and civil society at large used the Twitter hashtag in these mini-revolutions, and then scrutinizes the role of traditional media, or journalists, in these social media activism highlights of the South African political calendar. The protests created robust agonistic public spaces (to be discussed in the theoretical framework) as in diverse political voices all fighting just to be heard in some instances, and in other, for ideological hegemonic control. Critics of mainstream media argue through political economy philosophy that mainstream media play a role in the maintenance and production of hegemony. This chapter, through an interrogation of the two major bottom-up protests organically arising from the frustrations of poor black students, examines whether this hegemony was being unsettled through social media. The schisms, divisions, tendencies and factions ranged from narrow African nationalism,[3] to broad Pan Africanism, to Steve Biko's black consciousness philosophy to an anti-patriarchal force of black feminists.[4] These were loud vibrantly clashing agonistic spaces with cross-cutting ideologies and political party affiliations, which by and large crowded out the non-racial rainbow nation of the Nelson Mandela philosophy of the nineties in South Africa.

While this research does not deploy discourse analysis as part of its main methodology, the section below serves to illuminate further the substance or content of the hashtag activism, while giving 'voice' to the activists, as well as illustrating the ideologically agonistic spaces. To contextualize the protest, in terms of South Africa's post-apartheid era, the following quote serves well:

> 'The protests by students at universities highlighted the failure of the older generation to complete the revolution in a post-apartheid South Africa', according to Simpiwe Sesanti, associate professor of journalism, media and philosophy at the Nelson Mandela Metropolitan University in Port Elizabeth. (*City Press* 2015b)

The Students' Discourse

Whereas ideally a section on discourse should find its place in the data section of research, it is used here straight after the introduction, to give contextual flavour to the activism. The year of hashtag activism at universities was sparked by #RhodesMustFall which was then linked to organic, intersectional and overlapping struggles at other campuses nationwide also using hashtags; for example, #OpenStellenbosch (a fight primarily against the language policy, namely, Afrikaans, as well as racial inequality at the institution; *The Times* 2015a, b), #TransformWits (mainly about decolonizing curricula and increasing the numbers of black women professors, among other demands; *Mail & Guardian* 2015), and the #BlackStudentsMovement at Rhodes University—all these hashtag activisms appear to have led to the nationwide lead to #FeesMustFall protest at the end of 2015 which forced a national shutdown of universities and postponement of end of year examinations. Some of the comments below highlight in more detail the issues and the ideological moods of the activists.

> I call this the year of student activism. Students and South Africa are looking at where we should be—the South Africa we should have got post-1994—the promises we have been given and we are realising it is not happening (Sikhululekile Duma, a member of #Open Stellenbosch; *City Press* 2015c).

Duma's comment articulates the frustrations of the students about the promises of a new South Africa, which did not happen. Overlaps were also in evidence, as we see from UCT student, Alex Hotz when she explained her context at her university:

> Things have been simmering for a long time. Racism has been experienced constantly through academic and financial exclusion. The idea of having to assimilate to belong has also been a long-standing issue (*City Press* 2015a).

The head of the Free State University, Vice Chancellor Professor Jonathan Jansen, explained this trajectory as 'anger that simmered below the epidermis of the superficial politeness of English culture which boiled over with the #RhodesMustFall movement' (*The Times* 2015c).

#TransformWits activist, and also a member of the radical and populist party, the Economic Freedom Fighters (EFF), Vuyani Pambo, voiced his dissatisfaction thus:

> Management has been pretending to be listening to our calls and has been dragging its feet... the curriculum we get from these institutions is alienating. Black students cannot find themselves in the literature that they read... we need more black lecturers, especially female lecturers, an Afrocentric curriculum and more student activism (*City Press* 2015d).

The student activism, which had echoes of the Soweto June 16, 1976 uprising (*The Times* 2015c), spread to Oxford University in the United Kingdom, which included a debate on whether the statue of Rhodes should fall there as well. In the end, it was decided that the Rhodes statue would not fall at Oxford, because of the argument that students should be encouraged to think critically, and that censorship about that which causes offence should be condemned (*The Times* 2016).

Theorizing Digital, Hashtag Activism Trends and Radical Democracy

While #RhodesMustFall sparked the #MustFall hashtag trend and went on to spread to Oxford in the UK, in South Africa, at the end of 2015 social media analysts attempted to make sense of the trends. According to the annual Twitter review in 2015, the top trending hashtags for the year were #FeesMustFall and #NationalShutDown (Dirk and Petersen 2015). Twitter spokesperson, Alexandra Valasek, observed that both these hashtags created massive public debate. This has direct echoes of the robust agnostic spaces of a radical democracy in action. In addition, #RhodesMustFall social media manager, Mohammed Abdulla, commented: 'The media hype sparked by UCT student activist Chumani Maxwele's poo-flinging onto the statue of Cecil John Rhodes at the university made us realise we needed to use social media platforms to write our own narrative' (Dirk and Petersen 2015). Clearly, these comments, which are the background to the theorizing, illustrate that social media was more than just about sharing views and opinions. These comments are instructive, and this article then dissects the kind of agonistic spaces that were created by the protests. It is at this point then that it is apposite to turn to the theorizing of digital activism blending with radical democracy before an explication of the method, data findings and concluding reflections for this chapter.

Using radical democracy as a theoretical framework for this research, how do we then link that framework and theorize digital activism? In fact, it is not a tangential or tenuous link but a strong one. One of the key concepts in radical democracy is the notion of agonistic spaces. Agonistic spaces exist where legitimate adversaries fight, but within the symbolic space of democracy, according to radical democratic theorist Chantal Mouffe (2005). In this symbolic space, we must accept conflict, difference, pluralism and division as part of politics and society. We should consider those who don't agree as 'legitimate adversaries', rather than as enemies. In the case of #RhodesMustFall and #FeesMustFall, these legitimate adversaries would be university administrations often positioned by students as binary oppositions or enemies, whereas in fact they exist within the broad democratic space and are legitimate adversaries. Then, the antagonists themselves—for example, the EFF, the Progressive Youth Alliance (aligned to the ANC) and the new growing young black feminist movement (for instance #ForBlackGirlsOnly)—jostle for space, sometimes regarding each other as enemies and sometimes recognizing each other as legitimate adversaries in a democracy.

Mouffe developed her agonistic radical democratic model that focused on the transformation of political enemies into adversaries within a necessarily conflictual democratic framework (Mouffe 2005; Daniels 2012). In this regard, she has managed to form a valued counterbalance to the dominance of consensus-centred (and neo-liberal—there is no alternative) approaches towards the political. 'She critiqued these approaches for ignoring the presence of conflict as a structuring societal force and for not recognizing its crucial role in the shaping of the much-esteemed societal consensuses. It is exactly this focus on conflict that has been inspirational for many researchers working within the field of media, journalism and democracy' wrote Carpentier and Cammaerts (2006), in an interview with her. The interview focused on the threats and problems that the Western democratic institutions (including the media) are facing in the present-day conjuncture.

> Obviously, in a democratic society, you cannot have people treating each other as enemies... My counter-argument would be that not allowing conflict ultimately leads to an authoritarian order. You also have the 'good' democrats who say that, if we give way to the idea of conflict and the

> ineradicability of conflict, and then we have to abandon the very idea that we can have democracy. In contrast, I would argue that conflict is ineradicable, but there are different ways in which conflict can express itself.
>
> Democracy then becomes the legitimisation of conflict. Its aim is to enable forms of expressing conflict that are not going to destroy the political association. You do not need to negate conflict in order to imagine a democratic society. The question then becomes: how are we going to deal with conflict and what kinds of conflicts you allow for? When a society does not allow this agonistic form of conflict to express itself, you see the emergence of antagonistic forms of conflict. (Carpentier and Cammaerts 2006)

The importance of this elucidation is that it can be applied directly to the South African agonistic (friendly enemies allowing each space in a democracy) spaces to develop; for instance, the ANC and the EFF talking on the same platforms). However, in a slight departure from the classic radical democracy model in operation, both on the public physical platforms and on the social media platforms of Twitter and Facebook, it was not clear whether the space was just noisy and robust and acknowledging of legitimate difference or whether real enemies were developing in a polarized society of white and black and of the haves and the have-nots. Perhaps that is tangent not for this particular research, but it is worth noting that it is an area for further theoretical investigation. At this stage, it is worth turning to theorizing digital activism and then making the link with radical democracy before an analysis of the 2015 data—traditional media and activism and student activism and hashtag.

New Media, Digital Media and Hopes for Greater Participation and a Deepening Expansive Democracy

According to many theorists (Moyo 2009; Stassen 2010; Van Noort and Verweij 2013)' new and digital media, including social media, is enabling for citizen participation in a democracy, although others (Manji 2008; Sandoval and Fuch 2010) have argued that economic and social differences are amplified through social media. Some have also argued that the digital divide in Africa is growing (e.g., Van Dijk, 2006), while others have provided evidence that the gap is closing. The important point is, as Muneri (2016) has appositely pointed out, is that an 'understanding and theorisation of citizen journalism[5] should be connected to wider issues of broadening democratic communicative space and participation'.

This article must bear this background point in mind as well as the radical democracy model, as it homes in on two major protests which used hashtag activism and looks at who participated—media and non-media—and how they participated.

This article does not intend to be deterministic and definitive about either optimistic or pessimistic view, but by and large will suggest that new media is becoming a more inclusive and expansive space and is contributing to a strengthened public sphere, given the evidence of hashtag activism in the protests under scrutiny in this research—and indeed what appears to be an increase in the hashtag use from #RhodesMustFall (beginning of 2015) to #FeesMustFall (end of 2015). This took place through the radical democracy's leitmotif of the inclusion of more voices contributing towards more diversity (therefore the radical democracy model of robust fights and contentions in agonistic spaces) in tandem with the arguments by Dahlgren (2005), McNair (2006) and Moyo (2014). The argument here is that the internet—and in the case of this particular research, social media, specifically Twitter—is contributing towards more participation by citizenry towards a deeper democracy, even though there are issues of access and economic inequality vis-à-vis the digital divide. The public sphere concept of Habermas has to be strengthened but this time with greater inclusion of diverse voice; in other words, beyond Habermas's public sphere from white, male, elite to black feminist women who were beginning to emerge as powerful voices as the #RhodesMustFall, #FeesMustFall, #OpenStellenbosch movements. The mini-revolutions have been compared to the Arab Springs in 2010 and 2011 of Tunisia and Egypt when members of the public took to their smart phones and quickly organized marches and protests through Twitter, Facebook (Bohler-Muller and Van Der Merwe, 2011). The impact of some of these revolutions has been significant: for instance the fleeing of the Tunisian present Ben Ali to Saudi Arabia in January 2011 and the fall of Egyptian president Hosni Mubarak in February 2011.

In the South African context of the major protests which deployed the hashtag, it was not a complete radical democracy in action. Bearing in mind Derrida's caution, that democracy is never fully realized, it is always becoming (Derrida 2004), this research turns to examine the data of hashtag activism in the #MustFall protests vis-à-vis traditional media use of the hashtag, and everyone else's. Indeed, while there were muted calls for #ZumaMustFall, this did not accelerate into a full-on revolution by 2016. So far, the article has highlighted what the issues were in the #RhodesMustFall and #FeesMustFall protests. It then theorized digital activism, outlining that there were two main views—one highlighting the positives of technology and the other saying that it does not go that far due to the digital divide. This article then took a turn in the middle to say even given that there is the digital divide, hashtag activism made a huge impact during the two mini-revolutions in SA in 2015. It now moves on to explicating data which shows the citizen participation (including student activism) compared to media journalist activism, before reaching some reflecting conclusions. However, this chapter turns to the method first.

Methodology

The methodological approach here is a combination of an empirical one, through content analysis of Twitter feeds as developed for Wits Journalism's State of the Newsroom research project, 2013–2014 (Daniels 2014), combined with a qualitative theoretical conceptual analysis and some discourse analysis. This multi-methodological approach worked well to tease out the different dimensions of the research question. The journalists/editors/media personality Twitter accounts were purposively selected (also known as selective sampling) on the basis of having Twitter accounts and high social media activity. The data was collected via the Twitter Application Programming Interface (API) (Falcke 2014), which provided information such as content of the tweet (the actual 140 character message), the favourites, and number of tweets, retweets, and hyperlinks.

The Twitter Application system captured tweets for the top (highly active) 2,500 South African Twitter accounts on a daily basis, and based on the name of the account and other metadata, the accounts were classified into media-based accounts and non-media-based accounts. The former included, amongst others, media personalities, journalists, media houses and radio stations. A total of 322,124 tweets were captured between 12 March 2015 and 16 April 2015, resulting in 1,026 tweets emanating from media-based accounts tweeting specifically about #RhodesMustFall, and 4,414 from other members of the public accounts (e.g., students and civil society in general) tweeting about #RhodesMustFall.

For #FeesMustFall, a total of 1,490,377 tweets were captured between 14 and 29 October 2015, with 14,867 belonging to media-based accounts tweeting specifically about #FeesMustFall, and 86,837 belonging to other members of the public accounts tweeting about #FeesMustFall. While the system did not capture all tweets on Twitter for the respective periods, it does offer a snapshot of those accounts that generate the most activity on Twitter in South Africa. In the next section, the data extractions assist in answering the question: What role did media play in hashtag activism during the #RhodesMustFall and #FeesMustFall protests in South Africa in 2015?

Data and Analysis: What the Twitter Extractions Revealed

1. The most important finding from the above dataset is the fact that media were not asking questions, which we could then take to mean they were not the ones engaged in citizen journalism, nor were they encouraging citizen journalism. A total of 83 % of the tweets showed that media were not asking questions or engaging in their tweet outputs (Fig. 9.1).A second important finding here was that a slightly higher than half, 53 %, of media tweets, were related to linking content to web content (Fig. 9.2).
2. About half, 49.8 %, of media used the hashtag #FeesMustFall when they tweeted about fees must fall. The other half used other hashtags or no hashtags. This could be an indication that media did not know

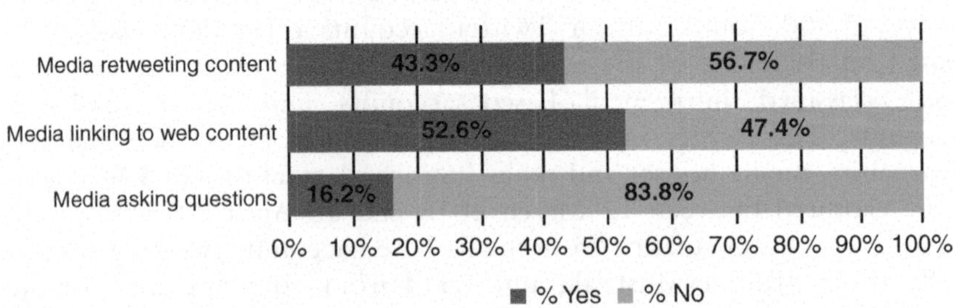

Fig. 9.1 Tweet content analysis for media users for #FeesMustFall

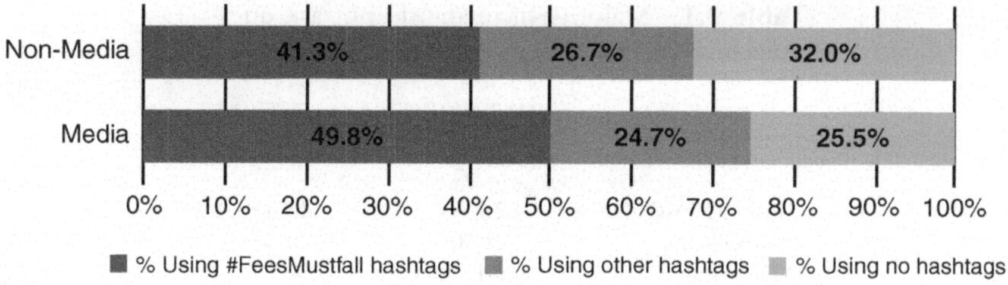

Fig. 9.2 Percentage of tweets using hashtags

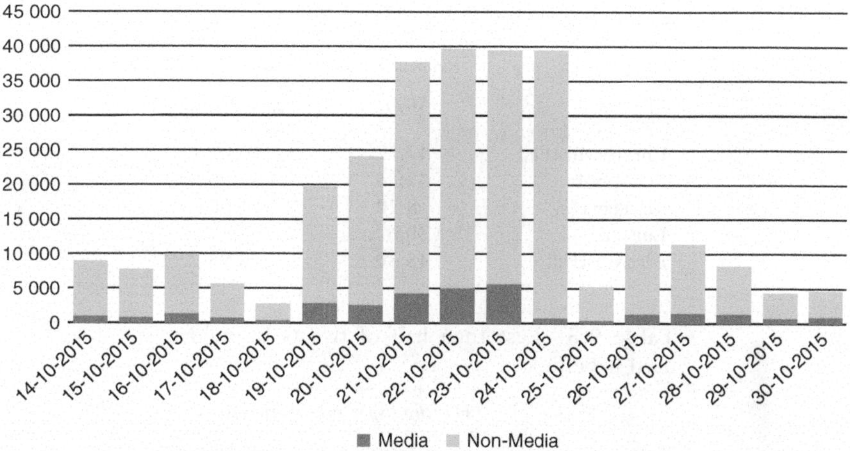

Fig. 9.3 Tweets by day

how to use the hashtag or that they were not too concerned about being part of the broader discussion on Fees Must Fall.

3. However, there were more media using the hashtag than non-media. About 42 % of non-media used the hashtag, compared to about 50 % of media (Fig. 9.3).
4. In the data, we can see that non-media were more active with tweets on the Must Fall protests than media (Table 9.1).
5. The table shows the top 'issues' (Table 9.2). First extractions were for the top 'issue' hashtags for 2015, and five events that were

Table 9.1 Majority of media do not ask questions in their tweets

	Asking questions in the tweet(%)	
	Media	*Non-Media*
RhodesMustFall	28.36	28.45
Xenophobia	20.86	20.56
Marikana	30.18	24.51
Luister	22.35	30.37
FeesMustFall	16.17	21.09

Table 9.2 About half of all tweets are merely re-tweets

	Retweeting other content(%)	
	Media	*Non-Media*
RhodesMustFall	47.37	46.07
Xenophobia	42.36	50.65
Marikana	8.20	41.50
Luister	30.67	57.44
FeesMustFall	43.30	68.93

Table 9.3 Less than half of tweets by media used hyperlinks

	Having hyperlinks in tweets(%)	
	Media	*Non-Media*
RhodesMustFall	49.42	41.32
Xenophobia	43.34	49.52
Marikana	9.52	44.36
Luister	38.34	35.94
FeesMustFall	47.43	53.20

relatively evenly spaced from each other were picked (Table 9.3). These include:

(a) RhodesMustFall
(b) Xenophobia
(c) The Marikana Report

(d) Stellenbosch's Luister Documentary
(e) FeesMustFall

Then, within each hashtag, the research deconstructed the following:

(a) A content analysis to detect if a question was being asked.[6]
(b) A content analysis to detect if the content was just a retweet of someone else.
(c) A content analysis to detect if a hyperlink was present in the tweet.
(d) A count of hashtag use by user type (media vs. non-media).
(e) Daily totals so you can see the progression of the hashtag per day.

Analysis

1. The most important finding here is that, overall, the use of hashtags is NOT increasing over time, but does surge when there are topical events happening. When those events happen, the hashtags do converge into the popular hashtag, giving it critical mass (Fig. 9.4).
2. Furthermore, journalists do not coin the eventual popular hashtag—they use what becomes the popular hashtag.
3. The conclusion to be reached must be that traditional media were 'hashtag takers' as opposed to 'hashtag setters'.

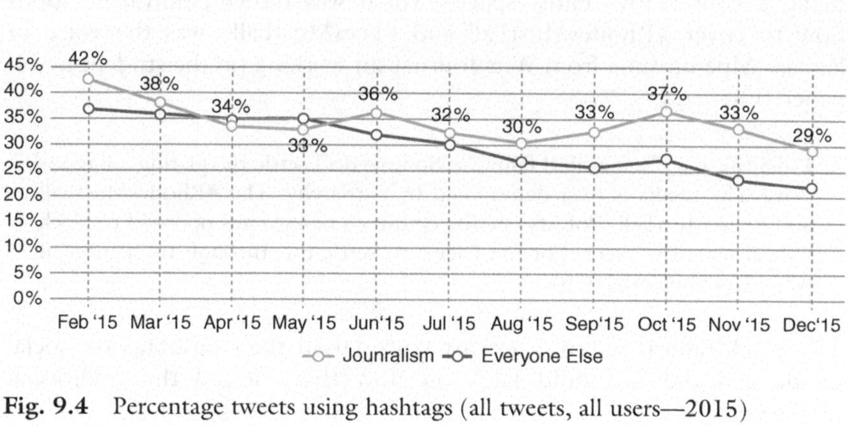

Fig. 9.4 Percentage tweets using hashtags (all tweets, all users—2015)

4. Some of the other quantitative analysis for #FeesMustFall showed that the first evidence of the tweet emanated from the Wits SRC (8 October 2015) with the Wits SRC statement: 'Once again, University Fee Increases prove that being intelligent is not good enough if you are poor #WitsFees.' This then evolved with the Progressive Youth Alliance actually coining the term #WitsFeesMustFall on the same day.
5. The first known journalist to use it was Gabi Mbele (on this research database): 'TheGabi (October 14, 2015): Wits Empire Road entrance is a mess #WitsFeesMustFall'

So the quantitative analysis showed that journalists use hashtags, but not more than other users on Twitter.

Reflecting on the activism from the year before—2015 the year under analysis—young black feminist women who were activists and journalists spoke at a seminar at Wits University (17 February 2016) about the importance of the hashtag, in their case radical black women and #PatriarchyMustFall. Aaisha Dadi Patel (*Media Studies/Daily Vox*) shared: 'I am fully committed to the hashtag fees must fall. I live tweeted everything every day. I believe in the movement. I am a student, an activist, a journalist, Muslim, black and a feminist' (Patel 2016).

Chairperson of the panel, Nicky Falkoff opined: 'The only way I could find out what was going during #FeesMustFall was to follow the hashtag' (Falkoff 2016).

Attacking the traditional mainstream newsroom in South Africa for being a conservative elitist space—which was rather ambivalent about how to cover #RhodesMustFall and #FeesMustFall—was the voice of Zimasa Mpemnyama from Wits Journalism working on the student newspaper, *Vuvuzela*.

> I identify as a black radical feminist. So how do I settle the glaring antagonisms? The media is over-determined by patriarchy. The #RhodesMustFall and #FeesMustFall protests saw the country's newsrooms opposed to black radical feminist voices. For me I have to settle this through the Fanonian way (Mpemnyama 2016).

The black radical feminist activist voices used their hashtags on social media and did not hold back on how they viewed the traditional newsrooms.

Falkoff elaborated: 'Social media has become potent. At the same time that student journalists were remaking journalism, mainstream media were struggling to catch up.'

The discourse from the panel discussion, especially that traditional media in general followed social media, appeared to match or fall in tandem with the quantitative results of the Twitter extractions.

Concluding Reflections

In 2015, two mini-revolutions took place in South Africa: #RhodesMustFall and #FeesMustFall. Both were successful in that both the statue of Rhodes and fee increases fell to ground zero. There was something else that was also somewhat unsettled and disrupted in the process: mainstream media's hegemony. However, a word of caution here: there is evidence that the mainstream media was unsettled but not overthrown from its top position. There was greater diversity of voices through the agonistic spaces created in social media. Traditional media—for example, newspapers, television and radio—did not 'fall' during the two protests but its number one place in public discourse and debate was knocked from its plinth to become a follower of news on social media rather than a leader. It was a temporary knocking-off, however given that the revolution was neither deep nor expansive.

On the one hand, it could be regarded as hashtag activism in full swing to the benefit of these 'revolutions' with student activism being at the forefront. Upon closer scrutiny, it appears as though the hashtag was indeed used but not to the extent one might imagine. However, more importantly, the use of the hashtag grew from one protest at the beginning of the year—namely, #RhodesMustFall—to the next protest at the end of the year, #FeesMustFall. Upon even closer scrutiny, student and citizenry engagement was more in evidence with the hashtag than traditional media. What is evidently clear from the extracted data, both media and citizenry using the hashtag rose exponentially from the #RhodesMustFall protests (322,124) to the #FeesMustFall protest (1,490,377). It could be argued then that the use of the hashtag in activism was gaining in popularity.

This may be an optimistic moment for citizen engagement on social media as it is assumed that elite and traditional media own the social media space. It may not be direct democracy realized but it may mean that traditional media's hegemonic control is over and its place has been unsettled. This is good for diversity and media freedom and radical democracy.

In terms of the theory deployed in this chapter, these protests occupied a robust agonistic space in the symbolic democratic order which is post-apartheid South Africa. Indeed, all those fighting to be heard found their voice as they brought down first the statue of the archetypical colonial figure of Rhodes. Then later in the year, in October 2015, the #MustFall movement fought against the 10 % increase in fees imposed by university administrations and the government. Both the protests were successful as they resulted in the fall of the statue and the fees. Through these two struggles, other activist struggles emerged—though not explored fully in this chapter—for instance, the radical black feminist voice deploying the hashtag #PatriarchyMustFall.

The activist hashtag during the two protests under research here drew great interest and citizenry participation, which can be gleaned from the fact that overall more non-media than traditional journalists were engaged on the social media platform Twitter. The traditional media was caught half-asleep, so to speak, and had to jump on the bandwagon. They struggled to keep up with social media and citizen participation. They did not ask too many questions, which would indicate social engagement, and they did not use the hashtag as much as one would have expected. This could be an indication that something had changed from when Mouffe gave an interview 10 years ago in 2006 and averred that social media was very much a space where the like-minded affirmed the like-minded and that it was still an elite space, where: 'In fact, it perversely allows people to just live in their little worlds, and not being exposed anymore to the conflicting ideas that characterize the agonistic public space' (Carpentier and Cammaerts 2006). This is not to say that the public sphere in South Africa is not an elite space. It is, but there are indications of change. The change, it is argued here, is an optimistic one for media spaces opening up with the advent of social media, Twitter in particular, to include new voices, rather than it being a space that was taken and preserved by the elite from traditional newsrooms (together with other elite, e.g., political parties).

Agonistic spaces, to use the radical democracy concept, was elucidated well in both the #RhodesMustFall and #FeesMustFall protests, as we witnessed and as was shown in the discourse earlier in the chapter, involved clashing views, serious contestations and differences, including violent actions; for example, the pouring of excrement over the statue of Rhodes. The protests in 2015 were the clearest indications of radical democracy in action; these used hashtag activism to organize protests led by students. This #RhodesMustFall activism at the beginning of 2015 led to the national shutdown of universities at the end of 2015 in the #FeesMustFall protest, and then to intersectional feminist struggles of activism for instance #ForBlackGirlsOnly and #PatriarchyMustFall, which continued into 2016.

A stronger public sphere was developing through hashtag activism, overtaking the Habermasian elite public sphere of days gone by. The Habermasian public sphere of the past in South Africa—for example traditional newsrooms, mainstream media, journalists, analysts, commentators, politicians and other members of the chattering classes—was unsettled by the new and radical voices. However, it must also be noted that Twitter itself is an elite medium not accessed by all who do not have the Internet but who are connected to news via radio. In fact, the majority of South Africa's 50-million-strong population did not participate in these debates. Even given this though, it is argued here that the year 2015 showed that activists from citizenry and the student movement had lead and traditional journalism was following, in a nuanced break from the past, during this period.

Notes

1. Twitter is a social media platform which allows those networked to each other to communicate in 140 characters, or 'Your news in 140 characters' as Wilma Stassen has put it (2010) in the article 'Your news in 140 characters: Exploring the role of social media in journalism,' *Global Media Journal*, African Edition 2010 Vol 4 (1).
2. Munsamy, R. *Daily Maverick* (2015) It's not about the statues, Stupid! 9 April 2015.
3. To the experience of white university members told they were not allowed to speak and air their views, nor should they be appropriating black culture by wearing beads and bracelets or braids as hairstyles.
4. This resulted in 2016 with a new activist hashtag, #ForBlackGirlsOnly.
5. Citizen journalism, part of the new media ecologies since the internet, can be broadly defined as a two-way stream between citizens and newsrooms—understood to mean better participation and diversity in news and access to traditional newsrooms. Nonetheless it is a contested term given its broadness but the main issue for this article is the extent to which citizens (in this case student activists) can be empowered by getting their views in the public domain, hitherto closed off to them.
6. The content analysis looked for a question mark or typical interrogative words.

References

Bohler-Muller, N., and Van Der Merwe, C. (2011). The potential of social media to impact socio-political change on the African continent.

Carpentier, N., & Cammaerts, B. (2006). Hegemony, democracy, agonism and journalism: An interview with Chantal Mouffe. *Journalism Studies, 7*(6), 964–975.

City Press. (2015a, September 6). Our lives don't matter.

City Press. (2015b, September 6). shut up and listen.

City Press. (2015c, September 6). We can't pretend.

City Press. (2015d, September 8). Serving white interests.

Dahlgren, P. (2005). The Internet, public spheres and political communication: Dispersion and deliberation. *Political Communication, 22*(2), 147–162.

Daily Maverick. (2015, April). It's not about the statues, Stupid!

Daniels, G. (2012). *Fight for democracy: The ANC and the media in South Africa*. Johannesburg: Wits University Press.

Daniels, G. (2014). *State of the newsroom South Africa 2014: Disruptions accelerated*. Johannesburg: Wits Journalism.

Derrida, J. (2004). The last of the rogue states: The democracy to come. *The South Atlantic Quarterly, 103*(2/3), 232–341. Maryland: The John Hopkins University Press.

Dirk, N., and Petersen, C. (2015, December 9). Rhodes tweets top of trends on Twitter. *The Star*.

Falcke, D. (2014). Developed the method for Twitter extractions.

Falkoff, N. (2016, February 17). Wiser seminar entitled: Intersectional writing in times of protest: Conversations with young women journalists. Johannesburg: Wits University.

Mail & Guardian. (2015, August 28–September 3). Suspended Wits 7 violent of vexed.

Manji, F. 2008. Alternative media for social change in Africa. Myths and realities. Paper presented to Cape Town International Book Fair.

McNair, B. (2006). *Cultural chaos: Journalism, news and power in a globalised world*. London: Routledge.

Mouffe, C. (2005). *The democratic paradox*. London and New York: Verso.

Moyo, D. (2009). Citizen journalism and the parallel market of information in Zimbabwe's 2008 election. *Journalism Studies, 10*(4), 551–567.

Moyo, L. (2014). Beyond the newsroom monopolies: Citizen journalism as the practice of freedom in Zimbabwe. In E. Thorsen and S. Allan (Eds.), *Citizen journalism: Global voices* (pp. 273–288). London: Peter Lang.

Mpemnyama, Z. (2016, February 17). Wiser seminar entitled: Intersectional writing in times of protest: Conversations with young women journalists. Johannesburg: Wits University.

Muneri, C. (2016). Chapter entitled: Beyond blind optimism: The case of citizen journalism in the struggle for democracy in Zimbabwe in the book. In B. Mutsvairo (Ed.), *Participatory politics and citizen journalism in a networked Africa* (p. 179). London: Palgrave Macmillan.

Ngcaweni, W. (2015, October 25). Superiority sadly seems alive and well. *The Sunday Independent.*

Patel, A. (2016, February 17). Wiser seminar entitled: Intersectional writing in times of protest: Conversations with young women journalists. Johannesburg: Wits University.

Sandoval, M., & Fuch, C. (2010). Towards a critical theory of alternative media. *Telematics and Informatics*, *27*, 141–150.

Stassen, W. (2010). Your news in 14 characters: Exploring the role of social media in journalism. *Global Media Journal*, African edition, *4*(1), 1–6.

The Times. (2015a, August 27). Listen up, old South Africa.

The Times. (2015b, September 2). Campuses seething.

The Times. (2015c, September 3). The storm rages, unabated.

The Times. (2016, January14). History is not a blank page on which we write our own version.

Van Dijk, J. (2006). *The network society. Social aspects of new media.* London: Sage.

Van Noort, E., & Verweij, P. (2013). Journalist Twitter networks, public debates and relationships in South Africa. *Digital Journalism*, *2*(1), 98–114.

Glenda Daniels is a senior lecturer in Media Studies at Wits University at Wits Journalism (University of Witwatersrand, Johannesburg). she was formerly project co-ordinator of the State of the Newsroom Project at Wits Journalism. She has a PhD in Political Studies (Wits) and is also author of the book, *Fight for Democracy: the ANC and the Media in South Africa* (Wits Press), 2012. Press freedom is both her passion, and intellectual interest; she is also a freedom of expression activist and served on the first national working group of the Right2Know campaign. In 2014, she serves as the chair of the South African National Editors' Forum's (Sanef) Diversity and Ethics committee. Daniels has been a journalist in South Africa for over 20 years, having started off her career as a trainee at the then Weekly Mail in 1990. She has since worked for most of the major newspaper companies in the country in various capacities such as labour and politics writer to senior features writer, profile writer, to copy editor to surveys manager.

CHAPTER 10

@SOS_ZA_#SABC: Civic Discourse and the Negotiation of PSB Principles

Viola C. Milton

Introduction

In October 2009 the South African Department of Communications ("DOC") found itself in conflict with civil society organizations (CSOs) following the publication of a draft "Public Service Broadcasting Bill, the Charter of the Corporation and the Charter of Community Broadcasting Services" (PSBBill), which called for fundamental changes to the South African broadcasting landscape (Public Service Broadcasting Bill 2009). The proposed PSB Bill was in part a response to the deep and very public crisis of South Africa's public (service) broadcaster, the South African Broadcasting Corporation (SABC).[1] The protracted period of negotiation that followed the introduction of this Bill extended into November 2010 and allows insight into the ways in which citizen participation can shape public policy in South Africa's fledgling democracy. Furthermore, because both modern democratic societies and broadcasting policies have been developed within the context of the nation-state, the process by which a national broadcasting policy is negotiated offers especially useful

V.C. Milton (✉)
Department of Communication Science, University of South Africa,
Pretoria, South Africa
e-mail: Miltovc@unisa.ac.za

B. Mutsvairo (ed.), *Digital Activism in the Social Media Era*,
DOI 10.1007/978-3-319-40949-8_10

insight into the nature of that nation's civil society (Heath 1999, p. 512) and by extension also its understanding of citizenship as practice. Civil society, as used here, refers to

> the wide array of non-governmental and not-for-profit organizations that have a presence in public life, expressing the interests and values of their members or others, based on ethical, cultural, political, scientific, religious or philanthropic considerations. Civil Society Organizations (CSOs) therefore refer to a wide of array of organizations: community groups, non-governmental organizations (NGOs), labor unions, indigenous groups, charitable organizations, faith-based organizations, professional associations, and foundations (The World Bank n.d., http://bit.ly/ggso2G)

Heller (2009, p. 124) adds to this that civil society consists of voluntary association that are governed by communicative practices. "If the telos of politics is power, and its logic the aggregation of interests, the telos of civil society is reaching new understanding through the public use of reason" (ibid.). He argues that civil society assists in the practice of citizenship in three ways: (1) provide a space in which citizens can meaningfully practise democracy on a day-to-day basis; (2) anchor the legitimacy of political practices and institutions in vigorous public debate; and (3) serve as a countervailing force to the power-driven logic of political society (Heller 2009, pp. 124–125). Citizenship within this framework describes the relationship between the individual and the state, or as Turner (1993, pp. 2–3) puts it, citizenship is

> ...that set of practices (juridical, political, economic and cultural) which define a person as a competent member of society, and which as a consequence shape the flow of resources to persons and social groups...
>
> Citizenship is concerned with...the various social arrangements whereby benefits are distributed to different sectors of society. (Turner, 1993, pp. 2–3)

Proponents of citizenship as practice conclude that more than just being equal in the eyes of the law, (with all the rights and privileges that such equality bring about), citizenship is also a social process that includes amongst others civic engagement, participation in social movements and protest. Hence, contemporary understandings of citizenship contends that it also be defined contends that it also be defined as a social process through which individuals and social groups engage in claiming, expanding or losing rights (Delanty 2000; Isin and Turner 2002). Against this backdrop, this chapter is an exploration of the process of citizenship. Employing a case study approach, it examines civil society and civic discourse relating to the negotiation process that followed the publication of the Proposed Bill and with particular focus on the efforts of the "SOS: Support Public Broadcasting Coalition's" (SOS) efforts in this regard. Looking at media and citizenship from the vantage-point of civic engagement, this chapter contends that social media can act as a central site for the production, management and sharing of media activism and the negotiation of media policy. It therefore considers the changing legislative framework for the public broadcaster from the viewpoint of social media, civil society and civic discourse, asking in short, "how are transformations in the Broadcasting Act and recent crises at the SABC, explored and discursively constructed by civil society through their involvement in social media networks?" The point of reference for this discussion is the discourses surrounding the PSB Bill as they are played out on the social network site Twitter (through @SOS_ZA and #sabc) and the SOS Google groups pages (http://groups.google.com/group/SOS-relay).

The objective of this chapter is to contextualize contemporary discourses surrounding public (service) broadcasting in South Africa in the context of citizen's negotiation of media policy as articulated by the SOS Coalition. The first half of the chapter comprises a textual analysis of the manner by which the SOS responds to the deepening crisis at the SABC with a strong focus on their negotiations for a revision of the PSB Bill of 2009. The second half of the chapter concludes with some thoughts regarding the role played by civil society in influencing South African broadcasting policy and media practice in relation to the SABC and what that says about the potential of *practising* citizenship in contemporary South Africa.

Public Broadcasting, Media Policy and Politics

> Information is the sustenance of revolution. Whether it is conveyed in a note surreptitiously passed hand to hand or in a broadcast the entire world can watch, evidence of corruption and calls for citizens to rally for change can pull individuals together, letting them share a reservoir of truth. This is politically intoxicating and it fuels the collective outrage and courage needed to challenge a government. (Hoskins et al. 2011, p.108)

Civil society has an established history of engaging with government over issues threatening media independence in South Africa's fledgling democracy. The Campaign for Open Media (hereafter COM)'s march on the SABC headquarters in Auckland Park on 25 August 1990 comes to mind as one example. On this date over a thousand people marched towards the SABC in Auckland Park in a bid to

1. attract public attention to the fact that a Task Group, that is, the Viljoen Task Group, had been established to investigate the future of broadcasting;
2. present the chairman of the SABC, and also the chair of the Task Group, with a memorandum registering their opposition to the composition of the Task Group; and
3. demand that the restructuring of broadcasting take place on a democratic basis (Louw 1993, p. 47).

This incident marked the first time that ordinary members of the South African public mobilized around broadcasting matters, and followed the controversial appointment of the Viljoen Task Group on Broadcasting in March 1990. Media activists took issue with the lack of representativeness of the group's membership as well as the fact that its deliberations were held in secret. The Film and Allied Workers Organisation (FAWO) and COM forming an alliance in protest against this state of affairs, organized the march and succeeded in placing broadcasting, heretofore treated as an issue that should be "de-politicized," squarely into the political arena (ibid., pp. 11–12). The August march on the SABC was followed by a series of other high-profile public events staged by members of civil society, including the trade unions, civic organizations, cultural and political formations, academics, journalists and media practitioners.

On November 14, 1990, following the release of the Viljoen Report, the COM was replaced by the Campaign for Independent Broadcasting (CIB), whose primary aims included

1. that it should be acknowledged that broadcasting was a constitutional issue and therefore needed to be dealt with through the process of constitutional negotiations;
2. preventing the National Party government and SABC management from taking any further unilateral action in restructuring the SABC, and the film and broadcasting sector;

3. putting the issue of the control and regulation of broadcasting firmly on the agenda of the democratic movement as a whole and particularly the ANC;
4. challenging the SABC on the questions of its perceived bias in favour of the National Party Government; and
5. impacting upon "democratising" broadcasting through the phasing-in of new broadcasters to sector. (Louw 1993, pp. 65–70)

The CIB's initial primary focus was on the selection and appointment of the SABC Board, which in June 1993 ended up being rather messy, controversial and ultimately an exercise in futility. Giving voice to the prevailing sentiment at the time, the CIB demanded that an independent selection panel and not the State President appoint a new SABC board representative of South African society. They also called for the establishment of an independent regulatory authority to regulate the broadcasting sector as a whole. Clearly, where the broadcasting debate in South Africa is concerned, the past is present. As was the case for the 1990s civil society movements, the current concerns regarding media policy in general and broadcasting policy in particular, seems poised on two primary questions: who should control the SABC and how should it be funded? Thus, not unlike the 1990s, it is civil society that is stepping up to the plate to reclaim the SABC and redefine how public broadcasting should be viewed within a developmental state. Indeed, the past is present.

The existing regulatory framework for broadcasting in South Africa was a direct product of popular mobilizations and pressures of the transition period (Louw 1993; Tomaselli and Teer-Tomaselli 2008; Sparks 2009) which resulted in the Broadcasting Act of 1999 (this Act has since been amended a number of times, most notably in 2002 and 2009—with all of these amendments primarily addressing issues of funding and governance as it pertains to the relationship between the public broadcaster and the South African government). In terms of the Broadcasting Act of 1999, the SABC became a "public company incorporated in terms of the Company Act, to be known as the South African Broadcasting Corporation Limited" (Section 8A(1) Republic of South Africa 1999). The Act aims to, among other things, facilitate democracy, the development of society, gender equality, nation building, provide education, and strengthen "the spiritual and moral fibre [sic] of society" (Broadcasting Act 1999, p. 9). The Act obliges the SABC to provide a plurality of news, views, information, and wide-ranging entertainment and educational programming. To ensure compliance, the Act provides for a number of key players in the governance of the SABC:

1. The DOC and the Minister of Communications
2. ICASA (The Independent Communications Authority of South Africa—provided for in the Broadcasting Amendment Act of 2002)
3. The SABC Board
4. The Executive Committee

The Board, in terms of the Broadcasting Act—"controls the affairs of the Corporation" and is entrusted with the following:

1. Compliance with the SABC Charter, which details the distinctive role for public broadcasting in South Africa (Section 6 of the Broadcasting Act)
2. Ensuring legislative compliance
3. Appointments and oversight of executive members to the Board and senior management
4. Strategy development and oversight of the latter's implementation

In theory, the mandate is a powerful one, but the Board faces a number of structural and practical problems, including:

1. Lack of clarity with regard to the Charter so it is difficult to ensure compliance thereof.
2. The legislation, Articles of Association and Shareholder's Compact contradict one another. The Articles and Shareholder's Compact in fact give "interventionist" powers to the Minister of Communications (on behalf of the State as shareholder) and restrict the power of the Board
3. Appointments of executive members to the Board remain a vexed issue. In the Articles of Association, it appears that such appointments are ultimately decided by the Minister, thus creating a situation in which the decision-making responsibilities of the Board is curtailed by the Minister
4. Finally, in a rather confusing division of responsibilities, the Board is also the accounting authority, giving it particular financial responsibilities and making it accountable for mismanagement. The confusion

> arises in that management and board responsibilities in this respect appear to overlap, thus actively encouraging the Board to play a more "hands-on" role (Lloyd et al. 2010, pp.110–128).

Against this backdrop, the SOS seeks to revive the spirit of earlier media pressure groups in their attempts to negotiate for an improved Broadcasting Policy environment. According to their manifesto, the SOS is a membership-based coalition representing unions, NGOs, CBOs, community media, independent film and TV production sector organizations; academics, freedom of expression activists and concerned individuals. They aim towards creating a public broadcasting system dedicated to the broadcasting of quality, diverse, citizen-orientated public programming committed to deepening South Africa's Constitution, particularly the Bill of Rights and socio-economic rights. Specifically, they focus on strengthening the SABC (and also community radio and TV). Their current efforts are geared in particular towards ensuring that new comprehensive legislation is drafted for the SABC (and community media) that ensures their effective governance and funding (S.O.S. Support Public Broadcasting, http://bit.ly/9EO4oK).

SOS enters the public arena at a time when the role of social media in civic and civil discourse is widely debated in academic and civil society settings. The organization has established a digital presence through their engagement with Twitter, Google groups, Facebook and their own website. Through the use of social media networks (which supplement their more hands-on efforts), the SOS provide not only an important context and necessary background about the issues that South Africa's television-viewing audiences should take heed of, but they also attempt to move audience members to take a stand. The remainder of this paper addresses civic discourse about the SABC and media policy in South Africa through the eyes of the SOS and with a specific focus on their negotiation of broadcasting policy in South Africa between 2009 and 2010.

@SOS_ZA: Saving the SABC in 140 Characters or Less

From a media history point of view, one advantage of social media such as Twitter is that it provides at once a community (for cultural analysis) as well as a digital archive (for curating the work of digital communities). Jakubowicz would probably argue that what social media offers is a fragmented community, but, one could conceivably counter that, where advocacy is concerned, there is less of a fragmentation of community, given that those choosing to join (or in Twitter-language, "tweet"), are joined by a common course and a shared desire towards action. Of course, one of the downsides of attempting to utilize social networking sites such as Twitter and Google groups as "digital archives" is that they are "…rather jumbled—there is a high ratio of noise to signal…" (Catone 2008, http://bit.ly/qIQbqH). This is especially the case with Twitter. For example, a cursory glance at the Twitter page for @SOS_ZA at the time of writing revealed that the Coalition had 427 Tweets, was following 355 "people" and had 197 followers. In fact, the fluidity of this medium of communication for advocacy is illustrated by the fact that by the time I completed my original work on this chapter, the number of active followers for SOS-ZA (who recently changed their Twitter-handle to @SOSCoalition) has increased to 1,044. The SOS Google groups network on the other hand has 340 members and generated more than 1,000 posts. To illustrate what is meant by "jumbled communication" and "high ratio of noise", a quick click on @SOS_ZAs tweets reveals a mix between information to keep people informed about the Coalition's activities through commentary on ongoing media matters, attempts to solicit debate and/discussion from followers and retweets from other twitter accounts commenting on the SABC crisis and the proposed Bill. Here, the organization utilizes hashtags as well as direct tweeting to reach its objectives.

What this means for the media historian/analyst is that "…with some specifically directed tweeting or clever use of hashtags, sorting the valuable data from the garbage isn't very difficult…" (Catone 2008, http://bit.ly/qIQbqH). Before discussing the SOS's social media advocacy, it is important to note that Twitter has a 140-character limit, which means that users must be creative in their use of language and characters in order to get their message across. Google groups on the other hand has no such limits, allows anyone within the group to start or respond to postings and may or may not be topically arranged. For ease of sorting, I entered SOS Google groups data via a relay site (i.e., SA Media Critique), whose primary function is to relay messages of the SOS, but does so in a more organized fashion than the SOS's own pages. With this in mind, how did I sort through the garbage and what did I learn?

My primary interest in the SOS Coalition's utilization of social networking towards advocacy, was on their efforts to negotiate the terms of the revisions to the existing South African Broadcasting Act, particularly as it pertains to their expressed efforts to force government to retract the gazetted, controversial 2009 PSB Bill. In this respect I was not only interested in *what* @SOS_ZA tweeted, or wrote about, but more so *how* their tweets and letters on Google groups framed the discourses about the PSB Bill and *how* it discursively constructed the SOS's mission with regards to their broadcasting advocacy activities.

By Twitter standards, the amount of tweets generated by @SOS_ZA for the period under purview, was relatively modest (only 427 over a period of 12 months), but trying to make sense of 427 tweets and all its corresponding links and references is still a daunting task.

As such, it was necessary to limit my scope to directed tweets meant to engage followers on matters pertaining to the SABC and broadcasting reform. In this respect, three hashtags emerged as indicators of the Coalition's interests: #zamediafreedom (also appears as #mediafreedomza and #zamediafreedomza), #mediamattersza and #sabc. Topically, this chapter is most concerned with the latter, given its focus on the public broadcaster. I therefore directed my attention towards the talk about the SABC generated by @SOS_ZA through a cursory textual analysis of #sabc to find out *what* was talked about and *how* it was framed. The hashtag includes references to a selection of linked documents in the tweets regarding public broadcasting policy and the SABC. I focussed primarily on tweets generated between July and December 2010. I conducted a similar exercise for the SOS Google groups activity, looking primarily at letters and linked press releases about the PSB Bill from October 2009 until its withdrawal in November 2010.

Google Groups: Negotiating Broadcasting Policy Reform

While the SOS's available twitter activity can only be tracked back to 2010, their available Google groups pages date back to 2008 (with two posts), and an increasingly active presence introduced in May 2009. The spike in activity coincided with yet another governance and financial crisis at the SABC which led to the eventual decision to place a discussion document for broadcasting reform on the table and the consequent introduction of the PSB Bill in October 2009. There is clearly a need for improved policy and legislation that can deal adequately with the SABC's funding and governance problems. The PSB Bill of 2009 is government's response to this need. The PSB Bill can be accessed in its entirety,[2] but for this discussion, it is worth noting that the most controversial issues raised in it were the proposal for a radical change in the SABC's funding model, inconsistencies in the phrasing of the Bill and the threat to broadcasting and media freedom. At present, the SABC is funded through a mixed model that includes commercial funding, licence fees, a small percentage from government funding and a small percentage from "other" sources. (A detailed discussion hereof can be accessed in Louw and Milton (2012), Chap. 8.) In essence, the PSB Bill proposed that in future, direct parliamentary appropriations and television licence fees be replaced by an earmarked tax on income. The accrued funds for public broadcasting were to be paid into a Public Service Broadcasting Fund, to be administered by the Media Development and Diversity Agency (MDDA). All broadcasters would be allowed to apply for funding through this mechanism. The Bill stipulated that public broadcasting should be funded from personal income tax (not more than 1 %), money appropriated from parliament, contributions from broadcasting services licensees, contributions from business and money accruing to the Fund. It further proposed a cap on commercial revenue, stipulating that this may not exceed the income from the PSB Fund and other non-commercial revenue. The Bill also outlined Board and Chief Officer appointments for the SABC that would make the SABC much more dependent upon the DOC and the Minister of Communications in its decision-making processes. Critics argued that the SABC "is headed for a complete editorial independence meltdown if the Bill is enacted" (Da Silva 2010).

The SOS in particular argued that the Bill should be put through a proper Green Paper/White Paper process to allow the civil society more time to make substantial responses (Lloyd et al. 2010). In fact, as can be gleaned from the SOS Google groups pages, their advocacy to get the Bill reviewed started immediately, with the Coalition's then Campaign Coordinator and spokeswoman, Kate Skinner, writing to the 340 members of the Coalition's Google group on November 1, 2009 that she had

> . . . written a draft letter to the Minister asking for significantly more time for discussion and debate and for a comprehensive (White Paper) policy review process. The Bill calls for fundamental changes to the broadcasting sector (new public funding mechanisms, new roles for the Minister, new charters for public and community broadcasting etc.) These discussions cannot be concluded by DOC's deadline of 7 December. I will be sending you the draft letter shortly. The plan is to have a press conference to highlight the issues included in the letter. Also, just a quick comment on funding—apparently the suggestion that license fees will be scrapped is causing

immediate problems for the SABC. Members of the public now think that they don't have to pay their TV licenses. However, this is still a major funding source potentially throwing the SABC into an even more precarious funding situation… (Skinner 2009, http://bit.ly/oIsrfu).

On November 4, 2009 she made good on her promise to send a letter to the minister on behalf of the group. This letter details many of the problems the group identified with the Bill (many of these already outlined above) and takes on the DOC's assertion that the Bill does not introduce major policy changes:

While the Department claims that the Bill does not introduce any fundamental policy shifts (and therefore a review of the Broadcasting White Paper, 1998 is unnecessary) the Bill does indeed introduce major policy shifts [which she proceeds to then outline in the letter]… These are major policy shifts. They stand to fundamentally restructure the broadcasting environment. The Coalition believes that what is required now is a thorough and in-depth consultation with all stakeholders to chart a way forward. This includes:

1. A review of the White Paper (1998) and a systematic review of the provisions in the Republic of South Africa 1999 that have proved effective/ineffective. In particular a review must be done as regards those provisions that have directly contributed to the crisis or proved unworkable, as many of these seem to have been reintroduced in the new Bill.
2. Access to the research done by the Department so as to effectively comment on the evidence-basis for new provisions made in the Bill. This includes research related to the costs of setting up the fund, administering the fund, predictions as to the amounts of funding required by the broadcasting sector, percentages of funding that will be set aside for the SABC's public division, versus the community media sector, signal distribution and so forth.
3. Finally, we need an indication from the Department that it has in fact received firm commitments from National Treasury that the latter is prepared to amend the Income Tax, 1962 Act and implement the provisions proposed by the new Bill.

The Coalition is keen to work closely and constructively with the Department in whatever capacity is appropriate to ensure that we have a vibrant, sustainable public service broadcasting system that operates in the

> public interest. If possible we would like to have a meeting with the Minister to discuss these important issues.
>
> Yours sincerely
> "Save our SABC: Reclaiming our Public Broadcaster" Coalition (Skinner 2009, http://bit.ly/oIsrfu)

These letters not only succinctly contextualize and synthesize the Coalition's position in relation to the PSB Bill, but they also frame the tenor of their engagement with government on the Bill and the issues about the Bill addressed in the letters. In effect, they introduce the process of negotiation in relation to the amendment of broadcasting policy in post-Polokwane South Africa. Primarily the Coalition and other commentators wanted to convince government that the Bill needs more time to be reviewed and that, in fact, even the work on and introduction of the Bill was premature as there needs to be much more research on issues concerning broadcasting (including issues of governance, funding and broadcaster-state relationships) before the legislative revision process can even commence. Their letters to the group and the DOC was supplemented with press releases detailing their position, thus ensuring a wide circulation of the Bill and its malcontents as perceived through civic discourse.

In response to the civic discourse about the Bill, then Minister of Communications, Siphiwe Nyanda, wrote a piece in *Business Day*, which was then circulated by Skinner (2009) to SOS Google groups members. Skinner opted for not only posting a link to the full article in her letter, but also excerpts of what she saw as the most pertinent issues raised by the Minister and on which SOS members should focus in formulating a response. In this respect, she highlighted that the Minister wanted to "set the record straight on the public broadcaster" and that he took issue with "ignorant responses to the [PSB] Bill," which he saw as having the hidden agenda of "scaring the public" (Skinner 2009, http://bit.ly/oIsrfu). The implication here is that responses such as those generated and publicly circulated by the SOS, were irresponsible and ignorant of the Bill's "true" intentions. Skinner (2009) notes that on a more positive note, the Minister also highlighted the DOCs intentions with the Bill, including:

1. Not wanting to control issues surrounding local content
2. Not wanting to control community media
3. Not wanting to control the public media

4. That the Bill raises several proposals as regards funding and that no decision has been taken yet with regard to the collection of revenue
5. That the Department of Communications is fully aware of the fact that it needs to discuss its funding proposals with National Treasury
6. That time will be made for proper consultations. In fact the Minister refers to the Bill now as a Draft Bill although it is not gazetted as such (Skinner 2009, http://bit.ly/oIsrfu).

With the lines of communication now not only open, but also reciprocated, the SOS Coalition then responded to the Minister in a follow-up open letter, noting their satisfaction with the above stated principles and intentions, but reprising their call for

1. a Proper policy review process
2. Substantively more time for consultation—that at the very least this needs to be the end of February because December and January are holiday periods.
3. Access to the research done by the Department as regards the Bill.
4. Broad-based publicity re: the Bill including the dates for deadlines for submission of proposals etc. (including public service announcements on radio and advertisements in mass circulation newspapers).
5. Broad-based consultations in all provinces with stake-holders (Skinner 2009, http://bit.ly/oIsrfu).

In later posts, they also express surprise at the Minister's reference to the Bill as a "draft" Bill, noting that nowhere in the gazette pages is the Bill labelled as such. The distinction between referring to it as the PSB Bill and a draft PSB Bill is an important one, as the latter signals intent to discuss and negotiate the terms of the proposed Bill as opposed to presenting the public with a fait accompli to which they may respond, but if not a "draft" their responses may not impact upon the eventual enactment of the Bill. Thus, not just semantics. Another recurring theme in the SOS's responses to government, is the call for the DOC to grant access to the research they claimed to have conducted with regard to the Bill—in fact, this theme is also present in tweets about the Bill during the parliamentary hearings, as will be seen in the next section.

The negotiation process is not always clear and linear, but can also be messy and fraught with tension—not only between the group and government, but also between group members themselves—as people do not always agree on one course of action. So for example SOS group member Mashilo Boloka (at the time of writing this letter, the head of policy in the DOC) threatens to unsubscribe from the group because he interpreted their publication and discussion of Anton Harber's (Journalism Professor at Wits University and a Coalition member) comments on the Bill's treatment of community media offensive, writing in this respect that,

> I do not think we should undermine the intelligence of everyone by acting on the comments from Anton Harber, unless the agenda of this forum is set elsewhere. Personally, I have a fundamental problems with Anton Harber's comments because not only are they misinterpreting the provisions of the Bill in respect of community broadcasting services, they are oblivious to the challenges faced by the sector, particularly sustainability (Boloka 2009, November 11, 09:21 a.m. http://bit.ly/oIsrfu).

He outlines why his argument holds strong over Harber's comments and later that day, another member (Mark), responds, imploring Dr Boloko not to unsubscribe, noting that

> As the head of policy in the Department of Communications, it would be great if you could at least be informed of different perspectives—even better if you are willing to engage in the debate. That would be an indication that the DoC is embracing the participatory democracy (community ownership and control) that the community media sector is founded on . . . I don't know how Anton "sets his agenda" but the agenda of this group is set by all who participate in setting it . . . (mark@wisenet.co.za 2009, November 11, 11:14 a.m., http://bit.ly/nqk5ny)

A similar situation arises about the Bill's provision for funding through a levy on income tax. Later on November 11, 2009, group member Jane Duncan (Rhodes University Professor and former Director of the Freedom of Expression Institute in South Africa) writes in this regard that

> I really think that SoS needs to seek a meeting with Treasury to signal its support for the income tax proposal. This should be done parallel to the meeting being sought with the Minister of Communications. Then SoS needs to consider a widespread public campaign in support of this proposal, as well as in support of the SABC's independence. Listening to some of the public sentiment on this proposal, it is clear that much more needs to be done to win the argument in the public space for an income tax-based form

> of public funding. Many are expressing concern about their tax money being used to fund a propaganda machine, and that issue needs to be addressed by getting the public behind this proposal, as well as proposals to enhance the independence of the SABC. Predictably, it seems to be middle class audiences that are complaining the most. We need to make the argument that public broadcasting is a merit good that the more monied in our society should contribute to, whether they use the service or not. Many middle class people do not use public transport or public hospitals, but we expect them to contribute to the upkeep of these public services because they are a public good, and we strive towards a society that is redistributive in nature. So the argument being made by DSTV subscribers that they will not pay because they have contracted themselves out of the free to air terrestrial space, is not an argument that can be allowed to win the day. The danger we face is that Treasury may refuse to concede the income tax proposal, leading to us having the worst of both worlds: a more tightly controlled broadcaster by the state, but one that is forced to become even more commercialized as adspend fragments in the multichannel environment (Duncan 2009, http://bit.ly/nqk5ny)

Duncan's letter suggests that there is consensus within the group to accept the income tax levy provision in the Bill as necessary for a free and independent broadcaster, but, as is clear from the next letter, her sentiment not only irked the "middle class audiences" she refers to in her letter, but also drew the ire of BEMAWU (the Broadcasting and Electronic Media Allied Workers Union), who writes on November 12, 2009 that

> [t]he income tax proposal can never work. Every other minister will do the same if it is allowed to happen. What will be next? A percentage income tax to build new roads, another percentage to build houses, another percentage to build schools, another percentage to do away with motor vehicle licenses and so it will continue. We are talking about 1500 jobs on the line if the income tax proposal will be accepted. There is also a real danger that people who are unhappy with the content they get on air will try to not pay tax now, instead of a tv license which will have a severe effect on the country. If 4 million Zulus for example decide to not pay any tax because they don't agree with what's been broadcasted or they feel they don't get a fair share of language and culture on the airways, what then? There is already a public outcry and we have read some comments of people saying they will not pay more tax for the SABC fat cats to squander their tax money . . . Would it not be a simpler solution to raise the Government subsidy by 5 % to provide more funding to the SABC and link the SABC with E-Natis where you will

> not be able to renew your vehicle license or get any income tax returns if your tv license has not been renewed?
>
> We are living in a computer age and anything is possible… (BEMAWU 2009, http://bit.ly/nqk5ny)

While Duncan's response to the Bill slights middle-class audiences' complaints about the radical change in funding for the broadcaster, BEMAWU's concern is for the impact the proposed change would have on the job market—a situation that feeds in to the divide between those with money and those without. Duncan's decontextualized assertion that it is primarily middle-class audiences that are responding negatively to the Bill, does not necessarily take into account *who* may have had access to the discussions about the Bill at this stage in the negotiation process. BEMAWU's response on the other hand speaks from the point of view of a union who looks after the best interest of its constituents—that is, the workers who may be left jobless if the Bill is enacted. What is interesting about BEMAWU's response is that it disregards 1990s policy decisions (as well as Duncan's clear comment in relation to this) that government funding might make the broadcaster more susceptible to government interference. In the light of other provisions in the Bill that are already granting the DOC more input into the governance of the public broadcaster, it is small wonder that the final presentations on the Bill all responded to its unconstitutionality (i.e., the tax provisions make it a "money bill") and its threat to media freedom and independence.

Given the "messiness" of getting public and civil society approval for the Bill in its original form, a running thread in the Coalition's advocacy was to pressurize government to extend the deadline for public submissions on the Bill beyond December. They eventually succeeded in this respect when on 3 December 2009, government announced that the date for submissions had been extended to January 15, 2010. While the SOS and its partners was hoping to push for a March 2010 date, they were none-the-less gracious in accepting government's heed to their call for an extension, noting in a press statement that,

> The "Save our SABC" Campaign representing a number of trade unions including COSATU, COSATU affiliates CWU and CWUSA, FEDUSA and BEMAWU; independent producer organisations including the South African Screen Federation (SASFED); and a host of NGOs and CBOs

> including the Freedom of Expression Institute, Media Monitoring Africa, the Media Institute of Southern Africa and the National Community Radio Forum; as well as a number of academic and independent experts welcome the fact that the Department of Communications has shifted the deadlines for comment on the Bill from December 7, 2009 to January 15, 2010. However, we do note that this extension is over the Christmas period and this certainly significantly hampers our ability to research, debate and consult on the issues raised by the Bill. We had originally asked for an extension until the end of March 2010.

Their statement concludes with another reiteration of the problems they have with the Bill, while stressing again the need for

> a proper policy review process including a review of the Broadcasting White Paper, 1998. In line with sound law making practices we believe that the policy review process should proceed the drafting of new legislation. The Coalition will certainly respond to the new deadline of the 15th of January but one of the key foci of our submission will be addressing the need for a proper policy review process. We also again call on the Department to release the research it has done that proceeded and informed the Bill's proposals.

The year 2010 however introduced fresh challenges for the SABC which makes the problems highlighted by the SOS in their January 2010 submission on the bill all the more pertinent. To note, their primary concerns about the proposed Bill, centred on issues such as:

1. Lack of proper public consultation and a comprehensive policy overview
2. Endangerment of the job sector (BEMAWU for example argued that between 1200 and 1500 employees will lose their jobs if the Bill is signed into law)
3. Lack of clarity regarding the Bill's preamble that "South Africa is a developmental state" and that the broadcasting system must therefore be aligned to the development goals of the country
4. The Bill's focus on an appropriation of money through taxes, means that it is in fact a "money bill" and thus the Department of Communications has no constitutional power to introduce the bill as a money bill may only be introduced by the Minister of Finance (who in 2009 rejected the idea of a dedicated tax for public broadcasting).

5. The increasing power of control over Broadcasting afforded to the Minister of Communications, including:

   (a) the proposed provision that the appointment process for the chief officers (Group Chief Executive Officer, Chief Operating Officer and Chief Financial Officer), be contingent upon approval by the Minister of Communications, thus opening the door for ministerial interference in the SABC's decision-making processes and that
   (b) the Bill's position regarding the separation between public service broadcasting and commercial broadcasting within the SABC and the Minister's role in overseeing the process of cross-subsidisation need further review as it violates the independence of the SABC board

6. Lack of consistency and contradictory views resultant of the Bill's inclusion of two Charters—an SABC Charter and a Community Media Charter—which often contradict each other and in some cases also contradict the main Bill (Skinner as quoted by Da Silva 2010).

True to their December 2009 promise, their submission contextualized their call for a comprehensive policy-review process, noting in their press release about their submission that,

> We argue that it remains a puzzle to the Coalition that the Department appears to be missing the opportunity with a new ANC leadership, a new Parliament, a new Portfolio Committee, A new Minister and a new Director General to make new, fresh, bold policy initiatives. We argue that significant debate needs to be held as regards a host of topics including the Bill's linking of broadcasting to the "developmental state" and its total reconceptualisation of the role of community media. Further we discuss, in some detail, the issue of funding. For instance we note the Bill presents only one funding option the dedicated broadcasting tax which has now been rejected by National Treasury...
>
> We argue that a policy review process would allow for a number of governance and funding options to be researched, debated and discussed which would certainly be to the long term benefit of public broadcasting.

The period following the January 2010 submission process was met with relative silence by government, who took their time looking over the various submissions they received. During this time of reflection, the SABC became embroiled in yet another governance and financial crisis. Looking at the SOS Coalition's Google groups pages and their Twitter activity (via @SOS_ZA), a clear picture now emerges about the SABC's situation following the introduction of the draft PSB Bill in October 2009 that contributed to government's 2010 decision to allow oral presentations on the Bill as well as the eventual withdrawal of the Bill in November 2010. Through a further examination of @SOS_ZA's microblogging on Twitter in relation to their Google groups pages, the issues that inform broadcasting policy debates, the areas of disagreement and the progress toward consensus can now be traced.

@SOS_ZA: Saving the SABC in 140 Characters or Less…

In December 2009, newly instituted President Jacob Zuma announced a new SABC board with the former minister of arts and culture, Dr Ben Ngubane, as chair. Given the general representativeness of the board, commentators were hopeful that Zuma's ascendancy to the proverbial throne signalled a new era not only for the country as a whole, but also for the communications sector in particular. However, as can be gleaned from what follows, this optimism was unfounded.

There are a total of 182 tweets using #sabc as directed marker on @SOS_ZA, for the period under purview. In order to keep the authenticity of tweets intact, wherever tweets are quoted in this chapter they will be inserted unchanged (and uncorrected). The first appearance of #sabc on @SOS_ZA was a linked tweet on August 3, 2010, linking to an article about dissent at the SABC resulting from the broadcaster's governance and financial problems:

- SOS_ZA Kate Skinner RT @timesSAguardian Home:#SABC bosses face rebellion: http://bit.ly/bhgLFV 5:41 pm Aug 3rd, 2010 from web (SOS_ZA 2010b)

While the linked article in the above tweet certainly contextualizes the growing woes of the public broadcaster, a number of tweets following this one (but sans the #sabc) visually documents the downward-spiralling relations between members of the SABCs governing body as well as the much-publicized financial woes of the post-Polokwane SABC:

- SOS_ZA Kate Skinner What do people think of Ben Ngubane's support for the CEO around bonuses? 5:19 pm Aug 3rd, 2010 from web (SOS_ZA 2010a)

- SOS_ZA Kate Skinner Cosatu's positions on secrecy bill, media tribunal and Sabc—excellent. Broadly supports Sabc Board. Ben and Solly the problem. Agreed! 8:15 pm Aug 26th, 2010 from Twitter for BlackBerry® (SOS_ZA 2010e)
- SOS_ZA Kate Skinner SABC CEO Solly Mokoetle has just been suspended. 4:14 pm Aug 27th, 2010 from web (SOS_ZA 2010f)
- SOS_ZA Kate Skinner Hope SABC Board followed labour law to the letter. Solly contesting suspension. Cant afford a protracted labour law battle! Aaarrrrgh! 7:15 pm Aug 29th, 2010 from web (SOS_ZA 2010g)
- SOS_ZA Kate Skinner Sabc management weighing in on the side of Solly. Things getting messy! 8:11 am Aug 30th, 2010 from Twitter for BlackBerry® (SOS_ZA 2010h)
- SOS_ZA Kate Skinner Sabc board member Magatho Mello has officially resigned! Two members have now thrown in the towel. Parly must act. 10:45 am Sep 6th, 2010 from Twitter for BlackBerry® (SOS_ZA 2010i)

The above tweets provide a digital time-line that dates back to May 2010, but it is one that makes sense only if one is fully informed about the SABC's precarious condition back then. In May, 2010, a number of non-executive SABC Board members pointed to serious misconduct with regard to corporate governance at the broadcaster. At issue was the unilateral appointment of Phil Molefe as the head of news, by Dr Ben Ngubane, the then Chair of the SABC Board as well as financial misconduct by Ngubane and group CEO, Solly Mokoetle. The article to which the first hash-tagged tweet links even suggested that President Jacob Zuma was siding with the out-of-favour duo by mentioning in its opening paragraph that both enjoy support from the president. Indicative of the growing dissatisfaction with the state of affairs at the SABC, this series of @SOS_ZA tweets between 3 August 2010 and 19 October 2010, documents the growing discontent of people in the industry and civil society in general:

- SOS_ZA Kate Skinner Debate at Constitutional Hill 2nite on Sabc crisis—finding lasting solutions, 630 pm. Board chair will speak from the floor. 12:32 pm Sep 7th, 2010 from Twitter for BlackBerry® (SOS_ZA 2010j)
- SOS_ZA Kate Skinner Pippa Green: Sabc town hall meetings. Citizens really had there say. #zamediafreedom 8:41 am Oct 17th, 2010 from Twitter for BlackBerry® (SOS_ZA 2010k)

In light of this situation and to help sort out the mess, it was resolved that the Portfolio Committee on Communications would conduct a special parliamentary hearing to discuss issues of governance at the SABC. Bear in mind that this additional process was taking place at the same time as the review of submissions from civil society and other parties on the draft PSB Bill, which in itself outlines a major overhaul for the SABCs governance and finances. Originally, the special parliamentary hearing was scheduled to take place behind closed doors in August 2010, and it did indeed get under way, as illustrated by this tweet:

- SOS_ZA Kate Skinner Ben Ngubane spoke in the closed session. No one else. Hearing needs to be concluded soon! Only one side of the story. 5:21 pm Aug 24th, 2010 from Twitter for BlackBerry® (SOS_ZA 2010d)

However, the South African National Editor's Forum (SANEF) along with the SOS and others urged Parliament to rethink that strategy, claiming that public interest and balanced reporting are at stake. In fact, SANEF eventually forced Parliament to reconsider by serving them with a court interdict,

- SOS_ZA Kate Skinner Sanef has got an interdict to force parly to hold an open session on the Sabc. Everything on hold. Now discussing Postbank Bill. Sigh! 1:30 pm Aug 24th, 2010 from Twitter for BlackBerry® (SOS_ZA 2010c).

This resulted in a date-change that meant that only Ben Ngubane spoke in the closed session. The new date was announced via @SOS_ZA on October 17, 2010,

- SOS_ZA Kate Skinner Sabc reporting to Parly Wed. Minister says they will be presenting united front. Why Board not telling us? #zamediafreedom 9:32 pm Oct 17th, 2010 from Twitter for BlackBerry® (SOS_ZA 2010l)

On October 20, 2010, it became clear that any optimism about the new SABC board appointed by President Jacob Zuma was premature and misplaced, as illustrated by the following selection of tweets:

- SOS_ZA Kate Skinner Just heard that #Sabc Board resignations been accepted with immediate effect. Ex Board members can't speak. Big prob. 9:50 am Oct 20th, 2010 from Twitter for BlackBerry® (SOS_ZA 2010m)

- SOS_ZA Kate Skinner #Sabc union Bemawu calling for Chair to resign due to dismal Parly performance. Also hasn't signed Ceo contract! 8:34 am Oct 22nd, 2010 from Twitter for BlackBerry® (SOS_ZA 2010n)
- SOS_ZA Kate Skinner #Sabc Chair saying the appointment of acting Ceo is illegal. He wants to bring back Solly! Did anyone hear this on the news? 9:46 am Oct 22nd, 2010 from Twitter for BlackBerry® (SOS_ZA 2010o)
- SOS_ZA Kate Skinner Civil society orgs refusing to nominate new #Sabc board members until Board, Parly etc commit 2 good corporate goverance. 9:29 am Nov 2nd, 2010 from Twitter for BlackBerry® (SOS_ZA 2010p)

Clearly, the controversies surrounding the appointment of new SABC Boards continued and in fact, the preferred method of protest, failing a commitment by those in power to act, was still resignation or forced removal of Board members. In particular, the appointment of a new SABC board in 2010/2011 was derailed by the unilateral appointment of Phil Molefe as Head of News, as can be seen by, amongst others, this random selection of tweets:

- SOS_ZA Kate Skinner #Sabc Board member Peter Harris argues that Phil Molefe's appointment was not ratified. New decision was taken. Decision now legal 11:23 am Nov 23rd, 2010 from Twitter for BlackBerry® (Skinner 2010ab)
- SOS_ZA Kate Skinner Gina: Molefe has now been appointed. This was 6 sept. #Sabc 2:10 pm Nov 23rd, 2010 from Twitter for BlackBerry® (Skinner 2010ac)
- SOS_ZA Kate Skinner Pippa Green: appointment process painful but we are moving on. Key issue is to turnaround news. We are putting clear KPIs in place. #Sabc 2:14 pm Nov 23rd, 2010 from Twitter for BlackBerry® (Skinner 2010ad)

With questions being asked about political pressure,

- SOS_ZA Kate Skinner Opposition Mps: was there political pressure re appointment of head of news? #Sabc 2:20 pm Nov 23rd, 2010 from Twitter for BlackBerry® (Skinner 2010ae)

- SOS_ZA Kate Skinner Gina: I had no political pressure put on me re the appointment of the Head of News. #Sabc 2:27 pm Nov 23rd, 2010 from Twitter for BlackBerry® (Skinner 2010af)

and calls from MP's for a further investigation into the matter of the appointment,

- SOS_ZA Kate Skinner Vos: as parly u can call for an investigation into the matter of the appointment. It was a huge problem. #Sabc 2:29 pm Nov 23rd, 2010 from Twitter for BlackBerry® (Skinner 2010ag)
- SOS_ZA Kate Skinner Killian: I personally asked the Public Protector to investigate the appoint of the Head of News. #Sabc 2:35 pm Nov 23rd, 2010 from Twitter for BlackBerry® (Skinner 2010ah)
- SOS_ZA Kate Skinner Parly chair: Good that there is unity in the Board but this must be built on good corp goverance.#Sabc 2:42 pm Nov 23rd, 2010 from Twitter for BlackBerry® (Skinner 2010ai)

Nonetheless, the appointment process for a new SABC Board forged ahead and Parliament declared that they should have a new board in place by February 2011. @SOS_ZA ended the tweets on a hopeful note, pointing out that parliamentary hearings did result in a commitment to good governance as illustrated by this random selection of tweets from the hearings:

- SOS_ZA Kate Skinner Sabc board nominations extended to 6 Dec. Now Parly, #Sabc board etc need to commit to good governance so people prepared to stand 10:02 am Nov 17th, 2010 from Twitter for BlackBerry® (Skinner 2010aa)
- SOS_ZA Kate Skinner Parly Chair: we shd have new #Sabc Board members in place by Feb. Our expectations are high re: this Board. Thanks & goodbye! #Sabc 2:58 pm Nov 23rd, 2010 from Twitter for BlackBerry® (Skinner 2010aj)
- SOS_ZA Kate Skinner @MediaMattersZA I am! But most interesting day in Parly. Commitments to good governance. Some glimmers of hope. #SABC 5:16 pm Nov 23rd, 2010 from Twitter for BlackBerry® (Skinner 2010ak)

One outcome of the sorry state of affairs at the SABC, together with increased pressure from civil society organizations such as SOS, was that government was forced to rethink its strategy regarding the PSB Bill. Government responded to calls for a review of the Bill, thereby opening the floor for oral negotiations in November 2010 through a parliamentary hearing process that allowed the public and members of civil society to respond to the bill in person. What follows is a random selection of tweets from the PSB Bill hearings:

- SOS_ZA Kate Skinner At public service broadcasting bill hearings. Guy Burger saying a policy review is essential! This first then the law. #sabc 7:44 am Nov 15th, 2010 from Twitter for BlackBerry® (SOS_ZA 2010q)
- SOS_ZA Kate Skinner Guy Berger: we need to avoid political capture of the #sabc. Maybe break it up 3 Sabcs! #mediamattersza 7:50 am Nov 15th, 2010 from Twitter for BlackBerry® (SOS_ZA 2010r)
- SOS_ZA Kate Skinner Multichoice: Public Service Broadcasting Bill should be an #Sabc Bill not deal with comm media etc. #MediaMattersZA 8:09 am Nov 15th, 2010 from Twitter for BlackBerry® (SOS_ZA, 2010s)
- SOS_ZA Kate Skinner Multichoice: we need a flat rate public broadcasting levy to fund the#Sabc. It should be managed by SARS. #MediaMattersZA 8:24 am Nov 15th, 2010 from Twitter for BlackBerry® (SOS_ZA 2010t)
- SOS_ZA Kate Skinner At public service broadcasting bill oral hearings. National Association of broadcasters: the Bill should only look at the #Sabc 9:37 am Nov 16th, 2010 from Twitter for BlackBerry® (SOS_ZA 2010u)
- SOS_ZA Kate Skinner NAB: Dept of Comms needs to do more research on funding options for the #Sabc. It is DOC's role! #MediaMattersZA 9:43 am Nov 16th, 2010 from Twitter for BlackBerry® (SOS_ZA 2010v)
- SOS_ZA Kate Skinner The Dept of Comms says they have done lots of broadcasting research. The public must keep asking for it. #Sabc 10:02 am Nov 16th, 2010 from Twitter for BlackBerry® (SOS_ZA 2010w)
- SOS_ZA Kate Skinner NAB: the #Sabc's oversight structures must play their roles. At some point Parly and the DOC accepted a deficit

budget. Not acceptable! 10:07 am Nov 16th, 2010 from Twitter for BlackBerry® (SOS_ZA 2010x)

- SOS_ZA Kate Skinner NAB: we need a clear policy review, a road map for broadcasting for the next 20 years. Dept of Comms must lead the way. #Sabc 10:16 am Nov 16th, 2010 from Twitter for BlackBerry® (SOS_ZA 2010y)
- SOS_ZA Kate Skinner Cape TV: public broadcasting should be aligned to the goals of the Constitution, not just the developmental goals of the state. #Sabc 10:55 am Nov 16th, 2010 from Twitter for BlackBerry® (SOS_ZA 2010z)

As evident from the above tweets, presentations on the proposed Bill was made by various members of civil society, ranging from academics (such as University of Rhodes professor, Guy Berger), media organizations (such as M-Net and Multichoice and the National Association of Broadcasters) and (not evident from the tweets, but accessible on the SOS Google groups pages), civil society organizations such as the SOS and Media Monitoring Africa. These presentations as reflected through @SOS_ZAs microblogging above, upholds the concerns about the proposed new Bill outlined earlier in this paper. Clearly, what these tweets illustrate is that while there is consensus that broadcasting policy in South Africa needs a thorough overhaul, a more rigorous period of reviewed is needed to unpack just how such an overhaul should take place and what exactly it should entail. Reiterating arguments stressed in their written submissions filed in January 2010, presenters above disagreed with the funding focus of the PSB Bill, the executive decision-making powers afforded to government in terms of thereof, and in some cases even disagreed with each other in terms of how these issues should be revised. One issue that all the role-players seemed to agree with, was that a thorough review of the policy landscape is needed before any proposed changes to the law is signed into effect and that government must be pressured to show the research they claim to have conducted.

For the SOS Coalition, as manifest in their discussion documents and press releases, the Bill's heads-on tackling of the escalating crisis at the SABC was laudable, but they lamented the fact that the Bill sought to resolve the crisis by increasing direct government interference (when it is clear from the foregoing discussions that it is precisely government interference that played a major role in the SABC's crisis of governance and funding in the first place). The SOS Coalition therefore lobbied with other organizations, media bodies and opposition political parties for restraint regarding the implementation of the proposed bill, asking that the issue be tabled, pending a thorough review of the South African Broadcasting policy landscape. Through engaging in a series of discourses and public action that involved press releases, public debates as well as social media networking and discussions with similarly minded groups and organizations, government was forced to negotiate more inclusively with civil society in developing and implementing a revised Public Service Broadcasting legislative framework. On November 22, 2010, the newly minted Minister of Communications, Roy Padayachee, who took over from Siphiwe Nyanda earlier that month, announced that the controversial PSB Bill had been withdrawn, and this was communicated to the SOS Google group as well as the twitter-verse:

> From: **'Kate Skinner' <.... @mweb.co.za>**
> Date: **Mon, 22 Nov 2010 06:20:31 +0200**
> Local: **Mon, Nov 22 2010 6:20 am**
> Subject: **Minister calls for a review of psb bill!**
>
> Dear All
> This is wonderful news—see below! One of the major aims of our campaign has been to fight for a proper policy review process. We argued that the PSB Bill was premature. The Minister has now decided to withdraw the Bill to allow the Dept to consider new models for funding the SABC and community media. He will be looking at the costs of digital migration. He will also be ensuring that there is consistency in the legislative and regulatory environment. Excellent!
>
> Warm regards
> Kate
>
> Kate Skinner
> Campaign Coordinator—SOS:Support Public Broadcasting
> (082) xxx-xxx
> www.supportpublicbroadcasting.co.za
> <http://www.supportpublicbroadcasting.co.za/>
> twitter.com/sos_za
> via Google groups (http://bit.ly/oXhU7l)

The incoming Minister cited as reasons for this decision that government wanted South Africa's broadcasting policy to be at the cutting edge of the digital age, emphasizing that this requires a committed effort from the state, industry and key role-players in society (Sabinetlaw 2010). In what can be considered a victory for civil society activism, Minister Padayachee further noted that processes would now be put into place to:

1. review the 1998 white paper on broadcasting, including a scan of the broadcasting legislation and regulations currently in place to ensure policy and legislative alignment;
2. review completed research on funding options for the SABC and community media; and
3. institute an economic modelling exercise to look at the costs for the SABC and community media as well the projected costs of digital migration.

The digital migration process finally kicked off in 2016, but media commentators and scholars alike agree that the roll-out has been highly irregular. This notwithstanding, it can be agreed that in the case of the proposed PSB Bill of 2009/2010, civil society and civic discourse succeeded in turning a highly contentious issue, leaving the door open for more active participation of all stakeholders in future policy decisions and negotiations. Here, it is worthwhile to note the role of social media in supporting media policy advocacy. As Dahlgren (2000) notes, the rampant intermeshing of the internet with so many social institutions, organizations and everyday settings invites us to consider how this technology is concretely used and integrated in contexts where people are repeatedly moving between on- and offline activities within the practical circumstances they have at hand. While advocacy scholars concur that social media can play a significant role in bringing about social change, they nonetheless stress that "... change is ... brought about by getting one's hands dirty, by inserting oneself into the material conditions and realities of the historical present" (Giardina and Denzin 2011, p. 2). In accepting this argument, it is meaningful to acknowledge that even though social media alone will not bring changes; it does expose issues and links organizers. Through the SOS Coalition's online activities, a platform was created which provided opportunities for academics, media professionals and representatives from a host of civil society organizations, to express their visions for a new broadcasting era in South Africa, as well as to discuss legal, technical and financial matters as it pertains to public (service) broadcasting in that country. In essence, it gives a glimpse into citizenship as practice, that is, a social process in which civic engagement and participation in social movements provides a space in which citizens can meaningfully practice democracy in everyday life. Through their social networking efforts, the SOS ensured wider publication (and perhaps eventual participation) in what they are doing, providing at once a platform for a public not necessarily interested in joining the coalition, but nonetheless concerned about broadcasting issues, as well as streamlining in-group communication between coalition-members in seeking consensus on how they wish to position themselves in terms of ongoing discourses and issues.

What we have learned through following @SOS_ZA is that they were indeed lobbying for a public broadcaster that would be more accountable to the public it professes to serve. Their efforts included informing ordinary citizens about broadcasting policy, problems in the governance of the SABC and issues pertaining to Parliament's responsibility towards the SABC and the South African public. Their efforts extended beyond mere informational tweets (although these form the bases of this paper's focus), to include organized dissent (like marches to Parliament or SABC headquarters), lobbying with Parliament on behalf of the SABC viewing public and forming a pressure group with partners such as SANEF to force politicians, law-makers and policy-makers to listen. In this respect and in relation to the 2010 parliamentary hearings into the SABC, they were therefore successful in forcing Parliament to reschedule the hearings and to open it for the public. This also opened the door for them to partake in the parliamentary hearings through attendance and spreading the word on what was transpiring during the course of the hearings. As a direct result of their lobbying and their engagement with other civil society organizations, trade unions and the general public, the SOS are connected to two important victories that may very well shape the future of participatory broadcasting policy reform in South Africa—the first was the SOS Coalition and SANEF's efforts to ensure that the parliamentary hearings into the SABCs trials and tribulations would be accessible to the South African public and civil society, and the second was succeeding in forcing government to retract a controversial bill and start the process from scratch.

Notes

1. To read more about the crisis, consult Lloyd et al. 2010.
2. The PSB Bill can be accessed in its entirety at http://www.info.gov.za/view/DownloadFileAction?id=110838.

References

BEMAWU. (2009, November, 12, 5:47 a.m.). *[t]he income tax proposal can never work.* http://bit.ly/nqk5ny. Accessed 15 March 2011.

Boloka, M. (2009, November 11, 09:21 a.m.). *Dear Mark and colleagues.* http://bit.ly/oIsrfu. Accessed 15 March 2011.

Catone, J. (2008). Twitter as a tool for social change. http://bit.ly/qIQbqH. Accessed 3 June 2011.

Da Silva, I.S. (2010). Lobby group cries foul over "unconstitutional" public service broadcasting. Bizcommunity.com. http://bit.ly/5zKi6M. Accessed 1 June 2011.

Dahlgren, P. (2000). The Internet and the democratization of civic culture. *Political Communication, 17*(4), 335–340.

Delanty, G. (2000). *Citizenship in a global age: Society, culture, politics.* Buckingham: Open University Press.

Duncan, J. (2009, November 11, 5:32 p.m.). I really think that SoS needs to seek a meeting with Treasury to signal its support for the income tax proposal. http://bit.ly/nqk5ny. Accessed 15 March 2011.

Giardina, M.D., & Denzin, N. K. (2011). Acts of activism - politics of possibility: Toward a new performative cultural politics. *Cultural Studies. Critical Methodologies, XX* (X), 1–9.

Heath, C.W. (1999). Negotiating broadcasting policy. *Civil society and civic discourse in Ghana. Gazette, 61*(6): 511–521.

Heller, P. (2009). Democratic deepening in India and South Africa. *Journal of Asian and African Studies, 44*(1), 123–149.

Hoskins, A., O'Loughlin, B., Richards, B., & Seib, P. (2011). Editor's note. *Media, war and conflict, 4*(2), 107–108.

Isin, E.F., & Turner, B.S. (Eds.) (2002). *Handbook of citizenship studies.* London: Sage.

Lloyd, L., Duncan, J., Minnie, J., & Bussiek, H. (2010). Public broadcasting in Africa series. South Africa. A survey. http://bit.ly/oBvBhU. Accessed 2 June 2011.

Louw, P.E. (Ed.). (1993). *South African media policy: Debates of the 1990s studies on the South African media.* Belville: Anthropos.

Louw, P.E., & Milton, V.C. (2012). *New voices over the air: The transformation of the South African broadcasting corporation in a changing South Africa.* New York: Hampton Press.

mark@wisenet.co.za. (2009, November 11, 11:14 a.m.). *Hi Mashilo.* http://bit.ly/nqk5ny40. Accessed 15 March 2011.

Public Service Broadcasting Bill. (2009). Public service broadcasting bill. *National Gazettes* no. 32663, from October 28, 2009. http://bit.ly/ofePfJ. Accessed 1 June 2011.

Republic of South Africa. (1999). *Broadcasting act* (9 of 1999). Pretoria: Government Printers.

SabinetLaw.net. (2010, November 24). Communications withdraws public service broadcasting bill. *SabinetLaw*. http://bit.ly/ncWn6J. Accessed 13 March 2010.

Skinner, K. (2009, November). *Various mailings*. http://bit.ly/oIsrfu. Accessed 15 March 2011.

Skinner, K. [SOS_ZA] (2010a, August 3). *What do people think of Ben Ngubane's support for the CEO around bonuses?* [Tweet]. https://twitter.com/search?q=SOS%20Coalition%20since%3A2010-05-01%20until%3A2011-12-31&src=typd. Accessed 2 June 2011.

Skinner, K. [SOS_ZA] (2010b, August 3). *Home:#SABC bosses face rebellion*: https://twitter.com/search?q=SOS%20Coalition%20since%3A2010-05-01%20until%3A2011-12-31&src=typd.

Skinner, K. [SOS_ZA] (2010c, August 24). *Sanef has got an interdict to force parly to hold an open session on the Sabc. Everything on hold. Now discussing Postbank Bill. Sigh!* [Tweet]. https://twitter.com/search?q=SOS%20Coalition%20since%3A2010-05-01%20until%3A2011-12-31&src=typd.

Skinner, K. [SOS_ZA] (2010d, August 24). *Ben Ngubane spoke in the closed session. No one else. Hearing needs to be concluded soon! Only one side of the story* [Tweet]. https://twitter.com/search?q=SOS%20Coalition%20since%3A2010-05-01%20until%3A2011-12-31&src=typd.

Skinner, K. [SOS_ZA] (2010e, August 26). *Cosatu's positions on secrecy bill, media tribunal and Sabc - excellent. Broadly supports Sabc Board. Ben and Solly the problem. Agreed!* [Tweet]. https://twitter.com/search?q=SOS%20Coalition%20since%3A2010-05-01%20until%3A2011-12-31&src=typd.

Skinner, K. [SOS_ZA] (2010f, August 27). *SABC CEO Solly Mokoetle has just been suspended. 4:14 pm Aug 27th, 2010 from web.* [Tweet]. https://twitter.com/search?q=SOS%20Coalition%20since%3A2010-05-01%20until%3A2011-12-31&src=typd.

Skinner, K. [SOS_ZA] (2010g, August 29). *Hope SABC Board followed labour law to the letter. Solly contesting suspension. Cant afford a protracted labour law battle! Aaarrrrgh!* [Tweet]. https://twitter.com/search?q=SOS%20Coalition%20since%3A2010-05-01%20until%3A2011-12-31&src=typd.

Skinner, K. [SOS_ZA] (2010h, August 30). *Sabc management weighing in on the side of Solly. Things getting messy!* [Tweet]. https://twitter.com/search?q=SOS%20Coalition%20since%3A2010-05-01%20until%3A2011-12-31&src=typd.

Skinner, K. [SOS_ZA] (2010i, September 6). *Sabc board member Magatho Mello has officially resigned! Two members have now thrown in the towel. Parly must act.* [Tweet]. https://twitter.com/search?q=SOS%20Coalition%20since%3A2010-05-01%20until%3A2011-12-31&src=typd

Skinner, K. [SOS_ZA] (2010j, September 7). *Debate at Constitutional Hill 2nite on Sabc crisis - finding lasting solutions, 630 pm. Board chair will speak from the floor.* [Tweet]. https://twitter.com/search?q=SOS%20Coalition%20since%3A2010-05-01%20until%3A2011-12-31&src=typd.

Skinner, K. [SOS_ZA] (2010k, October 17). *Pippa Green: Sabc town hall meetings. Citizens really had there say. #zamediafreedom* [Tweet]. https://twitter.com/search?q=SOS%20Coalition%20since%3A2010-05-01%20until%3A2011-12-31&src=typd.

Skinner, K. [SOS_ZA] (2010l, October 17). *Sabc reporting to Parly Wed. Minister says they will be presenting united front. Why Board not telling us?#zamediafreedom* [Tweet]. https://twitter.com/search?q=SOS%20Coalition%20since%3A2010-05-01%20until%3A2011-12-31&src=typd.

Skinner, K. [SOS_ZA] (2010m, October 20). *Just heard that #Sabc Board resignations been accepted with immediate effect. Ex Board members can't speak. Big prob.* [Tweet]. https://twitter.com/search?q=SOS%20Coalition%20since%3A2010-05-01%20until%3A2011-12-31&src=typd.

Skinner, K. [SOS_ZA] (2010n, October 22). *#Sabc union Bemawu calling for Chair to resign due to dismal Parly performance. Also hasn't signed Ceo contract!* [Tweet]. https://twitter.com/search?q=SOS%20Coalition%20since%3A2010-05-01%20until%3A2011-12-31&src=typd.

Skinner, K. [SOS_ZA] (2010o, October 22). *#Sabc Chair saying the appointment of acting Ceo is illegal. He wants to bring back Solly! Did anyone hear this on the news?* [Tweet]. https://twitter.com/search?q=SOS%20Coalition%20since%3A2010-05-01%20until%3A2011-12-31&src=typd.

Skinner, K. [SOS_ZA] (2010p, November 2). *Civil society orgs refusing to nominate new #Sabc board members until Board, Parly etc commit 2 good corporate goverance.* [Tweet]. https://twitter.com/search?q=SOS%20Coalition%20since%3A2010-05-01%20until%3A2011-12-31&src=typd.

Skinner, K. [SOS_ZA] (2010q, November 15). *At public service broadcasting bill hearings. Guy Burger saying a policy review is essential! This first then the law. #sabc.* [Tweet]. https://twitter.com/search?q=SOS%20Coalition%20since%3A2010-05-01%20until%3A2011-12-31&src=typd.

Skinner, K. [SOS_ZA] (2010r, November 15). *Guy Berger: We need to avoid political capture of the #sabc. Maybe break it up 3 Sabcs! #mediamattersza* [Tweet]. https://twitter.com/search?q=SOS%20Coalition%20since%3A2010-05-01%20until%3A2011-12-31&src=typd.

Skinner, K. [SOS_ZA] (2010s, November 15). *Multichoice: Public Service Broadcasting Bill should be an #Sabc Bill not deal with comm media etc. #MediaMattersZA* [Tweet]. https://twitter.com/search?q=SOS%20Coalition%20since%3A2010-05-01%20until%3A2011-12-31&src=typd.

Skinner, K. [SOS_ZA] (2010t, November 15). *Multichoice: We need a flat rate public broadcasting levy to fund the#Sabc. It should be managed by SARS.*

#MediaMattersZA [Tweet]. https://twitter.com/search?q=SOS%20Coalition%20since%3A2010-05-01%20until%3A2011-12-31&src=typd.

Skinner, K. [SOS_ZA] (2010u, November 16) *At public service broadcasting bill oral hearings. National Association of broadcasters: The Bill should only look at the #Sabc.* [Tweet]. https://twitter.com/search?q=SOS%20Coalition%20since%3A2010-05-01%20until%3A2011-12-31&src=typd.

Skinner, K. [SOS_ZA] (2010v, November 16). *NAB: Dept of Comms needs to do more research on funding options for the #Sabc. It is DOC's role! #MediaMattersZA.* [Tweet]. https://twitter.com/search?q=SOS%20Coalition%20since%3A2010-05-01%20until%3A2011-12-31&src=typd.

Skinner, K. [SOS_ZA] (2010w, November 16). *The Dept of Comms says they have done lots of broadcasting research. The public must keep asking for it. #Sabc* [Tweet]. https://twitter.com/search?q=SOS%20Coalition%20since%3A2010-05-01%20until%3A2011-12-31&src=typd.

Skinner, K. [SOS_ZA] (2010x, November 16 *NAB: The #Sabc's oversight structures must play their roles. At some point Parly and the DOC accepted a deficit budget. Not acceptable!* [Tweet]. https://twitter.com/search?q=SOS%20Coalition%20since%3A2010-05-01%20until%3A2011-12-31&src=typd.

Skinner, K. [SOS_ZA] (2010y, November 16). *NAB: We need a clear policy review, a road map for broadcasting for the next 20 years. Dept of Comms must lead the way. #Sabc* [Tweet]. https://twitter.com/search?q=SOS%20Coalition%20since%3A2010-05-01%20until%3A2011-12-31&src=typd.

Skinner, K. [SOS_ZA] (2010z, November 16). *Cape TV: Public broadcasting should be aligned to the goals of the Constitution, not just the developmental goals of the state. #Sabc* [Tweet]. https://twitter.com/search?q=SOS%20Coalition%20since%3A2010-05-01%20until%3A2011-12-31&src=typd.

Skinner, K. [SOS_ZA] (2010aa, November 17). *Sabc board nominations extended to 6 Dec. Now Parly, #Sabc board etc need to commit to good governance so people prepared to stand* [Tweet]. https://twitter.com/search?q=SOS%20Coalition%20since%3A2010-05-01%20until%3A2011-12-31&src=typd.

Skinner, K. [SOS_ZA] (2010ab, November 23). *#Sabc Board member Peter Harris argues that Phil Molefe's appointment was not ratified. New decision was taken. Decision now legal.* [Tweet]. https://twitter.com/search?q=SOS%20Coalition%20since%3A2010-05-01%20until%3A2011-12-31&src=typd.

Skinner, K. [SOS_ZA] (2010ac, November 23). *Gina: Molefe has now been appointed. This was 6 sept. #Sabc.* [Tweet]. https://twitter.com/search?q=SOS%20Coalition%20since%3A2010-05-01%20until%3A2011-12-31&src=typd.

Skinner, K. [SOS_ZA] (2010ad, November 23). *Pippa Green: Appointment process painful but we are moving on. Key issue is to turnaround news. We are putting clear KPIs in place. #Sabc.* [Tweet]. https://twitter.com/search?q=SOS%20Coalition%20since%3A2010-05-01%20until%3A2011-12-31&src=typd.

Skinner, K. [SOS_ZA] (2010ae, November 23). *Opposition Mps: Was there political pressure re appointment of head of news? #Sabc.* [Tweet]. https://twitter.com/search?q=SOS%20Coalition%20since%3A2010-05-01%20until%3A2011-12-31&src=typd.

Skinner, K. [SOS_ZA] (2010af, November 23). *Gina: I had no political pressure put on me re the appointment of the Head of News. #Sabc* [Tweet]. https://twitter.com/search?q=SOS%20Coalition%20since%3A2010-05-01%20until%3A2011-12-31&src=typd.

Skinner, K. [SOS_ZA] (2010ag, November 23). *Vos: As parly u can call for an investigation into the matter of the appointment. It was a huge problem. #Sabc.* [Tweet]. https://twitter.com/search?q=SOS%20Coalition%20since%3A2010-05-01%20until%3A2011-12-31&src=typd.

Skinner, K. [SOS_ZA] (2010ah, November 23). *Killian: I personally asked the Public Protector to investigate the appoint of the Head of News. #Sabc* [Tweet]. https://twitter.com/search?q=SOS%20Coalition%20since%3A2010-05-01%20until%3A2011-12-31&src=typd.

Skinner, K. [SOS_ZA] (2010ai, November 23). *Parly chair: Good that there is unity in the Board but this must be built on good corp goverance.#Sabc* [Tweet]. https://twitter.com/search?q=SOS%20Coalition%20since%3A2010-05-01%20until%3A2011-12-31&src=typd.

Skinner, K. [SOS_ZA] (2010aj, November 23). *Parly Chair: We shd have new #Sabc Board members in place by Feb. Our expectations are high re: This Board. Thanks & goodbye! #Sabc.* [Tweet]. https://twitter.com/search?q=SOS%20Coalition%20since%3A2010-05-01%20until%3A2011-12-31&src=typd.

Skinner, K. [SOS_ZA] (2010ak, November 23). *@MediaMattersZA I am! But most interesting day in Parly. Commitments to good governance. Some glimmers of hope. #SABC* [Tweet]. https://twitter.com/search?q=SOS%20Coalition%20since%3A2010-05-01%20until%3A2011-12-31&src=typd.

Sparks, C. (2009), South African media in transition. *Journal of African Media Studies, 1*(2), 195–220.

Tomaselli, K., & Teer-Tomaselli, R.E. (2008). Exogenous and endogenous democracy: South African politics and media. *The International Journal of Press/Politics, 13*(2), 171–180.

Turner, B. (1993). Contemporary problems in the theory of citizenship. In B. Turner (Ed.), *Citizenship and Social Theory.* London: Sage.

Prof Viola C. Milton started her teaching career at the University of Pretoria, where she also completed her undergraduate degrees as well as a Master's degree. She then moved to Bloomington, Indiana (USA) where she enrolled for a doctorate in Communication and Culture. At the University of South Africa, she is a Thuthuka grantholder for a project, entitled "The televised public sphere:

Afrikaans television and identity formation," which explores the politics of identity in post-apartheid Afrikaans television. Recently, her research focus shifted to the negotiation of media policy in South Africa as well as issues of media, citizenship and identity. This focus is reflected in the research project entitled "The Media Policy and Diversity Project" funded by Unisa's Women-in-Research grant as well as by the Open Society Foundation. The project is spearheaded by Dr Julie Reid and Prof Milton in collaboration with Prof Jane Duncan from the School of Journalism and Media Studies at Rhodes University. She is executive editor for the oldest South African journal in Communication Studies, entitled *Communicatio: South African Journal for Communication Theory and Research.* She also chairs the South African Communication Association's Journalism and Media Studies Interest Group.

PART III

Gender and LGTB Movements Online: Emerging Debates

CHAPTER 11

Digital Strategies and African LGBTI Organizing

Ashley Currier and Julie Moreau

Internet technology and social media can shrink the distance between social movements in different world regions (Earl and Kimport 2011), allowing activists almost instantaneous access to lessons, material support, and advice from fellow activists in other countries (Van De Donk et al. 2004). Activists involved with under-resourced and unpopular social movements, such as lesbian, gay, bisexual, transgender, and intersex (LGBTI) movements, may be especially drawn to digital media as a means to mobilize constituents dispersed throughout a country and to evade unwanted public attention (Dencik and Leistert 2015). With the rise of new media, transnational advocacy networks (TANs) rely on digital media to develop a unifying vision, plan their next moves, draw attention to matters that may interest a variety of actors, and research human rights conditions in different countries (Bob 2012; Wiseberg 2001). Actors embedded in TANs invest in 'information exchange' to 'create new issues

A. Currier (✉)
University of Cincinnati, Cincinnati, United States
e-mail: currieay@ucmail.uc.edu

J. Moreau
Washington University, St. Louis, United States
e-mail: juliemoreau@wustl.edu

B. Mutsvairo (ed.), *Digital Activism in the Social Media Era*,
DOI 10.1007/978-3-319-40949-8_11

and categories and to persuade, pressure, and gain leverage over much more powerful organizations and governments' (Keck and Sikkink 1998, p. 2). Digital communication and strategies 'extend the opportunities for dissent that are available to the wired citizen, and the organization and expression of voice and action against authority acquires an unprecedented scale' as activists can reach distant audiences (Mejias 2013, p. 104). Transnational movement organizations, such as Amnesty International, Human Rights Watch, and OutRight International, formerly the International Gay and Lesbian Human Rights Commission (IGLHRC), have favoured email alerts and press releases posted to their websites as ways to create a sense of urgency around LGBTI human rights violations in particular African countries (Thoreson 2014). Digital alerts motivate LGBTI rights supporters around the world to pressure African government leaders to take actions that respect LGBTI rights. Actions political leaders can take include decriminalizing same-sex sexual practices and refraining from engaging in political homophobia, which refers to the public disparagement of 'same-sex sexualities, non-heterosexual persons, gender variance, and gender and sexual diversity activism' (Currier 2012a, p. 442).

Despite the democratizing potential of digital strategies, they can pose problems for LGBTI organizing, when activists rely on them almost exclusively. With instantaneous transmission, digital strategies can also perpetuate the circulation of misinformation about LGBTI organizing. As Ryan Richard Thoreson's (2014) research shows, IGLHRC's reliance on digital strategies generated constraints for employees, whom Thoreson referred to as 'brokers' (p. 11). Brokers experienced difficulty making the organization's website accessible to people using mobile devices. IGLHRC employees were also unsure whether action alerts prompting people to email government officials in countries with spotty LGBTI human rights records were as effective as a 'flood of physical letters and faxes' (Thoreson 2014, p. 166). Additionally, IGLHRC employees had to confront and correct inaccurate information about LGBTI human rights violations that circulated online among LGBTI rights activists. IGLHRC worked to prevent incorrect information about Tiwonge Chimbalanga, a transgender woman, and Steven Monjeza, a cisgender man, who were on trial in Malawi in 2010 for violating the anti-sodomy law, from circulating internationally. An LGBTI rights activist 'repeatedly and publicly insisted that Monjeza had contracted malaria and was deathly ill in prison' (Thoreson 2014, p. 178). Representatives from the Centre for the Development of People (CEDEP), a leading LGBTI rights movement organization in Malawi, visited the couple in prison and confirmed that Monjeza had received treatment for malaria and was convalescing. Misinformation about Monjeza's poor health and mistreatment in prison created 'criticism' locally that CEDEP was 'spreading lies and blowing the incident out of proportion, which they did not need as they prepared to defend Monjeza in court' (Thoreson 2014, p. 178). IGLHRC brokers worked behind the scenes to ask the activist to stop circulating bad information about Monjeza and publicly asserted that Monjeza had recovered from malaria. Although IGLHRC brokers tried to stop the harm created by the circulating online misinformation about Monjeza's health in prison, CEDEP's reputation suffered, nonetheless.

Digital media can have damaging effects on African LGBTI activism. While activists can anticipate some negative effects, others catch activists by surprise. In particular, the rapid dissemination of movement information that digital media provide can render African LGBTI activist organizations vulnerable, as activists cannot control how others, such as Northern audiences concerned by anti-queer developments in African countries, will use and interpret their messages. When reports about anti-homosexuality legislation and mobilization in countries like Nigeria and Uganda become 'viral' in the West by spreading quickly online, the resulting furore led to the labelling of entire African nations and their citizens as 'homophobic' (Epprecht 2008). Writing about tabloid journalism's role in instigating international outrage over anti-queer hostility in Uganda, Kenne Mwikya (2013, p. 145) observes how '[i]ntellectual thought and analysis... were muffled by the din of blogs and news sites summarily concluding that Uganda is homophobic'. In addition, when Western audiences offer sanctimonious responses to anti-homosexuality mobilization in African countries, this can silence African LGBTI rights activists who have been organizing in response to anti-LGBTI efforts (Epprecht 2008). Tavia Nyong'o (2012) characterizes these strategies as generating the 'fantasy of participation' whereby people in one part of the world can support and imagine themselves participating in LGBTI organizing elsewhere in the world (p. 46).

In this essay, we offer insights into the benefits to and drawbacks of African LGBTI movement organizations' use of digital media and strategies. We turn to three case studies involving LGBTI movement organizations' reliance on digital media and strategies to explain the consequences of digital strategies on these organizations. Because we did not focus our empirical research on questions of digital strategies in African LGBTI organizing, we draw selectively from case studies in which digital strategies affected organizational processes and outcomes. First, we examine how digital media can fuel political homophobia targeting LGBTI activism, using the case of anti-gay harassment, vilification, and violence against Alternative-Côte d'Ivoire, an Ivoirian LGBTI movement organization. Second, we discuss the void left in the South African LGBTI movement by the closure of Behind the Mask, the first LGBTI movement organization to serve as an online information clearinghouse for African LGBTI organizing; Behind the Mask's closure due to financial problems illuminates the ephemerality and precariousness associated with using digital strategies funded by Northern donors. Third, we analyse critical LGBTI movement responses to the digital work of Luleki Sizwe, a black South African lesbian activist organization, which used an online petition to mobilize people around the world to pressure South African government officials to take action against anti-lesbian rape and violence. Original field research informs our case studies. We draw on ethnographic and interview research Currier conducted in South Africa in 2005–2006 and in Côte d'Ivoire in 2013 and on ethnographic and interview research Moreau conducted in South Africa in 2011 and 2012.

Emerging Political Homophobia in Côte d'Ivoire

The landscape for LGBTI organizing in West Africa has changed in response to local and international socio-political developments. In October 2011, British Prime Minister David Cameron announced that his government would terminate aid to African governments that refused to recognize LGBTI rights. On December 6, 2011, United States Secretary of State Hillary Rodham Clinton unveiled President Barack Obama's pro-LGBTI rights policy in a speech at the United Nations (UN) (Myers and Cooper 2011). Some experts interpreted Clinton's announcement as targeting particular African governments that persecuted gender and sexual minorities (Pflanz 2011). After Clinton's speech, African political leaders speculated whether this policy would mean that their countries would lose donor aid if they did not immediately recognize LGBTI rights.

Côte d'Ivoire, a nation still recovering from civil war, seems hospitable to gender and sexual minority organizing. Unlike many other African nations in which same-sex sex acts are criminalized, same-sex sexual behaviour is illegal in only if it occurs in public (Kouassi 2011). For most of the 2000s, political and religious officials remained conspicuously silent about homosexuality and LGBTI rights, unlike their peers elsewhere on the continent. Several LGBTI movement organizations, including Alternative-Côte d'Ivoire and Lesbian Life Association Côte d'Ivoire, operate openly (Department of State 2012). However, LGBTI organizing has been difficult in the past. In 2006, the Ivorian Association for Lesbians, Gays, Bisexuals, and Transsexuals tried to register with the state, a request the interior minister denied (Kouassi 2009). Homophobia hampers the work of HIV/AIDS activists who work with men who have sex with men (MSM), and anti-LGBTI violence inhibits activism (Corey-Boulet 2012; Department of State 2012). In light of social homophobia, LGBTI activism in Côte d'Ivoire is concentrated mostly in non-governmental organizations (NGOs) working on HIV/AIDS education, prevention, and treatment (Nguyen 2010; Thomann 2014). HIV/AIDS work has enabled NGOs like Alternative-Côte d'Ivoire (Alternative) to work with gender and sexual minorities under the auspices of a public-health mandate. Because anti-gay opponents sometimes portray LGBTI activists as corrupting and converting heterosexual people into 'homosexuals', couching LGBTI advocacy within a public-health framework allows some organizations to continue their gender and sexual diversity activism unfettered (Currier and Cruz 2014; Epprecht 2012).

Alternative's reputation as an HIV/AIDS NGO came under attack when local media learned that the French embassy was giving the organization US$50,000, resulting in anti-gay opposition directed at Alternative (Currier and Thomann 2016). Whereas some African LGBTI activist organizations experienced difficulty in obtaining funds for their campaigns, Alternative was quite successful. Although funding from the US President's Emergency Plan for AIDS Relief (PEPFAR) supported much of Alternative's HIV/AIDS outreach work, Alternative managed to procure funding from other sources, including the French embassy in Abidjan, which pledged funds to support the group's LGBTI rights advocacy. Alternative celebrated this grant with a signing ceremony at the organization's office on 25 June 2013. A number of staff and volunteers at Alternative took photos of the ceremony and uploaded photos to social-media accounts. Some Ivoirian journalists downloaded these photos and used them to smear the French embassy's support for Alternative.

Local homophobia erupted in the aftermath of the French embassy's grant to Alternative. Ivoirian media claimed that the French embassy was paying Alternative to advocate for the legalization of same-sex marriage. France's legalization of same-sex marriage in May 2013 and US President Barack Obama's call for African leaders to respect LGBTI rights during his June 2013 visit to Senegal added fuel to this conspiracy theory (Nossiter 2013). These developments prompted Ivoirian President Alassane Outtara to issue a statement that same-sex marriage had no place in Côte d'Ivoire. In this sense, digital activism resulted in what Joseph Massad (2002) has called an 'incitement to discourse' around homosexuality (p. 374). Referring to transnational LGBTI movement organizations, such as the International Lesbian and Gay Association and IGLHRC as the 'gay international', he argues that these organizations' orientalist impulse (re) colonizes sexualities in the Arab and Muslim worlds (Massad 2002, p. 374). Where previously there had been little political homophobia, increased attention to same-sex sexuality prompted a governmental response that ultimately made life worse for LGBTI people locally.

Ivoirian media continued publishing unfavourable stories about Alternative. Some journalists disclosed the secret location of the organization's fundraising event, prompting leaders to postpone the event. Although local homophobia appeared to subside late in 2013, anti-gay mobilization became violent early in 2014, when vigilantes attacked the Alternative office and homes of Alternative's leaders. Fearful for the safety of the organization's staff and volunteers, Alternative's leaders pressured UN officials and the Ivoirian government to investigate these attacks, resulting in the posting of UN peacekeepers and Ivoirian military outside Alternative's office in Abidjan (Thomann 2014, pp. 183–187). These events shook defenders of gender and sexual diversity who closely monitor local political developments. The rise of political homophobia in Côte d'Ivoire can be directly linked to journalists' use of digital media to cast doubt on LGBTI organizing and the French government's intentions in giving Alternative a grant.

Behind the Mask: Linking LGBTI Activists throughout Africa

African LGBTI social movement organizations creatively use digital media to mobilize their constituents to participate in protests, to publicize new campaigns, to drum up support for victims of violence, and to forge connections with potential funders. Increasingly, some LGBTI movement organizations have begun specializing in using digital strategies and media to advance movement goals. Movement organizations' specialization gives other organizations the opportunity to focus on specific programs for constituents, to develop effective law-reform campaigns, to stage impromptu protests quickly, and to provide infrastructure and organizational expertise to emerging activist organizations (Levitsky 2007). In some cases, organizations concentrate on providing services or running campaigns in a specific geographic area, such as a neighbourhood, town, or city. In countries like South Africa in which the LGBTI movement field contains numerous LGBTI activist organizations, organizational specialization can relieve other groups of the need to provide multiple services and run many campaigns, which can exhaust organizations' resources and tire dedicated volunteers. In addition, movement specialization can help prevent or mitigate 'turf' disputes between organizations, as activists become familiar with where other organizations work and the strategies they use (Currier 2011). Behind the Mask emerged as one such organization offering a much-needed service and strengthening a pan-African LGBTI movement's infrastructure through its online presence and transnational activist network.

Based in Johannesburg, South Africa, Behind the Mask concentrated on gathering information about LGBTI activism throughout the continent and publishing original content on its website. Bart Luirink (2000), a Dutch journalist, obtained funding from a Western donor in 2000 to create Behind the Mask as a way to facilitate internet reporting on LGBTI activism in southern Africa. Behind the Mask sponsored online meeting spaces, including a '[queer] woman's chat room', according to Sibusiso, a black lesbian woman and Behind the Mask staff member (interview with Ashley Currier, 28 November 2005, Johannesburg, South Africa).

Behind the Mask supplied information for 'African gays and lesbians, whatever class or ethnicity, or those supporting the rising GLBT-movement on the African continent.... [W]ith the help of the information we provide, western GLBT-movements could provide more support for African brothers and sisters' (Alexander 2002, p. 229). Jeremiah, a black gay man and Behind the Mask staff member, explained that Behind the Mask's website was a way of 'reaching people in different countries' (interview with Ashley Currier, 8 November 2005, Johannesburg, South Africa). Sibusiso echoed this notion, stating that Behind the Mask provided 'a voice for the voiceless, the homosexual community in Africa as a whole' (Currier 2012b, p. 127). In some cases, Behind the Mask's digital strategies played an important role in the lives of ordinary LGBTI people. Ndumiso, a black lesbian woman and Behind the Mask staff member, recalled a 'case in Egypt where a gay guy was in prison, and this lawyer found out about it from [Behind the Mask's] [web]site. He actually contacted us and needed more articles on what was happening there. And we had a contact in Egypt that he could talk to. So we got him in contact with that guy, and the [arrested] guy was out of jail later because they worked together' (interview with Ashley Currier, 27 October 2005, Johannesburg, South Africa). Ndumiso believed that this unnamed Egyptian gay man might have languished in prison if an interested lawyer had not stumbled on information about this arrest on Behind the Mask's website, which prompted him to lend assistance.

Behind the Mask's digital network of African LGBTI activists uniquely positioned the organization's staff as experts on the state of gender and sexual diversity organizing in different countries. Some Northern donors prevailed on Behind the Mask staff to share their insights on fledgling activist organizations. In other words, donors asked the organization to vet 'newer organizations for donor funding. Donors occasionally asked Behind the Mask to verify the existence, reputation, and visibility of new movement organizations that applied for funding' (Currier 2012b, p. 138). However, this situation placed Behind the Mask, an organization capable of securing donor funds, 'in an unequal power relationship with new or struggling LGBT[I] movement organizations' (Currier 2012b, p. 138). Staff recognized and worked to reduce these inter-organizational disparities. Nevertheless, staff members were proud of the close working relationships they had with different donors, hoping that these relationships would benefit other African LGBTI organizations.

Although Behind the Mask successfully secured external donor funding for its work, funders eventually withdrew support from the organization, resulting in its closure. Thuli Madi, former director of Behind the Mask, stated:

> You know, the thing about Behind the Mask is that our primary product is the website and us updating the whole world, what's happening in different countries. And with the social networks, everyone is doing that. I think at the last board meeting we really had to address the question of whether Behind the Mask, you know, is complete or has actually met its purpose. Because the myth, initially in 2000, 2009 was whether homosexuality was African or not. I think we've [dispelled the myth] with the stories that we carry on our website in different countries. People are actually updating on what's

happening in their countries (Interview with Julie Moreau, 5 March 2012, Johannesburg, South Africa).

According to Madi, social media displaced Behind the Mask as an important source of information about African LGBTI organizing and issues, resulting in donors' loss of enthusiasm for funding the organization. While Madi insisted that the organization had fulfilled its primary role, she was doubtful about its overall impact. She asserted, 'You know, there's still a need for us to actually enter into dialogue with the South African Human Rights Commission, the Commission for Gender Equality [on the issue of] hate crimes or corrective rape.' She further expressed uncertainty about the reliability of information coming from the LGBTI movement and the national government about LGBTI issues. She stated, 'It's disappointing because we do media and we do other offline projects, but we need to know, what have they done? I mean, I cannot count on the report that I read over the weekend, which is updated. They haven't really done anything, except the Western Cape you know, with their 777 campaign, hate crimes and stuff.'[1] Madi's statements suggest that digital activism is powerful when activists are well resourced and positioned to generate reliable information.

When Behind the Mask suspended its operation, the website, which contained information about LGBTI organizations in different African countries and original reporting in English and French, disappeared as well, disappointing activists and allies around the world. Gay and Lesbian Memory in Action archivists acquired some of Behind the Mask's files and are cataloguing the organization's contents in their collections. Behind the Mask's disappearance suggests that relying too much on digital strategies and media can weaken African LGBTI movement organizations. In addition, digital social media can erode the important of LGBTI movement organizations like Behind the Mask that stake their reputations on serving as online repositories for African LGBTI activism.

Luleki Sizwe: Digital Media and Black South African Lesbians' Anti-rape Organizing

Digital strategies figure prominently in internal movement disputes about how South African LGBTI activist organizations should respond to anti-lesbian rape and violence. Within LGBTI movement politics, there is much debate about how to understand and present the issue of violence against LGBTI people. Some groups emphasize the importance of presenting a unified image, insisting on a singular message about movement priorities. These activists fear that a fringe movement element will overwhelm mainstream movement messages. In social movement studies parlance, this is what some scholars term the 'negative radical flank effect', which can erode movement support, resources, membership, and audiences (Haines 1984, p. 32). Activists involved with unpopular movements may try to avoid the radical flank effect altogether by taking great care with the movement's public profile. Controlling the movement's public image and neutralizing potential dissident elements are ways that social movement organizations ensure that there is identity consistency within the movement (Currier 2010). How South African LGBTI movement organizations mobilized around anti-lesbian violence mattered immensely to activists because the material consequences of such mobilization could include re-victimizing black lesbian survivors of anti-lesbian violence. In addition, when African LGBTI movement organizations deploy digital strategies and sensationalist images of LGBTI Africans as vulnerable victims transnationally to pressure national governments to take their demands seriously, they can become unwitting participants in transnational narratives that position the entire continent of Africa as desperately 'homophobic' and Northern audiences as the 'saviours' of African LGBTI people (Wahab 2016).

Black lesbians living in South African townships faced the everyday possibility of anti-lesbian violence (Swarr 2012). Anti-lesbian violence in South Africa targeted black lesbian women for bodily injury and humiliation. This form of violence took a material form that black lesbian activists dreaded. Many black lesbians feared that strangers, acquaintances or even family members would harass, abuse or rape them. Black lesbian activists find this violence to be particularly upsetting, given the fact that South Africa has one of the world's most progressive constitutions (Gevisser 2000; Croucher 2011). Ratified in 1994, the constitution prohibits discrimination on the basis of sexual orientation. Since then, lawmakers have decriminalized homosexuality and legalized same-sex marriage (Judge et al. 2008). However, no law treats violence against gender and sexual minorities as a hate crime (Wesley 2012), although law-makers were considering such a law in 2014 (Bendix 2014). We understand anti-lesbian violence as both homophobic and misogynistic violence stemming from colonial- and apartheid-era inequalities (Gqola 2007; Muholi 2004).

Mobilization against anti-lesbian violence has continued over the last few years, especially in response to the rape and murder of several black lesbians. In February 2006, Zoliswa Nkonyana was a young black lesbian woman who was killed by a group of men in Khayelitsha, a Cape Town township, because of her sexuality. The circumstances of Nkonyana's murder mirrored the psychological and physical insecurity that many black lesbians faced daily. On 7 July 2007, Sizakele Sigasa and Salome Massooa, two black lesbian activists, were found raped and murdered in Soweto; their murders sparked the formation of the 777 campaign by LGBTI activists to stop violence against gender and sexual minorities. In April 2008, Eudy Simelane, a member of Banyana, the national women's soccer team, was murdered. On April 24, 2011, Noxolo Nogwaza, a black lesbian activist, was murdered outside Johannesburg. We enumerate the deaths of these women not to exaggerate the threat of anti-lesbian violence but to humanize the women who lost their lives to violence.

Efforts to publicize anti-lesbian violence in South Africa entered a transnational phase in 2010 when Ndumie Funda, a black lesbian woman who lives in Gugulethu, sought signatures through a Change.org website that demanded a face-to-face meeting with South African Minister of Justice Jeffrey Thamsanqa Radebe. Funda is the founder of Luleki Sizwe, whose stated mission is to provide safe haven for black lesbian survivors of anti-lesbian rape. Luleki Sizwe takes its name from the names of two black lesbian survivors of anti-lesbian rape. According to Funda, Luleki Sizwe also 'means to discipline the nation constructively.... Luleki of Luleki Sizwe means to discipline and Sizwe means nation so that is where the name came from' (interview with Julie Moreau, July 15, 2011, Cape Town, South Africa). The severe beating and rape of Millicent Gaika motivated Funda to take her campaign transnationally. After Gaika's rapist was released on bail for an equivalent sum of less than US$10, Funda wrote to Minister Radebe, asking him to declare anti-lesbian rape a hate crime. He did not respond.

Using Luleki Sizwe's name, Funda put up a petition on Change.org toward the end of 2010 (Luleki Sizwe 2010). Funda designed the petition so that for each signature the petition received, Change.org sent one email to Minister Radebe. The petition garnered 100 000 signatures from 163 countries in less than six weeks and eventually solicited 171 000 signatures from 175 countries. Funda recalled when a South African government official contacted her and pleaded, '"We can't even get our own emails. Can you stop now?" And I said, "Uh uh. We are not going to stop." We flooded their emails... their fax machines; they couldn't breathe.' Funda wanted the Ministry of Justice to take action on anti-lesbian violence. She warned government officials,

> If you are not giving me a date by January [for a meeting], we're gonna hit you [with more correspondence]... I am serious, because you are busy with this guy who came and plotted his wife to be killed in South Africa,[2] [instead of working on] the actual issues here in South Africa. People are not going to invest in South Africa.... So that is when they came to their senses.

Funda stated that government officials responded to the online petition, barrage of email and fax correspondence, and telephone calls by telling Funda, '"You might be tiny, but you are powerful." We said, "We might be tiny. We might not have the funding—being funded by one funder—but we can do the work."' The quantity of support on the petition motivated the minister to meet with Funda and pledge to take action. According to Funda, 'for the first time in our history, so to speak, the government that we voted [for] has sat down with us'.

The petition portrays black South African lesbians as facing a dire situation. It states, 'This heinous crime is prolific in South Africa, especially in the "townships". Most of the victims are tortured, grievously assaulted and sometimes murdered! They are also prone to getting HIV/AIDS from the assault, and many of them commit suicide as a result of the "corrective rape".'

The petition also provides some evidence to substantiate how urgent this request is:

- '31 lesbian women have been murdered because of their sexuality.'
- 'More than 10 lesbians a week are raped or gang raped in Cape Town alone.'
- '150 women are raped every day in South Africa.'
- 'For every 25 men accused of rape in South Africa, 24 walk free.'

In addition to using the statistics to elicit support for the campaign against anti-lesbian violence, Luleki Sizwe circulated photos of Millicent Gaika's bruised and battered body after her sexual assault. These photos confirmed the defencelessness of black lesbian women. Commenting on Luleki Sizwe's digital-media strategy, Henriette Gunkel (2013) argues that the 'petition has the effect of sensationalizing the crimes and exploiting the "victims" for the publicity value of their images. It also ignores the many organizations and activists that for decades have been working against hate crime and gender-based violence more generally' (p. 70).

Not all South African LGBTI activist organizations agreed with Luleki Sizwe's strategy to emphasize the vulnerability of black lesbians in their Change.org plea. Triangle Project, the oldest LGBTI movement organization in South Africa, objected to how Luleki Sizwe portrayed anti-lesbian violence in the petition. In fact, activists involved with the Triangle Project decided not to sign or endorse any online petitions condemning anti-lesbian rape. Triangle Project activists claimed that using images of battered lesbians' bodies was 'unethical' and 'sensationalist'. In a press release denouncing the tactic of using battered women's bodies to generate publicity for 'corrective rape', the Triangle Project stated 'If you read carefully through the online petitions and the articles associated with these campaigns, you will find that the voices of survivors are largely absent. Once again black women in Africa are being cast as voiceless victims, as voiceless faces' (Triangle Project 2011). This statement ties the depicted vulnerability of black lesbians to the historic objectification and dehumanization of women of African descent unable to stand up for themselves. Activists with the Triangle Project sought to intervene in the misinterpretation of black lesbian women and move beyond the portrayal of black lesbians as vulnerable and unable to defend themselves.

The press release also contested the term 'corrective rape'. According to the press release: 'We need to be careful of creating a false division between the categories "lesbian" and "woman" and "anti-lesbian" and "anti-woman".' Activists with the Triangle Project thought that these distinctions segmented anti-lesbian violence from violence against women, preventing activists from responding to all forms of violence against women.

In a country in which the media and conservative political parties have demonized lesbians for allegedly corrupting young women and abusing children, black lesbian activists worry about their public representation. Repairing black lesbians' cultural reputations in South Africa was a priority for black lesbian activists. Within this framework, the Triangle Project's objections to the use of graphic photos of black lesbians' hurt bodies make sense; the digital strategy of using black women's bodies to assign political urgency to anti-lesbian rape was counterproductive because it reinforced the notion of black lesbians' vulnerability. In this case, digital strategies allowed organizations access to global Northern funds and support, but such access unfolded in the absence of accountability mechanisms regarding the funds' use and potential exploitation of survivors' faces and personal narratives of violence. Thus, while digital activism may be effective in eliciting domestic governmental action, activists may lose control over circulating movement discourses under increased domestic and transnational attention; these discourses can feed into racist characterizations of citizens of African countries as 'homophobes'.

Conclusion

Our exploration of digital strategies in African LGBTI organizing reveals that the potency of digital activism comes with potential drawbacks. First, digital activism can fuel political homophobia. Through generating increased attention to the issue of sexuality, digital strategies and transnational attention can shift political incentives and prompt governments to speak out on the issue of homosexuality. Second, while digital activism can provide organizations with access to funding and therefore redistribute funds from the global North to the global South, it can also generate a reliance on one form of activism for funding. When Northern donors decided that specialized knowledge of African LGBTI issues was no longer necessary because of new sources such as social media, they withdrew their funding for Behind the Mask, resulting in the loss of valuable information for African LGBTI people and movements. Finally, digital activism can allow one framing of an issue to gain transnational prominence, especially when this perspective taps into transnational stereotypes. In the case of anti-lesbian rape, digital activism can allow organizations to put forward a particular framing of an issue that resonates with anti-African global common sense in order to procure funds and pursue their goals. This framing not only reinforces global Northern dominance but also obscures important debate on how to eradicate anti-lesbian rape and violence against women and gender and sexual minorities.

Notes

1. LGBTI activists initiated the 07-07-07 campaign in 2007 to stop violence against gender and sexual minorities after the rapes and murders of two black lesbian activists.
2. Funda is referring to the murder of Anni Dewani, a Swedish national, on South African soil in 2011. Allegation of a murder-for-hire plot against her husband Shrien Dewani made headlines in South Africa and internationally.

References

Alexander, J. (2002). "Behind the Mask": An African gay-affirmative website. *International Journal of Sexuality and Gender Studies, 7*(2/3), 227–234.

Bendix, M. (2014, February 14). South Africa's law to stop hate crimes against gays. *Inter Press Service News Agency*. http://www.ipsnews.net/2014/02/south-africas-law-stop-hate-crimes-love/?utm_source=rss&utm_medium=rss&utm_campaign=south-africas-law-stop-hate-crimes-love. Accessed 11 May 2016.

Bob, C. (2012). *The global right wing and the clash of world politics*. Cambridge: Cambridge University Press.

Corey-Boulet, R. (2012, December 1). Anti-gay stigma hinders bid to lower Côte d'Ivoire's HIV rate. *Inter Press Service News Agency*. http://www.ipsnews.net/2012/12/anti-gay-stigma-hinders-bid-to-lower-cote-divoires-hiv-rate/. Accessed 11 May 2016.

Croucher, S. (2011). South Africa: Opportunities seized in the post-apartheid era. In M. Tremblay, D. Paternotte, and C. Johnson (Eds.), *The lesbian and gay movement and the state: Comparative insights into a transformed relationship* (pp. 153–166). Farnham, Surrey: Ashgate.

Currier, A. (2010). The strategy of normalization in the South African LGBT movement. *Mobilization: An International Journal*, *15*(1), 45–62.

Currier, A. (2011). Representing gender and sexual dissidence in southern Africa. *Qualitative Sociology*, *34*(3), 463–481.

Currier, A. (2012a). The aftermath of decolonization: Gender and sexual dissidence in postindependence Namibia. *Signs: Journal of Women in Culture and Society*, *37*(2), 441–467.

Currier, A. (2012b). *Out in Africa: LGBT organizing in Namibia and South Africa*. Minneapolis: University of Minnesota Press.

Currier, A., & Cruz, J.M. (2014). Civil society and sexual struggles in Africa. In E. Obadare (Ed.), *The handbook of civil society in Africa* (pp. 337–360). New York: Springer.

Currier, A., & Thomann, M. (2016). Gender and sexual diversity organizing in Africa. In S. Fadaee (Ed.), *Understanding southern social movements: A quest to bypass northern social movement theory* (pp. 87–103). London: Routledge.

Dencik, L., & Leistert, O. (Eds.). (2015). *Critical perspectives on social media and protest: Between control and emancipation*. Lanham, MD: Rowman & Littlefield.

Department of State. (2012). Country reports on human rights practices for 2011: Côte d'Ivoire. http://www.state.gov/j/drl/rls/hrrpt/humanrightsreport/index.htm?dlid=186187#wrapper. Accessed 11 May 2016.

Earl, J., & Kimport, K. (2011). *Digitally enabled social change: Activism in the Internet age*. Cambridge, MA: MIT Press.

Epprecht, M. (2008). *Heterosexual Africa? The history of an idea from the age of exploration to the age of AIDS*. Athens: Ohio University Press.

Epprecht, M. (2012). Sexual minorities, human rights, and public health strategies in Africa. *African Affairs*, *111*(443), 223–243.

Gevisser, M. (2000). Mandela's stepchildren: Homosexual identity in post-apartheid South Africa. In P. Drucker (Ed.), *Different rainbows* (pp. 111–136). London: Gay Men's Press.

Gqola, P. D. (2007). How the "cult of femininity" and violent masculinities support endemic gender based violence in contemporary South Africa. *African Identities*, *5*(1), 111–124.

Gunkel, H. (2013). Some reflections on postcolonial homophobia, local interventions, and LGBTI solidarity online: The politics of global petitions. *African Studies Review*, *56*(2), 67–81.

Haines, H.H. (1984). Black radicalization and the funding of civil rights: 1957–1970. *Social Problems*, *32*(1), 31–43.

Judge, M., Manion, A., & De Waal, S. (Eds.). (2008). *To have and to hold: The making of same-sex marriage in South Africa*. Johannesburg: Fanele.

Keck, M.E., & Sikkink, K. (1998). *Activists beyond borders: Advocacy networks in international politics*. London: Cornell University Press.

Kouassi, S.M. (2009). Rapport pour l' examen périodique universel de Côte d'Ivoire. http://lib.ohchr.org/HRBodies/UPR/Documents/Session6/CI/SRI_CIV_UPR_S6_2009_F.pdf. Accessed 11 May 2016.

Kouassi, S.M. (2011, September 20). Ivory Coast: Abidjan is becoming a gay Eldorado. Radio Netherlands Worldwide. http://www.rnw.nl/africa/article/ivory-coast-abidjan-becoming-a-gay-eldorado. Accessed 11 May 2016.

Levitsky, S.R. (2007). Niche activism: Constructing a unified movement identity in a heterogeneous organizational field. *Mobilization: An International Journal*, *12*(3), 271–286.

Luirink, B. (2000). *Moffies: Gay life in southern Africa*. Claremont: Ink Inc.

Luleki Sizwe. (2010). South Africa: Take action to stop "corrective rape. http://www.change.org/petitions/south-africa-take-action-to-stop-corrective-rape. Accessed 11 May 2016.

Massad, J.A. (2002). Re-orienting desire: The gay international and the Arab world. *Public Culture*, *14*(2), 361–385.

Mejias, U.A. (2013). *Off the network: Disrupting the digital world*. Minneapolis: University of Minnesota Press.

Muholi, Z. (2004). Thinking through lesbian rape. *Agenda*, *61*, 116–125.

Mwikya, K. (2013). The media, the tabloid, and the Uganda homophobia spectacle. In S. Ekine and H. Abbas (Eds.), *Queer African reader* (pp. 141–154). Oxford: Pambazuka.

Myers, S.L., & Cooper, H. (2011, December 6). U.S. to aid gay rights abroad, Obama and Clinton say. *New York Times*, p. A11.

Nguyen, V. (2010). *The republic of therapy: Triage and sovereignty in West Africa's time of AIDS*. Durham, NC: Duke University Press.

Nossiter, A. (2013, June 29). Senegal cheers its president for standing up to Obama on same-sex marriage. *New York Times*, p.A6.

Nyong'o, T. (2012). Queer Africa and the fantasy of virtual participation. *Women's Studies Quarterly*, *40*(1–2), 40–63.

Pflanz, M. (2011, December 9). Africa reacts to Obama's pro-gay rights foreign policy. *Christian Science Monitor*. http://www.csmonitor.com/World/Africa/2011/1208/Africa-reacts-to-Obama-s-progay-rights-foreign-policy. Accessed 11 May 2016.

Swarr, A.L. (2012). Paradoxes of butchness: Lesbian masculinities and sexual violence in contemporary South Africa. *Signs, 37*(4), 961–986.

Thomann, M. (2014). *The price of inclusion: Sexual subjectivity, violence, and the non-profit industrial complex in Abidjan, Côte d'Ivoire*. Doctoral dissertation. Department of Anthropology, American University, Washington, DC.

Thoreson, R.R. (2014). *Transnational LGBT activism: Working for sexual rights*. Minneapolis: University of Minnesota Press.

Triangle Project. (2011, February 18). Enough! Online "corrective rape" campaigns and petitions. *Black Looks*. http://www.blacklooks.org/2011/02/online-corrective-rape-campaigns-petitions-enough/. Accessed 11 May 2016.

Van De Donk, W., Loader, B.D., Nixon, P.G., & Rucht, D. (Eds.). (2004). *Cyberprotest: New media, citizens, and social movements*. London: Routledge.

Wahab, A. (2016). Homosexuality/homophobia is un-African? Un-mapping transnational discourses in the context of Uganda's Anti-Homosexuality Bill/Act. *Journal of Homosexuality, 63*(5), 685–718.

Wesley, T. (2012). Classifying "corrective" rape as hate crime: A call for justice. *BUWA! A Journal on African Women's Experiences*, 75–81. http://www.osisa.org/sites/default/files/75-81.pdf. Accessed 11 May 2016.

Wiseberg, L.S. (2001). The Internet: One more tool in the struggle for human rights. In C.E. Welch, Jr (Ed.), *NGOs and human rights: Promise and performance* (pp. 238–247). Philadelphia: University of Pennsylvania Press.

Ashley Currier is associate professor of women's, gender, and sexuality studies at the University of Cincinnati. She is the author of *Out in Africa: LGBT Organizing in Namibia and South Africa* (2012). Her research has appeared in *Australian Feminist Studies, Feminist Formations, Gender & Society, GLQ, Mobilization, Politique Africaine, Qualitative Sociology, Signs: Journal of Women in Culture and Society, Studies in Law, Politics, and Society*, and *Women's Studies Quarterly*. She is working on a book manuscript about the politicization of homosexuality in Malawi and another project examining anti-LGBT and pro-LGBT movement dynamics in Côte d'Ivoire and Liberia.

Julie Moreau is a post-doctoral fellow in Women, Gender, and Sexuality Studies at Washington University in St. Louis. Her research interests include transnational queer studies, social movements, and citizenship. She is currently working on a book manuscript that explores the concept of queer citizenship and the construction of collective sexual identities in contexts of legal equality, and another project that examines the diffusion of same-sex marriage norms in Latin America.

CHAPTER 12

A Resilient Unwanted Civil Society: The Gays and Lesbians of Zimbabwe Use of Facebook as Alternative Public Sphere in a Dominant Homophobic Society

Nhamo A. Mhiripiri and Sithandazile B. Moyo

Queer gender and sexuality is largely condemned in the mainstream heterosexual Zimbabwean media and culture. Politicians have over the years politicized queer identities and sexuality to win over what is perceived to be a homophobic majority. President Robert Mugabe is probably Africa's most articulate and virulent critic of homosexuality and queer culture. The civil society organization Gays and Lesbians Association of Zimbabwe (GALZ) represents a social movement that has struggled to put its issues into the public sphere, at times winning cases in Zimbabwean courts of law. It is a social movement for lesbian, gays, bisexual,

N.A. Mhiripiri (✉)
Media and Society Studies, Midlands State University, Midlands, Zimbabwe
e-mail: nhamoanthony@yahoo.com

S.B. Moyo
Marketing Communications, Rhodes University, Grahamstown, South Africa
e-mail: sthandazilemoyo@yahoo.com

B. Mutsvairo (ed.), *Digital Activism in the Social Media Era*,
DOI 10.1007/978-3-319-40949-8_12

transgendered, transvestite and other so-called 'queer' sexuality and identities. These are social and individual identities that challenge but still co-exist with heterosexuality. The latter is undoubtedly the dominant preferred social, sexual and gender orientation for both males and females. Even though homosexuality had been previously discussed in Zimbabwe, it gained more public discussion when Mugabe called gays and lesbians 'worse than dogs and pigs'. It is nearly unimaginable people of alternative gender and sexuality to heterosexuality can openly organize and articulate their interests in a dominant homophobic patriarchal culture such as Zimbabwe. GALZ struggles to publish its ideas in the mainstream media and is technically banned on national radio and television. New Information Communication Technologies and Facebook are nonetheless offering alternative spaces of information, debate and discussion for this marginalized group. The study focuses on how GALZ uses Facebook as an alternative platform of communication.

The GALZ subaltern civil society organization was formed in 1990 to offer a communication and advocacy platform for the Zimbabwean queer community. The group planned to organize social events of interest to its members and to provide a drop-in centre for accessing relevant videos and literature. Initially, due to the homophobic nature of the majority of Zimbabweans, the organization tried to be as discreet and secretive as possible. The year 1995, when GALZ was banned from displaying literature at the 'Human Rights and Justice' Zimbabwe International Book Fair in Harare (ZIBF), projected homosexuality in Zimbabwe to local and global media headlines (Dunton and Palmberg 1996; Shaw 2005, p. 91). Previously GALZ was involved in HIV and AIDS campaigns and challenging homophobia. When GALZ failed to publish its counselling advert with the *Daily Gazette* newspaper, and suffered from government attacks, the organization became much more daring and confrontational, hence the 1995 attempt to exhibit at the book fair. The publicity that surrounded the attacks on GALZ and President Robert Mugabe's insults drew local and international attention to the organization. In 1996 GALZ applied once again to exhibit at the ZIBF, but government imposed a ban. GALZ resorted to court action and won the right to participate. In spite of the court victory the GALZ stand was trashed by attackers. By 1997, GALZ had transformed from being a predominantly white, middle class social club to an activist organization representative of the social, class and racial mix in Zimbabwe. GALZ has tried to participate in various public fora, including the 1999 Constitution process.

The GALZ Information and Communication department produces and disseminates literature about Lesbian, Gay, Transgender, Bisexual, Intersexual and Queer (LGTBIQ) life in the country and elsewhere. These include the *Gazette* (a quarterly magazine), *Whazzup* (a bi-monthly magazine), special reports, books and booklets. This department is also supposed to manage social media networks like Facebook, Twitter and the Website.

Since the late 1990s, Gay, Lesbian, Bisexual and Transgender (GLBT) sexuality—also to be referred to here as homosexual or queer sexuality—has been intermittently addressed in the Zimbabwean media. Reports intensified in the late 1990s when the late Reverend Canaan Banana—Zimbabwe's first ceremonial President when Robert Mugabe was still Prime Minister—was brought to trial on 11 counts of sodomy and indecent assault, including assault on his aide, Jefta Dube. Banana was imprisoned and the Zimbabwean media took the opportunity to condemn homosexuality and the victimization of a weaker citizen by a powerful politician. Canaan Banana died in disgrace after serving time in prison, and he remains an embarrassment to the Mugabe government.

Methodology

This chapter consists of a comprehensive literature review of how Zimbabwean media has reported on homosexuality in Zimbabwe since the 1990s when the topic became visible in the public sphere. Online archival posts and comments from 2013 to 2015 on the GALZ Facebook page were critiqued. Critical discourse analysis of the postings or lack of on the GALZ website is useful in establishing whether or not the publication of discussions and information on the GALZ Facebook page has translated to the opening of an alternative social media and communicative space. Topics for discussion are selected from the GALZ Facebook website from 2013 up to 2015, with selection based on topical issues of the day such as the castigation of homosexuality by Morgan Tsvangirai, who most in the local queer society had expected to be considerate about their situation and status. The discussion on the adoption of the new Zimbabwe constitution and the rights it confers to those belonging to queer society is another case. Interviews with members of Zimbabwean queer society are then quoted, although in most cases the names of respondents are made up to protect the individuals. This is because Zimbabwe is still largely a homophobic society and verbal persecutions of the group are common, from both ordinary heterosexual Zimbabweans and influential politicians, including the State President Robert Mugabe.

Interviews were conducted with the GALZ Director to find out the impact of Facebook in articulating queer issues in Zimbabwe. Snowballing was employed to identify Zimbabwean gays and lesbians, and questionnaires were administered to them to ascertain their attitudes towards being excluded from the mainstream media. Media student Sthandazile Bianca Moyo who has a network of gay and lesbian friends, amongst them fellow students, would first identify these friends and then invite them into participating in face-to-face interviews or focus group discussions. Some of these students also mentioned use of privately run Facebook accounts for personal communication with like-inclined people, and which they have more control over as they can 'block' undesirable communicators, especially those who are homophobic.

Literature Review and Theoretical Framework

Since the mid 1990s Zimbabwe's state policy has projected the most articulate homophobic stance of any African state. There is some critical literature that has addressed the notion of homosexuality in Zimbabwe; this literature argues that, contrary to popular opinion, homosexuality was a 'silent', 'unspoken' sexual practice found in both traditional and pre-colonial African society, albeit confined to the 'private sphere' just like most matters of sexuality, including open exhibition of heterosexual affinities (Epprecht 1998; Shaw 2005). In an article on the representation of queer inclination in the writings of fiction writer Dambudzo Marechera and in Zimbabwean literature in general, Drew Shaw makes a brief but informative exploration and critique of how Zimbabwean print media has reported on the subject. However, there has not been any systematic extensive study of how the mainstream media represents the complex topic of homosexuality or queer genders, and this chapter does not pretend to make such an ambitious submission.

GALZ as an organization was banned from articulating its ideas on the Zimbabwe Broadcasting Corporation (ZBC) channels, while the same channels tolerated discussion on gay-bashing. GALZ were not extended the right of reply since they were denied interviews and appearance on phone-ins. The state-controlled ZBC operated as a virtual monopoly until two new stations were licensed in 2012. GALZ were also restricted from advertising in the national press. Most mainstream newspapers belong to the state controlled Zimpapers chain, with titles such as *The Chronicle, The Herald* and *The Sunday Mail.*

In 1996 GALZ challenged its Book Fair ban through the High Court of Zimbabwe, where they won the right to exhibit. In spite of the court victory, homophobic youths torched their literature and ransacked their stand. The police watched without making any arrests. The 'moral majority' appeared to have won for the moment, but the Zimbabwean public and government woke up in 1997 to the huge scandal and embarrassment resulting in the imprisonment of Reverend Canaan Banana. Mugabe would still castigate homosexuality at any public gathering, especially at funerals of top government and party officials. It has now become a tradition that salvoes against homosexuals increase in intensity whenever there are general elections in Zimbabwe. ZANU PF fought elections on an anti-white, anti-British and anti-homosexual platform, and interestingly, opposition leader Morgan Tsvangirai had to back-pedal in 2011 after he attested on BBC's *Newsnight* with Gavin Esler that he supported gay rights. Tsvangirai was quoted as saying gay rights were 'a human right' that should be respected in Zimbabwe. 'To me, it's a human right... It's a very controversial subject in my part of the world. My attitude is that I hope the constitution will come out with freedom of sexual orientation, for as long as it does not interfere with anybody.' State-controlled media had a field day, reproducing Tsvangirai's pro-gay statements in order to discredit him in the eyes of a Zimbabwean population largely assumed to be conservative and homophobic. For reasons of political expediency he was later to publicly scorn and discredit homosexuality, saying it was not even a debatable issue worth inclusion in the national constitution. His ambivalence arose from a desire to satisfy both a presumably majority homophobic Zimbabwe voting constituency and a pro-gay donor European audience.

According to Drew Shaw (2005) Mugabe epitomized a 'virulent new homophobic movement within pan-Africanism', when he condemned homosexuality as 'anathema to African culture', inciting people to 'purge Zimbabwe of this foreign vice'. Mainstream media and Zimbabwean church organizations supported Mugabe's 'crusade'. Shaw observes:

> The Zimbabwe Broadcasting Corporation (ZBC) and national newspapers such as *The Herald*, *The Sunday Mail*, *The Chronicle* and the *Sunday News* depicted homosexuals as corrupt, immoral, un-African, deviant, and perverse. *Moto* magazine (affiliated to the Catholic Church) went further, alleging that gays were involved in satanic cults, barbaric rituals, child molestation, ritual rape, and murder. 'Perverts swell satanic ranks' and

> 'Get out of the closet so that we know who you are!' featured as articles in the September-October (1995) edition, which was almost hysterical in its homophobia (Shaw 2005, p. 92).

GALZ presented perhaps the most resilient fortress in defence of GLBTI rights in spite of deliberate vicious attempts to silence that besieged community. Queer civil society mounted a resolute local and international campaign for recognition, which included legal battles in Zimbabwean courts.

Midlands State University student, Sithandazile Bianca Moyo (2015), studied the use of Facebook by young homosexuals. This is the study on which most of the findings in this chapter are based. A recent study based on critical discourse analysis of Zimbabwean news publications from January to March 2014 reveals that there is some measure of restraint in the way local journalists write about homosexuality and queer genders in general, although this does not imply an open tolerance of these alternative gendered cultures (Mhiripiri 2014). The International Federation of Journalists African Chapter commissioned Mhiripiri to study press reports and conduct interviews with Zimbabwean journalists on their perceptions of homosexuality and queer sexualities. Some 40 male and female Zimbabwean journalists from different media stables including five freelancers reflected their own problems and difficulties in practising within an intolerant socio-cultural and political order. The journalists were randomly sampled from the state-controlled Zimbabwe Broadcasting Corporation, the Zimpapers chain, the privately owned radio station ZiFM, newspapers such as Associated Newspapers of Zimbabwe's *Daily News*, Alpha Media Holding's *News Day*, and the online newspaper www.newzimbabwe.com. The study concluded that media houses do not have policies on reporting queer sexualities, and journalists often confuse terminologies and identities associated with the various queer identities.

The journalists' own responses also show that there is a lot of caution, fear of stigmatization and alienation in the case that they openly write about homosexuality in an accommodative way. The main causes of the fear and even self-censorship are cited as the cultural context, heteronormative patriarchy, tradition, religion, and political pressure from the openly homophobic central political leadership of President Mugabe and ZANU PF (Mhiripiri 2014).

Zimbabwe's new Constitution, adopted in 2013, is ambiguous about homosexuality. Different people use different sections to either recognize or reject homosexuality and any forms of gendered queerness. 'Persons of the same sex are prohibited from marrying each other', posits Section 78(2) on marriage rights. Although it bans marriages between same-sex couples, the section is vague on the prohibition of consensual same-sex sexual relations. Theoretically, therefore, gay couples can legally engage in consensual sex outside the institution of marriage. Gay and lesbian activists paradoxically cite other sections of the same constitution to argue for their sexual orientation and gendered identities. Citable sections in the new constitution include Section 49, on the right to liberty, Section 51, on the right to human dignity, Section 57, on the right to privacy, and Section 56, on equality and non-discrimination. For example, Section 56(3) reads categorically:

> Every person has the right not to be treated in an unfairly discriminatory manner on such grounds as their nationality, race, colour, tribe, place of birth, ethnic or social origin, language, class, religious belief, political affiliation, opinion, custom, *culture, sex, gender*, marital status, age, pregnancy, disability or economic or social status, or whether they were born in or out of wedlock (Constitution of Zimbabwe 2013) [Emphasis added].

Since homosexual and queer movements arguably constitute sub-cultures at least in Western countries and partly in South Africa, arguments for non-discrimination of such cultural groups have been proffered (Appiah 1994, pp. 149–164). It is arguable that the anti-gay, lesbian, transgender rhetoric associated with Zimbabwean politicians and mainstream media denies these categories recognition as gender and cultural categories. Zimbabwe is not the only African country pressed to attend to issues pertaining to GLBTIQ. While South Africa has a constitution which allows for free choice in gender and sexual orientation, it is confronted with a homophobic moral majority some of whom have taken the law into their own hands and have insulted, violently attacked, used 'corrective rape' or lynched deviants to heteronormativity. Uganda has featured in the international media in the recent past for its Anti-Homosexuality Bill which President Museveni signed into law in 2014. The repertoire of pro and anti- GLBT activists in Uganda is remarkable. Western conservative Christian churches are in alliance with Ugandan politicians and policy-makers, while critics of the Bill included local activists, international political leaders and the usually conservative denominations such as the Catholic Church (Strand 2013). The Uganda media has reported hesitantly, at times reluctantly, 'in settings where policymakers' (homophobic) opinions and public opinion remain largely unchanged' (Strand 2013, p. 276).

Our theoretical point of departure is that identity (including gender identity), culture and tradition are socially constructed phenomena. They are transient and not neatly bounded, fixed or frozen. Likewise, identities cannot be pigeonholed, essentialized or homogenized. Identities of all sorts emerge within the play of specific modalities of power, hence they are 'more the product of the marking of difference and exclusion, than they are the sign of an identical, naturally-constituted unity—an identity...without internal differentiation' (Hall 1996, p. 4). Narrative is central to the structuring of media stories and the realities depicted in the stories are representational. The media trade in constructed images of people and in their possible identification. Kwame Appiah notes that constructed narrative 'naturalizes' gender differences as normal but this does not ensure their permanence. In such instances histories, biologies, and cultural affinities are invented, scripted and structured by conventions of narrative even though the world never quite permanently conforms to such machination (Appiah 1992, p. 283). This is partly because selected literary images are changeable and it is up to writers and people who contest the images to redefine them in ways that they deem to be more realistic, constructive and liberating to the society in question (Grossberg 1996, p. 90).

Theories of culture and identity are relevant to the discussion of homosexuality and queer identities. It is generally accepted in critical scholarship that identities and culture are individual and social constructs, and that subjects of identity have the prerogative to define themselves in ways they best prefer, although others also can define and describe them. The programme of humanization is also central to the discourses and narratives on identity. Concepts of inter-culturalism, cross-culturalism or multiculturalism assume that there is cultural parity and self-determinism, but therein lies the problem when one group assumes some ideological or moral self-righteousness that enables them to exclude others from self-expression. Such exclusions can be predicated on ideas about the fight against cultural imperialism or cultural pollution. Some homophobic African cultures justify their suppression or exclusion of homosexual expressions on the basis of fighting against negative, corrupting, foreign cultural values. It is paradoxical when one group silences another citing protection of its own values. Culture and tradition have been used to justify the subjugation of marginal gender identities such as those of gays, lesbians and the transgendered, and a power-knowledge discourse with corresponding representational images has also been instrumental in maintaining and reinforcing the status quo, the press and mainstream media appearing as specific examples. The construction of gender difference hence raises discursive implications with the possibility of the dominant power conveniently constructing its other as a repressed and desired difference (Grossberg 1996, p. 91). Gender difference is thus built into the overall social system of controlling 'deviant' sexualities in diverse areas such as the organization of the production of goods and services, kinship and family, emotional relationships and the minutiae of daily life. Arguments about cultural imperialism and gender deviance and intolerance can only stand in contradistinction to notions that identities are social constructs in constant change. This study is also cognizant of queer theory, and the public sphere and alternative public sphere concepts.

The Articulation of GLBT in Contemporary Zimbabwean Press Reports

Same-sex sexual relations have typically been reported on as cases of 'sodomy' which come into the public sphere when an aggrieved party to the act reports to the police. This does not mean that there are no cases of consensual homosexuality. The cases prominently reported on in the various Zimbabwean newspapers since January 2013 are on the supposed inclusion or exclusion of homosexual rights in the new Zimbabwe constitution, opposition leader Morgan Tsvangirai's initial embrace and later rejection of homosexual rights, ZANU PF supporters' physical attacks of GALZ members attending GLBTIQ functions, the citizen's arrest and subsequent court case of transgender activist Ricky Nathanson, the prosecution and acquittal of GALZ leadership for operating an 'unregistered' organization; several court cases on non-consensual sodomy and President Mugabe's public support of Museveni's anti-homosexual law. At least one of these stories originally written as hard news inspired follow-up stories and opinion articles. Incidentally, most of these cases are posted on GALZ websites to encourage debate or discussion. Elsewhere Mhiripiri (2014, p. 21) has noted

> It is indeed striking that most of the stories on 'homophobia' are thrust into the public sphere and mediated after first appearing as arrests and court cases. This alone might be an indictment on Zimbabwe's tolerance of homosexuality to those who believe in gay rights as human rights.

> Alternatively, to those who believe homosexuality should be stamped out as un-African and anathema, Zimbabwe probably represents a frontier for the preservation of values and attitudes that characterize Africanness and propriety. Once again, the various stories pose difficulties in classifying what constitutes 'homosexuality' when the act and exhibition is fraught with legal and cultural complications of all manners.

The press reports were varied in their treatment of homosexuality issues, with some hard news tolerant and empathetic while most feature articles were condemnatory and intolerant. Critical Discourse Analysis permits the present authors to deduce whether the articles are framed in a homophobic or empathetic or sympathetic manner. The words that set the tone and mood whether to accept or tolerate homosexuality or to alienate and stigmatize those associated with the orientation are noted. These might appear as adjectival or adverbial terms with specific denotative or connotative meaning meant to sway the reader to a final discernible perception.

Some hard news stories used the Nathanson case as an opportunity to clarify issues, dispel misconceptions, and demand that the dignity and privacy of all individuals be recognized, thereby bringing the discourse of human rights and constitutionalism into the argument. GALZ Director Samba Chesterfield rapped the police and the Zimbabwean media for their 'ignorance' on matters of sexuality and gender. Chesterfield emphasized that Nathanson would more aptly be described as transgender rather than gay. The activist presumably insisted on this qualification since there were no obvious and strictly 'homosexual' actions in Nathanson's use of a toilet for women. He also called for the police and the media to undergo 'diversity training' in order for them to outgrow homophobic and transphobic tendencies in future policing and reporting.

In a story in apparent reference to GALZ, Mugabe was quoted:

> We want the youth to grow up knowing that they will mature and marry in the same way as Simba has done, as Omar has done. But there are these despicable groups; I understand we have a homosexual group in this country. I didn't know about it only to be told the day before yesterday about such a group, so we want to investigate who belongs to that group (Mutimukulu 2014, p. 2). (Parts of quotation translated by Mhiripiri from Shona.)

The speech was read as a direct threat to gay activists, and publications such as www.newzimbabwe.com. *The Chronicle* of 3 March went on to publicize the 'threat' in its headlines.

Pronouncements by ZANU PF leaders and ideologues often criticize Western countries for trying to force homosexuality on Zimbabweans and other developing African countries (Mhiripiri 2014). The political opposition the Movement for Democratic change is similarly presented as a purveyor of homosexual interests besides being labelled as a lackey of imperialism.

Journalists, especially those from the state-controlled media, write in support of homophobia, although there is a growing number of tolerant writers. Mhiripiri's research on reporting homophobia in the Zimbabwean media notes,

> While journalists write on homosexual activities especially when they come through as court cases spurred through some prosecution and litigation, there is general apprehension to write on homophobia. The main reasons for the self-censorship are fear of stigmatization and being labelled homosexual in a country perceived to be homophobic. The hegemonic homophobic political system further constrains journalists from freely writing about homosexuality and homophobia. Much as journalists skirt writing on homosexuality and homophobia, they ought to operate from positions of conviction rather than fear. It is also disconcerting that most Zimbabwean journalists are not familiar with the language and diction that refers to the complexities of GLBT and queer sexualities. There is widespread confusion over what homophobia means, and to many the word means the opposite of what it actually means in reality. The main arguments given in Zimbabwe about homophobia are that homosexuality is un-African, and part of Western imperialism. The main problem is when to respect the rights, perceptions and aspirations of a large majority at the expense of cultural minorities such as gays and lesbians. Cultural nationalism in this case flies in the face of the tolerance and multiculturalism liberals would want to imagine. In Zimbabwe homosexuality and queer genders remain fringe cultures and identities, considered by many as freak, taboo and shameful, and the journalists and mainstream media look very unlikely allies of the few but very vocal homosexual and queer activists mainly because the former prefer conformity and social security in a dominant homophobic culture and, again to a considerable extent, an equally homophobic media industry.

In an interview with Sithandazile Moyo, the GALZ Director Chesterfield Samba was hopeful that Facebook would be an effective alternative public sphere for communicating issues related to Gays and Lesbians...

> Our assessment is that Facebook has allowed us to interact with individuals in a way that does not necessarily allow for them to reveal their true identity

> thereby giving them the opportunity to express themselves freely and engage in issues that they would not otherwise engage in publicly with their identities revealed. It does provide the people we interact with some sense of security in remaining anonymous. We have thus been able to reach individuals that we cannot meet in our daily work through physical contact and impart information that is helpful to them as they see fit. We are also able to bypass bureaucracy as what plays out in other media platforms such as radio, television and print.

Given the dominance of homophobia in the mainstream media, social media seems to offer an alternative discursive space for the marginalized queer community. This might seem encouraging although the space also appears to be barricaded and intruded upon by traditional homophobic elements. However, the GALZ Facebook page, for a while, offered space for discussion and debate as shown below.

Posts on the GALZ Facebook Page:

Tsvangirai on Homosexuality and the Complexities of Wooing the Heterosexual Moral Electoral Majority

GALZ lost patience with Tsvangirai, Prime Minister in the Government of National Unity, when he repeated his attacks on homosexuals just days before the 16 March 2013 referendum on the Constitution. Miles Rutendo Tanhira's article entitled 'Zimbabwe LGBTs reject premier who turned on them', linked from 76Crime.co.zw, bases its story on condemnations made by alleged 'infuriated' members of the community 'interviewed on a social network'. There, GALZ Facebook has no substantial responses to this link or article. A lonely post by one Mazvita Ruwambara reads 'Hie my dear friends'. The unanswered greeting reads like a desperate attempt to urge discussion or debate, but in vain. There is indication the article was 'shared' by two visitors to the page, and nine others 'liked' its publication. However, within Tanhira's article those 'interviewed on a social network' acknowledge they are a minority as compared to the electoral moral majority Tsvangirai was ostensibly courting. Nonetheless that minority was now threatening to reject Tsvangirai in any future election. General elections were anticipated the same year as the adoption of the new Constitution. The 'social network' on which members were interviewed is kept secret, perhaps as a measure to protect the discursive platform and alternative public sphere from further intrusion and possible attack from homophobic participants such as 'Felix' whose references are presented further below in this chapter. Indeed, when researcher Sthandazile Bianca Moyo interviewed GALZ Director Chesterfield Samba he disclosed that the organization uses Facebook alongside other social media platforms such as the GALZ website, Instagram and Twitter (Moyo 2015). The GALZ statement is also quoted copiously in the Tanhira article:

> We deplore the Prime Minister's statements, coming sadly on the eve of International Women's Day Celebrations and just days before Zimbabweans vote in a referendum.
>
> It is our view that political leaders in Zimbabwe continue to pander to public prejudices against LGBTI individuals through public statements that justify the exclusion and abuse of anyone suspected of being lesbian, gay, bisexual, transgender or intersex.
>
> GALZ shares the common desire of Zimbabweans for freedom, justice and equality, as promoted in the Preamble of the first draft of the Constitution. GALZ believes that, in recognising the diversity and rights of all people in Zimbabwe, we should also recognise that some Zimbabweans are attracted to people of the same sex.
>
> We believe that the Constitution is not the appropriate forum to give effect to the private beliefs held by some that same-sex couples should not be married.

One correspondent called Felix seems to have been removed and blocked after posting offensive insults. The reader can deduce that Felix posted insults by reading other contributors' references to him. It seems the GALZ Facebook administrator has deleted the offensive material as he comments: Gays and Lesbians of Zimbabwe (GALZ); 'Felix you must be gay otherwise whats your problem with gay people'. The GALZ administrator psychoanalytically concludes Felix practices gay-bashing as a way of suppressing his own homosexual orientation. In fact, Felix appears notorious and a pest to the GALZ Facebook page since he is continuously censured, admonished or rebuked by the administrator. For example in a discussion following another leading story from 2013 entitled 'Zimbabwe smear campaign targets alleged gay students' the administrator chides, 'Felix get a hobby'.

Constitutional Debates on the GALZ Facebook page

Another vibrant discussion involving about 29 comments was triggered by a shared link to an article written by Sebastian Mhofu entitled 'Zimbabwe Parliament receives draft Constitution' sourced from VOA.com. The GALZ administrator initiated discussion on 5 February 2013, asking, 'Zimbabwean LGBTI people, friends and allies what are your thoughts on the prohibition of same sex marriages, sharing is caring . . . ' The GALZ administrator assumes the role of a moderator in the debate, occasionally posing questions prompting for further clarification. One Yvonne Vonnie Rue Chademana observes she supports gay rights but not marriage. She takes a conservative position insisting 'marriage is a sacred thing meant for a man and a woman', and formal marriage is about 'a little paper anyway to two people in love who wanna spend the rest of their lives together'. Lobbying for constitutional support of gay marriage would be 'just taking it too far'. Radical commentators believe the gay community must fight for full rights, including those on marriage. They charge that 'Victory is certain'. Ntokozo Ray Dube argues 'Marriage is between two people who love one another; it can be between a man & woman, two women or two men. So everyone deserves to marry the person they love. This (is) a battle we have to win; we fighting for what rightfully belongs to us.' Tinoashira Peter Govinda Chikuni assumes a fairly postmodern and legalistic approach noting;

> All for it! The various arguments against same-sex marriages always end up reaching a blank wall when put to a test of simple logic. As for whether it should be done in Church, that argument is moot. No one can and should ever force a religious group into doing something against its tenets. So no forcing churches to carry out same-sex weddings!

Chikuni further argues for the prioritization of recognition of gay identities first before championing gay marriage rights. He says,

> The right to marriage is inter-linked to a whole bunch of other rights, but it can't exist on its own. The recognition of same-sex and alternate gender identities has to take place first, both legally and socially, before we even begin to attempt to advocate for marriage rights . . . My learned advice is fight let's fight for the expansion of the anti-discimination clause in the Constitution . . . I think our best option in light of the final draft of the Constitution is to argue that all the laws that criminalize same-sex relations

and gender non-conformity infringe on human dignity and equality (the rights to privacy and freedom have been thoroughly shot down by the Supreme Court already as grounds for the recognition of LGBTIA rights). The non-discrimination clauses in the Constitution are not strong enough for us to offer a successful argument. Once those laws are out of the way, it would be relatively easy to petition for the Constitution to be amended to permit same-sex marriage/unions. But I reiterate the words that have been spoken by many on this post, this change will only happen once our community is united, self-empowered, and only when our fellow countrymen have a better understanding of what it truly means to be LGBTIA.

Another contributor who takes an informed legalistic approach is Tonderai Calvin Mukudu, who incidentally qualifies his sexuality as follows: 'For the avoidance of doubt guys, I am very much gay.' He makes his views clear:

I think there is a misconception, the constitution has not criminalised homosexuality but rather it excludes the right to marry for gay pple. The only document that criminalises homosexuality is the Crimina Law (Codification and Reform) Act, while the S.A constitution is not the yardstick for democracy it is way better than ours in guaranteeing fundamental freedoms. U may never be lucky to get the Constitution amended to include gay marriages but pple r likely to accept a broader non-discrimination clause which encampasses freedom from discrimination on the grounds of sexuality. Once discrimination is outlawed it will mean the Marriages Act (Chapter 5.11) will be ultra vires the constitution in as far as it excludes gay marriages. For me civil unions r a good compromise, and they work okay

Ed Manny implodes the argument for gay marriage through his submission that criticizes some poly-amorous homosexuals. He writes,

focus on helping gay zimbos accept themselves and live productive live not chasing after the next person they will sleep with. most gay people are not ready to commit to one person so i don't think we as the gay community should be fighting for something we are not prepared to even do. i agree with Yvonne. and im speaking as a gay man who know too many gays who are going around town unemployed at 30 looking for boyfriends. tell them being gay shouldn't define you and they should make something out of their lives.

Interestingly, besides the rather mild moralism of Yvonne Vonnie Rue Chademana, there are no hecklers or offensive insults from homophobic commentators. The only submission which appears discordant is that of Cammillious Mugwara who is appealing for introduction to others of his ilk. He or she writes, 'Please galz can you connect me to other gays bcz i m really like this.' Notwithstanding the diversion, debates on the constitution in relation to gay rights are amongst the most vibrant that took place on the GALZ Facebook pages.

The 'Social' Capacity of GALZ Facebook

The page owners of the GALZ Facebook page use this platform to organize events such as dinner parties and meetings. The gays and lesbians mostly use this page to find sexual partners through exchange of numbers and email addresses. However most posts found on this page from January 2015 to April 2015 are insignificant and trivial, so much so that there is no rational debate and the only information being exchanged is about having sexual intercourse. Homophobic people also tended to abuse the site, posting outright insults or other dehumanizing or denigrating material. Some comments are sarcastic and distasteful.

Hate Language and the Collapse of an Alternative Subaltern Public Sphere

Due to abusive language and hate speech that has led practising GLBTI into retreat or hiding, the GALZ Facebook is a lost opportunity. It was ostensibly made to link up LGBTI members, although it was also working as an interface between that community and those of heterosexual or even asexual orientation. There is a level at which the Facebook space functioned as an attempt to reach out to the dominant majority and appeal for acceptance, compassion and understanding. This might have backfired, judging from the way the Facebook page has neglected updating its posts and other publications in the post-2013 period. Researcher Sithandazile Bianca Moyo (2015) has concluded that between January and December 2015 the site was publishing 'insignificant' materials, operating more like a dating site. The dating itself is even critiqued as sarcastic and gross, since those who are asking for partners seem to be heterosexuals poking fun, or the merely voyeuristic who will not be proposing sincerely or with any meaningful emotional attachment and respect for sex. Rational discussion and debate was possible but it was easily usurped by shrill moralistic and condemnatory or outright abusive voices. This was attested through insightful exchanges on the constitutional provisions of homosexual rights, the denigratory statements from top Zimbabwean politicians such as Tsvangirai or Robert Mugabe, and the attacks and ostracization of members of their community. However self-righteous and moralistic or hurtful and hateful statements intruded on the posts. This resulted in GALZ finding yet more secretive alternative public space for their members. The GALZ Facebook page looks like a derelict abandoned garrison with its crusading army in strategic retreat or repositioning. The LGBTI confess that they are generally afraid to publish their identities or their personal concerns and aspirations on this platform. None of the ten queer students Sthandazile Moyo interviewed was still willing to publish their personal identity on the GALZ site for fear of recrimination or physical attacks. Hounded from the GALZ Facebook page, Zimbabwe's LGBTI community seems to have strategically relocated to other communicative spaces, as shown in the secretive and concealed social media sites mentioned above. They therefore remain resilient in constructing their subaltern public sphere in spite of both state and cultural restrictions on their full participation as full dignified citizens.

The Challenges of Using the GALZ Facebook amongst Midlands State University Homosexuals

One post on the GALZ Facebook page is a link to an article reporting how homosexual students at the Midlands State University were being harassed with threats of exposure through another homophobic Facebook account. MSU is arguably the largest university in Zimbabwe, with more than 22,000 students. Due to the fact that MSU received such attention on the GALZ Facebook, it was reasonably justifiable for the researchers to conduct interviews and focus group discussions with both heterosexual and homosexual students at MSU. Sithandazile Moyo a member of the student community was better placed to conduct snowballing to identify participants and engage them. The researcher conducted focus group discussion with five gays and one lesbian and four heterosexual students at Midlands State University in Gweru. The researcher knew one person who is homosexual who then referred the researcher to the others through a process called snowballing. Group discussions were used to find out how effective Facebook has been for the homosexual community in articulating their issues. In their responses, several queer respondents from the Midlands State University student community tended to confuse the use of their personal Facebook accounts with that of the GALZ Facebook account. For instance, Respondent A acknowledges Facebook is an easy and effective way to converse with 'close ones'. However, if homophobic people make negative comments Respondent A says, 'I try and ignore them and those that happen to inbox me with negative comments, I block them.' The conflation of use of a purely personal Facebook account and the GALZ account is problematic, and in our reading of responses we deduced the respondents preferred to talk about their personal accounts more than the GALZ account, where they thought they were more vulnerable from homophobic attacks.

A male gay (Respondent B) said,

> I'm a member of the GALZ Facebook page. I just liked the page but I will be lying if I say I have ever posted anything nor like any post because I am scared to be exposed. The page is open for public therefore anyone who views it can see my comments or posts. We all know how the Zimbabwean government is so against us therefore I will never risk my life and come out as long I am residing in Zimbabwe . . .

Despite noting the terror, abuse and isolation that homosexuals face when they visit the GALZ Facebook, he was nostalgic that the platform initially provided a space for healthy interaction and compassionate company before it was invaded by undesirable homophobic people. He intimated that it was even possible to find love partners (see Moyo 2015).

One lesbian Thoko Moyo explained how Facebook is not reliable and safe,

> I used to follow the Facebook page in its infant stages. The administrators used to post significant information about Gays and Lesbians. It was more like a private group. I was happy and felt safe up until one day I received a threatening phone call from an anonymous person threatening to kill me if I participated on the page. The caller told me that he had all the information about me including the address where I reside and I must bear in mind that even if I was murdered no law would (be used to) arrest him because homosexuality is not allowed in Zimbabwe. I could not report the matter to the police in fear of being arrested too for being Lesbian but had no choice but unlike the page . . .

This again reveals how Facebook cannot be regarded as a liberator of Gays and Lesbians, as most users feel unsafe. Information gathered from a focus group discussion with heterosexuals revealed that even those who do not practice homosexuality can participate on the GALZ Facebook page in a bid to continue with the criticism. In the discussion one heterosexual participant remarked that homophobic visitors to the GALZ Facebook page can just insult gays on the page:

> Facebook can . . . be accessed by someone who is literate; one needs a smartphone with internet connection or a computer again with internet connection. So anyone, regardless of their sexuality, is free to say what they want on the Facebook page, thus they cannot run away from the negative criticism from mainstream media coz it's there even on their page. Therefore I disagree that Facebook has liberated this subaltern group by giving them a space for articulating the issues related to them.

These selected responses capture the general insecurity the GLBTI community, who initially thought had found in the GALZ Facebook a liberated alternative public sphere, now experience. This has led them to opting to use other social media channels that they can control and manage on their own, including private Facebook accounts, Twitter, etc.

Conclusion

Queer sexuality remains a contentious issue in Zimbabwe, which is undoubtedly a very homophobic country as evidenced by the attestations of the country's leading politicians both in government and in opposition. Zimbabwe remains a morally conservative closed society, too entrenched in the homophobic majority's perspective. Tolerance of homosexuality requires a radical revolution in the political and cultural set-up if one believes GLBT tendencies and homosexuality deserve space and expression in the Zimbabwean public sphere. Those who believe in gay and lesbian rights must therefore wage a struggle as other disadvantaged or marginalized groups have done over the years. However, the odds they face will be immense, since they are a minority trying to assert their free will while facing a hostile majority.

A vigorous debate has not yet been initiated in the Zimbabwean public sphere where sensitive matters ought to undergo rational discussion. Traditional African culture restricted discussion of sexual matters to specific spheres, and the new turn of events, a consequence of the inception of the HIV and AIDS scourge, has thrust gender and sexuality into the public sphere. GALZ has been known to place advertorials and supplements in mainly privately owned newspapers. Such actions have gone without much recrimination in the past. Nonetheless, with President's Mugabe's recent pronouncements against the organization, GALZ might find they have a hard road to travel in their publicity efforts. They risk physical violence. Protection of human life is prudent, especially in situations where the dominant heterosexual culture is comfortable with the repression and concealment of other types of sexuality. Such dominant culture often takes the cosy view that what one does not see does not exist. Going back to basics and thinking about what is right or wrong and what is good or bad for human kind is paramount at this time. Some people argue we are in a highly rational, scientific and amoral world. Free choice, as long as it does not do harm to any other person or to society at large, is therefore acceptable. Logical and rational articulations of decisions ought to be respected, especially with regards to same-sex consensual relations and transgender decisions. However, since human beings are also emotional and subjective entities it is unthinkable to totally exclude personal tastes and preferences. We cannot dictate how people feel, even though we may try to influence them. For instance, the scientific falsity of racial superiority can be asserted but this does not make even the most informed persons desist from racist inclinations and perceptions. What is immoral, moral and amoral needs to be rethought and re-debated, suspending emotions and biases, while being reflexive so that others understand the same said biases.

References

Appiah, K. A. (1992). *In mv Father's house*. London: Metheum.

Appiah, K. A. (1994). Identity, Authenticity, survival: Multicultural societies and social reproduction. In C. Taylor (Ed.), *Multiculturalism: Examining the politics of recognition*. New Jersey: Princeton University Press.

Constitution of Zimbabwe: Amendment: (No. 20), 2013. Harare: Government Printer.

Dunton, C., & Palmberg, M. (1996). *Human rights and homosexuality in Southern Africa* (Current African Issues 19). Uppsala: Nordiska Afrikainstitute.

Epprecht, M. (1998). The "Unsaying" of indigenous homosexualities: Mapping a blindspot in an African Masculinity. *Journal of Southern African Studies*, *24*(4), 631–642.

Grossberg, L. (1996). Identity and cultural studies—Is that all there is?. In S. Hall and P. Du Clay (Eds.), *Questions of cultural identity* (pp. 87–107). London: Sage.

Hall, S. (1996). Introduction: Who needs "Identity"?. In S. Hall & P. Du Guy (Eds.), *Questions of cultural identity* (pp. l–17). London: Sage.

Mhiripiri, N. A. (2014). Reporting homophobia in the Zimbabwean Media. In IFJ Africa Office (Ed), *Reporting homophobia in the Zimbabwean and Nigerian media*. Dakar: International Federation of Journalists.

Moyo, S. B. (2015) Gay and Lesbian of Zimbabwe (GALZ) Use of Facebook as an Alternative Public Sphere, Dissertation submitted in partial fulfillment of the Bsc. Hon. Media and Society Studies Degree, Department of Media and Society Studies, Midlands State University, Gweru.

Mutimukulu, M. (2014). President stands by Museveni, *The Herald*, 3 March, p. 2.

Shaw, D. (2005). Queer inclinations and representations: Dambudzo Marechera and Zimbabwean Literature. In F. Veit-Wild and D. Naguschewski (Eds.), *Body, sexuality, and gender: Versions and subversions in African literature 1* (pp. 89–112). New York: Rodopi.

Strand, C. (2013). The rise and fall of a contentious social policy option—Narratives around the Ugandan Anti-Homosexuality Bill in the domestic press. *Journal of African Media Studies*, *5*(3), 275–294.

Nhamo A. Mhiripiri is Associate Professor in the Media and Society Studies Department, Midlands State University. He has diverse interests in media and cultural studies, and is also a published fiction writer. His latest publications include a report for IFJ Africa entitled *Reporting Homophobia in the Zimbabwean Media* and a book co-edited with Tendai Chari entitled *African Football, Identity Politics and Global Media Narratives: the Legacy of the 2010 FIFA World Cup* published by Palgrave MacMillan, and the chapter "Narratives of the Zimbabwe Crisis, National Sovereignty and Human and Media Rights Violations", in Said Adejumobi's (ed), *National Democratic Reforms in Africa: Changes and Challenges published by* Palgrave MacMillan. He is currently co-editing the book *Media Law, Ethics and Policy in the Digital Age* to be published by IGI Global.

Sithandazile B. Moyo graduated with a Bsc Honours degree in Media and Society Studies from the Midlands State University in 2015, and is currently studying for a Masters in Marketing Communications at Rhodes University, South Africa.

CHAPTER 13

Blogging, Feminism and the Politics of Participation: The Case of *Her Zimbabwe*

Shepherd Mpofu

Introduction

The proliferation of the internet has shown promises and 'potentials' of empowering women in ways that are unimaginable in most patriarchal societies. Politics, activism and engagements through technology seem to have been gendered spaces as evidenced by research in the developing world (Anita 2008; Keller 2012; Morahan-Martin 2000). This chapter attempts to demystify this 'silent' myth, especially prevalent in the African context, that the internet, technological activism and political domains are meant for men. It will discuss activism in support of women's issues in Zimbabwe through a single case study approach. The website 'Her Zimbabwe' attempts to empower women as citizens, giving them a platform to speak on issues otherwise ignored in mainstream media or frowned upon by society, using material from citizen journalists, that is bloggers and readers who comment under blog stories which compose an alternative public sphere to the mainstream and, to a certain extent officialized, public

S. Mpofu (✉)
University of Johannesburg, Johannesburg, South Africa
e-mail: mpofu.shepherd@gmail.com

B. Mutsvairo (ed.), *Digital Activism in the Social Media Era*,
DOI 10.1007/978-3-319-40949-8_13

sphere dominated by mainstream media. 'Her Zimbabwe', as the name suggests, focuses entirely on women's issues giving women, as citizens, a platform to speak and articulate the issues which seem to be ignored by society, industry, policy-makers and the media. The site has a lot of content on women's issues especially from 'feminist' bloggers.

Methodologically this study will use purposive sampling to select material that speaks to issues of women's activism since 2012 and these will be subjected to critical discourse analysis, an analytic approach that critiques power, its distribution and imbalances. Theoretically the chapter is anchored on the issue of the voice in counter-digital public spheres.

There are two main developments that have influenced the way Zimbabweans have addressed the evolution of the socio-economic and political spheres and, in the process, managed to partly disrupt the status quo. Even though the status quo has not been dismantled, the fact that issues that could hitherto not be addressed in public or even in private are now on the menu for public discourses and consumption speaks volumes about this evolution. These two developments, besides education of course, are migration and technology. This chapter explores how the internet has empowered women to discuss and advance a 'feminist' agenda in a setting that has for a long time been favourable to patriarchal configurations where politics, activism and engagements in the technological era have continually been gendered and imagined as male spaces (Harris 2008) This is prevalent especially where technological use and activism are structured by gender. Moreover, this chapter argues that technological advancements and access have opened new vistas for women to advance issues of their collective interest. It is important to add here that there has not been any research on how issues regarding women empowerment, feminism etc. are discussed online especially in the context of Zimbabwe. Most research focuses on the crisis, politics and, if online activism is the area of study, political engagement and the diaspora (D. Moyo 2009; L. Moyo 2009; Mpofu 2013, 2014a, b, 2016). In addition, research from the developed world also helps to cast light on how, at its nascent stages, the internet has predominantly been a male domain (Morahan-Martin 2000; Anita 2008; Keller 2012) and when women have been 'let in' their participation has had different value attached to it (Anita 2008).

Scholars such as Newsom and Lengel (2012, p. 31) have looked at how Arab women have used the internet to advance their cause and realized that 'gendered messages are constructed, essentialized, reconstructed, and made invisible by the consumer media system'. The current set-up of media in Zimbabwe does not advance women's interests. Men dominate in the news, both as staffers producing the news and as news sources. There are few female editors in most media houses in Zimbabwe. There are few senior-ranking editorial appointments for females such as Victoria Ruzvidzo who is Zimpapers (a government-controlled stable of newspapers) managing editor, Elizabeth Mushonga who is the general manager of the provincial Zimpapers title *Manica Post* and Susan Makore is the Chief Executive Officer of a private radio station, ZIFM Stereo. Otherwise most women are employed as journalists, sub-editors or desk editors, features or supplements editors without much influence on final news content. This has an influence on the coverage and angling of stories pertaining to women's concerns.

The major problem in this research is that traditional or mainstream public spheres disempower women through (mis)representation, in that the agenda is set and management mostly done by men.

'Her Zimbabwe' is the brainchild of Fungai Machirori who started it in 2012 after graduation from the University of Reading in the UK. She argues that 'Her Zimbabwe' has an important space to occupy in agenda-setting while noticing that women's positive representation 'remains perilously low with women still occupying scant positions of authority in newsrooms and news media organisations. At the same time as we see a sharp rise in political alarmism in the mainstream media, we also [notice] the rise in hypersexualized and sexist content which is derisive towards women' (Interview, 23 February 2016). Thus the voices and issues of women are not only silenced or delegitimized through such coverages but there is a lack of gender sensitivity in Zimbabwe's male-dominated newsrooms.

As Harris (2008) suggests, women's activism is policed and supervised by men who are in power and this usually excludes women from voicing their issues 'outside formal politics' from which they are also disempowered. Of course, in Zimbabwe, for example, there has been an 'improvement' in advancing women politically (we have seen an increase in the number of female legislators for instance) but there has not been an inspiring deployment and employment of women in positions of influence in parastatals, industry, army, media, academy and the like. In January and February 2016, for example, the government-owned mainstream daily newspapers *The Herald* and *The Chronicle* respectively ran a story and a cartoon that spoke to issues of gender, sexuality and identity which could be an illustration of the dangers to women's representation in male-dominated media spaces.

Fig. 13.1 From *The Herald* 30 January 2016

In the first instance, shown in Fig. 13.1, *The Herald*, in reference to a hoax story emanating from a Kenyan newspaper suggesting that all men in Eritrea were being required by government to marry more than one woman, ran a picture of what appeared to Eritrean women with a caption reading thus: ‘No argument there, the Eritrean girls look good. Even the worst looking would definitely be a beauty queen here in Zimbabwe, (no offence to our bleached, weaved and over-painted sisters’ (*The Herald*, 30 January 2016). Fig. 13.2, a cartoon from The Chronicle of 4 February 2016 by Wellington Musapenda, who was subsequently suspended for breaching protocol by not running it through his editorial team, shows a pornographic depiction of tribalism and sexism all entangled together with two supposedly isiNdebele-speaking women reacting to the low academic performance by their regional high schools. There has always been an age-old stereotypical, pejorative and demeaning perception that Ndebele-speaking people are dull and all their women are good for is prostitution.

Fig. 13.2 From *The Chronicle* 4 February 2016

These issues were raised and debated on social media but their discussion in mainstream media remained narrow, most probably because of gender and ethnic biases that characterize newsrooms or a preoccupation with Zimbabwe's unfolding political drama playing itself out in the shaky ruling party.

At the pith of this research is the argument that it is time we noticed the important role technology-enabled conversations play to those powerless or voiceless and, in most cases, majority members of society. These techno-voices and conversations 'represent new directions in activism, the construction of new participatory communities (and cultures), and the development of new kinds of public selves' (Harris 2008, p. 482). Anita Harris, who was writing on young women's participation on political issues using the internet in the American context, noticed that in most cases it is challenging especially for women to construct 'public selves at a time when young female citizenship is operationalized through consumption and display rather than political agency' (2008, p. 483) and intellectual engagement with issues of the day and those that affect women especially.

Research Design, Method

In this chapter I use a single case study approach. Robert Yin, the foremost proponent of this approach, defines it as a scientific inquiry that 'investigates a contemporary phenomenon within its real life context especially when the boundaries between phenomenon and context are not clearly evident' (2003, p. 13). A case study is essential in this research as it helps us understand, holistically, cultural systems *in situ*. It is helpful in satisfying three pillars of any research: understanding, describing and explaining a phenomenon.

The Case

Fungai Machirori says the 'Her Zimbabwe' website (hereafter HZ) sprang from 'an idea from my Masters dissertation which explored Zimbabwean women's movement building across different geographical spaces... As one of my recommendations, I suggested that new media could play a role in a more robust movement building across space. And this is the recommendation I implemented... ' (Interview, 23 February 2016). Zimbabwe has a number of women-centric organisations such as Musasa, which works towards eradicating gender-based violence, Zimbabwe Women Lawyers Association, which seeks to create a legal environment that empowers women and children, Women's Action Group, which advances women and girl child's rights, and a network of women's rights activists called Women Action Group, among others. These have been dormant and not vocal about issues bedevilling Zimbabwean women on a daily basis owing to political threats, lack of funding and in some cases narrow avenues to engage society leaders. HZ's innovative use of the internet to amplify women's concerns is ground-breaking.

HZ, just like many other sites born in the diaspora that have attempted to advance democratic deliberations (Mpofu 2014a, 2015a), attempts to empower women as citizens, giving them a platform to speak on issues otherwise ignored in male-dominated mainstream media and newsrooms or frowned upon by society. Machirori argues that her website's exclusion of men is not necessarily '... segregation against men because the mainstream media, and so much [media coverage] focuses on men or areas that are traditionally perceived to be the preserves of men. It can't be a segregation "against" if the group that is being omitted... holds a special position and privilege in society' (Interview, 23 February 2016). The site uses material from citizen journalists that is, bloggers and reader input. Citizen journalism is a form of 'storytelling which moves from seeing journalism as a lecture but as a conversation where everyday people assume power and take charge and be influential in telling their stories from their own perspectives, through blogs, reader comments, email list-servs etc.' (Mpofu 2015b, p. 87). Most bloggers are young, university-educated, urban women. HZ's characterization as an alternative counter-public sphere to the mainstream draws from Fraser's (1992, p. 116) conceptualization of different types of alternative public spheres—'counter-publics' which are parallel arenas for discourse contesting the historically 'exclusionary norms of the bourgeois public, elaborating alternative styles of political behaviour and alternative norms of public speech'. HZ gives women, as citizens, a platform to debate, challenge patriarchy and amplify their issues of concern which are ignored by political or traditional leaders, society, industry, policy-makers and the media. But the critical question is, bearing in mind that most non-governmental organisations in Zimbabwe are reliant on donor funding, *amplifying for who and to what effect*? The site's content is largely from 'feminist' bloggers to satisfy what Machirori says is a 'particular deficiency in documenting Zimbabwean women's history. So this is why "*Her* Zimbabwe", and not "Our Zimbabwe" or "His Zimbabwe"' (Interview, 23 February 2016). It makes it clear, however, that men are 'secondary audiences'. The administration of the site includes three women and a man who is a finance officer.

HZ's aim is to harness:

> ...the potential of digital media to share and tell Zimbabwean women's stories, as well as nurture young women's digital activism. Her Zimbabwe's primary target audience is Zimbabwean women aged 20–35, although participation and contributions are accepted from women of all ages. Understanding that outcomes for women are increased by improving outcomes for society, Her Zimbabwe also targets men as a secondary audience. As women's issues cannot be separated from those of the men with whom they co-exist as partners, relatives, friends, work colleagues, the Her Zimbabwe website features a 'His Zimbabwe' section which allows men to express their viewpoints and stances on issues to with gender and equity.

The above suggests the site is exclusionary of the mostly disconnected and offline 0–19 and 36+ age-groups, delivering us into a debate of ethical dilemma on representation and speaking on behalf of those considered 'others' in one's community. This is to suggest that while it is welcome to speak for 'others' this could best be done within the confines of ethical representation and involvement without reproducing the same 'hierarchies of oppression and privileged ontological positions' (Hinterberger 2007, p. 74) characteristic of patriarchal settings that feminist movements are challenging for instance. Even my writing of this chapter needs to be tempered by an awareness that I may not fully grasp the 'others' whose struggles and creative ways of challenging patriarchy I am pontificating on. HZ's activities include:

Amplifying women's voices online: HZ's mainstay is its website through which the sharing of personal narratives, social commentary and perspectives on gender has been promoted. The website is supported by robust conversation and interaction via HZ's social media channels.

Stimulating conversation: Understanding the need to also promote discussion in the offline realm, HZ hosts a series of talks termed 'Critical Conversations' as a means to bring together bloggers, journalists, opinion leaders and activists to discuss issues that pertain to the media and technology environment, both locally and internationally. These speaks (sic) convene influential media and technology leaders, and the general public, to discuss, debate and critique issue of relevance to the sectors they represent.

Promoting literacy in digital storytelling and security: Another of the gaps HZ is filling is to bridge the digital access divide through building and strengthening women's online content production skills.

Despite targeting women, evidence from this research suggests men also contribute to the website and their men's contributions do not represent the 'mainstream' patriarchal views on feminism. They, just like women writers, attempt to dismantle patriarchy and the status quo they argue suppresses women.

Method and Questions

Methodologically this study will use purposive sampling to select material that speaks to issues of women activism since 2012 and these will be subjected to critical discourse analysis, an analytic approach that looks at power, its distribution and imbalances. Friker (2008, p. 200) defines purposive sampling as a 'type of convenience sampling which the researcher selects the sample based on his or her judgement' while Kripendorff

(2004, p. 119) furthers adds that 'relevance sampling... aims at selecting all textual units that contribute to answering given research questions... [since] the resulting sample is defined by the analytical problem at hand'. Purposive sampling is flexible as it can be used in 'even less structured ways without the application of any random sampling' (Friker 2008, p. 200).

This research follows questions around the first of these three core activities. It questions the viability of a gendered space in 'fighting' against a system that is oppressive to women. Does this call for the 'oppressors' exclusion or for a conversation and what parameters should be set for the conversation to obtain? Again, the research questions the ethics and use of an alternative digital public sphere that is elitist in a country ravaged by poverty where the mostly affected women are the poor, illiterate, in the rural areas, have no social capital, technological know-how and economic access to arenas of debate and, even if they had to have access, their dimensions of social experience would bring with them the burden of values attached to modes of participation in society (Anita 2008). The risk often becomes the transference of offline and often patriarchal social and political practices into the new domain. Further, the research gauges the effectiveness of such a website through the levels and intensity of debates on blogs. Lastly, what issues affect women and how are these raised and debated in HZ?

Theory: Technology, Voice and Changing Paradigms of Participatory Practices

Where women's voices are constrained, the internet has given them a voice, that is, an online voice where internet-based platforms are used to freely 'explore contemporary feminism and articulate their own perspectives' (Keller 2012, p. 430). In so doing they assert themselves into a space where they make arguments to be seen as equal and serious socio-political actors and agential citizens. The concept of the voice as articulated by Mitra empowers those marginalized members of the community into gaining a 'heteroglossic and hyperconnected' voice (2001, p. 29) that could be used to 'voice the unspeakable stories and eventually construct powerful connections that can be labelled as "cyber communities"', (2001, p. 30) with other people sharing similar interests. Mitra (2001, p. 30) further asserts that 'it is far more crucial to understand how the internet can, (1) open up the possibility of having a voice, (2) produce alliances (aka cyber communities) with unique characteristics, and (3) how the combination of voice and cyber community can help to renegotiate identities in a structured social system'. For a long time, most women, especially in developing contexts with subordinate/dominant structurations, find themselves in the category of the marginalized, subordinate and disempowered members in society without a voice on matters affecting them. Instead of speaking up for themselves these subordinate and marginalized women are spoken for and the systems that have made this possible continuously neglect questioning such structures of representation as the media. However one has to question if indeed having a voice on issues that affect women in HZ debates is actually considered as having a place 'at the table and utilizing that place to be heard and acknowledged' (Mitra 2001, p. 31) in the broader society. Women have succeeded at problematizing the centres of power in society through using new technologies whose immediacy and interconnectivity disrupt the 'traditional' flow and ordering of things.

This 'traditional' flow and ordering of things has upheld a culture where women occupy a position where they could only be seen and not heard and—to draw from Keller's assessment of how young girls communicate online—are 'encouraged to be political in appropriate' and patriarchally approved and supervised ways, 'while being excluded from formal [socio-] political arena due to (gender) based exclusions and patriarchal constructions of activism that privilege formal [male-dominated] political activities' (2012, p. 435). Women's communicative spaces, then, therefore become alternative to the mainstream and they then occupy a subaltern status as a counter-public. Writing about subaltern public spheres Squires (2002) argues that there are three formats they take; counter-public, enclave and satellite. I position HZ in the counter-public because, while it addresses issues related to women, it remains open and accessible to those it is not intended for—men. It operates on the sidelines of traditional public spheres manned and dominated by men that deny women a voice.

New media technologies have not only given women a voice but have helped alter our traditional understandings and configurations of space and time while also creating a community of counter-publics that may share, to a certain extent, some commonalities entering the communicative space as empowered and agential citizens. But which women are we speaking about? The suburban and connected or rural and disempowered ones? Machirori dismisses the notion of HZ being an elitist project thus:

> We have never presumed to represent all women's voices. Being an online platform in a country with limited access to online tools, this would be a

> gross overestimation of our capacity. It's a reductive argument that believes that someone is 'elite' merely by the fact of their access to online tools and spaces. Would we instantly identify an unemployed young graduate who spends the little money they get from their parents (or by selling second hand clothes at a market) to buy data bundles as an elite? Being online is becoming more of a necessity nowadays as it links us to opportunity and widens our communication base. As such, being online cannot be narrowly constructed as a pursuit of the elite alone. Conversely, to assume that the so-called elite women do not have issues that require redress is another myth that needs debunking. (Interview, 23 February 2016).

Despite this limited scope, new media activism has allowed us to 'productively rethink of [women] as active agents, cultural producers and citizens rather than passive victims and cultural dupes in the online world' (Keller 2012, p. 440). However, it is not my argument here that by being agential subaltern counter-publics women are 'binarized' with and against the mainstream. Admittedly women are empowered differently and cannot be taken as homogeneous collective affected by patriarchy in uniform ways. Most problematically is the targeted population by *Her Zimbabwe* if one was to engage with the meaning and significance of 'Zimbabwe' in the name. The website targets women between the ages of 20–35 those deemed, in a way, ungovernable. It seems this age-group has the means to access and interact online such as an education, hardware and economic means to 'purchase' their entry online. As one blogger, Vimbai Chinembiri, says 'the writers are drawn from upper middle class. This is probably by virtue of level of education and not necessarily because of background as content shows...' (E-mail communication, 5 May 2016). This brings us to the discussion on the effects of structural inequalities on online participatory practices. Watkins (2009) argues that access to technologies or 'digital gates' permits or restricts access to maintain disparities between race and class power relations online for example.

Digital divide or the opening of these 'digital gates' is informed by the location, class and techno-literacy of the women. Zimbabwe's current economic status does not positively influence people into prioritising informational needs when there are bread and butter issues to worry about. In addition, government interference into ordinary people's online communications has, to a certain extent, hindered participation. Access to the internet stood at 34 % in Zimbabwe, whose population is believed to be around 15 million (Mhlanga and Mpofu 2014). Growth in access has been influenced by the importation of 'cheap Chinese mobile gadgets, a recent reduction in mobile telephony rates and the expansion of the network by the country's three mobile operators' (Mpofu 2015b, p. 8). It should also be noted that in as much as the internet opens up vistas of communication and empowerment for women it can also be a landmine. Moraha-Martin (2000, p. 68) argues that 'the impact of the internet for women is not all positive. The internet also has created and amplified problems for women. Women have been targets of online oppression, harassment, and some have become real life victims because of their online participation.' The following section engages with HZ's discussions in blogs casting light on one of its main objectives of amplifying women's voices.

An Analysis of *Her Zimbabwe* Blogs and the Politics of Gender

My main focus here is to engage with the objective that the website sets for itself, that of amplifying the voices of women online. There are two suggestions raised by this objective. Firstly, women are speaking but their voices are not loud or prominent enough to be heard. Secondly, it could be deduced from the statement that very few of them are speaking and not heard or if heard are ignored. This analysis is done in tandem with the considerations of networked spaces, mostly dominated by men, as arena for fighting for freedom and the exclusionary nature not of the spaces alone but of the focus of the website in dealing with women's issues in Zimbabwe. The main assumption and contention in this section, which also forms the core of this chapter is that a speaking or writing subject on issues of feminism in HZ assumes a posture and occupies a space of power and authority 'which requires a commitment to an ethical involvement in the representation of "others"' (Hinterberger 2007, p. 74). To highlight this, one of the bloggers, Vimbai Chinembiri, observes that most of the bloggers 'have an above average level of education compared to most women in Africa or the women who are the subject of most of the writings' (E-mail Communication, 5 May 2016).

The current chapter uses 51 purposely sampled articles from the inception of the website until February 2016. These address a variety of issues regarding women's issues like sexuality, women's rights, child marriages, sport, violence and equality. Most blogs were contributed by women and very few have reader comments under them. This could mean two things:

that readers do not critically engage with issues raised or they do so on the website's *Facebook* page which replicates and updates stories as they are uploaded on the website.

It is possible that most women rights activists in Zimbabwe aim to dismantle the oppressive cultures that suppress women. Hence, the blog post from 'Pretty Chavango', 'Gender roles run deep', is critical as it speaks to the need for women to 'learn to traverse timidity, gender insensitivity and reality in order to break free from social norms and find success' (HZ, 9 July 2015). She further observes that societal power configurations favour boys and men more than they do women and girls. To illustrate this she claims that

> This society taught its sons that you need not worry about satisfying your women; they can do with little sex if at all. The *biggest mistake* my society made is that they told their boys that they can have sex with whoever they want whenever they want...go home and forget to satisfy their wives. Women have had to live with that kind of suffering for a very long time...When a woman sees a wrongly and provocatively dressed man she is moved, but she looks aside. When you move around with your chest bare and your shorts too tight as a man, know that you are offending some women somewhere. Just that they were taught to pretend it's not happening. Just as much as you are moved by a wrongly dressed woman or a provocatively dressed one, women actually do feel things...The same way you do. Just that our fathers taught our mothers to teach us to look aside. (Emphasis in the original)

Societies that are patriarchal have presented women through 'long established cultural stereotypes' (Wood 2007, p. 259) of what it means to be women and feminine as demonstrated by *The Herald* story and picture above. These feminine ideals are, as suggested in the quotation above, cultural expectations of women to be sex objects, submissive and passive whereas men are expected to be aggressive, macho and exude a sense of power. The 'acculturation' of women into passivity, silence and submissiveness is succinctly exposed in a comment to Chivango's blog by 'Rue', who summarizes society in her perceptions thus:

> Its funny that no matter how much you try to involve women in activities that will enhance them still they choose to be reserved and not participate. The reason being the society has taught our women to be content with what they have, that's why you find many women in abusive marriages still stay in

> them because they have been taught be content and strive on. But at times its not about striving on but about your happiness and success. If more women would only realise how much potential they have and stand for themselves and by so doing stand for others. Our society has over-emphasized the importance of men and yet forgetting that without the women men would not exist and most probably would not have the lives they have. After all men succeed to impress us!!! [sic] (HZ, 9 July 2015).

The above suggests the taken-for-grantedness the gendered roles and positions society has allocated to different sexes. Reference could be made to the hoax Eritrean story referred to above. Anthea Taderera's blog 'On Eritrea: When we make a "joke" of forced marriage' captures salient issues regarding women's commodification, 'thingification'—that is, being made into things of not much value, objectification and evils of forced marriages that tend to be overlooked as:

> Zimbabweans took to social media to discuss the 'news,' shared links to Eritrean visa offices as well as screenshots/images of fake partially completed visa applications, 'jokingly' checked into Eritrean airports on 'national duty,' engaged in casual collective misogynoir, downplayed the horror of forced marriage and commodified women . . . This callous response was particularly disappointing given the conversations around marriage, particularly the importance of being able to *consent* to marriage that we've been having as a result of the continued fight against child 'marriage'. (Taderera, 11 February 2016, emphasis in the original)

Activities online are viewed as negative because it seems those who participated in the fun did not think deeply about the story and what it means to women's rights and their treatment in a continent where they are treated as second class citizens. Women, as a semiotic reading of most reactions on social media and mainstream media suggests, are meant to be attractive sex objects, be there to satisfy men and always subordinate. In terms of physical looks there is a perception that most African settings encourage women to be 'curvy' and, as Chamunorwa Mufaro (2015) argues in her blog post entitled *Not curvy, not beautiful?* (5 October 2015):

> Africa has always appreciated the curvy woman with the full figure associated with fertility, health and affluence . . . just take a look at the language that our own African literary discourse uses to describe a beautiful African woman . . . (In) Ngugi wa Thiong'o's 1964 classic 'Weep Not Child' . . . Ngotho's idea

> of a good wife is a 'fleshy, black body with sweat.' In Chimamanda Adichie's…'Half of a Yellow Sun'…lead character, Olanna, is painted with a sensually stimulating edibility…(with a) 'curvy fleshy body' that is like 'a yellow cashew, shapely and ripe.' Her beauty is in the arch of her hips, the lusciousness of her bosom, the plumpness of her derriere and the thickness of her thighs.

This contrasts with Vimbai Midzi's arguments in her 'Sex and the City: respectability, womanhood and decency' (23 June 2015) blog '[W]omen are therefore held to standards of expressing sexuality within the confines of what men like, expect and will tolerate. Sex (note that this only applies to women) is seen as a sacrosanct gift from God. Our bodies are not seen as our own.' It is common cause that in most patriarchal African settings, Zimbabwe included, women have to express their sexuality within the confines of what men—through patriarchal configurations of sexuality—like, expect, decree and tolerate. Social media activities and some celebrities for instance advance self-sexualized images where the body parts of females are given more prominence than other capabilities they might have. This is the currency of beauty some society give prominence. Mufaro further observes, through experience and conversations in her (narrow) family setting that all this assumed beauty in an African woman is not meant for her, but for the consumption of the male species both as gazers and consumers as 'boys like a little more booty to hold at night' (Mufaro 2015). In relation to the Eritrean story, Taderera further accentuates this objectification while also debunking the 'thick' woman myth as a homogeneous expectation of all African men thus:

> The attractiveness of Eritrean women soon became the main topic of discussion. Men came out of the woodworks to tell us they wouldn't mind two wives *who looked like that.* One skit circulating on whatsapp called Zimbabwean women cows, as opposed to the 'objectively' desirable Eritrean women who were presented as a homogenous group of caramel skinned women with long straight flowing hair, thin but sufficiently…This framing is appalling as it ignores the diversity of black peoples…Eurocentric beauty norms are being applied…There is, therefore, no room for a multiplicity of beauty, or for challenging the idea that there is a single beauty standard that women must achieve or attempt to adhere to in order to validate our gender identities. Further there was the continuous implication that any form of beauty ritual was for the benefit for the male gaze and not perhaps because women found personal pleasure in their

> adornment...Women are thought of as things. A wife is apparently a thing...The entire conversation was quite telling, as not once even in passing was women's emotional and domestic labour in traditional heterosexual relationships mentioned. All that work continued to go unnoticed, expected as a given and yet still devalued. It was a very clear indication that for all our claims to be fairly progressive in the area of marriage we continue to look at interpersonal relationships with an uncritical eye and are comfortable following patriarchy's entrenched norms.

Of course this cannot be a universal conversation but it touches some experiences of Zimbabwean women and societies. The media and society have equally attempted and in some cases managed to create two binary images of women, the good and the bad. Those women that are virgins at the time of marriage are mostly considered good compared to those who are not or have children outside wedlock. Bloggers, to some could be bad girls. Chinembiri observes that sometimes ideas some bloggers especially 'mostly single women tend to clash with those of married women who often contribute through comments although there is a general consensus on some issues' (E-mail Communication, 5 May 2016) and in some cases men 'confront' bloggers accusing them of misleading other women. The bloggers debate and are not agreed on the commoditization of women through *lobola*. This is demonstrated by Mufaro's (2015) blog where she speaks about her aunts when they '...beam with anticipation at the prospects of charging high *lobola* (bride price) for my cousins who are well endowed with "assets"...As for me, I weigh a little below 50 kgs and I have a petite frame. My aunts "console" me by telling me that at least I am educated and intelligent.' The concept of *lobola* has been differently dealt with by some feminist bloggers on HZ. One argument is that women are taken as property to be auctioned where men sit and decide how much a woman who is about to get married is worth.

In '*Lobola*: to pay or not to pay?' Keith Mundangepfupfu (9 July 2015) a male blogger, argues that the *lobola* practice oppresses and commodifies women giving men undue power. Some reader comments under the blog are critical, presenting the need to maintain those cultures labelled backward in this modern world. These are highlighted below:

> *Tadzoka*: I think it is important to note the difference between the bastardization of *lobola*, and *lobola* proper. The author did briefly highlight the distinction, however, the argument sweepingly blamed the

institution of *lobola* for its abuse. Would it be fair for us to blame religion for terrorism? Indeed, not. We should blame the people who abuse the institution. *Lobola* is meant to be an exchange creating a family bond.

Morris M: I think the argument is very faulty. Just because some men view their wives as their possessions thru paying *Lobola*, there are many others who respect and consult their wives in all important decisions they make. And its a token of appreciation, everyone who believes is marrying a good wife MUST pay *lobola*. [sic]

In response to Mundangepfupfu, Vimbai Chinembiri's (2015) *Why I want lobola as part of my marriage* blog argues that *lobola* is important to her as:

> being the self-assured feminist that I am, I am certain that the kind of man who should marry me would be the kind who has respect and love for me, and the family I come from... I want him and his family to send a *munyayi* (negotiator) to my family to ask for '*sadza*' (asking for mealie thick porridge, that is my hand in marriage). I want him to adhere to the grocery list that my family will draft for the marriage ceremony. I want the visitors to *pfunya chisero* (bending their knees like females and sitting on the goat-skin mat in a way they would do while addressing a chief to whom respect is due) on a nice mat while my family lounges on the couches. They should call me and ask me if I know 'these people'. I want to enjoy being identified among my sisters as the young woman they have come to marry, and my parents should be blessed with *zvireverere zva Mai na Baba* (portions for *lobola* that go directly to the bride's parents). (9 October 2015)

This suggests something deeper, in terms of relationships, than the 'cosmetic' arguments on commercialisation and commoditisation of women. She suggests that it is about creation of family bonds and commitment between families. Also, this shows that the bloggers in HZ are not of the same mind. Their views of and on feminism are not narrow and straight-jacketed fitting all. It is crucial also to say that even though there are disagreements in some instances, there is general consensus in some issues. The editorial team, however, wields power in as far as gatekeeping is concerned. For example Chinembeiri recalls how her blog was rejected 'because it sort of made excuses for wife beaters. However my intention was to look at abuse from the perspective of the abuser' (E-mail Communication, 5 May 2016).

Issues of power, class, law and sex are also tackled by the website as advocacy for women and girl-children's rights. In a blog post '"Fast girls",

Tomana and the age of consent' (2 July 2015) Taderera contends with the court-set age of consent of 12 years and the controversial remarks by Zimbabwe's Prosecutor-General Johannes Tomana to the effect that 'let the children get married, because they're poor and what are they doing with their lives anyway?!' Further, Taderera observes that instead of condemning Tomana's reckless statement and the practice of child marriage, society condemns young girls caught up in child marriages or under age sexual intercourses as 'fast girls'. Taderera suggests that society sees these 'fast girls' as responsible for trapping men into sexual relationships. She argues:

> What has been particularly disheartening for me in the past few weeks is seeing the extent to which the myth of the 'fast girl' who goes around waylaying innocent *adult* men, forcing them to have sex with her is ingrained in the psyches of many. *Men who have sex with children are being presented as hapless victims of feminine wiles as opposed to the predators that they are.* (Emphasis supplied)

In most cases society lays the burden of blame on women when they are raped and most often than not victim-blaming borders on issues of their sexually enticing dressing to being in spaces where they 'know' full well they are not supposed to be. Sex, it seems, is not something women have to negotiate on rather men are left with all the power to interpret and decide whether or not to engage in any form of sexual relationship with a woman: be it consensual or rape. The argument by Tomana above that girls have to be married at a tender age because of poverty brings into play issues of class. Middle class and well-off families that can afford to send their girl-children to school and cater for them are safe. The poor can get married to escape poverty and this perpetuates the cycle of poverty and abuse of those considered poor. Taderera rightly points out that '[W]e are callously content to leave certain segments of society behind', and there is need for legislative transformation for the sake of all citizens. The intervention made by Tsitsi Chivango (2015) on *Gender equality: an important tool for sustainable development* (30 July 2015) is revealing (Chivango 2015) particularly the conclusion that despite Zimbabwe '…being a signatory to gender-sensitive instruments such as the Convention on the Elimination of all forms of Discrimination Against Women (CEDAW), the famous Beijing Declaration and Platform for Action (which people like quoting but know very little about), the African Charter on Human and

Peoples' Rights and the SADC Protocol on Gender and Development, our road to equality is still a long way ahead'.

Most bloggers do not only mourn about the oppressive nature of society without offering any solutions for what they see as problems. For instance, Midzi ends her blog posting thus,

> [T]he stereotypes and gender roles we have allowed to flourish in our society inhibit the ability of women to be full, rights-bearing citizens. We have allowed culture and religious beliefs to supersede the protection of our girls' rights…allowed the male gaze to determine how women's sexuality should be expressed. Our lawmakers must be made aware of the weaknesses of the law, and the extent to which these laws are harmful to women and girls. Beyond that, our society needs to change. We need to teach our girls that marriage does not add intrinsic value to their lives. (Midzi 2015)

In a blog entitled 'Why can men sex freely, but women can't?' Lazurus Sauti concludes by offering the following as solutions 'Therefore, communities need intervention programmes that change the attitudes of men, women and society at large… there must be educational programmes for young men and women that dispel unhealthy and unequal representations of women… there must be space for young men, in particular, to learn about sex, sexuality and healthy relationships in an open way and at a young age' (25 November 2015).

The themes raised above demonstrate the differences between western and African feminisms. This could be informed by the fact that their struggles are different. Chinembiri puts it this way: 'writers (African bloggers) struggle with different issues that are not entirely big issues in the western world…education for young girls, *lobola* debates, sanitary wear provision, harassment in public places… '.

Concluding Remarks

While it could be argued that in most Zimbabwean societies power distribution favours men more than it does women and that 'women worldwide have been last to come online' (Morahan-Martin 2000, p. 683) there seems to be potential of creating and starting conversations about issues pertinent to women. While some stories and blogs are analytical and largely informed by information and statistics released by such reliable agencies of the United Nations, African Union, World Bank etc., most of the bloggers rely on rather narrow familial or generalized take on societal issues to construct arguments. This creates ethical issues in and of representation in that familial surroundings and experiences are taken for granted as experiences of most societies in Zimbabwe. The issues around *lobola* and marriage or the preferred size of women by African men for instance, suffice as highlights of this problematic. Morahan-Martin (2000) then suggests that '[C]ritical thinking abilities are essential for internet users . . . [they] need to learn to evaluate the information they find online.' Not only do readers need to be critical, but those who compose the content too. However this does not preclude the positive impact of the fact that women 'are starting' to speak online. Online communication has democratized the way we have known communication in patriarchal settings where women are meant to be silent and where their issues are involved they have minimal input and the larger part of decisions are made by men. Thus online communication frees society from the tyrannies of face to face (f2f) communication leading to people conversing as equals outside the boundaries set by f2f communication which pay attention to race, gender, sex, class, social status and the like. On the flip side this does not diminish the digital divide between the techno-haves and the techno-poor, continuations of f2f communicative patterns online, occupational hazards and inequalities of online agitation in Zimbabwe. Rather, it amplifies these disparities pointing to the fact that power resides; more often than not, with men. The fact that policy makers are excluded from online conversations acts as a drawback too.

Again, the fact that the website attempts to present the voices of the youthful and urban women leads to the exclusion of other women who some of the bloggers and news reports attempt to speak for in generalized ways. For instance, issues of the poor children being given out for marriage as an attempt at poverty alleviation by their parents, guardians or communities remain silenced while men (officials) and bloggers (women with access to the internet) speak on their behalf or for them. While the practice is retrogressive, there is need for thorough research and to give prominence to these marginalized people's voices whose rights and agenda is foregrounded by such platforms as HZ. Of course this would be a difficult feat considering the strains placed on the HZ by funders in a context where political and economic decline and donor fatigue have made it difficult for independent media organisations to cover issues affecting especially those in remote areas of the country. While the bloggers challenge the operations of society under patriarchal dominance, they help to reinforce 'contemporary notions of masculinity, femininity, heterosexuality and power' (Devoss 2000, p. 835) in some instances. For instance Vimbai Chinembiri's post on *lobola* clearly demarcates and takes for granted the role men and women play in determining the future of the woman who is about to get married. Another aspect ignored in the discussions on the blogs is that of same-sex marriages and relationships are considered taboo in Zimbabwe. Chinembiri argues that this is so because of the differences between African and western feminisms. She responded to e-mailed interview questions thus: '[F]eminism beliefs by most writers are situated in the Zimbabwean context where there is little room for extremism. I would call it grounded feminism informed by a cultural background.' The question is what is lost or gained by silences around this issue?

HZ promises to play a pivotal role in advancing women's issues and amplifying those faint or solitary voices that shed light on the plight of women through off-line programmes. In 2014 the organisation started what they call 'critical conversation' after observing that, according to Machirori, 'Zimbabwe…has, for a long time, been closed off from a lot of issues and conversations—as a result of our politics—[and this gives us an opportunity] to…interact with different ideas, views and opinions…[While] online space facilitates conversation brilliantly, the face to face encounters are still just as valid, if not even more, as they allow space for collective introspection, follow up and more elaborate explanation]' (Jena 2014). The realities of poverty and digital divide seem neglected by Jena who seems to take internet accessibility for granted in country like Zimbabwe when she says '[B]esides being an easy to penetrate platform, the internet also permits certain liberties that are generally not available in other forms of media. For example, one just needs internet access, some technological knowhow and a gadget to start an online conversation.' The tools to access the internet, that is computers and modems, skills to manipulate the soft- and hardware come at a cost in a country whose economic environment propel every citizen who happens to be lucky to get a dollar to 'invest' on bread and butter than informational and activist needs and projects.

Acknowledgment I owe a lot of thanks, in no particular order, to Fungai Machirori, Nhlanhla Ngwenya, Delta Milayo Ndou and Vimbai B. Chinembiri for their assistance which made it possible for me to conduct this research.

References

Chamunorwa, M. (2015). Not curvy, not beautiful? http://herzimbabwe.co.zw/2015/10/not-curvy-not-beautiful/. Accessed 29 April 2014.

Chavango, P. (2015). Gender roles run deep. http://herzimbabwe.co.zw/2015/07/gender-roles-run-deep/. Accessed 25 August 2016

Chinembiri, V. (2015). Why I want lobola as part of my marriage. http://herzimbabwe.co.zw/2015/10/why-i-want-lobola-as-part-of-my-marriage/. Accessed 24 April 2016.

Chivango, T. (2015). Gender equality: An important tool for sustainable development. http://herzimbabwe.co.zw/2015/07/gender-equality-an-important-tool-for-sustainable-development/. Accessed 27 April 2016.

Devoss, D. (2000). Re-reading Cyborg(?) women: The visual rhetoric images of Cyborg (and Cyber) bodies in the World Wide Web. *CyberPsychology & Behaviour*, *3*(5), 835–845.

Fraser, N. (1992). Rethinking the public sphere: A contribution to the critique of actually existing democracy. In C. Calhoun (Ed.), *Habermas and the public sphere* (pp. 109–142). Cambridge, MA: MIT Press.

Fricker, R.D. (2008). Sampling methods for web and e-mail surveys. In N. Fielding, R.M. Lee and G. Blank (Eds.), *The Sage handbook of online research methods* (p. 195–216). London: Sage Publications Ltd.

Harris, A. (2008). Young women, late modern politics, and the participatory possibilities of online cultures. *Journal of Youth Studies*, *11*(5), 481–495.

Hinterberger, A. (2007). Feminism and the politics of representation: Towards a critical and ethical encounter with "others." *Journal of International Women's Studies*, *8*(2), 74–83.

Jena, D. (2014). Her Zimbabwe goes offline with first critical conversation. http://herzimbabwe.co.zw/2014/12/her-zimbabwe-goes-offline-with-first-critical-conversation/. Accessed 29 April 2014.

Keller, J.M. (2012). Virtual feminisms: Girls' blogging communities, feminist activism, and participatory politics. *Information, Communication and Society*, *15*(3), 429–447.

Krippendorff, K. (2004). *Content analysis: An introduction to its methodology* (2nd edition). Thousand Oaks: SAGE Publications.

Mhlanga, B., & Mpofu, M. (2014). The virtual parallax: Imaginations of Mthwakazi nationalism—online discussions and calls for self determination. In A. M. Solo (Ed.), *Handbook of research on political activism in the information age* (pp. 129–146). Hershey, PA: IGI Global.

Midzi, V. (2015). Sex and the city: Respectability, womanhood and decency. http://herzimbabwe.co.zw/2015/06/sex-and-the-city-respectability-womanhood-and-decency/. Accessed 27 April 2016.

Mitra, A. (2001). Marginal voices in cyberspace. *New Media and Society, 3*(1), 29–48.

Morahan-Martin, J. (2000). Women and the Internet: Promise and perils. *CyberPsychology and Behaviour, 3*(5), 683–691.

Moyo, D. (2009). Citizen journalism and the parallel market of information in Zimbabwe's 2008 election. *Journalism Studies, 10*(4), 551–567.

Moyo, L. (2009). Constructing a home away from home: Internet, nostalgia and identity politics among Zimbabwean communities in the diaspora. *Journal of Global Mass Communication, 2*(1/2), 66–86.

Mpofu, S. (2013). Social media and the politics of ethnicity in Zimbabwe. *Ecquid Novi: African Journalism Studies, 34*(1), 115–122.

Mpofu, S. (2014a). Public and diasporic online media in the discursive construction of national identity: A case of 'Zimbabwe. An Unpublished PhD Dissertation. University of the Witwatersrand, Johannesburg.

Mpofu, S. (2014b). Memory, national identity and freedom of expression in the information age-discussing the taboo in the Zimbabwean public sphere. In A. M. Solo (Ed.), *Politics and policy in the information age* (pp. 114–128). Hershey PA: Springer Publications.

Mpofu, S. (2015a). Transnational public spheres and deliberative politics in Zimbabwe. In O. Ogunyemi (Ed.), *Journalism, audiences and diaspora* (pp. 34–52). London: Palgrave.

Mpofu, S. (2015b). When the subaltern speaks: Citizen journalism and genocide "victims voices online," Digital African Review. *A Special Issue of African Journalism Studies, 36*(4), 82–101.

Mpofu, S. (2016). Participation, citizen journalism in the contestations of identity and national symbols: A case of Zimbabwe's national heroes and the Heroes' acre. *African Journalism Studies, 37*(3), 85–106.

Mundangepfupfu, K. (2015). Lobola: to pay or not to pay? http://herzimbabwe.co.zw/2015/07/lobola-to-pay-or-not-to-pay/. Accessed 24 April /2016.

Newsom, V.A., & Lengel, L. (2012). Arab women, social media, and the Arab spring: Applying the framework of digital reflexivity to analyze gender and online activism. *Journal of International Women's Studies, 13* (5), 31–45.

Ogunyemi, O. (Ed.), (2015). *Journalism, audiences and diaspora.* London: Palgrave Macmillan.

Sauti, L. (2015). Why can men sex freely, but women can't? http://herzimbabwe.co.zw/2015/11/8688/. Accessed 24 April 2016.

Taderera (2016, February 11). When we make a 'joke' of forced marriage. http://herzimbabwe.co.zw/2016/02/8954/. Accessed 12 October 2016.

Watkins, S.C. (2009). *The young and the digital: What the migration to social networking sites, games and anytime, anywhere media means for our future.* Boston, MA: Beacon Press.

Wood, T.J. (2007). *Gendered lives: Communication, gender and culture* (9th edition). Hampshire: Wadsworth Cengage Learning.

Dr Shepherd Mpofu completed a PhD in Media Studies at the University of Witswatersrand. He is currently a postdoc fellow at the University of Johannesburg. He holds a BSc (Hons) in Journalism and Media Studies from the National University in Science and Technology in Zimbabwe and a MA in Film and Television from the University of the Witwatersrand. His research interests include national identity and diasporic media; new media; race, class and gender; media and politics; and audiences.

CHAPTER 14

Gender and Media Representations of Land Based Reforms in Zimbabwe

Patience Mutopo

Introduction

Land has always been (since 1930 and the enactment of the Land Apportioning Act), and continues to be, a non-contestable debate and a critical resource for the well-being of Zimbabwe and most former colonial states. Latent and manifest conflicts began as black Zimbabweans were dispossessed of their land by the British colonizers. After independence, the Zimbabwean government implemented land and agrarian reforms meant to improve the livelihoods of the majority. However media representations of the land-reform programme have been varied, with the local media presenting factual analysis based on the unfolding of events, but with biased assertions from the state-centred media such as the *Herald* newspaper and national television, with independent media projecting a dismal land-reform process that has ignored the plight of women, (Mutopo 2014). The gender issues have mainly been presented by the national newspapers in Zimbabwe, thus the *Sunday Mail* and the *Herald* which have carried out analysis of women's role in the land-reform programme and how they have used the land in the process of enhancing

P. Mutopo (✉)
Centre for Development Studies, Chinhoyi University of Technology, Chinhoyi, Zimbabwe
e-mail: pmutopo@ymail.com

B. Mutsvairo (ed.), *Digital Activism in the Social Media Era*,
DOI 10.1007/978-3-319-40949-8_14

farming and livelihoods. (Chari 2013) points out that framing involves ignoring certain aspects of an issue, creating an artificial balance, exaggeration, lack of analysis of events and the use of a narrow selection of experts. In the *Sunday Mail* of 15 March 2015, an exposé of women's access to land in Zimbabwe was provided by Jeanette Manjengwa, giving explicit details of how women have participated in the fast-track programme of land reform and accessed land, hence improving rural livelihoods. This does not chime with reports from the *Sunday Mail* series of March–June 2015, in which various stories of fast-track farmers were presented with a focus on men, detailing the outcomes of the tobacco revolution, ignoring the fact that women are the critical actors in farming as the providers of labour, in as much as they do not hold usufruct rights to the land.

Reform was carried out in three phases, with the last one, the Fast Track Land Reform Programme (FTLRP) being the thrust of this case. The FTLRP ran under two models for resettlement: model A1 (decongestion) aimed to resettle 160,000 communal people, based on subsistence farming. Model A2 aimed to create a force of 51,000 small-, medium- and large-scale black commercial farmers, (Murisa 2007), Table 1). Many scholars have considered the nature of this programme, however, no authority has done a desk review and analysis of gender and land reform. This study analysed the FTLRP at Mwenezi resettlement in Masvingo Province. Table 14.1 provides evidence of the landownership patterns by gender in post-colonial Zimbabwe.

In pre-colonial Zimbabwe, rights to land were vested in the hands of the headman. Under this scenario women had rights and access to a minimum area of land on which they grew women crops such as groundnuts. The advent of the colonial regime undermined the rights of women, viewing them as minors in dire need of a male representative. Disparities amongst women themselves emerged as the unmarried women and those in a polygamous marriage were literally outcasts in land access. Their married counterparts were little better, as their husbands could gain access but they were not even considered. The divorced and widowed gained access only if they had custody of children. The emergence of the FTLRP saw the resettlement of people, emergence of new institutions and a certain gender ideology towards food production. Aspects of the FTLRP appealed most to men, who are generally mobile as no customary law requires them to stay at the homestead; they can venture outside in search of a living for their family (Nyawo 2016). In as much as single, divorced or

Table 14.1 Land ownership by province, model and gender: The Zimbabwe fast-track land-reform programme

Province	*Model A1*				*Model A2*			
	No. of males	*%*	*No. of females*	*%*	*No. of males*	*%*	*No. of females*	*%*
Midlands	14,800	82	3,198	18	338	95	17	5
Masvingo	19,026	84	3,644	16	709	92	64	8
Mash Central	12,989	88	1,770	12	1,469	87	215	13
Mash West	21,782	81	5,270	19	1,777	89	226	11
Mash East	12,976	76	3,992	24	–	–	–	21
Mat South	7,754	87	1,169	13	215	79	56	17
Mat North	7,919	84	1,490	16	574	83	121	–
Manicaland	9,574	82	2,190	18	961	91	97	9
Total	**106,986**	**82**	**22,723**	**18**	**6,043**	**88**	**796**	**12**

Adopted from Utete Report 2003

widowed women (unmarried women hereafter) were disadvantaged in the initial land-reform process by the state and traditional leaders, the FTLRP created strategic opportunities which improved their access to large arable fields.

With access to land for the married being a given using the household model,[1] it was necessary to get a piece of land from the husband's plot. However, responses from the women in the Rutenga resettled farms highlighted that it was not a limiting factor, as they were satisfied. They reported an improvement in their capacity to grow crops and to get yields that could sustain their family. The unmarried women managed to capitalize by being involved in political warfare (*jambanja*) and use of social networks to gain power which won them recognition and the right to acquire land in the A1 scheme (Scoones et al. 2010; Mazhawidza and Manjengwa 2011). Married women tended to be much more disadvantaged by their marital status. They were obliged to stay in the communal areas and tend to the family whilst the unmarried women were more opportunistic and less risk-averse. Relatively few women that have gained access to land; this can be attributed to patriarchal Zimbabwean customary practices and norms, viewing women as submissive, with men's primacy defining asset accumulation, for example (Mutopo 2015). These power dynamics leave women subdued and prevent them from accessing land.

Theoretical Framework

This study is based on a gendered approach to land reform, (Moser 2005; Mutopo 2011; Berhman et al. 2012; Mutopo et al. 2015). It aims to examine gender disparities in a documented era in Zimbabwe; the FTLRP. This approach takes women as the starting-point in the processes of land acquisition and analyses the role that women play in land utilisation. It takes into account that women operate in male-sanctioned environments. Attitudes of patriarchy emanated from the pre-colonial regime where men dominated the household. Due to the racial discrimination that was prominent in the colonial era, the patriarchal issue had to be addressed; land reform was no exception. Socially constructed attitudes are usually unequal in terms of power, decision-making, and freedom of action and not the biology of the sexes. Media representations of how women emerge as a social movement in the process of land utilization are an important factor in understanding how truth is constructed and projected into the world. This is enhanced by discourse analysis, since the power of the word resonates with the identity of the author and transmitter of information to the audience. Therefore, defining the success of the land reform process becomes gendered, because women are still 18 % of those who gained land, (Utete Report 2003) which also demonstrates the gender perspectives that are created during the reporting processes by different media actors, a process rooted in variation in media house policies.

This study dwells on this line of thought as its thrust is on lobbying for a change in the structuring of gender and access to land resources, with great attention paid to the importance of media projections and interpretations of gendered approaches to land reform. This aids in understanding how media influences can glorify masculinities in land at the expense of feminine notions that exist empirically. The ultimate goal is the emergence of a scenario in which decision-making and benefits of development are distributed on a basis of gender neutrality. There is a need for serious action to be taken towards how gender discrepancy is to be addressed in resource allocation, power dynamics and in customary law, rules and norms. This may be done within the land-reform context and in a democratic media environment, where reporting structures of the news are geared towards meeting and explaining livelihood-based approaches of societies.

Methodological Approach

This work utilizes an ethnographic methodological approach in which data and focus is derived from a case study of fast-track women farmers in Mwenezi district since 2009, the various land-reform documents, and published work. The methodology employs documents already in existence to highlight issues of FTLRP and gender. Some of the reports and quotes are based on documented data from case studies on the farms in Rutenga, Mwenezi district by the author. Benefiting from the vastness of the information source on FTLRP, documented sources used span the period from the programme's inception to date in a bid to thoroughly track changes in outcomes. Desk research uses published books, documents, newspaper articles, magazines and scholarly articles in order to delve into the nature and context of the case under discussion. Ethnographic methodology triangulated with the other methods helps in understanding the women-centred approaches of land-based livelihoods and the different agricultural systems the women employed. This is a key issue with regard to gender and media representation because anthropological techniques are important in laying out how people engage with the environment and how the information is decoded and brought out by the different media forms, such as newspapers, and the radio talk shows. The way people live and improve themselves in agricultural-based societies becomes critical for media dissemination, since it also influences different local and international policy agencies.

Gender and Land Reforms in Zimbabwe

The colonial regime had land policies like the Land Appointment Act of 1930 and the Land Tenure Act of 1969 which alienated the native black Zimbabweans from much of the productive land, pushing them into marginal areas of the country, creating a racially differentiated land-tenure system (Gaidzanwa 1991; Utete 2003; Ruswa 2007). The need for land inspired a liberation struggle; land was without a doubt, the single most important motive for the liberation struggle. After Independence, people expected a change, with women (86 %) (Scoones et al. 2010) working on the land expecting a lot, especially after being a stronghold of the struggle. In post-independence Africa, the land question has been non-debatable, but dominant and constant in the discourses and practices of development. As a way to address these inequities, the Zimbabwean government embarked on a land-reform programme and the first set of resettled families were in place in the early 1980s. Questions were raised regarding the addressing of historical racial imbalances in land ownership by land reform in Zimbabwe and whether it had attempted to address the issue of gender inequalities in its endeavours (ibid.). The Zimbabwean FTLRP presented an appealing prospect of a sustainable livelihood for many women, an opportunity that had never presented itself in the country's history of land invasions (Mutopo 2011). The FTLRP promised many more women gaining access to land, unlike preceding resettlement programmes soon after independence which did not recognize a woman as an independent entity but always subordinate to a male figure.

Women's Access to Land under the FTLRP

Under the two resettlement models (A1 and A2), there were differences in land acquisition. A1 applicants were resettled by the District Administrator (DA) who got lists of people from village heads. The A2 model applicants had to formally apply to the Ministry of Lands, Land Reform and Resettlement who would make awards depending on the resource base of the applicant, as this model had minimal to no government support. To date, even with the benefit of the 2004 National Gender Policy and the 2013 Zimbabwean Constitution, a sound gender and asset policy has not been structured. The percentage of women who acquired land under the two models ranged between 18 and 20 % nationwide (Chingarande 2003; Mutopo 2015). Even when allocated land (including through inheritance), women did not always remain in control.[2] In some cases, the son actually took over the mother's land entitlement and exercised control of the land and its production systems (Jirira and Halimana 2008; Mutopo 2014).

In Masvingo Province, there is a diverse pattern of how women have adopted and been affected by the FTLRP. Benefits from land reform were mainly evident in the communally marginalized women, especially the unmarried who realized independence with the coming of the resettlement scheme. In male-headed households women also gained some economic independence, which tended to shift gender roles and relations. Data analysed from cases in Goromonzi and Mazowe show that the FTLRP was widely viewed as 'masculine' favouring men over women, with women being mostly responsible for the small crops used for household consumption, whose market value in the event of a surplus comes far behind a man's agricultural income. Box 14.1, illustrates the extent to which women are affected by the ideology of the FTLRP.

Box 14.1 Local Villager Interview
The household setup is not fair as men have full control of cash crops and as women, are responsible for crops that are mainly for family consumption for example groundnuts. The unfair part of it is, even if as women, we sell surplus (women crops), men's hands will be seen when money gets on the table. That is the reason why we also engage ourselves in other non-agricultural generating activities in a bid to widen our income base.
Source: Adapted from Mutopo (2014, p. 75)

When the resettlement era began, customary law was non-existent. Benefits to women were realized in this period until Chiefs and Headmen began administering authoritative powers which undermined women's role in the land-reform initiative and their subsequent socio-economic transformation. The A1 permits, unlike the A2, which were an open-access exercise dependent on the resources one had, viewed women as spouses. There was a great disparity in gender treatment in the FTLRP—it was largely insensitive to the land needs and rights of women, albeit the A1 women landholders benefited and gained a livelihood. A disheartening response was given by one government official responding to the question of how and why women had been left out of land reform and the gaining of rights to land. His response deferred to the existence of tradition and culture (customary law) by saying,

> ... because I would have had my head cut off if I gave women land. Men would turn against the government, and it is not the government that calls on men to come and apply for land but it's set at household level; hence the outcome is inevitable.

This strongly implies that women can only get land in their own right in a world devoid of men.

With the regional range of studies done on land reform and gender, a basis for comparison and trend setting can be established. In Africa, it is realized that women tend to use their negotiation skills in accessing land. The Zimbabwean women employ the ‘right’ language to speak to their husbands and doing so at the ‘right’ time, usually in the bedroom (Mutopo 2011). Access to land especially by the married people conforms to creation of bargaining power. These bargains made by women frequently include sexual connotations in the accessing of land. In that regard, it validates the assertion that for women to access land, there has to be some sort of relationship tied to men and even the land that women might personally possess, e.g.. water gardens, are reported to be controlled by men too.

Utilization of Land by Women Entrepreneurs

If women have access to and control over land, household livelihoods and patterns improve and can be sustained. Since they are natural caretakers, they have proved to have better management policies regarding farm produce, its marketing exchange, and the subsequent use of the income earned (Mutopo 2015). Most land accessed by women through the FTLRP was being used for production of food crops, mainly for household consumption, with few women contributing to the trade in urban food networks or contributing to national food security or to export. This was attributed to the women's inability to access resources, especially financial credit facilities. The same phenomenon has been observed for other African countries as credit facilities often need a husband's signature and collateral of fixed assets, which the women normally do not have (Murisa 2007; Mutopo et al. 2015).

New research has argued that land reform has indeed opened up opportunities for women as new livelihoods are realized and pursued, leading to some gaining greater economic independence (Mutopo 2014; Mutopo et al. 2014). The findings in the Rutenga resettled farms include the role of women in the creation of new trading enterprises. Livelihoods were able to be sustained through creation of socio-economic linkages. The same case study, validated by others, revealed several cases in which women were accumulating land collectively in their own right and using the proceeds to invest in various developmental aspects of their lives e.g. taking children to school. Whilst the women advanced and created market networks, the men were left to do the domestic chores which normally would have been solely a woman's job.

Given the aforementioned gender gist that is associated with the FTLRP, the women in this programme managed to develop farmer-induced institutions intended to increase agricultural produce and aid its value chains. From similar observations, an earlier study pointed out the creation of an active agricultural rural civil society which developed to become a local farmer movement (Matondi et al. 2013). This creation of a movement enabled the women post-FTLRP to gain entitlement through their women-initiated developments, giving rise to entrepreneurship. This also concurs with the statistical fact that 80 % of Zimbabwe's agricultural production in the fast-track farms lay in the capable hands of women, playing a vital role in agro-business and entrepreneurship (ibid.).

Women's involvement in accessing land and cropping activities, with some even crossing borders to South Africa for trade purposes, has epitomized the way that women have progressed and learnt how to deal with an entrepreneurship environment. This phenomenon demonstrates how social relations are shaped and understood, devising ways of coping with life, even under the most difficult circumstances. Women, in this regard act as agents in the land-reform process, devising strategies and means of attaining and sustaining a livelihood for themselves (Mutopo et al. 2014) in a difficult environment. The work of, for example Jacobs (2010), Makura-Paradza (2010) and, Mutopo (2011) demonstrate the way in which women have assumed a powerful position in managing farms and earnings such that they emerge as independent financial accumulators. These studies nationwide can be prone to criticism as they derive a case study conclusion which cannot be generalized for the country as a whole. What can be done from the case study-based results is to acknowledge that women have, due to the FTLRP, assumed an upper hand in financial acquisition especially for day-to-day use, a scenario that was never dreamt of pre-FTLRP (Makura-Paradza 2010; Mazhawidza and Manjengwa 2011).

Marketing Strategies Employed by Women

Women have played a vital role in employment creation. In the event that they acquire land, they are said to employ workers whereas men usually rely on their spouses as labourers (Chiweshe et al. 2014).The study demonstrates one prominent marketing strategy that seems to be employed by the 'victorious' women under the A1 resettlement scheme in Zimbabwe. They created trade routes and strong marketing networks reaching as far as Johannesburg, South Africa. They would sell the produce deemed 'women crops' (vegetables and all sorts of nuts), managing to come back with enough income to uplift the household, even from one trip. This illustrates the risk-embracing nature of women as they are able to take a leap of faith and step out of poverty. Since women capacitated themselves through access to land they have managed to engage in regional trade, and have hence attained much independence. The women managed to make use of land reform and have reaped visible results from their access to land and the subsequent establishment of agri-businesses. Empirical validation of the viability of the FTLRP on uplifting and redefining rural livelihoods in Zimbabwe can also be confirmed from work done across all the different agro-ecological regions in Zimbabwe by various researchers, including but not restricted to, Murisa (2009), Scoones et al. (2010), Mutopo, 2011, Moyo (2011), Hanlon et al. (2013, p. 4) and Nyawo (2016). Field evidence given below demonstrates the different marketing strategies that women have employed in South Africa, which the media has not really zeroed in on yet; they show processes of agency and resilience by women in fast-track farms. The case of Mrs Maidei Chigushe (56 years) gives an indication of the kinds of entrepreneurial strategies carried out by women from Mwenezi farms.

Crossing the Border to Sell in South Africa

Mrs Chimbindi is from Merrivale resettlement area, Mwenezi. She and her husband acquired an A1 plot and practise subsistence farming and animal husbandry; they mainly grow sugar cane, maize, groundnuts and sorghum, since their plot is in Natural Region IV. She also goes to Dick Farm, where the A2 newly resettled farmers have irrigation and so they have plentiful vegetables year round, to buy and order more vegetables. She began a marketing enterprise in 2005, and travels to Johannesburg weekly to sell her produce in Berea Street.

Media Projections and Gendered Realities

Based on the author `s engagement with local women fast-track farmers it can be seen that they exist on a different, higher, economic and social plane than what the local independent media and the international media report on the role of women in land access and utilization after fast-track land reform. What I have observed in the past seven years based on ethnographic accounts is that women have accessed land and are utilizing it for different agricultural activities, (Mutopo 2015). As a consequence, media representation of the land reform in Zimbabwe has been a terrain for the contesting of hegemonic and counter-hegemonic discourse. The challenges faced by the media in representing the multi-layered conflicts and complex elements of this issue has been alluded to by various scholars who acknowledge that the centrality of the land question is intricately linked to the race question (Mamdani 2008; Muzondidya 2011; Chari 2013; Li Ping 2003). Mkodzongi (2010) clearly states this thesis when he points out that both academics and journalists have exhibited a tendency to engage in emotive debates that centre on personalities rather than issues, thereby missing opportunities to critically evaluate Zimbabwe's radical land-reform programme. The reality on the ground in the case study demonstrates that the women are not passive agents of the process of agrarian and land reform but rather they have emerged as strategic actors who have been able to create and shape new livelihoods in the process of improving their status as women.

Policy Imperatives

Zimbabwe's National Gender Policy of 2004 undoubtedly demonstrates that the original Constitution failed to realize the primary role of women, rural women essentially, in accessing land and in agricultural production. The Zimbabwe Constitution of 2013, although stating that that land distribution should have gender balance, has no clear-cut gender-specific policy regarding land access to women, only a statement of women's basic rights. This is a great move in the right path and should be commended. The lack of gender mainstreaming, paying particular attention to women's effects the economy through their potential role in the economic recovery of the country via agro-business and entrepreneurship, is suppressed. Concerning agro-business, the policy does not take a stand on addressing entrepreneurship issues, hence women's ventures in the agricultural sector are hampered. Zimbabwe needs a gender policy that is all-encompassing of women's issues (practical gender mainstreaming). This will enable women to be visible and recognized and even benefit from government policy. Statutory and customary law are parallel to each other when issues of gender and asset inheritance come up. If this parity is to be addressed, there is need for a nexus to be established between what the statutory law says about gender and what the customary law also says. The two cannot over-ride each other. It will not make sense to give women rights to land that can then be invalidated by customary laws.

There is need for a media policy that takes cognisance of the gender-based facets of land reform processes. This will help in the crafting nationally based gender policies that enhance rural women's livelihoods. A media policy that is in harmony with women's needs will also serve as springboard for women to read and appreciate media outputs, particularly if the news appreciates their livelihood pathways.

Conclusion

Public and private media projections of women's movements in land-reform processes are influenced by the political, economic and social history of a nation. This has been evidenced by the case study presented here and also the different state and non-state newspapers that report on gendered processes of land reform. This demonstrates that a gendered approach to land reform should bring attention and appreciation to bear on the different livelihood pathways that Zimbabwean women engage in in the aftermath of the land-reform process. Based on the author's ethnographic engagements with the communities for more than seven years, the evidence from the field demonstrates that women have accessed land and are engaged in various agro-based activities which the media has not focused on much. Rather they report on the negativities outweighing true case-based evidence. This therefore leads to the notion that media representations of gender-based land-reform programmes should take into account the role that women play in the agricultural sector based on field evidence and not helicopter-based fieldwork of one day's duration. Such unorthodox field experiences lead to malice on the part of the women who have benefitted from the land-reform programme. Women face discriminatory tendencies both in the public and private spheres, hence the adoption of the new Constitution of Zimbabwe should lead to media changes in the way women are portrayed in agro-based activities. Hence their control on land and its produce would be less likely to be compromised. There is need for a deliberate effort to recruit and recognize women as key players in building the national productivity base as they constitute more than half of the Zimbabwean population. It is against this background that the case study recommends that priority be given to women especially when allocating resources like land. This capacitates them and helps them sustain their households. It also enables them to access agricultural inputs such as seed, fertilizer and also opens access to credit facilities.

Notes

1. The family farm or household model means the land is given to the family or household not individuals within these institutions.
2. A legal court case of *Magaya v Magaya*. Venia could not access her father's land by virtue of being a woman. The ruling concluded that customary law in Zimbabwe supersedes statutory law in inheritance issues. In that regard, the male child is viewed as the suitable inheritor of the parents' property.

References

Berhman, J., Meinzein-Dick, R., & Quisumbing, A. (2012). The gender implications of large-scale land deals. *Journal of Peasant Studies, 39*, 49–79.

Chari, T. (2013). Media framing of land reform in Zimbabwe. In S. Moyo and C. Walter Chambati (Ed.), *Land and Agrarian Reform in former Settler Colonies.* Dakar: CODESRIA.

Chingarande, S. D. (2003). Women and access to land in the context of the fast track land reform programme. In AIAS (Ed.), *Policy brief prepared for The African Institute for Agrarian Studies (AIAS).* Harare: African Institute of Agrarian Studies Publishers.

Chiweshe, M. K., Chakona, L., & Helliker, K. (2014). Patriarchy, women, land and livelihoods on Al farms in Zimbabwe. *Journal of Asian and African Studies, 2*(3), 1–16.

ECA. (2003). *Land tenure systems and sustainable development in southern Africa.* Lusaka: Economic Commission for Africa, Southern African Office.

Gaidzanwa, R. B. (1991). Promised land: Towards a land policy for Zimbabwe, Unpublished MA thesis. The Hague: Institute of Social Studies.

Hanlon, J., Manjengwa, J., & Smart, T. (2013). *Zimbabwe takes back its land.* Johannesburg: Jacana Press.

Jacobs, S. (2010). *Gender and agrarian reforms.* London/New York: Routledge.

Jirira, K. M., & Halimana, M. C. 2008. A gender audit of women and land rights in Zimbabwe. *Paper prepared for the Zimbabwe Women's Resource Centre and Network (ZWRCN), Harare.* Harare.

Li Ping, J. D. (2003). *Rural land tenure reforms in China: Issues, regulations and prospects for additional r. Land Reform Special Edition* (Special Edition). Seattle, WA: Prentice Hall Publishers.

Long, N. (1992). From paradigm lost to paradigm regained? The case of an actor oriented sociology of development. In N. Long & A. Long (Eds.), *Battlefields of knowledge: The interlocking of theory and practice in social research and development.* London/New York: Blackfields Publishers.

Makura-Paradza, G. G. (2010). Single women, land and livelihood vulnerability in a communal area in Zimbabwe. In AWLAE (Ed.), African Women Leaders in Agriculture and the Environment. Leiden: Brill University Printers.

Mamndani, M., 2008, Lessons of Zimbabwe, Pambazuka News, 3 December 2008. (http://www.pambazuka.org/en/category/features/52407). Accessed 15 April 2016.

Matondi, P. B., Chiweshe, M. K., & Mutopo, P. (2013). *Gender and the agricultural sector in Zimbabwe.* Harare: Food and Agricultural Organisation.

Mazhawidza, P., & Manjengwa, J. 2011. The social, and political transformative impact of Fast Track Land Reform Programme on the lives of women farmers in Goromonzi and Vungu-Gweru Districts of Zimbabwe. *International Land Coalition Research Reports. Research Report No 2, Land Series.*

Mkodzongi, G., 2010, Zimbabwe's land reform is common sense', Pambazuka News, 3 November 2010. http://www.pambazuka.org/en/category/features/62917). Accessed 26 March 2016.

Moser, C. (2005). *A handbook on the gender analysis framework.* Cambridge: Cambridge University Press.

Moyo, S. (2011). Three decades of agrarian reform in Zimbabwe. *Journal of Peasant Studies, 38*, 493–531.

Murisa, T. (2007). *Social organisation and agency in the newly resettled areas of Zimbabwe: The case of Zvimba district* In African Institute for Agrarian Studies. Harare: African Institute for Agrarian Studies.

Murisa, T. 2009. *An analysis of emerging forms of social organisation and agency in the newly resettled areas of Zimbabwe: The case of Goromonzi and Zvimba districts*, PhD thesis.

Mutopo, P. (2011). Women's struggles to access and control land and livelihoods after fast track land reform in Mwenezi District, Zimbabwe. *Journal of Peasant Studies, 38*, 1021–1046.

Mutopo, P. (2014). Belonging and rural livelihoods: Women's access to land and non-permanent mobility at Merrivale Farm, Mwenezi District, Zimbabwe. *Erdkunde, 68*, 197–207.

Mutopo, P., Manjengwa, J., & Chiweshe, M. 2014. Shifting gender dimensions and rural livelihoods after Zimbabwe's fast-track land reform programme. *Agrarian South: Journal of Political Economy, 2*(2), 45–61.

Mutopo, P. (2015). Rethinking gender and accumulation: The relevance of Small Scale entrepreneurship and social capital within a rural context. In T. Murisa and T. Chikweche (Eds.), *Beyond the crises: Zimbabwe's prospects for transformation* Harare: Trust Africa, Senegal and Zimbabwe.

Mutopo, P., Chiweshe, M. K., & Mubaya, C. P. (2015). Livelihoods, gender configurations and large-scale land deals in Zimbabwe. In E. Osaboiheim (Ed.), *Creating African Futures in an era of global transformations: Challenges and prospects.* Senegal: CODESRIA.

Muzondidya, J. (2011). The elephant in the room: A critical reflection on race in Zimbabwe's protracted crisis. *Political Economy*, *3*, 45–61. http://www.solidaritypeacetrust.org/834/the-elephant-inthe-room-a-critical-reflection-on. Accessed 20 March 2016

Nyawo, V. Z. (2016). Families divided: Disruption of the family in Zimbabwe's fast track land reform programme. *American Journal of Social Sciences*, *1*, A18–A27.

Ruswa, G. (2007). The golden era? Reflections on the first phase of the land reform programme in Zimbabwe. In AIAS (Ed.), *Land and Governance in Zimbabwe. Occasional research paper series.* Harare: African Institute for Agrarian Studies (AIAS).

Scoones, I., Marongwe, N., Mavedzenge, B., Murimbarimba, F., Mahenehene, J., & Sukhume, C. (2010). *Zimbabwe's land reform. Myths and realities.* Harare: Weaver Press and Johannesburg: Jacana Press.

The Utete Presidential Land Report. (2003). Land acquisition and beneficiary patterns in Zimbabwe. Harare.

Patience Mutopo is a Senior Lecturer in the Centre for Development Studies, Chinhoyi University of Technology. She is also currently completing a V.W. Foundation funded post-doc at Cologne University Germany and Wageningen University, the Netherlands. She is also a Research fellow, with the Cologne African Studies Centre, University of Cologne, Germany, where she completed her PhD in African studies. Her research interests focus on gender, land rights, bio fuel production, agricultural value chains health and agro ecosystems. She is a member of the Legal Empowerment of the Poor coordinated by the Department of Environment and Development at the University of Oslo and the Norwegian Centre for Human rights. Patience has expertise in reproductive human rights issues in Africa specifically focusing on adolescent girls. Her region of focus is Southern Africa.

CHAPTER 15

Global Activism or Media Spectacle? An exploration of 'Bring Back Our Girls Campaign'

Dorothy Njoroge

Introduction

In April 2014 over 270 girls were abducted from their school in Chibok Nigeria by a militant Islamist group, Boko Haram. This led to an outpouring of condemnation and the #bringbackourgirls campaign was born. For the last several years, Nigeria has battled the terrorist menace posed by this group whose handiwork includes decapitation of citizens, burning of buildings, bombings of public places, shooting of worshippers in churches as well as the killing of moderate Muslim clerics among other horrors, all in an effort to create an Islamic Caliphate in Nigeria. The United Nations envoy to the area, Toby Lanzer, reported that over 1,000 schools have been destroyed in Nigeria, Chad, Cameroon and Niger, according to the *Daily Mail* of 16 November 2015.

Boko Haram, which roughly translates to Boko (Western education) is haram (forbidden) in the Hausa language, has been a shadowy Islamist group operating in north-eastern Nigeria but was thrust into international

The original version of this chapter was revised.
An erratum to this chapter can be found at DOI 10.1007/978-3-319-40949-8_16

D. Njoroge (✉)
Assistant Professor Mass Communication, United States International University-Africa, Carbondale, USA
e-mail: dwnjoroge@usiu.ac.ke

B. Mutsvairo (ed.), *Digital Activism in the Social Media Era*,
DOI 10.1007/978-3-319-40949-8_15

limelight following the #Bringbackourgirls campaign. Formed in 2002, the insurgency outfit has grown in strength, taking over territory from the Nigerian army and becoming a major headache for the Nigerian government. Since the new Nigerian president Mohamed Buhari was elected in 2015, the army has scored a number of success against the group but it has not by any means been vanquished. Two years after the abduction, the girls remain missing.

These atrocities committed by this group largely remained in the margins of global public discourse. But the capture of young women in a boarding school changed all that catching the collective imaginary of the global public lending support to the 'bring back our girls' campaign which quickly acquired visibility on social media. The #BringBackOurGirls was created by parents and activists in Nigerian who were frustrated by the seeming inaction of the Nigerian government following the abductions, to complement protests in cities across the country.

In the streets of Nigeria, parents dressed in red bore placards reading 'Bring Back Our Girls', while a coordinated campaign on social media had celebrities around the world appealing for the release of the girls carrying a '#BringBackOurGirls' sign in a symbol of global solidarity. The Bring Back Our Girls (BBOG) campaign was an online sensation, attracting global attention that garnered more than five million tweets.[1] BBOG was a local campaign aiming to expand globally and, as parents protested in the Nigerian seat of government in Abuja, similar protests were taking place in Washington DC, Los Angeles, London, and other cities across Europe and North America.

Opposition to girls' education has been waged by Jihadist Islamist groups ranging from the Taliban in Pakistan and Afghanistan to Boko Haram in Nigeria among other places on the globe. The BBOG case represents the experiences of girls and women around the whose educational endeavours are terminated or curtailed by groups adhering to ideologies that are inimical to women's progress with discourses steeped in patriarchy supported by misapplied cultural and religious systems. The viral campaign lifted the lid on the perils of girls' education in Nigeria that had escaped widespread public scrutiny.

Women have made tremendous strides as a result of women's movements around the world resulting in increased access to education, employment and self-efficacy for millions of women who can now live independent lives. While these gains are less visible in Africa, statistics still show an incremental jump in school enrolments at all levels, with the most impressive gains being made at lower levels of school, according to the Brookings Institute (Winthrop and McGivney 2014). Moreover, gender has become an important component in public policy and national planning further strengthening the advancement of women in various countries. A few women who have attained high political or corporate offices have given visibility to women in public spaces, leading to the conclusion, among some, that gender equity has been achieved or nearly so (Gqola 2007). Correspondingly, there has been an unease among large swathes of younger women in the West as well as African women in identifying with the feminist project for divergent reasons. Younger women, or the so-called Third Wave feminists in the West, find feminism distasteful and have embraced a commercialized 'empowerment' Lazar 2006.

This and other neo-liberal factors have resulted in the moment of post-feminism where it is assumed all is well and all women need to do is take advantage of all the opportunities availed to them so they can be on the same level playing field with their male counterparts. McRobbie (2007) posits that feminist discourse has been marginalized in the media and replaced by post-feminism. D-I-Y feminism eschewing earlier forms of collective organizing, lobbying and dissent is the essence of post-feminism. The post-feminist script, especially in entertainment depicts first 'feminism as an individualistic activity; second, portrays feminism as unnecessary for individual women; third, embroils feminism in consumerism; and fourth, demonstrates that men have already attained feminist enlightenment' (Kornfield 2012, p. 448). It posits that post-feminist women have overcome most of the disadvantages women suffered and can compete with men on an equal pane. Writing from Singapore, Lazar (2006) argues that post-feminism has become a global discourse circulated by international advertising firms and popular culture.

Post-feminism discourse in the West and cosmopolitan capitals around the world cloaks the real struggles women in many parts of world still face. It has served to obscure the dangers to human progress represented in the cases of Malala in Pakistan and the Chibok girls in Nigeria, for example, by movements such as Taliban and Boko Haram which violently oppose the education of girls. This assault, coupled with other insidious cultural practices that inhibit the education of girls and women, demonstrates the urgent need to re-invigorate and galvanize women's movements for the purpose of safeguarding girls' right to education, self-determination and even life itself.

Hence, a case like this lifts the lid on these underlying inequities that post-feminism discourse papers over. In addressing this issue, one of

Nigeria's and Africa's leading lights in the feminist movement, Amina Mama asserts that 'it is entirely outrageous to suggest that "we have done the gender thing and now we can move beyond it"' and observes that 'African societies are so clearly demarcated by gender divisions that it would be strategically suicidal to deny this and pretend that gender does not exist, or worse still, that gender struggles are a thing of the past' (Salo 2001, p. 63). Vibrant African and other third-world feminisms are needed to vigorously expose the inequities and translate these to policies that support and nurture women's education and other basic rights.

Generally, African women feel alienated from the western brand of feminism, with its history, demands and theorizing (Kolawole 2002; Guy-Sheftall 2003). Abortion rights and to a large extent rights to same-sex relationships do not resonate with African women, many of whom are still grappling with basic issues of survival in a highly gendered context. Women in advanced economies are not there yet, but have made significant strides in overcoming some of these hurdles. Nevertheless, as Susan Arndt (2002) points out, African feminism is an unsettled concept, at least in terms of nomenclature. It is variously known by Chikwenye Ogunyemi's term African womanism, Omolara Ogundipe-Leslie's Stiwanism, Hudson-Weem's Africana Womanism, Catherine Achonulu's Motherism and African feminism, among other monikers. But Amina Mama argues that critiques of third-world feminists have sufficiently informed feminist theorizing globally so it is not necessary to cede the term feminism to others. Thus the term African feminism will be the umbrella term in this chapter (even though the author recognizes that there are various shades of feminisms in Africa as well). But whatever the label, 'it is evident, however, that womanism, like feminism, strives for the total liberation of women from religious and socio-cultural institutions that relegate women to the periphery of existence' (Nkealah 2006, p. 138).

Despite shared values, several differences exist between African feminism and western feminism. In the main, African feminism addresses various challenges and integrates the struggle for gender equity 'with liberation from other forms of oppression, namely slavery, colonialism, neocolonialism, racism, poverty, illiteracy, and disease' (Guy-Sheftall 2003, p. 31). In essence, it is a 'pluralist struggle against all forms of oppression' (Kolawole 2002, p. 95). It seeks to address the 'history of interlocking oppressions in the burdens we carry' (Gqola 2001, p. 12). Amina Mama says feminism in the African context, 'signals a refusal of oppression, and a commitment to struggling for women's liberation from all forms of oppression internal, external, psychological and emotional, socio-economic, political and philosophical' (Salo 2001, p. 59). She further states that gender politics should take a three-pronged approach—transformation of women's subjectivity, of their personal lives and the political economy. Thus, women's liberation requires addressing gender injustice all the way from micro- to the macro-political level. In sum,

> African feminisms critique and reject dominant narratives that generalise and essentialise the condition of African women, men and children and seek awareness of specific contexts, cultures and peoples. Such an approach requires describing particular national or regional trends, while simultaneously raising awareness of contextual variations within broader trends. African feminisms in addition emphasise the power and agency of African women in particular to theorise from their cultures and lived experiences to produce knowledge that is contextually relevant, builds relationships, heals the self, the community and the larger socio-cultural context (Chilisa and Ntseane, 2010, pp. 618–619).

African feminism is also an expansive territory geographically and expands to accommodate continental and diasporan feminists who theorize and advocate for women in a myriad of contexts. Actually, the term Africana womanism was coined to reflect this reality. Globalization, employment pressures and inhospitable political environments in Africa have occasionally served to eject intellectuals and political activists and scatter them all over the world. In those new locales, African women continue to grapple with issues of identity and belongingness. In a campaign like this, such voices were able to unite giving a transnational complexion to the campaign.

Due to the parallels in the woman condition across the world, there is need for an overarching transnational, feminist perspective that takes into account experiences, concerns and locations of women around the world. Since Western feminism with its universalizing tropes is not a proper fit for gender analysis in the Third World, gender theory has expanded and continues to expand to incorporate other perspectives. Hedge calls for a "fusion of a global feminist worldview with postmodern and postcolonial influences' (Hedge 1998, p. 284). This global reconceptualization of feminist theory would produce multiple knowledges to combat the universalism of one perspective, she further argues. Post-colonialism provides the analytical tools that can be used to explore the gendered conditions in the rest of the world focusing on the hybrid nature of human experience thus dismantling the essentializing notions inherent in dominant outlooks (Hedge 1998). While important work has been done in this direction, it is not at all clear if such a gender globalist view exists. Nonetheless, African feminisms as previously mentioned, are transnational in nature due to the forced or willing migration of African peoples.

Ideological and geographical diversity of African feminisms cause tensions but also provide opportunities for an engaged transnational push for gender transformation. As Kuumba (2003) puts it, 'the sun never sets on African feminisms' due to its geographical spread through migration, resulting in 'global African feminisms'. Joy James (2013) classifies black feminism in categories of liberal/cultural feminism and radical/revolutionary feminism. Liberal feminism adopts accommodationist politics and seeks to work state and corporate power to improve the lot of women—men are identified as the obstacle to female advance. Radical approaches identify state and corporate systems as barriers to women's progress and seek to do away with institutionalized state and corporate structures of control as these are considered complicit in systems of patriarchy and capitalism that produce gender oppression.

Buiten (2013) on the other hand, classifies feminism thought within the South African context into two broad categories. The liberal inclusionary feminism approach 'characterised by an emphasis on women and their involvement in the so-called "public sphere", with a strong focus on equal participation; the representation of women's voices in legal, political, institutional and cultural roles; and legislative and policy reforms' (2013, p. 58). Both Women in Development (WID) and Women and Development (WAD) have promoted policies that encouraged equality in terms of quantitative increase of women in schools, leadership positions and so on (Chilisa and Ntseana 2010). But this reformist approach, while useful, is not sufficient as it focuses in increasing women's participation through institutionalized formal mechanisms while other salient issues, such as gendered power relations and discourse are given short shrift (Buiten 2013, p. 59).

Conversely, progressive feminist approaches, an umbrella term for post-colonial and similar approaches, focus on 'gendered social meanings and their relationship to power' (Buiten, 2013, p. 60). This approach does not seek to simply create more opportunities for women within the existing structures but to bring about social transformation based on equitable principles by dismantling the extant social order (Nkealah 2006, p. 135). It represents of a change in tack from advocating changes in laws and policies to improve equality to working to dismantle inequity not just in the public sphere but also in the private sphere (Buiten 2013, p. 60). This approach interrogates difference and constructions of feminisms as well as masculinities. Ultimately, it seeks to address 'the structural, social and cultural underpinnings of gender inequality at all levels, not merely at the level of public participation' (Buiten 2013, p. 61).

One strategy for bringing about this transformation is by using personal stories of experiences with injustice to speak to the hearts and appeal to the emotions, not just the minds, of those sustaining misconceptions in creative ways which are evident in African women's literature that details the negative consequences of patriarchy on female characters (Nkealah 2006). This approach fits in with Hedge's call 'for more local and specific understandings of personhood as being constituted within overlapping global discourses' (Hedge 1998, p. 288).

The Bring Back our Girls campaign represents a site where the specific local situation overlaps with globality as campaigners share snapshots of their activities as well as thoughts and feelings regarding the kidnapped Chibok girls. The purpose of this chapter is to analyse the feminist content of the campaign messages. To what extent is it framed as a social justice issue? To what extent are gender lens used to analyse the problem and/or solutions? But before delving into the details of these questions, the next section briefly outlines feminist discourse in African contexts.

Feminist Discourse in Africa

Feminist discourses in Africa are characterized by constraints in addressing the gender question as mostly a policy issue without the attendant social transformation. It characterized by a paradox of the discourse of empowerment co-existing with daily injustices. For example, in South Africa, despite a number of legislative changes to improve gender equity, gender-based violence is very high, including rape and sexual harassment on the streets (Gqola 2007, p. 115). As Gqola further elaborates,

> 'the empowerment of women', as currently employed and aired in South Africa, rests on the assumption that ensuring that some women have access to wealth, positions in government and corporate office is enough gender progressive work for our society. This assumption is flawed on various levels, even if increased representation of women across all sectors of our society is a worthwhile and necessary project (2007, p. 115).

It is flawed because various factors hinder women's rise, including the expectation that to succeed, women have to fit into the current system rather than the structures being adapted to suit the needs and requirements of women (ibid.).

Buiten's study of the journalism industry in South Africa confirms these observations. Her interviews of South African journalists and editors indicated that while, at a personal level, some appreciated the need for progressive approaches to gender issues, the overarching discourse was that of liberal discourse. As such, 'liberal-inclusionary feminist discourses shaped, and set limitations on, how journalists understood gender issues' (2013, p. 61). Further, these media workers did not have an appreciation of their role as producers of gendered texts which affect societal gender relations.

Similar trends are noted in Kenya in a study of mothers of political prisoners who acted together to go on hunger strike in a public park to demand the release of their sons, who had been jailed by President Moi in 1992 for their political activities in fighting for multi-party democracy. These women and their sympathizers engaged in protest activities for a year before their sons were released. Nancy Worthington studied the coverage of this activism in Kenya's independent news magazine the *Weekly Review*. Stamp (1995) had proposed that 'combative motherhood' is able to give such actors moral authority that can be effective in social change and also bridge the public and private spheres that usually govern media work thereby transcending media invisibility given to women actors (Worthington 2001, p. 171).

However, in this case, the publication effaced the women's agency by painting them as agents of opposition politics suggesting 'to readers that the women did not and possibly could not think for themselves' (Worthington 2001, p. 178). These women's names were not used in news coverage by *Weekly Review* except in one case when three of them collapsed during the hunger strike. Gqola (2007) speaks of similar invisibilization of women in South Africa.

Worthington (2001) notes that the *Weekly Review* coverage of Mothers of Political Prisoners severed the symbolic link between motherhood and their political action through framing that divided their maternal authority, actual or symbolic, from their 'combative' behaviour (Worthington 2001, p. 180). Without this symbolic link, 'the advocates were portrayed simply as combative women or political dupes, two much less appealing representations that were reinforced by their appearance in the masculine genre of news' (Worthington 2001, p. 180).

This negation of women's political agency by this publication fits with a larger discourse where women's voices are de-legitimated in media discourse and their activism usurped by other forces. While women's movements per se are not always bastions of confronting gender injustice, the #BringBackOurGirls campaign raises critical issues of women's rights. I examined the Facebook page of this campaign in the first two months of the disappearance of the girls to see how issues of social justice feature in the posts regarding this campaign. Beyond the urgency of rescuing the girls, to what degree were larger issues of gender justice part of the posts and interactions on the campaign's page on Facebook? How is problem conceptualized on social media? Are broader issues of women's oppression and its systemic nature part of the discussion? Most studies have looked at gender discourse in mainstream media. This looks at social media, without media gatekeepers, to examine campaigners' unfiltered expressions.

There are divergent views on the efficacy of online campaigning. Some have described it as simply fleeting, clicktivism (Christensen 2011; Drumbl 2012) while others see a real potential for creating cosmopolitan public (Madianou 2013, p. 250). A criticism directed at mediated suffering—that it does not lead to action—is obviated in social media networks as people can mobilize by sharing, donating, signing petitions and so forth. Action on social media is characterized as 'understanding/awareness; talk; and action' (Madianou 2013, p. 252).

Kony 2012 marked a watershed moment for campaigns on Africa and showed the potential of using digital networked tools to create a visible campaign for causes. The 30-minute video, which went viral, reaching 110 million hits in six days, was made by a US charity, Invisible Children Inc (Nothias 2013). By contrast, the #bringbackourgirls social media campaign is home-grown and started by a tweet from a Nigerian lawyer, Ibrahim M. Abdullahi, using the hashtag #BringBackOurGirls on 23 April.[2] This became the catchphrase for the campaign globally not just for the social media campaign but also for street protests.

Political action on the internet is affected by the digital divide, with parts of the world having unrestricted access while others have inadequate access, thereby reducing the impact of collective virtual activism (Van Laer and Van Aelst 2010). Though it must be noted the fastest growth in mobile phone adoption is in Africa 'total mobile subscription penetration in Sub-Saharan Africa is estimated to be around 80 percent in 2015' and 'by 2021, it is expected to reach 100 percent in the region' (Sub-Saharan Ericsson Report 2015). This is significant because people in sub-Saharan region largely access the internet through their phones for online activities such as social networking. As such, 'growing smartphone ownership and a lack of fixed broadband availability has resulted in mobile broadband being the most common way to connect to the internet' so that '83 percent of Nigerian mobile phone subscribers rely solely on this channel' (Ericsson Mobility Report 2015).

The Case

As indicated earlier, the abduction of the 276 girls and attendant lack of government action in Nigeria to recover the girls led to protests by parents and their sympathizers in Nigerian cities. It also led to a social media campaign mostly on Facebook and Twitter which picked up global support including the US first lady, Michelle Obama, Secretary Hillary Clinton, actress Anne Hathaway among dozens more celebrities and world leaders. The campaign called for a social media march, organizing events such as marches and vigils and signing petitions among other activities.

Two years on and the Facebook campaign is still on. However, the activity peaked in the first two months of the campaign. The corpus analysed comprised the Facebook page https://www.facebook.com/bringbackourgirls for the campaign focusing on the initial months of the campaign.

This chapter examines posts and comments on gender on the official campaign page. Among issues on this page regarding the calls for release of the girls and planning of various events in various places are posts and interactions regarding the nature of this crime and the larger socio-political issues surrounding it. This chapter reflects Facebook users' views on the gender question as represented within the comments and posts regarding this campaign. The methodology is thematic analysis of texts. Four main themes that relate to feminist concerns in the posts. These include right to education for girls, condemnation of human trafficking, religious oppression and women power.

Education as a Tool for Girls' Empowerment – 'Nothing can terrify a gorilla like a little girl with a text book!'

One of the enduring themes of feminist movement worldwide has been the education of women. Education remains one of the areas that women's organizations around the world have campaigned for so the girl child is not left behind.

Girls' empowerment is overwhelmingly defined as participation in education in online discourse. In tandem with demands of feminism, particularly the liberal-inclusionary version, preparing the girls to be active participants in society through education is a message that has seeped everywhere and seems to define what women empowerment. Education is seen as the social equalizer that helps girls achieve their dreams. More importantly, it helps them to think for themselves and think for themselves. As Mama posits, education provides women with the critical intellectual tools women can use to seek gender justice (Salo 2001). While an important step, education does not always translate to advancement for women.

Human Trafficking a Threat to Girls Empowerment – 'human trafficking! please sign petitions!'

While education was conceptualized as the means to women's advancement, the abduction of the Chibok girls is seen as a key setback to women's progress. According to comments on Facebook, abduction of the girls is understood in legal terms—human trafficking.

This crime against the young women is therefore defined as an international crime and echoes the global discourse of international justice. However, it is reductionist as it fails to interrogate the interplay of forces that made this heinous act possible. The failure of African governments to control rogue elements within their countries has escalated the discourse of international justice, as demonstrated by *Kony 2012*. However, this international justice discourse fails to interrogate the specific conditions in northern Nigeria that have prepared the ground for the atrocities witnessed including the abduction of the girls.

Religious Oppression Holding Women Back - 'Freedom from ignorance and religious oppression..... Bring back our girls!!!!!'

Feminism has identified religious dogma as one of the way through which women's oppression is accomplished. As Nkealah notes, feminism 'strives for the total liberation of women from religious and socio-cultural institutions that relegate women to the periphery of existence' (2006, p. 138). Clearly this position seems universally accepted and characterizes the Facebook comments on the campaign site.

Religious extremist dogma has been used for millennia to subordinate women's intellects, emotions and bodies. As such, female sexuality remains 'an issue that cannot be separated from African women's racialized and gendered histories and other social, political, religious, and economic relations' (Ampofo and Beoku-Betts et al. 2004, p. 695). Religious propaganda, from political Islam, in this case remains one of the key tenets used to disempower and subjugate women and deny them their human rights and is a key sub-theme in online interactions and posts.

Women's Power - 'Women's kick ass army!!!'

Despite women's vulnerability in this situation, their power is also recognized in some of the posts as noted below. This aspect goes furthest in demonstrating understand of the causes of gender inequity in our world today that seems premised on female subjugation. This theme goes furthest in recognizing the need to bring transformation in gender relations where one gender is not seen as a threat to the other—'When will men stop fearing women?' as one campaigner poses. The theme suggests a changing of guard may be necessary for things to turn around. Women's strength is constructed to emanate from bonds they share and the value accorded to the human person.

Conclusion

This campaign brought into sharp relief the real everyday struggles women in northern Nigeria experience in an attempt to get an education. School completion rates are very low, in fact, 'only 4 % of females complete secondary school in the Northern zones' (British Council Gender in Nigeria Report 2012, p. 2). The implications for human development are vast, given the Nigerian's high population and its place as a leading country in Africa.

The analysis of social media discourse shows that feminism concerns resonate with those campaigning for the release of the girls on social media and elsewhere. However, the discussion fits more on the liberal inclusive side of the continuum than the progressive side. It is widely expected that legal and institutional changes and making space for women within the current configuration of power will produce the changes needed to uplift the lot to girls. While the prospects of transformation of power relations are acknowledged, they remain marginal. Hence, while access to education is an important feature of social media discourse in this campaign, in Sri Lanka, women's educational achievement, almost at par with men, has not translated into social mobility through employment as women are held back by traditional gender roles such as motherhood, and by negative attitudes towards women taking up certain professions. Institutionalized sexism and racism also remain a problem for Sri Lankan women she further notes. Thus, questions of access serve as the first step of a long journey to afford women their full human rights, a reality that remains largely unacknowledged in public discourse that this campaign is symptomatic of.

The international justice discourse generalizes the conditions in northern Nigeria with those in other parts of the world where criminal elements have caused havoc. There is no discussion of the larger socio-political issues in northern Nigeria that the girls' abduction is symptomatic of. As Madianou (2013) notes in her study of two social media campaigns, *Kony 2012* and Waterforward, the national contexts for these causes are not provided in the campaign. She notes that historical context is absent in *Kony 2012* despite its 30-minute length. Yet 'African feminisms critique and reject dominant narratives that generalize and essentialize the condition of African women, men and children and seek awareness of specific contexts, cultures and peoples' (Chilisa and Ntseane 2010, p. 619).

Despite the discourses of the campaign resonating with feminist discourses, they cannot be classified as revolutionary. For example, they hardly question the system of patriarchy defined as 'self-sustaining structures of power, by means of which women's interests are always ultimately subordinated to male interests, constitute the social order known as 'patriarchy', a designation which applies to almost all human societies, past and present' (Morris 1993 in Nkealah 2006, p. 136). It is this system that made the girls vulnerable and also led to President Jonathan Goodluck's failure to act with sufficient urgency to rescue the girls.

Notes

1. http://www.bbc.com/news/world-africa-33446305
2. http://mashable.com/2014/05/06/nigeria-girls-bringbackourgirls/#c2kvqwDBTOqp

References

Ampofo, A.A., Beoku-Betts, J., Njambi, W.N., & Osirim, M. (2004). Women's and gender studies in English-speaking Sub-Saharan Africa: A review of research in the social sciences. *Gender & Society, 18*(6), 685–714. doi:10.1177/0891243204269188

Arndt, S. (2002). Perspectives on African feminism: Defining and classifying African-Feminist literatures. *Agenda, 54*, 31–44..

British Council Nigeria. Gender in Nigeria Report (2012). Improving the Lives of Girlsand women in Nigeria: Issues Policies Action, 2nd edn. https://www.gov.uk/government/uploads/system/uploads/attachment_data/file/67333/Gender-Nigeria2012.pdf. Accessed 14 May 2016.

Buiten, D. (2013). Feminist approaches and the South African News Media. *Ecquid Novi: African Journalism Studies, 34*(2), 54–72.

Chilisa, B., & Ntseane, G. (2010). Resisting dominant discourses: Implications of indigenous, African feminist theory and methods for gender and education research. *Gender and Education, 22*(6), 617–632. doi:10.1080/09540253.2010.519578.

Christensen, H. S. February (2011). Political activities on the internet: Slacktivism or political Participation by other means?. *First Monday, 16*, 2–7. http://firstmonday.org/ojs/index.php/fm/rt/printerFriendly/3336/2767. Accessed 29 January 2016.

Drumbl, M. A. (2012). Child soldiers and clicktivism: Justice, myths, and prevention. *Journal of Human Rights Practice, 4*(3), 481–485. doi:10.1093/jhuman/hus023.

Gqola, P. D. (2001). Ufanele Uqavile: Blackwomen, feminisms and postcoloniality in Africa. *Agenda: Empowering Women for Gender Equity, 1*(50), 11–22.

Gqola, P. D. (2007). How the "cult of femininity" and violent masculinities supportendemic gender based violence in contemporary South Africa. *African Identities, 5*(1), 111–124. doi:10.1080/14725840701253894. Accessed 25 April 2016.

Guy-Sheftall, B. (2003). African feminist discourse: A review essay. *Agenda, 17*(58), 31–36.

Hegde, R. (1998). A View from elsewhere: Locating difference and the politics of representation from a transnational feminist perspective. *Communication Theory, 8*(3), 271–297.

Heugh, K. (2011). Discourses from without, discourses from within: Women, feminism and voice in Africa. *Current Issues in Language Planning, 12*(1), 89–104. doi:10.1080/14664208.2010.543455. Accessed 25 April 2016.

James, J. (2013). *Seeking the beloved community: A feminist race reader*. New York: SUNY Press.

Kolawole, M. M. (2002). Transcending incongruities: Rethinking feminism and the dynamics of identity in Africa. *Agenda, 17*(54), 92–98.

Kornfield, S. (2012). The E-man-ci-pation of Jeannie: Feminist Doppelgangers on U.S.Television. *Communication, Culture & Critique, 5*, 445–462.

Kuumba, M. B. (2003). African feminisms in exile: Diasporan, transnational and transgressive empowering women for gender equity. *Agenda, 58*(3), 3–11.

Lazar, M. M. (2006). Discover the power of femininity!. *Feminist Media Studies, 6*(4), 505–517. doi:10.1080/14680770600990002. Accessed 19 April 2016.

Madianou, M. (2013). Humanitarian campaigns in social media. *Journalism Studies, 14*(2), 249–266. doi:10.1080/1461670X.2012.718558. Accessed 31 March 2016.

McRobbie, A. (2007). Top girls?. *Cultural Studies, 21*(4–5), 718–737. doi:10.1080/09502380701279044

Nkealah, N. N. (2006). Conceptualizing feminism(s) in Africa: The challenges facing African women writers and critics. *English Academy Review: Southern African Journal of English Studies, 23*(1), 133–141.

Nothias, T. (2013). It's struck a chord we have never managed to strike': Frames, perspectives and remediation strategies in the international news coverage of Kony2012. *Ecquid Novi: African Journalism Studies, 1*(34), 123–129. http://dx.doi.org/10.1080/02560054.2013.767438. Accessed 31 March 2016.

Roma Rajpal, W. What is Holding Women Back in Sri Lanka? 18th December 2014. http://ourworld.unu.edu/en/what-is-holding-women-back-in-sri-lanka. Accessed 15 May, 2016.

Salo, E. (2001). Talking about feminism in Africa. *Agenda, 16*(50), 58–63. http://dx.doi.org/10.1080/10130950.2001.9675993. Accessed 19 April 2016.

Sub-Saharan Ericsson Report. (2015). http://www.ericsson.com/res/docs/2015/mobility-report/emr-nov-2015-regional-report-sub-saharan-africa.pdf. Accessed 14 May 2016.

Van Laer, J., & Peter, V.A. (2010). Internet and social movement action repertoires: Opportunities and limitations. *Information, Communication & Society, 13*(8), 1146–1171. http://dx.doi.org/10.1080/13691181003628307.

Winthrop, R., & McGivney, E. (2014). *Raising the global ambition for girls' education*. Washington DC: The Brookings Institution.

Worthington, N. (2001). A division of labor: Dividing maternal authority from political activism in the Kenyan Press. *Journal of Communication Inquiry, 25*, 167–183.

Dorothy Njoroge is a senior lecturer of Journalism at United States International University-Africa. She obtained her Ph. D in Mass Communication and Media Arts from Southern Illinois University Carbondale and has taught in Africa and the USA. Her research interests include issues of social justice and has presented a number of papers on global justice campaigns for Africa focusing on the Make Poverty History campaign fronted by Bono and most recently the Bring Back our Girls Campaign. She has also co-authored a university-level text book, *An Introduction to Communication* (Oxford University Press East Africa).

CHAPTER 16

Erratum to: Global Activism or Media Spectacle? An exploration of 'Bring Back Our Girls Campaign'

Dorothy Njoroge

Erratum to: B. Mutsvairo (ed.), Digital Activism in the Social Media Era, DOI 10.1007/978-3-319-40949-8_15

The Publisher regrets that chapter title of chapter 15 is incorrectly published. The correct chapter title is Global Activism or Media Spectacle? An exploration of 'Bring Back Our Girls Campaign'.

The updated online version of this chapter can be found at http://dx.doi.org/10.1007/978-3-319-40949-8_15

D. Njoroge (✉)
Assistant Professor Mass Communication, United States International University-Africa, Carbondale, USA
e-mail: dwnjoroge@usiu.ac.ke

B. Mutsvairo (ed.), *Digital Activism in the Social Media Era*,
DOI 10.1007/978-3-319-40949-8_16

Index

B. Mutsvairo (ed.), *Digital Activism in the Social Media Era*,
DOI 10.1007/978-3-319-40949-8

S

T

The manufacturer's authorised representative in the EU is Springer Nature Customer Service Centre GmbH, Europaplatz 3, 69115 Heidelberg, Germany. If you have any concerns regarding our products, please contact ProductSafety@springernature.com

Printed and bound by CPI Group (UK) Ltd, Croydon, CR0 4YY
25/09/2026
02222854-0013